Ron Paul for President in 2012

Yes to Ron Paul and Liberty

by Walter E. Block

ISHI PRESS
INTERNATIONAL

Ron Paul for President in 2012

Yes to Ron Paul and Liberty

by Walter E. Block

Published in April 2012 by

Ishi Press in New York and Tokyo

First Edition

ISBN 4-87187-323-4
978-4-87187-323-9

Ishi Press International
1664 Davidson Avenue, Suite 1B
Bronx NY 10453-7877

1-917-507-7226

Printed in the United States of America

Table of Contents

Dedication

This book is dedicated to Dr. Ron Paul, many times congressman from Texas, future president of the U.S., and friend and mentor of mine.

Foreword

by Rafi Farber

From Israel: Vote Ron Paul and Let My People Go!

Lately I've been having trouble sleeping. I sit here in my living room in Karnei Shomron, Israel, on the 8th night of Chanukah, wondering what other miracles lay in store on January 3rd and in the months ahead. The name Ron Paul is constantly at my fingertips. I've typed it in so many times in the past month it's insane. I'm experiencing an excitement I've rarely ever felt, and I don't even live in America anymore. During the last Republican debate, I woke myself up at 3am Israel time to watch an 8pm EST live stream on YouTube, with no fatigue whatsoever. I'm on overdrive, and I can't calm myself.

I've only recently figured out what this excitement actually is.

I first got interested in the whole freedom movement when I heard that Ron Paul wanted to end all foreign aid, including to my country, Israel. This seemed like a spectacular idea to me. I hate the idea of taking American taxpayer money I don't need. The only reason we take it, by the way, is not because we need it. It's that we don't want to feel alone, and Jews always feel a deep existential isolation and loneliness. "As I see them from the mountain tops, gaze on them from the heights, this is a people that dwells alone, not counted among the Nations," says Balaam of the People of Israel in Numbers 23:9. We still feel that loneliness. So we take the money. It's shameful, it's theft, it's destructive, it's morally wrong, and it makes people hate us for tying them into a conflict they have no business trying to solve. I wanted it to end and didn't trust any Israeli leader to give it up on his own, so I looked up more about Ron Paul.

What I found was fascinating. On the forums, I learned of people who, back in 2008, made incredible sacrifices for this man. Some poured money into his campaign they could not afford to give, and some even lost their marriages because of their single-minded insane dedication. This shocked me. I couldn't understand it, but after a few days of listening to him, it began to click.

What is it about Ron Paul that inspires such extremes? Such maddening support on the one hand, and such fear and loathing on the other? I can give the answer in one word: Soul.

The essential soul of a human being is by definition free. The idea that men are free as determined by God is a concept that is foreign to most men. This is because most men want to control others, to take away their freedom. This is usually referred to as the drive for power. The drive for power is antithetical to freedom because power means the ability to control others. There is only one legitimate thing that power can and should be used for, whether it be military, legislative, or executive power. That is, to legalize freedom.

Ron Paul doesn't want to be president to "give" me freedom. He doesn't own my freedom and he didn't give it to me. The only reason Ron Paul wants to be president is to stop punishing people for using their freedom that is rightfully theirs. He wants no power. This is clear to anyone who listens to him speak.

There are two kinds of human beings. Those who want power, and those who want freedom. You can tell which one's which very easily. Those who want freedom are straight-edged. They are consistent, principled, and you can feel their human soul when they speak to you. There's a continuum out there of human souls somewhere in spiritual cyberspace, and when you come into contact with one of these souls, you know immediately, because souls are by definition free. You sense sincerity, realness, consistency, a free human being. If you're a man who seeks freedom and you come into contact with a real human soul, you become instantly addicted and you swallow up anything you can get your hands on. You want to unite immediately, no matter what you disagree on. There are people in the freedom movement that don't exactly like Israel, especially me because I am a "settler" but I don't care. If they want freedom, I sense it and my human drive for individualism suddenly turns into an intense desire to unite into a collective – but a collective of free individuals. It's a beautiful dialectic, and it doesn't matter what we agree or disagree on, as long as we agree on freedom.

You get hooked on Ron Paul and you desperately seek more and more, any video you can find from the past, any speeches you missed, anything he said that you haven't heard yet, even though you've heard it a thousand times already in different words. You can't help yourself. The voracious hunger to be able to use your God-given freedom takes you over entirely. It's like you suddenly realize you're human and the Divine Image with which God created you comes alive and catches fire.

But something else happens to you. Once you get hooked on Ron Paul, you can no longer bear to listen to a man who wants power, and you become instantly disgusted when they start saying words. Before, they were just boring. Now they're revolting. Listening to Romney or Gingrich or Bush or Obama makes you sick and you don't know how Ron Paul gets through those debates without getting nauseous. You see a political veneer in these politicians that's so transparent it's like a ghost flapping its ethereal tongue at you. You can't bear it.

What's so maddening about hearing Romney or Gingrich talk is that there's someone standing there saying things, but there's no soul in it. These are not free men. These are power men. Not that Romney or Gingrich don't have souls. They do. They are men just like you and I. But they have practically forfeited their souls to try to attain power, to control others with spin and talking points and contradictory statements like "I want to cut the budget and expand the military!" And they'll say it with a polished tone and a straight face, just like a soulless recording. Their humanity is so buried under the mountain of lies they have told themselves, that neither they nor you can even sense their souls in the human continuum. The scene of a human body speaking but no soul communicating can drive a free man mad.

The reason that Ron Paul never goes down in the polls is that he's not "convincing" people in the everyday sense that he's right on whatever issue. He's activating human souls, lighting spiritual fires one by one speaking about freedom. Once a soul gets activated, and the man realizes that he IS free no matter what people do to him or tell him, there is no turning back. The other candidates are trying to turn heads with snappy one-liners that sound cool. Slaves follow these one-liners like mobs, and follow each other from candidate to candidate. Slowly but surely, Ron Paul activates a few of the individual souls in the mob as they bob from snappy comeback to snappy comeback and he goes up in the polls.

Yet, we cannot expect every man woman and child to understand or get excited about the message of liberty. In fact, most just can't handle it. Being truly free is as terrifying as it is electrifying. The Bible tells us this very clearly in the story of the Exodus from Egypt. When

Moses finally accepts the role of deliverer from God, he was assigned to say the following to my ancestors' the Israelites:

"Therefore say to the Israelites: I am God. I will free you from the labors of the Egyptians and deliver you from their bondage. I will redeem you with an outstretched arm and with amazing signs. And I will take you to be My people and I will be your God, and you will know that I am the Lord who freed you from the labors of the Egyptians." (Ex. 6:6-7)

And what was my ancestors' response?

"And Moses told this to the people, but they didn't listen due to lack of spirit and cruel bondage." (6:9)

Not everyone can handle the message of freedom. It's too frightening for some people, and some are just too enslaved. Those are the people that despise Ron Paul, the same types who rebelled against Moses in the desert and attempted to go back to Egypt. Freedom is too much for them and they can't handle the divine gift. They want and need someone to control them. Their souls have been too battered by slavery, taxation, and wars.

But nonetheless, God forced my stiff-necked ancestors to leave Egypt, and as a result I'm here today, preaching freedom once again, fighting not only for America's freedom, but for my own from America's influence in my own region.

Vote Ron Paul and let my people go once again! Stop meddling here and stop trying to buy influence by giving me money. Stop trying to be the all-powerful peacemaker and let us work out the problems here on our own! If we think Iran is a threat, we can handle it and we'll take the consequences. It's not America's problem and you can't afford another war.

Now I understand why people will give everything to this man. Whenever he's asked the question, "Would you legalize heroin?" Ron Paul answers, "I want to legalize freedom!" Little do these people understand that freedom is a thousand times more addictive than heroin.

Rafi Farber is a member of Jews for Ron Paul and manages the website World of Judaica.

Introduction

If you are looking for a biography of Ron Paul, you will not find it here. If you are looking for a bibliographical analysis of his many magnificent speeches, testimonies before congress, books, lectures, articles, you will not find it here. If you are looking for Ron Paul's contribution to the history of the libertarian movement, you will not find it here. If you are looking for an assessment of the significance of the contribution made to the libertarian movement by the Congressman from the 14th district of Texas (which has been nothing short of magnificent), again, you will not find it here.

This book, instead, consists of a series of essays about Dr. Paul and his campaigns for the presidency of the U.S. in 2008 and 2012, with primary emphasis on the latter. The gist of them all is to make the case for his occupancy of the White House. Each and every last one of these chapters is an attempt, on my part, to expand and expound upon his views, to publicize them, to promote his candidacy, to defend it against attacks from within and without the libertarian movement.

Will Ron Paul win? At the time of this writing, right before the Nevada primary, it is far too early to know whether or not he will become the next president of the United States. From the perspective of this point in time, Dr. Paul faces an uphill, and then a downhill battle. My assessment is that he will have a more difficult time winning the Republican nomination than he will in beating Obama. This is because Paul attracts people from all over the political spectrum. Republicans, yes; but he is very attractive to Independents, and even, more surprisingly at the outset, to Democrats. And, while some of the primaries are open to voters from all three categories, these elections are of course statistically biased in the direction of Republicans, and Ron Paul has no comparative advantage vis a vis his three remaining competitors, Mitt Romney, Newt Gingrich and Rick Santorum, in this section of the electorate. That is his weakness, but also his strength; for if and when he gets the nod from the Republicans, he can attract more voters from the Democratic and Independent camps than these other three, and thus has the best chance of overturning the sitting president in the fall of 2012. In recent polls, only Paul and Romney are in a statistical dead heat with Obama. Gingrich and Santorum fall by the wayside in this regard.

But Dr. Paul is not only running for the presidency of the U.S. His campaign is also an attempt to change the hearts and minds of the more than 300 million people in America, but also the nearly 7 billion inhabitants of the entire Earth. And in this latter quest he has already succeeded, beyond even the most ambitious of hopes of his most fervent supporters (of which, I am one). Despite the blackout to which the mainstream media has attempted to subject him, there is nary a minute, let alone an hour or a day, where his face and voice is not beamed forth to the multitudes via radio, television, newspapers, magazines, and particularly, the Internet. In his 2007 book, Brian Doherty singled out five people who had made the greatest contributions to libertarianism: Milton Friedman, Friedrich Hayek, Ludwig von Mises, Ayn Rand and Murray Rothbard. I have no doubt that were Doherty writing that book at the present time, he would have included Ron Paul. In my view, the Texas congressman has acquainted more people with libertarianism, and converted them to this philosophy, than all of the others put together.[1]

According to Gandhi: "*First they* ignore you, then they *laugh at you*, then they fight you, then you win." Well, the leading lights of our culture are no longer laughing at Ron Paul. They tried, valiantly, to ignore him, but with each top-tier voting finish, with each jam-packed stadium of enthusiastic young supporters, it becomes more and more difficult to do so any more. They, the bad guys, are now engaging in fighting him with vicious smears. He is an isolationist (no, he isn't, he is a noninterventionist; the "dear leaders" of North Korea are isolationists.) He is a pacifist (you've got to be kidding me, here.) He is against defending the country (no he isn't; he draws a *sharp* distinction between *offensive* military adventurism that amounts to imperialism, on the one hand, and justifiable *defense* on the other). He

1This is not to denigrate people such as Mises and Rothbard, whose contribution was less widespread, but far deeper, in that they were theoreticians, not popularizers. In my view (Block, 2006A, 2010C), the libertarianism of Friedman and Hayek was a bit too watered down to be included in this illustrious listing, and Rand specifically rejected this label.

is a racist (*fuggedaboutit*, as we say in Brooklyn: he was not as attentive a publisher as he might have been. Here is my favorite quote on this brouhaha: "Ron Paul is vilified for missing a few paragraphs out of hundreds of newsletters by people who pass 2,000-page bills without reading a single word." -- Hosanna Myers.

I have no doubt in the ensuing months that Dr. Paul will be subjected to more and more of the same, with it escalating if another one or two of the Republican candidates drop out. Then, when Congressman Paul faces President Obama in the fall, the stops will really be pulled out.

According to Gandhi: "*First they* ignore you, then they *laugh at you*, then they fight you, then you win." Well, the leading lights of our culture are no longer laughing at Ron Paul. They tried, valiantly, to ignore him, but with each top-tier voting finish, with each jam-packed stadium of enthusiastic young supporters, it becomes more and more difficult to do so. They, the bad guys, are now engaging in fighting him with vicious smears. He is an isolationist (no, he isn't, he is a noninterventionist; the "dear leaders" of North Korea are isolationists.) He is a pacifist (you've got to be kidding me, here.) He is against defending the country (no he isn't; he draws a *sharp* distinction between *offensive* military adventurism that amounts to imperialism, on the one hand, and justifiable *defense* on the other). He is a racist (*fuggedaboutit*, as we say in Brooklyn: he was not as attentive a publisher as he might have been. My favorite quote on this brouhaha is this: "Ron Paul is vilified for missing a few paragraphs out of hundreds of newsletters by people who pass 2,000-page bills without reading a single word." -- Hosanna Myers.

I have no doubt in the ensuing months that Dr. Paul will be subjected to more of the same, with it escalating if another one or two of the Republican candidates drop out. Then, when Congressman Paul faces President Obama in the fall, the stops will really be pulled out.

Part I.

Economics

Ron Paul has distinctive views on three issues: foreign policy, personal liberties, and economics. Why am I starting this book off on economics? It is because the dismal science is important. I admit it; I am biased in this direction. I do not denigrate the importance of the other two issues. It is just that I see them, as I see pretty much everything, through the eyeglasses of economics. Those of you more interested in the other two arenas of political economy will just have to be patient.

Chapter 1.

The Economics of Discrimination

This essay more concerns Rand Paul than Ron Paul. I include it in this book for two reasons. One, the Senator from Kentucky has been a staunch supporter of the Congressman from Texas and two, while this issue initially erupted with Rachel Maddow's interview with the son, the father certainly got into the scrum, in support of his progeny.

The Case for Discrimination

In the days of yore, to say that a man was discriminating was to pay him a compliment. It meant that he had taste; he could distinguish between the poor, the mediocre, the good and the excellent. His ability to make fine distinctions enabled him to live a better life than otherwise.

Nowadays, in our politically correct times, discrimination implies racial and/or sexual hatred. It evokes lynching the innocent, hanging black people who had committed no crime, and, yes, perhaps, even, in the extreme, a return to slavery. This at least was virtually the reaction that greeted candidate for U.S. Senate Rand Paul, when he averred that there were parts of the so-called "Civil Rights" Act of 1964 that were objectionable. But all Senator Paul was saying is that while it would be illicit for *government* to discriminate on the basis of race or sex or any other such criterion, it is a basic element of private property rights that *individuals* be free to engage in exactly such preferences. If they were not, an important element of liberty would be lost.

The howls of outrage that greeted this reasonable distinction were so great that Dr. Rand Paul felt compelled to backtrack on his statement. However, we are now discussing a book, not an election. Here, truth and justice are our only guides, not the hurt feelings of journalists working for the mainstream media and other sob sisters. As such, it is clear that discrimination on the part of individuals, but of course not the state, is part of our birthright of liberty.

If not, coercive bisexuality would be the logical implication of the anti-discrimination movement. Why? Well, male heterosexuals despicably discriminate against half the human race as bed/sex/marriage partners: all other men. Nor can female heterosexuals plead innocence against this dread charge; they, too, abjure half of their fellow creatures in this regard. Can male homosexuals deflect this deadly indictment? No, they, too, refuse to have anything to do with all females in such a context. Similarly, female homosexuals, lesbians, rotten creatures that they are, also avoid entangling alliances of this sort with all men, again, half the human race. No, it is the bisexuals, and *only* the bisexuals, who are entirely innocent of discrimination of this sort. They are the only decent people in the entire sexual spectrum to refrain from this evil practice. (We now disregard the fact that bisexuals also make invidious comparisons based on beauty, age, sense of humor, etc.) Therefore, if we really opposed discrimination in matters of the heart, we would all embrace bisexuality. Since we do not, the logical implication is that we should be forced to do so. For, to hang back from this conclusion is to give not only tacit but active approval to discriminatory practices, surely one of the worst things in the politically correct panoply.

It might well be objected that the laws against private parties discriminating should apply only to business, not personal interactions. But why just in commerce, and not, also, in human relations? Surely, if there is any such thing as the right not to be discriminated against, it applies in *all* realms of human existence, not merely in the marketplace. If we have a right not to be murdered, or stolen from, and we do, we do, then this right pervades *all* realms of human existence. It is *equally* improper to be killed or robbed in the bedroom as it is in the store. And, as a matter of fact, present anti-discrimination law does not even apply, across the board, in the commercial realm. Rather, it depends upon "power" relationships, a rather meaningless concept, at least as employed by our friends on the left. For example, if I hate Chinese people, and therefore will not patronize their restaurants, I violate no law. However, if the owner of the Chinese restaurant despises Jews, he will not legally be able to forbid them from entry onto his premises. Why? Because, in this case, sellers are deemed to be more "powerful" than buyers. But it does not always work in this way. If a large buyer, say, Wal-Mart, refused to purchase from any female-headed firm because of their taste for discrimination against women, they would not for a moment be able to get away with such a policy. But why should "power" in this misbegotten sense determine the legality of economic decision-making? Surely, a "powerless" man in the sense of being poor would not be allowed to rape a "powerful" woman, in the sense that she is rich. Or would he? Well, this defense has not yet been tried, so who knows?

Another objection is that it might be acceptable for any one individual to discriminate against a downtrodden minority, but if many, or, worse, all of the members of the majority engaged in this practice, its victims would suffer unduly. For example, suppose that whites refuse to rent hotel rooms to blacks, or to employ them. Then, the latter will undergo grievous misery. But this objection is economically illiterate. If whites boycott blacks in this manner, the free enterprise system will rise up in defense of the latter. How so? If no landlord will rent to a black person, the profits from doing so will rise; it will then be to some entrepreneur's financial advantage to supply this part of the market. Similarly, in the labor field, if whites refuse to hire blacks, their wages will fall below the levels that would otherwise prevail. This will set up large profit opportunities for someone, be he white or black it matters not, to hire these people, and thus be able to out-compete those with great(er) tastes for discrimination. (I am in these cases discussing only, employer/owner discrimination, and abstracting from customer and employee discrimination, complications I analyze in Block, 2008A.) But, this phenomenon did not overcome the plight of black people who were forced to sit in the back of the bus during the Jim Crow era in the south. Why not? Because entry into the bus industry was strictly limited by the political forces responsible for this reprehensible legal code in the first place. If private discrimination was all that was standing in the way of black people sitting in all reaches of the bus, competing firms would have supplied bus service.

Chapter 2.

Environmental Economics

2.1. Ron Paul and the Environment

We don't hear too much about Ron Paul's views on the environment. But, no surprise, he is very sound on this issue as he is on so many others, at least from a libertarian point of view. A strong advocate of private property rights, Dr. Paul correctly sees this as the cornerstone of a sound libertarian-based environmental policy.

The idea behind free market environmentalism (FME) is that pollution, whether of noise, smoke, dust particles, smells, whatever, is nothing more nor less than a trespass. It constitutes an uninvited border crossing of an owner's property, and thus a violation of private property rights. In the libertarian society, people who engaged in this sort of thing would be stopped, forthwith; injunctions would be granted for clear and present dangers, and damages, when demonstrated, would be assessed against the perpetrators. These would be torts, not crimes (unless of course the perpetrator did not cease and desist from these acts pursuant to a court order).

As for species going extinct, all of them would be allowed to be *owned*, and thus bought and sold. If any animal were nearing extinction, the price of the animal would rise. Then, the ordinary profit and loss incentives of the free enterprise system would kick in, and voila, end of problem. That is to say, "greed" would work in the direction of saving these species. The owners of elephant farms, for example, would jealously guard their private property against poachers; their game farms would be well protected, as are cows, at present. The cause of the problem from the free market point of view is that these animals all too often run free; the tragedy of the commons (when there are no clear property titles, the resource tends to vanish or be overused) applies to them, as poachers hunt them down for their valuable tusks.

In such a free or libertarian society, there would be no need for "clean air" acts, nor regulations protecting rare species, or any of the plethora of laws beloved of the "watermelons" (green on the outside, but red on the inside).

However, quite recently, Congressman Paul has come under attack by a law professor from the University of California at Berkeley. According to Daniel Farber, who is the Sho Sato Professor of Law and chair of the Energy and Resources Group at UC Berkeley (he is also their faculty director of the Center for Law, Energy, and the Environment), Ron Paul's policy planks, if implemented, would be a disaster for the environment.

First, not unreasonably, Farber links to Ron Paul's web site on environmentalism. There, we read this:

The free market – not government – is the solution to America's energy needs.

Unfortunately, decades of misguided federal action have helped lead to skyrocketing fuel prices, making it even more difficult for hardworking families to make ends meet.

Washington's bureaucratic regulations, corporate subsidies, and excessive taxation have distorted the market and resulted in government bureaucrats picking winners and losers.

In fact, much of the "pain at the pump" Americans are now feeling is due to federal policies designed by environmental alarmists to punish traditional energy production – like oil, coal, and natural gas – in hopes of making energy sources they favor more "economical."

Sadly, even with $4.00 a gallon gasoline, many are attempting to make our energy crisis even worse by working to impose job-destroying carbon taxes, or a "Cap and Tax" system.

As long as we allow federal regulations and bureaucratic red tape to get in the way of energy exploration, our country will never solve its energy crisis, and Americans will continue to pay the price in high costs.

A pro-energy president

As president, Ron Paul will lead the fight to:

- *Remove restrictions on drilling, so companies can tap into the vast amount of oil we have here at home.*

- *Repeal the federal tax on gasoline. Eliminating the federal gas tax would result in a savings of 18 cents per gallon for American consumers.*

- *Lift government roadblocks to the use of coal and nuclear power.*

- *Eliminate the ineffective EPA. Polluters should answer directly to property owners in court for the damages they create – not to Washington.*

- *Make tax credits available for the purchase and production of alternative fuel technologies.*

It's time for a president that recognizes the free market's power and innovative spirit by unleashing its full potential to produce affordable, environmentally sound, and reliable energy.

This all sounds pretty good to me. My only "complaint" is that Congressman Paul does not call for the imprisonment of those responsible for creating the unconstitutional and thus illegal EPA in the first place (they don't call me Walter "Moderate" Block for nothing), but I'll let that lacunae slip. You can't have everything. Dr. Paul is, after all, a politician, and what can you expect from such people? That's why I give him only a 97% libertarian rating.

In contrast to me, Farber is aghast, aghast I tells you. He is appalled that there should be any such thing as free market environmentalism (for the best publication on this subject ever written, the one that informs my own views on these matters, Rothbard 1982). Ecological concern, don't you know, is a monopoly of progressives, socialists and liberals. Now, here are Farber's comments, in *italics*, and my reaction is interspersed with his comments:

OK, what's wrong with this proposal? Here are a few things:

1. Why just property owners? Why not other people with health effects? Is there some reason why a tenant with asthma can't sue, but a company with paint damage can go to court? Because property values matter, but not human health?

There is a clear answer why Ron Paul specifies *"property owners"* not *"tenants."* This is because the property owner has the ultimate responsibility for the property in question. "The buck stops" with the property owner. And, you may well ask, who is the "property owner" in the case of tenancy? Why, of course, it is the *tenant.* It is the tenant who is the temporary "property owner" for as long as the lease contract is in effect. But, there is a complication. If a third party, the polluter, is bombarding the home in question with smoke particles, this not only affects the temporary property owner, the tenant (e.g., his lungs), it *also* negatively impacts the permanent property owner, the landlord (his property is being physically invaded and damaged, and as a result he will not be able to charge his tenants as much money compared to the situation where his property rights were sacrosanct). Both of them may, in the free society, obtain an injunction against the polluter, warding off future offenses, as well as seek damages for past wrongs. Does Farber really think it is fair to criticize a broad policy plank for not engaging in this level of specificity? Evidently, all's fair in love, war and politics, at least for this law professor.

Nor is his criticism of Ron Paul a fair one based on the claim that "*property values matter, but not human health.*" Indeed, as we have seen, the two go together! Farber seems unacquainted with Adam Smith's invisible hand; we are led through the market process to promote the general good. In this case, the way to earn profits is by pleasing customers, not alienating them. Why else would the landlord want to sue the polluter apart from protecting his tenant from this nuisance, if not that the higher rents he can collect would reflect a more desirable pollution-free environment? To maximize profits, of course. (This is why the landlord has an incentive – in the absence of government interferences like rent control, to paint, to fix the plumbing, make other repairs, etc.). But these considerations lead precisely in the direction of "*human health.*" This Berkeley law professor does not at all appreciate the benefits of the marketplace in protecting "*human health.*" He seems to think that if the government doesn't do it, then it doesn't really count.

2. Who would be the defendants? If you live in a big city, how do you sue all of the polluters for damage? Do you sue everyone who has a car or truck for contributing to air pollution? How do you pay for the expert witnesses and legal fees?

The defendants would be the polluters, of course. Who else? No, you don't sue all the polluters; only the ones who have actually trespassed their garbage onto your property (whether you own the property temporarily or permanently, it matters not one whit). How would you determine who is who? Under free enterprise, there would arise an industry composed of firms that engage in environmental forensics. Thanks to popular television shows, we are all now well-acquainted with ordinary forensics (the study of blood, semen, hair follicles to determine who has committed a crime). Environmental forensics would be carried on in much the same way. The victim would hire a company familiar with the chemistry of pollution. This firm would take samples from the affected property. Then, woe betide the company guilty of such trespasses.

No, you don't have to "*sue everyone who has a car or truck for contributing to air pollution.*" That is silly; it would be *way* too cumbersome. In the free society, all roads, streets, highways, avenues, thoroughfares, etc., would be privately owned. There would be far fewer street owners than motorists. You would just sue them (if your environmental forensics agent found evidence on your property of the end products of vehicle fuel); it would be a lot more efficient and reasonable than trying to take every single motorist in the big city to court.

But, to directly respond to Farber's challenge, one way of financing such law suits would be on a contingency basis. Under proper libertarian law, the forensic firm would offer chemists, lawyers, etc. If they were convinced there was an actual case of pollution, they would likely go to court in support of their clients and initially bear these costs. We must not lose sight of the fact that many victims of pollution are very large corporations, some with thousands of tenants. Surely, they could self-finance any necessary lawsuits.

3. Why only damages? If he truly believed in property rights, he'd allow injunctions to stop the harm from continuing.

In the FME philosophy, there would of course be injunctions in cases of clear and present dangers. No person in a crowded city should be allowed to keep dynamite on his premises. If anyone did, an injunction against him would surely be justified. Just because this point is not mentioned in a brief entry on a web site is surely not a valid criticism of the Paul campaign. These statements, by their very nature, must be brief. They cannot possibly cover all bases. I note that the site does not mention species extinction, either. Does this mean that Congressman Paul wants all species to disappear? Or is unconcerned with endangerment of elephants, rhinos, etc.? Of course not. Farber is a cheap-shot artist. In the libertarian literature on the environment recommended below, the justification for injunctions is certainly included. The ethos of libertarianism opposes initiatory force, *or the threat thereof.* And, what is to be done, the only thing that *can* be done, about the latter? Injunctions, of course.

4. How would courts handle the immense body of litigation? The pollution suits would be the world's biggest class actions, with millions of plaintiffs, swarms of defendants, huge fees for expert witnesses, etc. Is that really what conservatives want?

These questions and challenges assume that there would *be* any pollution under a regime of free enterprise with strict protection for private property rights. There would not be. If the law of the land was strictly enforced against the trespass of smoke particles, this practice would be virtually eliminated. Right now, the law of trespass against home invasions *is* strictly enforced. It is must be a rare thing indeed that someone goes on vacation, and comes home to find strangers living in his house. Why? Because such would-be trespassers know full well that if they tried any such shenanigans, they would be summarily removed from the premises, and face criminal charges. As a result, there are no "*millions of plaintiffs, swarms of defendants, huge fees for expert witnesses*" in these cases. But the same applies to trespassing dust, smoke and other pollutants.

We've already tried this approach, and it didn't work. This is more or less where the law stood fifty years ago. We didn't pass modern environmental laws because we loved regulation; we passed them because the old system led to massive air and water pollution. This isn't a policy proposal. It's a libertarian fantasy. And a callous one at that.

If this was truly the system we had "*fifty years ago*" then Farber should well know the answers to the questions he poses didn't he raise it as his 4th point?. Did we not have "*big cities*" in 1962, five decades ago? How did it work, then, Farber? Were there "*millions of plaintiffs, swarms of defendants, huge fees for expert witnesses*" in those days? Of course not.

This Berkeley law professor is off by a little bit more than one century in his charges; I guess they don't teach history, or even acknowledge it, at this world-famous university. 'Twas not in 1962 that we had a legal system similar to the one Ron Paul is proposing and Farber apoplectically opposing. Rather, this took place, at least in proximate form, during the middle of the *nineteenth* century (see on this a very important work by historian Morton Horwitz, 1977). In that bygone era, people *were* allowed to sue for pollution. When the case of pollution victims, e.g., environmental plaintiffs, was demonstrated in court, they received damages after the fact, and/or injunctions beforehand. They didn't always win, of course. The burden of proof always properly rests with the plaintiffs, not the defendants.

This property rights system had several very salutary effects. For one, manufacturers were led, by Adam Smith's invisible hand, into substituting more expensive but cleaner-burning anthracite coal for cheaper but dirtier burning sulfur coal. For another, the infant industry of environmental forensics was born. Someone, after all, had to testify, and demonstrate that this here particular dirt particle emanated from that there smokestack. Railroads were incentivized for similar reasons to capture the sparks from their engines, instead of allowing them to spread hundreds of feet from the tracks onto their neighbors' property. The manufacturers of chimneys had reason to place meshes in them, to capture the end products of the burning process before they could land in other people's lungs and on physical property. Was this legal system perfect? No, of course not, no human creation ever is. But it worked tolerably well, until the "Progressive" period at the end of the nineteenth century and beginning of the twentieth.

Then, when the environmental plaintiff went to court, a new legal philosophy took place. We were not "number one," then, the leading hegemon, the most powerful imperialist nation in the world. No, that title belonged to England, at the time. But our political leaders had ambitions in that direction, and their views began to permeate the courts. So the next time a little old lady complained about a factory dirtying her washing on the clothes line, or a small farmer complained about sparks from a railroad burning his haystacks, the response was much more likely to be: "Yes, yes, they violated your private property rights, your stinking, lousy, selfish private property rights; but there is something more important, far more important, than them: the public good. And, in what does the public good consist? Why, in manufacturing, railroads, heavy industry. We're not going to become the leading military power by taking the side of little old ladies and small agriculturalists." Here is an actual Supreme Court of Georgia opinion of this sort: "The pollution of the air, so far as reasonably necessary to the enjoyment of life and indispensable to the progress of society, is not actionable" (Holman v. Athens Empire Laundry Co., 1919, cited here). Not actionable? That means that environmental polluters cannot be sued. No one can be granted an injunction against them. They are liable for no damages when they rampage over other people's property, with their pollutants.

As a sop to the victims of pollution, however, the legislatures did institute minimum smokestack height requirements, thus making it far more difficult to determine the guilty parties, the violators of private property. As can be expected, horrific air and water pollution followed. If there were a "good" heavy industrialist who engaged in research and development in smoke-prevention devices, who used more expensive but cleaner-burning anthracite coal, who placed traps in his chimney etc., he would be at a competitive disadvantage vis-à-vis other members of his industry who followed these new laws and judicial findings, and used other people's property as a free depository for their air and water-borne garbage. Under such a legal regime, it is no accident that pollution became a gigantic problem. The leftist critics, the Daniel Farbers of the day, claimed that free enterprise and private property rights had failed. Only government could solve the problem, with its EPA and myriad regulations. But, as we have seen, the real cause of the difficulty was not at all that free enterprise and private property rights could not cut the mustard. It was that they functioned reasonably well from the beginning of our country in the late eighteenth century but were then extinguished at the onset of the Progressive period, in the late nineteenth.

Lookit, Mr. Farber; this is not the time or place for a full dress rehearsal of free market environmentalism. There is an immense amount of literature on this subject. As I hope you can appreciate in this op-ed I can only touch, very briefly, on a few of the pertinent high points. But, if you are serious in pursuing this matter, I urge you to read some of the Austrian economic literature. And, in the meantime, I suggest you refrain from attacking Ron Paul on an issue about which you are woefully ignorant. A law professor with a specialty in "Law, Energy, and the Environment" really should know a bit about this subject.

2.2. Global Warming, Air Pollution and Libertarianism

I have been asked a series of very interesting, important and challenging questions by a loyal reader of LewRockwell.com who will remain anonymous. My thought is that these queries of his, and my responses to them, might prove to be of interest to readers. My answers follow these marks (<<) and are in *italics*. He begins here:

The problem I have is global warming.

Let's ignore any scientific debate and just accept, for the sake of argument, that emissions of carbon dioxide cause changes to the climate and those changes cause things like rising sea levels that damage property and could potentially lead to the extinction of mankind on Earth.

<< *Ok. I'll try to deal with this contrary to fact conditional, at least arguendo.*

I have read your essay "Environmentalism and Economic Freedom: The Case For Private Property Rights"

<< *Bless you, bless you. Those are the sweetest words an author can read. For the full cite on that publication,* go to Block, 1998.

I can see that if I were emitting a pollutant that caused damage to the property of another, the case is quite clearly an invasion of property rights and easily dealt with.

<< *Yes, that is basic libertarian theory regarding trespass.*

I am not so sure about carbon dioxide. Clearly this is not a pollutant per se and does not cause any direct damage to property. If emitting carbon dioxide onto another's land was an invasion of property rights, then surely we would all have to stop breathing.

<< *Let me say at the outset that my mentor and guru on the issue of applying libertarian property rights theory to environmental challenge is Murray N. Rothbard. His 1982 article is THE best thing that has ever been written on this subject.*

<<*I agree with every single word of it, with great enthusiasm. I think this magnificent essay should be required reading for all of those interested in a libertarian perspective on the environment.*

<<As to your specific question, there is in law a concept called de minimis: the law does not concern itself with trifles. Exhaling, on that ground alone, cannot be considered a trespass.

<<But there is another even more important reason we are all innocent when we breathe out: homesteading. Before there could be private property rights, there had to have been people. And, human beings, to the best of my limited scientific knowledge, always exhale. So, there was carbon dioxide being emitted from this source before there was any homesteading of land. (Exhaling creatures did the homesteading; but, first, they breathed in and out.) Therefore, we inherited the right to exhale from our forebears. They exhaled rather promiscuously. They bequeathed this right to us. They did it; so may we.

As you quote Rothbard in your excellent essay, "David Friedman & Libertarianism a Critique"

"... consider the case of radio waves, which is a crossing of other people's boundaries that is invisible and insensible in every way to the property owner. We are all bombarded by radio waves that cross our properties without our knowledge or consent. Are they invasive and should they therefore be illegal, now that we have scientific devices to detect such waves? Are we then to outlaw all radio transmission? And if not, why not?

"The reason why not is that these boundary crossings do not interfere with anyone's exclusive possession, use or enjoyment of their property. They are invisible, cannot be detected by man's senses, and do no harm. They are therefore not really invasions of property, for we must refine our concept of invasion to mean not just boundary crossing, but boundary crossings that in some way interfere with the owner's use or enjoyment of this property. What counts is whether the senses of the property owner are interfered with."

My problem is that if emitting carbon dioxide is not a violation of property rights but excessive amounts in the atmosphere actually does cause climate change that damages property and perhaps eventually causes the extinction of mankind on the planet, is there any Libertarian solution to the problem ?

<< You misspelled "Libertarian." Upper case means the Libertarian Party, lower case indicates the general movement or the libertarian

philosophy. (Hey, I'm a professor; I have to be pedantic. Otherwise, they'll kick me out of the profession.)

<<I don't see the problem. Exhaling, like radio waves, "cannot be detected by man's senses, and do no harm." So, no harm, no foul. So let's forget about exhaling. Instead, consider massive outputs of carbon dioxide, so gigantic that they wreck the entire atmosphere, and kill us all. For example, what if there was some sort of super carbon dioxide generator? Now, that is an entirely different kettle of fish. The problem with our leftist, progressive friends on environmentalism is that they never offer us a criterion on the basis of which we can infer rights violations. They blather endlessly about global warming, global cooling, climate change, ad nauseam. But they never state the criteria of success or failure. Is it the present temperature? Two degrees less? One degree more? However, with regard to this gargantuan carbon dioxide machine that kills us all, we libertarians would certainly admit that human rights (that is, property rights) have long ago been violated way before we died from it en masse. In the free or libertarian society, the owner of this machine would surely be enjoined from starting it up.

How can you prevent an action that is not a violation of property rights, without violating the rights of the emitter?

<<There is confusion here between the illicit super-duper CO2 generator, and legitimate exhaling. The former is the only rights violator here, not the latter. So, there is no "action that is not a violation of property rights," (exhaling) that is being unjustifiably stopped by law. The only thing subject to an injunction would be the massive polluter.

Of course people could simply get together and agree not to emit, but as you say in your essay on environmentalism:

"For to engage in environmentally sound business practices under a legal regime that no longer requires this, is to impose on oneself a competitive disadvantage. Other things being equal, this will guarantee bankruptcy."

<<I do not at all resort to agreements. The massive polluter is a trespasser, and must be stopped by the force of law.

My questions boil down to:

1. Is emission of carbon dioxide an invasion of property rights. (If so why, and what about breathing?)

<<Yes, GIGANTIC, MASSIVE CO2 emissions violate property rights; exhaling does not.

2. If it is an invasion of property rights how can it be enforced? (There is no way of connecting individual instances of damage to specific emitters.)

<< It is enforced the same way laws against murder and rape are enforced. If there is a (hopefully very limited) government, then its main, perhaps even only, task is to stop such violations as murder, rape, kidnapping, arson, fraud, and, yes, trespassing massive (not teeny) amounts of carbon dioxide. If we live under free market anarchism, then the private courts-police will do this.

<<Perhaps you are uncomfortable with the notion that we would be putting in jail someone (the massive emitter), for doing something to a greater degree that we all do (exhaling) to a lesser degree. But there is precedent for this. We can all talk in a normal voice; but we cannot get a super bullhorn, and scream at people so loudly through it that we literally deafen them. We all smell a bit, even after taking a shower, but that is entirely legal. However, it should not be within the law to set up a pig farm or a tanning factory in a residential neighborhood that was built in a relatively odor-free environment. It is quite all right to shine a flashlight at someone's house. But not such a powerful one that it burns down this dwelling.

<<There is, too, a "way of connecting individual instances of damage to specific emitters." Consider automobile pollution. There are millions of cars out there, emitting pollutants into hundreds of millions of people's lungs. Yes it would appear to be difficult, if not impossible, (transactions costs, beloved of the pinko Chicago School of economics) to handle this through lawsuits. But, as Rothbard says, that is because at present we have road and highway socialism. If these transit lanes were privatized (see my book on that subject, Block, 2009), then victims of such pollution would take these owners to court, and there would be many fewer of them than motorists. It would be relatively easy to do so. Road owners would thus have an incentive to

anticipate this risk to themselves, by, presumably, charging VERY high prices to polluting cars. Adam Smith's "invisible hand" would thus lead us in the direction of air-quality sanity.

3. If it is not an invasion of property rights, then how can we solve the problem of global warming without infringing on the property rights of the emitter?

<<If we are still in arguendo mode, positing a vast polluter, then we are not at all violating his rights when we compel him to cease and desist. Hey, he is in effect a murderer. We stop him in self-defense, just as we would a guy running at us, screaming and brandishing a knife or gun.

4. It is theoretically possible for many deminimis acts to collectively cause a problem. Take a smaller-scale analogy. I own a river. A small boy urinates in the river. This causes no harm to the river or the fish in it. It is invisible, cannot be detected by man's senses and does no harm. However, if 1,000 or 10,000 unconnected boys all urinate in my river at the same time, then all the fish in my river will die and my property rights will clearly have been violated. However, on what basis do I have any right to stop any single boy whose individual actions are below any sensible deminimis threshold and do not constitute a violation of property rights alone?

<< There is a disanalogy between urinating on someone else's property and exhaling, when a few molecules of CO2 waft over onto someone else's property. Forget about the "small boy." The criminal law works differently for children than for adults. Also, un-owned rivers present difficulties, so I'll ignore them as well. If an adult urinates in my front yard with no permission, I can have him arrested, and properly so. I might well not do so, if the guy was desperate, there were no men's' rooms around, etc. But, if I knew that 1,000 men were going to inundate my garden in advance, I would again have the right to stop them through force of law, and this time I probably would, otherwise I'd have no garden left. However, if there were one or 1,000 men who exhaled near my property, and all of their CO2 "trespassed" on my garden, one, I would not know about it, and two, the law would properly defend their right to this "invasion," not mine to stop them. Why? Because people have been exhaling from time immemorial; thus, our grandfathers have homesteaded this right for us, the present generation. Of course, they have been urinating too, for all these

epochs, but, NOT on other people's property. The homeowners, presumably, took sharp offense at THAT practice.

5. Why is even a large emission of carbon dioxide a violation of property rights? As Rothbard says:

"The reason why not is that these boundary crossings do not interfere with anyone's exclusive possession, use or enjoyment of their property. They are invisible, cannot be detected by man's senses, and do no harm. They are therefore not really invasions of property, for we must refine our concept of invasion to mean not just boundary crossing, but boundary crossings that in some way interfere with the owner's use or enjoyment of this property. What counts is whether the senses of the property owner are interfered with."

The emissions of carbon dioxide, even in large quantities at say a power station, are "invisible, cannot be detected by man's senses, and do no harm" themselves. It is only when these emissions join with other emissions from other sources and react with the other gases in the atmosphere that the alleged greenhouse effect takes place, which allegedly causes, for example, the sea levels to rise and damage another's property.

The emitters' actions <u>only</u> cause a violation of property rights if other people act in a certain way and the emitter has no control over the actions of the other people. How can it be a violation of property rights to do something that causes no harm itself, but leads to harm <u>only</u> if other people do something?

<< Let's take noise as an analogy, here. I live next door to a sports stadium where thousands of people gather. I was there first. I homesteaded the rights to a reasonably quiet environment. I live in a large city, so there is always SOME noise about; it is not deathly quiet. My neighbor schedules athletic events at 4 a.m., while I am trying to sleep. (I know this is unlikely, but work with me here.) Now, if there were one or two people talking, even loudly, downstairs, I not only would not object (I live on the 30th floor, and can hardly hear them), but the law would properly not allow me to protest, since small groups of people homesteaded such rights (they were doing that long before my building was constructed). But when tens of thousands of people cheer on for the home team, they keep me awake. So here is a case where "The emitters' actions <u>only</u> cause a violation of property rights if other people act in a certain way and the emitter has no control over

the actions of the other people." Any one fan yelling in the stadium is de minimus. No one fan can control the yells of other rooters. And, yet, surely, I may enjoin the entire stadium from keeping me awake, whereas I cannot object to a few people screaming. Here, we truly have a case where it can "be a violation of property rights to do something that causes no harm itself, but leads to harm only if other people do something."

6. How does the analogy with private roads help with respect to the atmosphere?

I can see how a private road system could work (love your book!), but I don't see how the analogy carries over.

a. On what basis could ownership of the atmosphere be homesteaded?

b. Even if people owned specific tracts of atmosphere, how could the person whose property was damaged link the damage to the tract of atmosphere that took the emissions? The system is fluid and, it would appear, impossible to draw back a chain of causation to a specific tract of receiving atmosphere any more than to a specific emitter. And as Rothbard said:

"Thus, a strict causal connection must exist between an aggressor and a victim, and this connection must be provable beyond a reasonable doubt. It must be causality in the commonsense concept of strict proof of the 'A hit B' variety, not mere probability or statistical correlation."

<< a. I never said that the atmosphere could be homesteaded. I don't think it can be, at least nowadays, since it is a superfluous good. It is not scarce. On the moon and Mars, oxygen will be bought and sold like any other market commodity (or given away as a loss leader), but not here, not now. In talking about private roads, I was merely demonstrating that transactions costs considerations would not preclude our society from viewing air pollution as a tort that could be dealt with by the courts. It is awkward in the extreme to have 300 million inhabitants of the U.S. sue some millions of car owners for pollution. But, if the nation's highways were owned, say, by 100 corporations, it would be a lot more feasible.

<< b. Here is where environmental forensics come in. If we had all along been dealing with the question of air pollution as we should have been, as a trespass of smoke or dirt particles, there would have also developed an industry devoted to demonstrating such rights violations. We have a profession that analyzes semen, hair follicles, blood types, etc., because we properly see murder and rape as rights violations, and wish to determine "who dunnit." We have no such accomplishments with regard to air pollution because, as Rothbard demonstrates, we have long lost out way on this matter, in terms of proper law.

Thanks for your assistance with this; it really helps me to appreciate the power of libertarianism by examining the problem cases.!

<< You are entirely welcome. Your questions were very good ones. If we cannot answer the difficult objections, we must rethink our libertarian positions. I think it is crucially important that the challenges you pose be refuted, because Ron Paul is now being criticized by left-wing environmentalists for having either no views, or incorrect ones, on these important issues. I don't say, of course, that Congressman Paul would agree with every point I make. But he and I are both followers of Murray N. Rothbard on this (and many other) issue(s), so I would not be totally surprised if he supported most of the analysis I offer.

Chapter 3.

The Federal Reserve System

If Ron Paul is famous for anything in economics, it is for his deep and abiding suspicion of the Federal Reserve System. He has gone so far in this direction as to call for an end to the Fed (Paul, 2001). The three entries in this chapter deal with that subject.

3.1. The Fed is a Criminal Organization

I often get very nasty letters that make my blood boil. I guess that is the price regular columnists of LewRockwell.com have to pay for contributing to this blog, since we all take rather unpopular positions on many issues. Often these letters are filled with nasty expletives, question my parentage, and much worse.

But rarely do I receive a letter that really infuriates me. The one below is entirely polite. There is not a slur in it. No questioning of my sanity, my morality, my ethnic or religious persuasion. There is no threat in it, implied or explicit. And yet, this one is far worse than those others. I repeat it below, along with my response to it. See if it doesn't enrage you, too. (My antagonist is an economist with the Fed. I render him anonymous, to save him embarrassment.)

From: Mr. R

Sent: Saturday, January 21, 2012 2:28 PM

To: wblock@loyno.edu

Subject: Federal Reserve Board Research Assistant Opportunities

Dear Professor Block:

I am writing to request your assistance in informing your department's students about Research Assistant (RA) positions at the Federal Reserve Board. Our positions are highly competitive; each year we hire approximately 20-30 recent undergraduates as RAs. While at the Board, RAs work on a broad range of topics and have the opportunity to increase their quantitative skills by working on both real-world policy issues and high-level research projects. After their time at the Board, many of our RAs move on to top graduate school programs.

Additionally, we offer summer internships for economics, mathematics, and finance students to work on advanced research projects with Board economists.

Thank you for supporting our program.

Best,

Mr. R

Research Recruiting Administrator
Division of Research and Statistics
Board of Governors of the Federal Reserve System
Washington, D.C. 20551
202-736-1912
www.federalreserve.gov

Dear Mr. R:

I will indeed pass along your message to my students. I will do so, despite the fact that I think yours is a criminal organization, because, one, I owe it to my students to pass along information about all (presently) legal job openings and two, because I like to have my students make up their own minds about issues of this sort.

But when I do so in my next mailing to them, I will append a message of my own, alongside yours.

Here it is:

Dear Students:

I regard the Fed as a criminal organization, since it engages in (well, aids and abets) counterfeiting. The Fed is to the U.S. economy what the old central planning apparatus of the late and non-lamented Soviet Union was to the entire economy of the U.S.S.R. The Federal Reserve System has been responsible, since its inception in 1913, for destroying some 96 percent of the value of our dollar, the life blood of our economy. This organization has exacerbated the business cycle. It has created both inflation and unemployment. These people, along with HUD, Fannie and Freddie, are responsible for the depression that currently afflicts us. (For more on this, read Ron Paul's *End the Fed* and Murray Rothbard's *The Mystery of Banking and What Has Government Done to Our Money* and *The Case for a 100 Percent Gold Dollar*).

I pray, hope and trust that Ron Paul will be the next president of the U.S. If so, I think I have a shot at being one of the people he brings to Washington, D.C., to help him implement his programs of reducing the governmental footprint. If so, I hope he appoints me the next head of the Fed. If so, I will do my level best to end this monstrosity of an institution with all deliberate speed, and institute a 100 percent gold-backed dollar in its place. I shall also do what I can to institute a Nuremberg type trial for all employees of the Fed. Not only should we audit them, we should throw in jail all of those responsible for counterfeiting, creating unemployment and inflation, and all but destroying our currency.

And here is a message for you, personally, Mr. R.

You "Thank (me) for supporting (your) program." But what makes you think I support the Fed? Is it because I am an economist, often write on macro-money issues, and your organization has suborned almost this entire subset of the economics profession with high-paying jobs, assistance-ships, and entre into prestigious journals which are necessary for promotion in academia (White, 2005). Well, if so, yours was a good guess. Most economists, particularly those who do research in macro-money, have indeed been purchased by your organization. However, I am an exception to this general rule. I oppose central planning whether in farming, manufacturing, or, in the provision of money and central banking. I am a rarity in the economics profession: someone who actually supports Ron Paul.

I have no doubt that "After their time at the Board, many of (y)our RAs move on to top graduate school programs." All I can say about this is, so much the worse for "top graduate school programs." What they teach there, and what you use at the Fed, is Keynesianism and Monetarism. It is greatly to be regretted that at none of these institutions is Austrian economics even considered, let alone mentioned. What the Fed and these "top" programs do to Mises, Hayek and Rothbard, namely ignore them, is what the mainstream media try to do to Ron Paul; namely, act as if he is the 13th floor of the hotel, in the words of that great philosopher, Jon Stewart. For this reason alone, yours is not a legitimate scientific institution.

Mr. R, it is not too late for you, personally. You can quit your job in that evil institution and seek honest employment elsewhere. There, you can actually contribute to the creation of goods and services purchased by voluntary customers instead of mercilessly battening down on them.

Best regards,

Walter E. Block, Ph.D.

From: Mr. R

Sent: Monday, January 23, 2012 11:40 AM

To: Walter Block

Subject: RE: Federal Reserve Board Research Assistant Opportunities

Professor Block,

Thank you for passing information regarding the Board's Research Assistant and Internship programs along to your students.

Regards,

Mr. R

Research Recruiting Administrator
Division of Research and Statistics
Board of Governors of the Federal Reserve System
Washington, D.C. 20551
202-736-1912
www.federalreserve.gov

Dear Mr. R:

I take it that you have not read what I sent you?

Yours truly,

Walter E. Block, Ph.D.

From: Mr. R

Sent: Monday, January 23, 2012 12:03 PM

To: Walter Block

Subject: RE: Federal Reserve Board Research Assistant Opportunities

Professor Block,

I did. Your e-mail and blog post do not diminish my appreciation of your willingness to communicate information about our programs to your students/recent graduates regardless of your assessment of my employer. As you wrote, "(you) like to have (your) students make up their own minds about issues of this sort," including, I'm sure, where to seek employment and further their research skills, engage in policy issues, and gain exposure to central banking. Your dedication to your students in spite of your personal feelings is the hallmark of a good professor.

Best regards,

Mr. R

Research Recruiting Administrator
Division of Research and Statistics
Board of Governors of the Federal Reserve System
Washington, DC 20551
202-736-1912
www.federalreserve.gov
Dear Mr. R:

I take it, then, that you don't care to respond, substantively, to what I have said?

Yours truly,

Walter E. Block, Ph.D.

Mr. R did not reply to this query of mine.

3.2. Ron Paul and the Fed: A Rejoinder to David Frum

(with William Barnett II)

According to David Frum:

"Ron Paul … is best known for his vehemently isolationist foreign policy views. But his core supporters also thrill to his self-taught monetary views, which amount to a rejection of everything taught by modern economists from Alfred Marshall to Milton Friedman.

"… Paul (has) not the faintest idea of what (he) is talking about. The problem is not that (his) answers are wrong — that can happen to anyone. The problem is that (he does not) understand the questions, and (is) too lazy or too arrogant to learn."

There is more wrong here than you can shake a stick at. Let us list the errors.

Congressman Paul is *not* an isolationist; rather, he is a *non interventionist*. He has repeated this over and over again, but, evidently, Frum has still not caught on. An isolationist wants to, well, *isolate* our country from all others. Dr. Paul desires nothing of the sort. Rather, he wants the U.S. to be fully involved in world affairs. He seeks cultural, social and economic relationships with members of all other nations. He only rejects the imposition of our values on others at the point of a gun; that is, he opposes *interventionism.* In this, he may be out of step with the other candidates for the Republican nomination, but not at all with our founding fathers:

"My ardent desire is, and my aim has been … to comply strictly with all our engagements foreign and domestic; but to keep the United States free from political connections with every other Country. To see that they may be independent of all, and under the influence of none. In a word, I want an American character, that the powers of Europe may be convinced we act for ourselves and not for others; this, in my judgment, is the only way to be respected abroad and happy at home." — George Washington (letter to Patrick Henry, 9 October 1775) Reference: *The Writings of George Washington, Fitzpatrick*, ed., vol. 34 (335)

"Peace, commerce and honest friendship with all nations — entangling alliances with none, I deem [one of] the essential principles of our government, and consequently [one of] those which ought to shape its administration."— Thomas Jefferson: 1st Inaugural Address, 1801. ME 3:321

"But [the United States] goes not abroad, in search of monsters to destroy. She is the well-wisher to the freedom and independence of all. She is the champion and vindicator only of her own.

"She will commend the general cause by the countenance of her voice, and the benignant sympathy of her example. She well knows that by once enlisting under other banners than her own, were they even the banners of foreign independence, she would involve herself beyond the power of extrication, in all the wars of interest and intrigue, of individual avarice, envy, and ambition, which assume the colors and usurp the standard of freedom. The fundamental maxims of her policy would insensibly change from liberty to force. ... She might become the dictatress of the world. She would be no longer the ruler of her own spirit...." *When John Quincy Adams served as U. S. Secretary of State, he delivered this speech to the U.S. House of Representatives on July 4, 1821, in celebration of American Independence Day.*

Nor is Dr. Paul opposed to our imperialist venture in Iraq merely "because what we are doing in Iraq isn't working." He opposes this since such policies are incompatible with the views of the founding fathers, with the Constitution, and because no one from On High has appointed us to be the policeman of the world. In any case, whether something "works" or not depends entirely upon one's goal. The present debacle in that tormented country is "working" just fine, thank you, for the likes of Bechtel and Halliburton.

His monetary views are not at all "self-taught." He readily admits he stands on the shoulders of giants in this regard, members of the Austrian School of Economics, preeminently, Ludwig von Mises and Murray Rothbard. However, even if Frum was correct on this and Paul's economic views were self-taught, that at least implies he has *learned* some of the dismal science, unlike many of his fellow congressmen, and even some journalists (hint, hint, Frum). Moreover, he is actually a many times published author on this subject.

Alfred Marshall (1842—1924) is hardly a "modern economist."

"Lazy?" "Arrogant?" Sounds more like the author of these words than Ron Paul. The congressman from Texas, who is now crisscrossing the country giving speeches at a rate that would exhaust a much younger man, may be the most well-read member of the House of Representatives. Okay, okay, to say that is to damn with faint praise. Let us put it in these terms then; were he not a politician, *and* a doctor, *his published research in economics* would alone falsify Frum's charge.

This "indictment" constitutes nothing more than name-calling. Frum does not mention even *one* specific error made by Paul. He contents himself with the material quoted above.

Despite the glee with which we have pointed out these errors, the main focus of the present essay, however, concerns the oft made charge that Mr. Paul is "kooky" in his criticism of the Fed. After all, this monetary institution has been around since 1913, almost 100 years. Is it not irresponsible to advocate its demise?

Well, no. Very much to the contrary, Ron Paul's plan to abolish the Fed is the essence of monetary soundness. And this is for several reasons.

Under the control of this "venerable" institution, inflation has soared.

According to the inflation calculator, "What cost $100.00 in 1913 would cost $2014.81 in 2006. Also, if you were to buy exactly the same products in 2006 and 1913, they would cost you $100.00 and $4.96 respectively." In other words, under the aegis of the Fed, every dollar under its control is now worth slightly less than a nickel.

Let us compare this with a similar 93-year time period before the creation of the Fed. This calculation shows that "What cost $100.00 in 1820 would cost $63.02 in 1913. Also, if you were to buy exactly the same products in 1913 and 1820, they would cost you $100.00 and $158.69 respectively." In other words, the dollar held its value to a far greater degree under the relatively more free market situation before the advent of the Fed. (Indeed, it was worth *more* at the end of that period than at its beginning.) What is so "kooky" about ridding ourselves of an institution that debauches the currency to such a degree, particularly when the free enterprise system has shown money not only need not lose its value but can actually increase in purchasing power?

Far from "ironing out" the business cycle, under the watch of the Fed it has been exacerbated.

But is not Frum correct in asserting that Paul is "out of touch" with the respectable mainstream of the economics profession, as represented by Milton Friedman. Yes, this cannot be denied. Just as Dr. Paul is "out of touch" with the mainstream media, this is true in terms of what passes for the community of "expert" economists.

Milton Friedman, although linked in the public mind as the chief exemplar of free enterprise, was actually no such thing. Rothbard shows that his claim as a leading spokesman for liberty and the marketplace is highly overblown. This is a conclusion that emerges from this exchange as well: Friedman, Milton vs. Walter Block. (2006B). Further, Prof. Friedman is particularly weak in the monetary arena as an exemplar of capitalism.

Here is an interesting quote from Milton Friedman, which is very much apropos to our present concerns:

Major premise: Socialism is a failure. Even lifelong Communists now accept this proposition. Wherever socialism has been tried, it has proved unable to deliver the goods, either in the material form of a high standard of living or in the immaterial form of human freedom.

Minor premise: Capitalism is a success. Economies that have used capitalism — free private markets — as their principal means of organizing economic activity have proved capable of combining widely shared prosperity and a high measure of human freedom. A private market system has proved to be a necessary, though not a sufficient condition for prosperity and freedom.

Conclusion: The U.S. needs more socialism. An obvious non sequitur, yet there is no denying that many apparently reasonable people — including most members of Congress and of the Bush and Obama administrations — accept all three propositions simultaneously.

This, we readily admit, is a *brilliant* way to put matters. It is not for nothing that this economist has a wide reputation as a defender of private property rights and free enterprise. The only problem with it is that it applies to Friedman himself, certainly in the field of monetary economics.

For the Fed is to money as is the central planner to the entire economy. In other words, unpalatable and uncharitable as it sounds, for much of his career Milton Freidman was a monetary socialist. What, after all, is the case in favor of governmental monopolization of the money supply? It is no stronger for state control over education, or retirement funds, or health or welfare, or the post office or, indeed, much if anything else. And, a case can easily be made that money is more important than any of these other things. After all, it constitutes the very lifeblood of the entire economy, upon which all of these other things intimately depend. That is, without an economy, we need not "worry" about education, the post office, food, etc. And without money, there is only barter; a modern economic system is precluded.

There are those who wish to consign this crucial institution to the tender mercies of the government. Ron Paul, happily, is not one of them. For this, he is forced to bear the howls and outrage from economic illiterates such as David Frum, and, yes, Milton Friedman, at least for long stretches of his career. (At least the latter has written voluminously on this matter; the former confines himself to sneers.)

The advantage of the gold standard, vis-à-vis fiat currency supplied by government is that the state cannot inflate the former. Thus, it functions, at least relatively, as a veritable Rock of Gibraltar. In fact, had we remained on a gold standard we would have been far better off than at present. Any example illustrating this claim would be an underestimate of the benefits of free market money for if we had remained on the gold standard, there would be a lot more gold today than there now is. The extra demand for it would have led to more exploration and development, better technologies for extracting gold from ore, and more substitution from non-monetary uses, and the complementary use of other commodities as money. Nevertheless, we offer the following: 1 ounce of gold was worth approximately $20 in 1913 and today is worth about $1000 (actually above that amount, as of March, 2012), so it takes approximately 50 times more dollars to buy an ounce of gold at present.

In this regard states J. H. Huebert: "And with the subprime mortgage meltdown and the dollar's value collapsing, another of Dr. Paul's campaign issues is gaining traction — his desire to abolish the Federal Reserve, an unaccountable, privately owned bankers' bank that inflates the money supply. This makes the dollars in your pocket, your savings, and your investments worth less and less each year as the politically favored recipients of the Fed's new money profit at ordinary Americans' expense. The other candidates, who have benefited from the status quo, ignore the issue, but Ron Paul has been fearless; clips of him grilling Fed Chairman Ben Bernanke at congressional hearings have been a surprise hit on YouTube."

But Frum's case is far worse than all this would indicate. We have mentioned above that the Frumster was correct in at least one of his allegations: for many years, Milton Friedman was indeed a bitter opponent of the gold standard, in opposition to Ron Paul's position on the matter. However, Friedman was a "second thoughtster" on this matter, as demonstrated by Richard Ebeling. This economist demonstrates that toward the end of his career, Friedman came to support, if not in full, and enthusiastically, then at least in great part, Ron Paul's views on monetary institutions.

Let us allow Friedman to speak for himself on this matter, courtesy of Richard Ebeling's research:

"Most of my own work dealing with public policy has had the same character of proceeding as if I were addressing governmental officials selflessly dedicated to the public interest. I have attempted to persuade the Federal Reserve System that it was doing the wrong thing and it ought to adopt a different policy. This time was ill spent because the public-interest characterization of government, is basically flawed.... We do not regard a businessman as selflessly devoted to the public interest. We think of a businessman as in business to improve his own welfare, to serve his own interest.... Why should we regard government officials differently? They, too, aim to serve their own interest, and in government as in business we must try to set up institutions under which individuals who intend only their own gain are led by an invisible hand to serve the public interest. The Federal Reserve System puts a great deal of power in the hands of a few people and it is so constructed that it has been in their self-interest to pursue a policy which, I believe, has been very harmful for the public rather than helpful.... Clearly, it was not in the self-interest of the Federal Reserve hierarchy to follow the hypothetical policy [of a monetary rule]. It was therefore a waste of time to try to persuade them to do so."

States Ebeling: "But by the mid-1980s, Friedman had second thoughts about whether government could ever be trusted to follow the necessary restraint to provide this supposedly superior paper money system. He began to regularly quote a sentence from Irving Fisher's 1911 book, *The Purchasing Power of Money*: 'Irredeemable paper money has almost invariably proved a curse to the country employing it.'"

Here, again, thanks to Ebeling, is another quote on this matter from Friedman and his co-author Anna Schwartz from their publication: "Has Government Any Role in Money?"

"The apparently great value to the economy of having a single unit of account linked with an (ultimate) medium of exchange does not mean that government must play any role, or that there need be a single producer of the medium of exchange. And indeed, historically, governments have entered the picture after the event, after the community had settled on a unit of account and private producers had produced media of exchange.... Historically, producers of money have established confidence by promising convertibility into some dominant money, generally specie [e.g., gold or silver]. Many examples can be cited of fairly long-continued and successful producers of private moneys convertible into specie. We do not know, however, of any example of the private production of purely inconvertible fiduciary moneys."

Friedman and Schwartz continued:

"Our own conclusion ... is that leaving monetary and banking arrangements to the market would have produced a more satisfactory outcome than was actually achieved through government involvement."

"Let me emphasize that this note is not a plea for a return to a gold standard.... I regard a return to a gold standard as neither desirable nor feasible —with the one exception that it might become feasible if the doomsday predictions of hyperinflation under our present system should prove correct."

In another publication, "Has Gold Lost Its Monetary Role?" Friedman said, in an almost direct refutation of Frum:

"If you could re-establish a world in which government's budget accounted for 10 percent of the national income, in which *laissez-faire* reigned, in which governments did not interfere with economic activities and in which full employment policies had been relegated to the dustbin, in such a world you might be able to restore a real gold standard. A real honest-to-God gold standard is not feasible because there is essentially no government in the world that is willing to surrender control over its domestic monetary policy."

In his "Real and Pseudo Gold Standards," Friedman explained:

"Under such a real gold standard, private persons or government might go into the business of offering storage facilities, and warehouse receipts might be found more convenient than the gold itself for transactions. If individuals find warehouse certificates for gold more useful than literal gold, private enterprise can certainly provide the service of storing the gold. Why should gold storage and the issuance of warehouse certificates be a nationalized industry? Finally, private persons or governments might issue promises to pay gold either on demand or after a specific time interval which were not warehouse receipts but nevertheless were widely acceptable because of confidence that the promises would be redeemed. Such promises to pay would still not alter the basic character of the gold standard so long as the obligors were not retroactively relieved from fulfilling their promises, and this would be true even if such promises were not fulfilled on time, just as the default of dollar bond issues does not alter the monetary standard. But, of course, promises to pay that were in default or that were expected to be defaulted would not sell at face value, just as bonds in default trade at a discount.... Such a system might, and I believe would, raise grave social problems and foster pressure for government prohibition of or control over the issue of promises to pay gold on demand. But that is beside my present point, which is that it would be a real gold standard."

Let us consider yet another refutation of Frum's position from Friedman's pen: "A real gold standard is thoroughly consistent with [classical] liberal principles and I, for one, am entirely in favor of measures promoting its development."

To conclude: Frum attempts to prove that Congressman Paul is a monetary crank because he differs with Milton Friedman. While it cannot be denied that Dr. Ron Paul and Professor Milton Friedman have some differences on this matter, Frum's contention is nonsense. Paul's critique of the Fed, and support of a free market stateless money system is hardly a "rejection of everything taught by modern economists (such as) Milton Friedman."

3.3. The Economist on Ron Paul and the Fed, a Critique

Here is an interesting story from the Economist (Nov 26, 2009) magazine that mentions Ron Paul, not in a very positive light, sad to say. See my very critical comments on it, below.

The Federal Reserve under attack: Poked by pitchforks; Curbs on the Fed's independence are advancing through Congress

Populists and bankers have been at odds since America's earliest days. Its first two central banks were shuttered in the nineteenth century in part because of their perceived closeness to financiers. In the wake of the financial crisis, those tensions have bubbled back to the surface. The central bank is again in the crosshairs.

On November 19, the financial services committee of the House of Representatives voted — over the objections of its chairman, Barney Frank — to add a provision to a regulatory overhaul that would subject the Federal Reserve to examination by Congress' investigative agency, the Government Accountability Office. Congress gave the GAO authority to audit the Fed in the 1970s, but exempted its monetary-policy and lending decisions. The new provision, pushed by Ron Paul, a conservative Texas Republican and Alan Grayson, a populist Florida Democrat, would eliminate the exemption. This could make the Fed less effective as a lender of last resort by making banks reluctant to borrow for fear that an audit would disclose their identity, and the Fed might become more wary of raising interest rates for fear of such an audit.

The animus towards the Fed is striking, considering that its unprecedented market interventions almost certainly averted a financial meltdown last year and a far more severe recession. But many congressmen care less about the disaster avoided than the injustice of bailed-out bankers taking home record bonuses as unemployment keeps rising. The Fed is now guilty by association, seen as too close to banks, too quick to bail them out and too generous and secretive when it does so. The Fed's structure supplies fodder for this critique. The compromise that led to its creation in 1913 split responsibility for monetary policy between politically-appointed governors in Washington, D.C., and the presidents of 12 regional banks, whose boards are appointed in part by private bankers.

The Fed and the Treasury now face the delicate task of trying to excise the Paul-Grayson provision from a regulatory overhaul they dearly want, in particular because it would create a process for avoiding future ad hoc bail-outs. Their best hope is that the provision dies when the House bill is merged with one from the Senate. Chris Dodd, chairman of the Senate Banking Committee, has beaten back demands from senators in both parties for a similar provision. Mr. Dodd's own bill, though, is far from Fed-friendly. He would strip the Fed of its bank regulatory responsibilities and erode its independence by eliminating private bankers' say in appointing regional Fed bank boards, and making the chairmen of those boards political appointees.

Ben Bernanke, the Fed chairman, has so far been personally spared the vitriol and seems likely to win a second four-year term; the Senate will hold a confirmation hearing on December 3. Tim Geithner, the treasury secretary, has been less fortunate. In his previous job as the New York Fed president, he was at Mr. Bernanke's side for most of the bailouts. A handful of members of Congress have called (fruitlessly) for him to be fired. One of America's great strengths, so Mr. Geithner dryly remarked, is that anyone can criticize his decisions with the benefit of hindsight.

Now for my comments on this piece. First, the positive ones:

1. They mentioned Ron Paul. Any article in the mainstream press that does that, and *The Economist* certainly qualifies in that regard, can't be all bad.

2. They spelled Ron Paul's name correctly. Again, points for them.

Now for the criticisms (I am nothing if not evenhanded, giving credit where credit is due, but, critical where appropriate).

1. Ron is not a "conservative." He is, instead, a libertarian, as he never tires of mentioning. The follow-up query often heard is, "Well, then, how can you be a member of the Republican Party? How do you justify running for office under their banner?"And, as Congressman Paul often replies, there are liberal Republicans and conservative Republicans, why can't there be libertarian Republicans?

2. *The Economist* claims that Ron Paul's bill will "make the Fed less effective as a lender of last resort." This implies, without offering a shred of a reason in support, that the Fed is already "effective" in this regard. Where is the evidence for this contention?

3. In the view of this journal, the Fed's "unprecedented market interventions almost certainly averted a financial meltdown last year and a far more severe recession." Sure. Yeah, yeah. Without a doubt. Evidently, no one on the other side of the pond has read the congressman's *End the Fed* nor the brilliant analysis of Tom Woods' *Meltdown*.

4. What is wrong, pray tell, with being concerned about the "injustice of bailed-out bankers taking home record bonuses as unemployment keeps rising." This almost makes Ron Paul out to be a leftist populist, concerned that some people's salaries are too high. Nothing could be further from the truth. In the view of this libertarian (Republican) congressman, wages can rise to the stratosphere and be justified, as long as they emanate from the free choices of market participants. However, when government steps in with its subsidies, then, it is certainly legitimate to inquire into such matters.

5. "The Fed is now guilty by association." The Fed is merely an innocent bystander? No, as a plethora of Austrian economists have demonstrated, our central bank has been intimately involved as the causal agent of the present economic malaise. The Fed has artificially lowered interest rates, encouraging entrepreneurs to misallocate resources in the direction of heavy, long-run projects (houses, cars), in the early stages of the Austrian structure of production. If you look at the business cycle for the 100 years before and after the creation of this monetary economic central planning bureau, it is relatively easy to discern its effect: destabilization of the economy. It had a dips and doodles before 1913, but afterward it looks more like a roller coaster. The contrast between the two centuries would have been even greater had the nineteenth been earmarked by full laissez-faire capitalism. It was not; it merely lacked the Fed.

6. As for Tim ("Busy Timmy") Geithner and the "benefit of hindsight," this shows a stupendous ignorance of the history of Austrian Economics, in general, and Austrian Business Cycle Theory (ABCT) in particular. Members of this school of thought have been analyzing the causes and cures of depressions since at least 1912, with the publication of this book by Ludwig von Mises. Hindsight, indeed.

The Economist has sometimes been called the modern day equivalent of De Tocqueville, an earlier and often very accurate European commentator on the U.S. condition. And, with some reason. It is often the case that this publication has seen, truly, into our condition in a way that has eluded many of us. Sadly, this is not one of those occasions.

Chapter 4.

Other Economic Issues

4.1. "Justice" Department Goes After Gates Foundation

SEATTLE, Wash. – After the Bill & Melinda Gates Foundation announced plans to donate $5 billion to help rebuild libraries destroyed by Hurricane Katrina, the Department of Justice's Antitrust Division launched a formal investigation into this organization. Thomas O. Barnett, Assistant Attorney General, said in a press release that, "The Bill & Melinda Gates Foundation, the world's largest charity cartel, has overstepped its boundaries and entered into the realm of predatory pricing. How is FEMA supposed to compete with private charities?"

The Gates Foundation had been under close scrutiny for restraint of trade in the charity industry for several months. According to some reports, the foundation's Herfindahl Index was too monopolistic, exerting "undue influence on the philanthropy sector." According to one trust-buster, "The four firm concentration ratio (CR4) is in the stratosphere. A Herfindahl Index above 2000 indicates acute concentration. The Gates' numbers are at least double that. This is *dangerous.*" Charities, including the United Way and the Salvation Army were among those pushing for the investigation, citing the foundation's recent gift of $37 billion from Warren Buffett.

Up until the donation to the Gulf Coast, however, the Justice Department had largely been silent. However, after hearing that Bill Gates looked to the evil monopolists John D. Rockefeller and Andrew Carnegie as inspiration for his philanthropy, it took only days before Mr. Barnett officially decided to launch the investigation.

The investigation, cheered on by Senators Hillary Clinton and John McCain, has bipartisan support. Both McCain and Clinton released a joint statement, averring that, "The free market is a wonderful thing, but how can we expect the government and other organizations to match the giving power of Gates? The free market in philanthropy is going to give us the same results as the free market in computers and electronics: exploitation."

Leading economists are hailing the decision as a step toward perfect competition. Dr. Paul Krugman of Princeton University has noted that, "Except for the political arena, all areas of the economy need perfect competition. Although to you lay people 'trust-busting' may seem to drive up prices and prop- up inefficient, government-subsidized corporations, a Ph.D. in economics will reveal that you are all morons."

Similarly, Columbia University's Nobel Prize winning economist Joseph Stiglitz warned against "Big Charity." To the cheers of an electrified meeting of antitrust lawyers and economists, Professor Stiglitz roared, "We must fight oligopoly wherever it rears its ugly head. We must fight the reckless capitalist – be he philanthropist or proctologist. Evidently, Bill Gates learned nothing, absolutely, nothing, from our recent antitrust case against Microsoft. Well, it is time, nay it is past time, to teach him another lesson; this time to his so-called 'Foundation.'"

Congressman Ron Paul, a staunch defender of free market capitalism noted, "This is nuts. But if they really wanted to push this antitrust nonsense to its logical conclusion, they would 'bust up' Giuliani and Romney's campaigns as they are clearly anti-competitive. In fact, the ultimate logic of neoclassical monopoly theory would be to break up the U.S. government into tens of thousands of small city-states. Why, the Herfindahl Index for that entity tops the charts at 10,000, and its CR1 is an astoundingly horrendous 100%."

Please note: this is a parody.

4.2. NAFTA and Dr. Ron Paul: Reply to "Superhighway Scaremonger's" by Corcoran

Although I agree with just about 99.9% of everything my long-time friend Terry Corcoran has ever written on economics, I must protest one small part of his otherwise very brilliant column.

Mr. Corcoran notes in his *National Post* (August 25, 2007) article "Superhighway Scaremongers," quite correctly, that both Maude Barlow of the Council of Canadians, and Ron Paul, congressman from Texas now running for president of the United States, both oppose NAFTA. Mr. Corcoran refers to the puzzle that the former is infamous for her opposition to free trade, while the latter, "nominally a free-market libertarian," favors tearing down tariffs, quotas and other barriers to the movement of goods and investment. He concludes: "I think Mr. Paul and Ms. Barlow should get together and sort this out. I can't."

The reconciliation, as I see it, is that Ms. Barlow is against NAFTA because she thinks it promotes free trade, while Dr. Paul opposes it because he maintains, quite correctly, that it has the very opposite effect. Ron Paul favors an immediate unilateral declaration of free trade with all nations and a complete elimination of all barriers against peaceful international commercial relations. No time-wasting and expensive negotiations. No limitations to just a few countries. No imposition of labor or environmental standards. Just full free trade with everyone.

Dr. Paul has been accused of being an isolationist because of his opposition to U.S. imperialistic wars. The latter is true, but the former is nonsense. He is a staunch advocate of economic co-operation between all peoples. Dr. Ron Paul is not merely "nominally a free-market libertarian." He is a veritable standard-bearer for this movement, perhaps the best publicist it has ever had, bar none.

Corcoran, unhappily, is by far not the only supporter of free enterprise who has criticized Congressman Paul for not being full in favor of free trade. Gary Johnson, former governor of New Mexico, and sometime candidate for the Republican nomination for president in 2012, has also made this error; time and again. And Ed Crane, president of the semi-libertarian think tank the Cato Institute, had this to say in his

Wall Street Journal op-ed of December 31, 2011: "Which is not to say that Mr. Paul is always in sync with mainstream libertarians. His … opposition to the NAFTA and CAFTA free trade agreements in the name of doctrinal purity are at odds with most libertarians." Perhaps Joe Salerno said it best in criticism of Crane (see his magnificent "postscript" below.)

These so-called "free trade" agreements are in essence mere customs unions. Tariffs and other trade barriers are reduced, slightly, for some but not all items. Bureaucrats get to live high off the hog in esoteric five-star locales, as they endlessly debate the fine points of these "agreements." Free trade, full free trade of the sort supported by Congressman Paul, consists of nothing but a unilateral declaration of free trade with all nations, whether or not they reciprocate.

4.3. Economists: Do NOT Vote for Ron Paul!

I cannot help ending this section on economics on a somewhat whimsical note.

Remember that *South Park* episode when the people from the future came back to the present and took our jobs away (*therrre taken' errrr jobs*!)?

Well, there's a new menace afoot. This time, it is a real one. It doesn't come from the future. No, it emanates from, of all places, Texas, and takes the form of a mild-mannered, seemingly rational, ten-term Republican congressman, who is also, horrors!, a *libertarian.*

If Dr. Paul is elected president, it will be *curtains* for our jobs, for *all* our jobs.

This appears in the Bureau of Labor Statistics Occupational Handbook:

"Economists held about 15,000 jobs in 2006. Government employed 52 percent of economists, in a wide range of agencies, with 32 percent in Federal Government and 20 percent in State and local government. The remaining jobs were spread throughout private industry, particularly in scientific research and development services and management, scientific, and technical consulting services. A number of economists combine a full-time job in government, academia, or business with part-time or consulting work in another setting." (I thank Shawn Ritenour for this cite).

Dr. Ron Paul (yes, he is also a doctor) is *on record* stating that he will cut back government *drastically*. He has his sights set on the *federal government* in particular. But 32 percent of 15,000 jobs equals 4,800 employment slots for economists! Now, he might not inaugurate programs that require pink slips for this entire number of economists. But, suppose he retains 100 of our fellow dismal scientists (don't ask why he might do this; it is greatly to be doubted, except perhaps as a temporary measure, necessary to close down entire departments. In this case, he might not "retain" anyone presently on the payroll, but rather bring in a bunch of libertarians ugh, to help with the dismantling job). This means that 4,700 hundred (and they say that Austrian economists can't do math; pshaw!) of our colleagues will suffer the ignominy of being fired.

But this is only the tip of the iceberg. My colleagues James T. Bennett and Tom DiLorenzo remind me that for every economist directly employed by government, there are perhaps several who work as "consultants" for and with them. If, or, rather, I should say *when*, a President Paul eliminates most of our jobs in the federal government, an estimated 4,700 of them (and this may well be an underestimate), some multiple of that number will also be consigned to the unemployment lines.

On the other hand, my colleague Roy Cordato indicates that this figure may be an overestimate. To be fair and accurate in our assessment of the menace to our profession in the offing if the evil Ron Paul is elected, we must also take this into account. (We Austrians are nothing if not good empiricists.) Cordato states: "One also needs to be careful in that often what the government classifies as 'economist' we definitely would not. We (the John Locke Foundation) have been trying to track down the legitimacy of someone contracted by the state who claims that he is an economist based on the fact that he was hired by the EPA with the title of 'economist.' He has an undergraduate degree in engineering and an MBA. What we have discovered is that there are some positions labeled 'economist' by the EPA that are little more than clerks, with no credentials in economics required."

What of the 20 percent of economists who work not for the *federales*, but at the state and local levels? At first blush, one might think that they would be safe from the Paul Meat Cleaver. After all, President Paul (doesn't that phrase constitute a horrible grating sound to some?) is a staunch decentralist and supporter of state and even local authority. However, a large number of these jobs are dependent upon federal employment of economists. When the latter are way more than decimated, the former are sure to follow. Suppose that only half, or 10 percent, of state and local employment is eliminated as a result of the Paul Ax; that still amounts to 1,500 additional jobs. (I *told* you that we Austrians are math whizzes.)

Nor is the blood-on-the-floor scenario finished. What about the cushy (sorry, I meant important, crucial and necessary) jobs held by our colleagues in international organizations such as the U.N. the World Bank, the World Trade Organization? And this is to say nothing of that spate of conferences held to establish, and later on modify ad nauseam, treaties such as NAFTA, CAFTA, GATT and all the rest where we fly to exotic places and dine high off the hog (a thousand pardons; I should have said, work our fingers to the bone under sweatshop conditions). These are not part of the federal establishment, and there must be thousands of additional job slots for Americans at risk. But why be so nationalistic? The careers of many *foreign* economists are also at stake here. We must also protect the jobs of our colleagues across the sea.

How will Ron Paul impact academia, where further thousands of economists earn their daily bread? It is fair to say that he will cut quite a swath here as well. Federal subsidies will become a thing of the past. The entire Department of Education will be deep-sixed! This devastation cannot help but be transmitted to the state and local levels. Has Ron Paul never heard of market failure? Of the great benefits of public and subsidized education due to its external economies and neighborhood effects that we have, lo these many years, tried to inculcate into our students? To borrow the words my good friend David Frum used to describe the congressman in a different context, he is "too lazy or too arrogant to learn." True, a President Paul would leave private universities strictly alone. But there are many public institutions of higher learning, and even the so-called "private" ones are deeply in bed with the government at all levels, directly and indirectly through subsidies.

There are some nattering nabobs of positivism (sorry, I just couldn't help that one) who will reject my warning. They will dismiss my concerns as those of a weird modern day Paul Revere: "Ron Paul is coming. Ron Paul is coming." They will try to convince you that "Ron Paul can't win." I googled the phrase 'Ron Paul can't win' and found literally scores of pages making this claim. Do not believe these lies. Ron Paul is a *clear and present* danger to our profession. He is raising money hand over fist. Rather, his cult followers are doing so for him; he just sits back, relaxes, and watches the money pour in (he has shifty eyes; I wouldn't be surprised if he socked most of these funds in his Swiss bank account; that would be good thing: at least he wouldn't be elected). True, he is now relatively low in the polls. But he keeps doubling his prospective vote totals. Have we learned nothing from the experience of Mike Huckabee? At one time, the pollsters were ignoring him, too. Not anymore. Do not be complacent, fellow economists. This can soon be replicated by Ron Paul. Surveys are conducted on Republicans who voted in the last election and use land phones. This demographic ignores all too many of his supporters. Nor do the pollsters measure the *degree* of support for this charlatan; the willingness of his minions to go out into the sleet-filled winter of some of our northern states. Moreover, he has done well on every straw poll ever conducted.

No, despite the claims of those who would give us comfort since "Ron Paul can't win," he *will* win. Unless, that is, we mobilize to STOP HIM. We must do all we can to halt him in his tracks. So, please, I beg of you, write letters, essays, articles, even books, sign petitions, attesting to his lack of economic sophistication. Why, neither he nor any of his economic advisors hold posts at Harvard, Yale, Princeton or Berkeley. None of them publish in the *American Economic Review*, or the *Journal of Political Economy*. Ron Paul and his so-called economic brain trust are a bunch of lazy, rotten, willfully ignorant red-neck yahoos. Most of them do not know how to order a decent bottle of wine. We must start a new campaign, ABP: anyone but Paul.

Part II.

Foreign Policy

Chapter 5.

Closing Hormuz

The closure of an international body of water is an act of war. If Iran implemented such a policy in the Strait of Hormuz, it would thus constitute an act of war. This is because in order to do so, this country would have to physically violate the rights of peaceful shippers. One might object that, at present, Iran has only *threatened* to close the Strait of Hormuz. However, in my understanding of libertarian theory based upon the nonaggression principle (NAP), not only are people (or governments!) not permitted to actually invade or violate the rights of peaceful individuals, they are not entitled to *threaten* such actions either.

However, before we unduly criticize the Iranians for this threat, let us put the matter in context. The U.S. government has also *threatened* a blockade of Iran. With many statements emanating from Washington, D.C., to the effect that the U.S. government "is not taking anything off the table," they are menacing actions a lot more serious, and invasive, than a mere blockade.

Why is the U.S. acting in so bellicose a manner? This is because it seems to be a settled part of present American policy that Iran should not persist in its (supposed) goal of arming itself with nuclear weapons.

Now, somewhat paradoxically, I agree with the Obama administration on this matter. Iran should not have nuclear weapons. But, neither should anyone else! Why not? Because they are necessarily offensive. This type of ordnance cannot be used in a way that distinguishes between the guilty and the innocent. States Rothbard in this regard: "… while the bow and arrow and even the rifle can be pinpointed, if the will be there, against actual criminals, modern nuclear weapons cannot. Here is a crucial difference in kind. Of course, the bow and arrow could be used for aggressive purposes, but it could also be pinpointed to use only against aggressors. Nuclear weapons, even 'conventional' aerial bombs, cannot be. These weapons are *ipso facto* engines of indiscriminate mass destruction."

However, this demand of Iran on the part of the U.S. comes with particular ill grace given the fact that the latter country has thousands of such nuclear devices. If the Obama Administration had suddenly become infused with libertarianism in general, and with Rothbard's analysis of nuclear weapons in particular, it would certainly be justified in continuing to press the Iranians not to develop such firearms. But it would begin this quest by getting rid of its own stocks *first*.

But are not the Iranians unstable? Are they not likely, under the leadcrship of Mahmoud Ahmadinejad, to *use* these items against innocent people? Did not this person threaten to wipe Israel off the map with them, that is, use such weapons against that country? No. This was a mis-translation of what he actually said. Nor is it possible to ignore the fact that there is only *one* country on the face of the Earth that has actually *employed* atomic weapons against innocent men, women and children. And that country, strangely enough, is not Iran. Rather, it is the good old U.S. of A., land of the free and home of the brave.

So, while I certainly endorse Rothbard's analysis that any and all atomic weaponry is illicit in keeping with the NAP, it does not at all logically follow that a country with thousands of such armaments, that has the distinction of being the only one to have ever murdered people with such a heinous weapon, is justified in using force to prevent another nation from obtaining one for itself. (I here stipulate, arguendo, that this is indeed the case; Iran of course insists it is interested in nuclear power for entirely peaceful purposes.)

Now that we have explored the context, let us return to the Iranian threat to close the Strait of Hormuz. From a libertarian point of view, in order to assess the validity of this threat, we must ask: Does this constitute initiatory aggression, or threats, or retaliation? For libertarians are not pacifists. We reserve the right to employ threats, aggression or, violence, provided that it is in response to a prior act. So, did Iran "start up" with the U.S., or did the U.S. begin the hostilities?

When put in this stark manner, it is difficult in the extreme to see the Iranians as the aggressors. At worst, they were going to build a nuclear weapon, not merely avail themselves of the peaceful use of this technology. Along comes a country, much larger and more powerful than theirs, certainly lacking "clean hands" in this regard, and orders them to cease and desist, under dire threat. So, in *response*, the Iranians issue a threat of their own: to close off international waters to peaceful shipping. Yes, Iran is in the wrong for so doing. But, they are not the real villain of the piece. That guilt lies elsewhere. The threat of the blockade against Iran came *first*. Only *then* did the Iranians make their own threat.

Chapter 6.

Ron Paul: Stooge for Adolph Hitler? Don't Be Silly

Believe it or not, Congressman Paul's critics are now claiming he is a Neville Chamberlain, who would have, were he president at the outset of World War II, have given Adolph Hitler a free ride. With Dr. Paul at the helm, the last century would have marked the beginning of the Nazi Reich.

Nonsense.

First of all, a President Paul would never have foisted an oil embargo on Japan. So, there would have been no attack on Pearl Harbor, and no fighting with the Japanese military would have been necessary. This consideration alone means that hundreds of thousands of innocent people would not have perished. And, also, it would not have been the case that the U.S. would have been the only country in history to have actually used atomic weapons.

Second, Congress did indeed declare war on Germany; this is compatible with the U.S. Constitution, which Ron Paul, if no other candidate for President in 2012, fervently supports.

Third, and most important, it is unlikely that Hitler would have ever risen to power in Germany without U.S. entry into World War I, in 1917. Although contrary to fact history can only be speculative, consider the following points.

Before the U.S. poked its nose into a war that was none of its business (neither side threatened us), the war was fought on a roughly equal basis. Thousands of soldiers, on both sides, perished in fighting over a few acres of trenches. Likely, this war would have petered out before too long, if only due to the fact that both sides were running out of material, human and otherwise, necessary to carry on. But, our ruling class had more bonds with the British than with the Germans, so our way ahead was clear, with no President Paul to save us from our folly.

As a result, the Allies beat the Axis powers. Following up on this, the punitive Treaty of Versailles was imposed upon the losers, who were declared solely responsible for the hostilities. This lead to the German hyper-inflation of 1923, which, along with the aforementioned Treaty of Versailles, reduced the German society and economy to a rubble. It was only in the aftermath of these body blows to the German people that a scoundrel such as Hitler could have arisen.

A Paul presidency in 1940 would have meant a war with Germany, but not Japan. However, a President Paul in 1917 would not have encouraged U.S. entry into that conflagration. If he was successful, there would have been no need for any declaration of war against Germany, as there would have been no Adolph Hitler and his Nazis in charge. He would have been, instead, an unknown house painter. With a President Paul at the helm, there would have been no Holocaust; no 50 million people perishing during this war; no dropping of atomic bombs on innocent civilians, women and children, to our eternal shame.

Speaking of this "war" nomenclature, the historians have got it all wrong. There were not two separate wars, so-called World War I, and then so-called World War II. There was only *one* World War. It started in 1914 and ended in 1946; yes, yes, there was a slight cessation of hostilities between 1919 and 1939, but the so-called "interwar period" consisted of the Allies taking steps that brought Hitler front and center, in effect *created* him, and thus assured the continuation of this *one* World War. In like manner, the historians who claim there was a "Civil War" in the U.S. between 1861 and 1865 are similarly mistaken. A civil war takes place between two parties, each desiring to rule the territory occupied by the both of them. The Spanish Civil War qualifies in this regard, because the Communists and the Fascists both wanted to rule over that entire country. But in 1861, while the North wanted control over the entire U.S., the South only desired to *secede*. So, a more proper name for this conflagration would be, the War to Prevent Southern Secession, or the U.S. War of Secession.

Can we be sure of any such alternative history of the sort I am assuming with Ron Paul as president during these earlier epochs? Of course not. But, it is more likely, far more likely, than the scenarios painted by the enemies of Ron Paul in their feverish attempt to deny him the presidency, and to deny the rest of us the peace and prosperity we all want. Contrary to fact, history can only be a guesstimate. The critics of Congressman Paul maintain he would have been a pushover for Hitler. I maintain, to the contrary, that he would not have *created* a

Hitler, and had he taken office only in 1940, he would have presided as commander in chief over a war declared by Congress. He would have won it more quickly, since he would have only had to fight Germany and Italy, not Japan too. Yes, Germany only declared war against America because of the U.S. declaration of war against Japan. But, as long as Congress declared war on Germany, as commander in chief of the U.S. armed forces Paul would have acted in a Constitutional manner in pursuing this war. Dr. Paul does not oppose war per se, only offensive wars not declared by Congress, as he has stated over and over again. Ron Paul is a veteran of the U.S. Air Force; he has served his country in a military capacity, unlike the hordes of chicken hawks now calling for unconstitutional imperialist wars but who sought deferments when they were young men.

The racism and anti-Semitism charges have failed. This Hitler criticism is just plain silly. They can't call him a flip-flopper. They have already attacked his suits and his eyebrows. Yes, his eyebrows. I guess they are not sufficiently presidential. What smears are next for Dr. Paul, as he sweeps his way into the White House? We can only speculate. How about, Ron's love child? Children? Or, his 15 mistresses? No, wait; here is a better one: Ron as child abuser. Remember those 4,000 babies he delivered? Well, he molested them all by bringing them into this vale of tears. This just in: they are now criticizing his investment portfolio. More fast breaking news: Ron is "indifferent to throwing people out of work." Will wonders never cease? It's really hard to keep up with all the attacks. I mean, the man is a real ogre. Maybe we Paulians shouldn't support him? Nah. He's the best man to clean out the Augean stables. Congressman Paul might have some difficulty winning the Republican nomination, but when it comes to his face-off with President Obama next year, he's going to kick butt. Obomba's supporters will desert him for his imperialist militarism, for his bailouts, for his opposition to drug legalization. Independents, and even Democrats, will prove Dr. Paul's margin of victory.

Chapter 7.

Randy Barnett Traitor to Libertarianism

7.1. Randy Barnett: Pro-War Libertarian?

Suppose Paul Ehrlich was to renounce his views on overpopulation. Or a leading Marxist was to accept the legitimacy of capitalism. Or a rabbi was to claim that eating pork is compatible with the Talmud. Or Dick Cheney was to advocate an immediate U.S. withdrawal from Iraq. There would be great wailing and gnashing of teeth in the environmental, Marxist, Jewish and neoconservative communities, respectively. Charges of "turncoat," and "traitor," would fill the air. Members of each of these groups would reason that while it would almost be acceptable for members of the great unwashed to articulate sentiments of these sorts, it would leave them horror stricken that a prominent member of their own movement could be guilty of so great a defection.

Something of this sort has recently occurred in the libertarian movement. Randy E. Barnett has published an article in the *Wall Street Journal* (7/16/07) entitled "Libertarians and the War: Ron Paul doesn't speak for all of us." While Professor Barnett could not fairly be characterized as a leader of this movement, he certainly is (or at least was) one of its more high-profile practitioners. Even if libertarianism had more advocates, each one would still be very precious, given that this perspective is the last best hope for justice, economic prosperity and, indeed, the survival of the human race. That this episode occurs while we are still relatively weak, but on an upward trajectory (thanks most recently to the magnificent efforts of Ron Paul), makes it even more shameful.

Barnett attacks libertarianism on its most basic postulate; the nonaggression principle (NAP). This is the lynchpin of the entire enterprise. It is a litmus test for libertarians to oppose the initiation (or threat) of violence against those who have themselves not been guilty of such an evil act. In rejecting the NAP, nay, perverting it, this legal scholar can no longer be considered a libertarian. It is my utmost hope, however, that he will reconsider his rash remarks and once again join the libertarian movement. The world cries out for liberty, and Barnett has been a stalwart contributor to this cause. He can be, once again. This response is an attempt to promote just that result.

This author starts out on a strange note: Thanks to Ron Paul, "… many Americans might resist the libertarian label, because they now identify it with strident opposition to the war in Iraq. …" Strident? Ron Paul? A more soft-spoken, thoughtful and judicious politician would be hard to imagine.

In Barnett's view, the exchange between Paul and Giuliani redounded to the latter's benefit: "It was an electrifying moment that allowed one to imagine Mr. Giuliani as a forceful, articulate president." "Forceful?" Yes. But "articulate?" Give us a break. He exposed himself as a demagogue who simply had not done his homework. Indeed, Dr. Paul later held a press conference offering the New York City mayor a reading list for his edification. As for Giuliani's out-of-turn interjection, one wonders just who was in charge of the loudspeaker microphone system that allowed this outburst.

Mr. Barnett characterizes Ron Paul as "until then … a rather marginal member of the 10-man Republican field." True, if you count polls of people who had never heard of this candidate. But our former libertarian forgets all about electronic results; there, Dr. Paul has been anything but "rather marginal." He also finds "striking," Paul's linkage of "almost every question put to him — even friendly questions about taxes, spending and personal liberty — to the war." First of all, there were no "friendly questions" put to Paul. The moderator was visibly biased against this libertarian candidate (and so was the wielder of the sound system). Second, any libertarian worth his salt would see a connection, a strong one, between this execrable war and precisely those issues. But Barnett evidently sees no connection between war expenses and taxes, which seems very "striking" to me. Barnett evidently sees no connection between the liberty-sapping Patriot Act and loss of habeas corpus and this war either, which also appears rather "striking." These issues are irrelevant to his libertarian credentials, but his view of them certainly places his understanding of economics and current events in a poor light.

We now arrive at the core of my disagreement with this author. He states, "Does being a libertarian commit one to a particular stance toward the Iraq war? The simple answer is 'no.'" In my view, in contrast, the simple answer, the no-brainer answer, is a clear and resounding "yes." What is Barnett's reasoning? Let us take this bit by bit.

First, he says: "But like all libertarians, even Mr. Paul believes in the fundamental, individual right of self-defense, which is why libertarians like him overwhelmingly support the right to keep and bear arms. And most also believe that when the territory of the U.S. is attacked militarily, the government — which claims a monopoly on providing for national defense and extracts billions of tax dollars for this purpose — is justified in using the military in self-defense. For this reason, many libertarians (though not all) who now oppose the war in Iraq supported U.S. military actions against the Taliban regime in Afghanistan, which had aided and harbored the al-Qaeda network that organized the 9/11 attack."

There are several problems here. Why is it that *even* Mr. Paul believes in self-defense? This implies that there is some dispute among libertarians as to pacifism, and that Ron Paul only reluctantly eschews this viewpoint. Not so.

Then, the point must be made that it is one thing if, entirely out of the blue, an enemy attacks the U.S. Then, yes, the libertarian would have no objection to a strong defense, compatible with just war theory, and, indeed, retaliation. Our revolutionary war is one case in point. However, suppose there were a series of entirely unprovoked "abuses and usurpations" on the part of invasive country A against victimized country B. Finally, B has had enough, and retaliates against A. In street vernacular, A "started up" but B "got even." A is entirely in the wrong, not B. Then, is it justified on libertarian grounds for A to escalate matters further, and further attack B? Barnett to the contrary notwithstanding, it is not. This is a far more accurate rendition of the 9/11 attack and the aftermath than that furnished by Barnett. The U.S. had been for *decades* making unwarranted and unprovoked attacks in the near east. It had stationed soldiers in the foreign lands of countries that had never even come close to threatening or actually invading us. Any support of U.S. military action "against the Taliban regime in Afghanistan" thus cannot be justified on *libertarian* grounds. (Some might say that there were those in these countries, such as Saudi Arabia, who had *invited* American armed forces to occupy their lands. True enough. But it is hardly a *libertarian* notion to acquiesce in such "invitations.") Al-Qaeda was certainly unjustified in killing more than 3,000 innocent people in New York City. However, anyone with even the slightest passion for justice must never forget that *prior* to that horrendous event, the U.S. had killed vastly more innocents in Arab and Muslim countries.

Mr. Barnett's ire at "Afghanistan, which had aided and harbored the al-Qaeda network that organized the 9/11 attack" is surely misdirected. Remember, we *started up first*. However unjustified, they were attempting to even up the score. As well, fifteen of the nineteen terrorists responsible for the World Trade Center massacre came from Saudi Arabia, *not* Afghanistan, even less so from Iraq, which had nothing whatever to do with this horrid bloodletting. (Not that the U.S. would have been justified in attacking the Saudis on this ground. After all, another mass murderer, Tim McVeigh, was from New York State, but only he, not all inhabitants of the Empire State, was responsible for his nefarious deeds.)

Randy Barnett next steps into the batter's box with this: "But here is the rub. While all libertarians accept the principle of self-defense, and most accept the role of the U.S. government in defending U.S. territory, libertarian principles of individual rights and the rule of law tell us little about what constitutes appropriate and effective self-defense after an attack. Devising a military defense strategy is a matter of judgment or prudence about which reasonable libertarians may differ greatly."

I regard this as an evasion. It cannot be denied that "a military defense strategy is a matter of judgment or prudence about which reasonable libertarians may differ greatly." But the point is we have yet to establish that what the U.S. government was doing was *defense.* If it is true that America *started first*, then what we were doing after 9/11 was *not* defense. It was, rather, a further escalation of a conflagration *we had started.* Barnett does not offer any reason to believe that post-9/11 military action of the U.S. was *defense*. Indeed, he shows no awareness that his case depends entirely on that being true.

This brings us, finally, to Iraq. On this matter, Barnett states the following:

"Many libertarians, and perhaps most libertarian intellectuals, opposed the war in Iraq even before its inception. They believed Saddam's regime neither directly threatened the U.S. nor harbored or supported the terrorist network responsible for Sept. 11. They also feared the risk of harmful, unintended consequences. Some may also have believed that since the U.S. was not attacked by the government of Iraq, any such war was aggressive rather than defensive in nature.

"Other libertarians, however, supported the war in Iraq because they viewed it as part of a larger war of self-defense against Islamic jihadists who were organizationally independent of any government. They viewed radical Islamic fundamentalism as resulting in part from the corrupt dictatorial regimes that inhabit the Middle East, which have effectively repressed indigenous democratic reformers. Although opposed to nation building generally, these libertarians believed that a strategy of fomenting democratic regimes in the Middle East, as was done in Germany and Japan after World War II, might well be the best way to take the fight to the enemy rather than solely trying to ward off the next attack."

I am entirely in accord with this first paragraph. This is a reasonably accurate assessment of the libertarian position on the matter, the *only* libertarian position on the matter. The second paragraph, however, is a logical howler. There is no "other libertarian" who could believe any such thing. To the extent he did adopt this perspective, he could *not* be a libertarian.

Let us consider in some detail the supposedly libertarian claim we should "take the fight to the enemy rather than solely trying to ward off the next attack." What *next* attack? The horrific events of 9/11 were in *response* to *prior* western attacks on Arab territory. Had we not *first started up with them,* they would not be retaliating against us. These people (yes, they are people) are not attacking us because of our freedoms, because of the fact that we allow miniskirts and rock and roll music. There are numerous countries where such activities are practiced, and those countries have not been attacked. No, as Ron Paul has been at great pains to explain to Barnett's hero, Rudy Giuliani, this is *blowback.*

Surprisingly, Barnett himself acknowledges no less: "To a libertarian, any effort at 'nation building' seems to be just another form of central planning which, however well-motivated, is fraught with unintended consequences and the danger of *blowback* (emphasis added)."

How, then, can Barnett coherently talk of "tak(ing) the fight to the enemy rather than solely trying to ward off the next attack." It surpasses all understanding. The "next attack" will emanate from our continued aggression against them, as did the previous one. If we cease and desist, apologize, and pay compensation due to them, they will in one fell swoop stop attacking us.

To construe our invasion of Iraq as "defensive" is to so totally misconstrue what "defense" is as to violate not only libertarian principle, but even common sense. Iraq not only never attacked us, they never even threatened to do so. For us to *initiate* an invasion of their country was thus not *defense;* it was *offense.*

Preemptive war of the sort advocated by ex-libertarian Barnett is the foreign analog of domestic preventive detention. I note that males between the ages of 15 and 25 commit a disproportionately high number of crimes. Why wait to "ward off the next attack" by this cohort? Why not "take the fight to (this domestic) enemy?" Can I, as a libertarian, advocate that we lock up *every* male in the country at age 15, regardless of whether they have committed a crime, and set them free at age 25? I cannot, and still remain a libertarian. Well, then, neither can Barnett, *qua libertarian*, support a policy of "tak(ing) the fight to the enemy (who never attacked us) rather than solely trying to ward off the next attack."

Barnett next delivers himself of this opinion:

"Moreover, the pro-war libertarians believed there was 'legal' cause to take military action against Saddam's regime — from its manifold violations of the cease-fire to firing on American planes legally patrolling the 'no-fly' zone and its persistent refusals to cooperate with weapons inspections. Saddam's regime was left in power after its unprovoked invasion of Kuwait on these and other conditions that it repeatedly had violated, thereby legally justifying its removal by force if necessary. Better to be rid of Saddam and establish an ally in the war against Islamic jihadists in the heart of the Middle East, the argument goes, and then withdraw American troops."

There are several objections here. First, "Pro-war libertarians" is a contradiction in terms. There can logically be no such thing in the present context.

Second, Barnett, himself, has in the past been active among libertarians in distinguishing that which is legal or illegal from that which is compatible with libertarianism, or not. For example, smoking pot is now illegal in the U.S. But, certainly, so doing is consistent with the NAP of libertarianism. Barnett, when he was a prosecuting attorney in Chicago, and a libertarian, was not very happy with the prospect of incarcerating a person for breaking this law. But now, shockingly, he is relying upon what is legal, not that which is compatible with the libertarian law code. He has become a legal positivist it would appear, supporting the notion that what is legal is necessarily proper. But, can the legislature, or the courts, never make a mistake? This would appear to be the implication of Mr. Libertarian Barnett.

I will not debate with Barnett whether or not the no-fly zone was legal. I concede this to him. But it by no means follows that the "legal" no-fly zone is compatible with libertarianism. Barnett claims to still be a libertarian. Yet, he argues *not* that the no-fly zone was compatible with libertarianism, merely that it was "legal," according to U.S. law (which when he was a libertarian he rejected in regard to addictive drugs, prostitution, and other such victimless crimes).

Third, according to Barnett, all we need do is set up no-fly zones anywhere we want; say, in China or Chile, in Venezuela or Venus for that matter. Then, if the Chinese, Chileans, Venezuelans or Venusians disobey us and take to the air over their own territory, they are committing aggression against us, and we may bomb them as a *defensive* matter. This seems highly problematic, to say the least. Suppose that the Chinese, Chileans, Venezuelans or Venusians set up no-fly zones in the U.S. When we disobeyed them, as a violation of our sovereignty, according to Barnett's "logic," then these countries, or worlds, as in the case of Venus, would be justified in bombing *us*, and could claim they were only defending themselves. One is at a loss to know what to say of this, from an eminent legal theorist.

Fourth, Barnett bases his entire justification of the U.S. invasion of Iraq on the basis of our defending ourselves. How in bloody blue blazes can this be squared with his objection to "Saddam's regime's … unprovoked invasion of Kuwait." Stipulate, arguendo, that Saddam was unjustified in attacking Kuwait. Forget about the fact that he was for many years, "our" man, certainly during the Iraq-Iran War. Please explain how this somehow constitutes a threat or an actual attack *on the U.S.*, Barnett's justification for our invasion of Iraq.

Another problem with the Barnett piece is that he strongly implies that Abraham Lincoln, who "… promptly replace(d his) military commanders … when it became clear that … (their) … tactics were not working" was virtuous, or acted in a manner compatible with libertarianism. Yet, as Tom DiLorenzo and others have shown, this is exactly the opposite of the truth. On this ground alone, Barnett's libertarian credentials become highly suspect.

Let me say a word about the fact that Barnett's article implies things, but does not clearly state them. For example, he never quite comes out and claims to be a pro Iraq war libertarian; on the other hand, this is clearly his intention. I find this rather evasive.

In his conclusion, Randy Barnett says: "These (pro-invasion) libertarians are still rooting for success in Iraq because it would make Americans more safe, while defeat would greatly undermine the fight against those who declared war on the U.S. They are concerned that Americans may get the misleading impression that all libertarians oppose the Iraq war — as Ron Paul does — and even that libertarianism itself dictates opposition to this war. It would be a shame if this misinterpretation inhibited a wider acceptance of the libertarian principles that would promote the general welfare of the American people."

There are grave problems here, as there were throughout.

First, what is this business of "mak(ing) Americans more safe?" Supposedly, the entire justification for this war, at least on libertarian grounds, was that it was an instance of *self-defense.* There are ways to make the citizens of this country safer that have nothing to do with that goal. For example, if we outright murdered every single inhabitant of Earth, apart from Americans of course, we would probably be "more safe." Let us stipulate that this is so. According to Barnett's conclusion, this would now be justified. And, mirabile dictu, on libertarian grounds! No, libertarianism justifies *defense* and *only* defense, not necessarily becoming "more safe." Let me put this in other words: the best way to ensure our safety is to follow the dictums of two of our founding fathers:

Thomas Jefferson: "Peace, commerce, and honest friendship with all nations, entangling alliances with none." John Quincy Adams: "America … goes not abroad seeking monsters to destroy." "We favor the freedom of all nations, but will fight, only, to protect our own."

Second, no one "declared war on the U.S." Nor, to be clear, has the U.S. recently "declared war" on anyone else. If this is to be done in a manner consistent with the *law* that Barnett elsewhere supports, then a declaration of war must be passed by Congress, at least according to the U.S. Constitution. Ron Paul has many times called for a vote on this matter, but to no avail. One might be excused for expecting Barnett to support Paul in this regard, but if so one would be disappointed.

I certainly agree with Barnett's contention that "a wider acceptance of the libertarian principles … would promote the general welfare of the American people." But I cannot bring myself to believe that all libertarians do not oppose this war. Those who support this undeclared, invasive, offensive, imperialist war simply are not libertarians.

But wait. Perhaps I am being too harsh. After all, if libertarianism applies to, say, 500 issues, and a person consistently and fully applies the NAP to, say, 495 of them, can he not be considered a libertarian, despite these few deviations? After all, there are disputes between fully credentialed libertarians on issues such as abortion, immigration, incitement and voluntary slave contracts. In general, I would answer in the affirmative on this matter. I am nothing if not a "big tent" libertarian.

But a perversion of the very meaning of "defense," and hence, the NAP itself, is another matter. It is as if a man claims to be a Catholic, yet rejects the Holy Trinity; claims to be a mathematician, yet rejects 2+2=4; or claims to be a geometrician, yet rejects the Pythagorean theorem. These things are simply too close to the core beliefs of the several philosophies to admit of any demurrers from those who claim to be adherents.

Who am I to read anyone out of the libertarian movement? Who appointed me boss? No one. I can only speak for myself. I can only give my own views on this or indeed any other matter. My claims stand or fall, not on the basis of who I am, but on the reasons I put forth in support of them.

The Randy Barnett I knew for at least four decades would not be capable of penning anything like that disgraceful *Wall Street Journal* article. I can only hope that he wrote it in a fit of pique, or that some other explanation of this sort is the correct one. It is my fervent hope he will next write a refutation of it. We need him back in the libertarian movement.

7.2. A Libertarian War in Afghanistan?

The previous chapter laid out why Randy Barnett was wrong in claiming that libertarians could support the U.S. side of the war in Iraq. But what about Afghanistan?

Let me now quote from two of my critics on this matter, both pro-war self-styled "libertarians"- who shall remain anonymous.

My first critic says this:

"I tend to agree with you on most everything you write and that's pretty much true of this latest. However, there is an area that I do disagree with — the attack on the Taliban and al-Qaeda following 9/11. While I do agree that the events of 9/11 may well be attributed to our foreign policy, I cannot stand for the "specific" targeting of non-military/non-political. And let's remember, al-Qaeda declared "war" on the U.S.

"It would appear by your reasoning on the Afghan issue that if faction A pokes and jabs at faction B and B finally declares war on A that A must stand aside and not defend itself. We can rightfully hold A responsible for the creation of a state of war but that does not require A to lie down and die. Our call for the turning over of those that planned and orchestrated the events of 9/11, I feel to be well within libertarian principles."

My second critic wrote as follows:

"I read with interest your response to Randy and find it very compelling. I follow you on the whole, but have some questions respecting the paragraph on Afghanistan.

"You say, because of our interventions into the region of the near east, 'Any support of U.S. military action against the Taliban regime in Afghanistan thus cannot be justified on *libertarian* grounds.' At what point is a government justified in responding despite blowback?

"As I recall the events after 9/11, the perpetrators were identified (or identified themselves), and the 'host country,' in addition to aiding them, refused to turn them over. Wouldn't this qualify as an act of war? I accept that our involvement in Iraq and Saudi Arabia by the first Bush galvanized the al-Qaeda network, but does this mean that Americans should not expect their government to respond to 9/11? If I am shot by a Cherokee while walking down a street in Oklahoma, am I not entitled to restitution and protection through the law… I think your conclusion regarding Afghanistan might be a bit hasty. If the Afghan government of the time chose to harbor and assist a near eastern aggressor within their midst, regardless of what motivated Bin Laden, aren't the Taliban then complicit in the aggression? I'd be interested to know more about your thinking on this however."

My short answer to these critics is that there is no country that is now justified in invading any other country because of the World Trade Center attack of 9/11, but if there were, it would be the Afghans who would be more justified in committing further terrorist acts in the U.S. than we would be in killing further innocents in that nation in this terroristic manner.

In my view, complete justice would require that the U.S. (well, those individuals responsible) pay reparations for initiating these murderous hostilities. We killed far more innocent people abroad than the more than 3,000 guiltless Americans who perished in New York City on 9/11.

The problem we face in making sense of these horrible events is bias. We are all naturally biased in favor of "our" side: Americans in favor of their fellow citizens, and foreigners on their own side. In an attempt to obviate this, let us no longer speak of groups such as the United States, Al-Qaeda, Afghanis, Iranians, Iraqis, Arabs, Palestinians, Israelis, Jews, etc. Instead, let us attempt to look at this matter through less jaundiced eyes, in a more dispassionate manner.

Accordingly, let us speak not in terms of the above categories, but instead, for simplicity's sake, of A and B. Let us posit that A begins our little drama by murdering 5 of B's children. Now, the just thing would be for B to capture A, and to subject him to the full penalties provided by law for such an outrage. However, B does something very different, and totally unjustified. He murders one of A's children. Why so few? Let us stipulate that A is much more powerful than B, and that the murder of only one of A's innocent children was the "best" he could do.

Assume, that even though A is more powerful than B, both are so well entrenched that justice will not easily be meted out to either of these murderous scoundrels. So now what? What insight does libertarian theory afford us in this context? Several conclusions may be drawn, I think.

One, neither party should be encouraged to invade the territory of the other. To do so, given that both are strong enough not to be brought to the bar of justice, would only mean the senseless killing of still others. However, if we take a God's eye point of view, and entertain the contrary to fact conditional that only one of these nefarious characters can indeed be punished for the murder of the others' child(ren), then it is clear that A must be brought to justice. There are two reasons for this. The minor one: A killed far *more* innocent children than did B. Major reason: A was the *first* to engage in murder; in the street vernacular, he "started up." B is no saint. He, too, spilled innocent blood. But he *retaliated*, he did not *begin*. There is surely a lower rung in hell reserved for those who begin such dastardly chain reactions than those who "merely" follow suit. I thus respectfully disagree with Murray Rothbard, who says:

"If Smith and a group of his henchmen aggress against Jones, and Jones and his bodyguards pursue the Smith gang to their lair, we may cheer Jones on in his endeavor; and we, and others in society interested in repelling aggression, may contribute financially or personally to Jones's cause. But Jones has *no* right, any more than does Smith, to aggress against anyone else in the course of his "just war:": to steal others' property in order to finance his pursuit, to conscript others into his posse by use of violence, or to kill others in the course of his struggle to capture the Smith forces. If Jones should do any of these things, he becomes a criminal as *fully* as Smith, and he too becomes subject to whatever sanctions are meted out against criminality."

As I see matters, although both his "Smith" and my "A," and his Jones, and my "B" are all vicious, depraved despoilers of children, the former pair are *more* guilty than the latter pair.

Rothbard's failure, as I see it, is not sufficiently distinguishing between he who *first* engages in an entirely unwarranted action, and he who only *then* follows suit. Both are evil. But there is still a difference between them. Jones is not as *fully* a criminal as is Smith. They are both, of course, guilty of first-degree murder. But, surely, a careful analysis can see at least a "dime's worth" of difference between them.

Who is A and who is B? As would be obvious to any impartial observer, we, the U.S. must take on the role of A, and various Muslim nations and nongovernmental organizations (NGOs) can only fairly and properly be cast as the B of our little morality play. *Long before*

9/11 took place, our own country was busy killing innocents abroad in those parts of the world. Thus, if the U.S. is justified in going into Afghanistan to hunt for Osama bin Laden, and other perpetrators and aiders and abettors of the crimes of 9/11, then *they* are even *more* righteous in doing *precisely the same thing to us.*

If anyone doubts that America *started up* and the "terrorists" (note scare quote marks here) were guilty of the slightly lesser charge of retaliation, consider the following:

"In 1996, then-U.N. Ambassador Madeleine Albright was asked by *60 Minutes* correspondent Lesley Stahl, in reference to years of U.S.-led economic sanctions against Iraq, 'We have heard that half a million children have died. I mean, that is more children than died in Hiroshima. And, you know, is the price worth it?'

"To which Ambassador Albright responded, 'I think that is a very hard choice, but the price, we think, the price is worth it.'"

Note the *date* of this statement. It was 1996, fully five years *before* the (unjustified) retaliation of the World Trade Center in 2001.

Should the U.S. defend against any further, retaliatory terrorist incursions? Of course. But then, by that token, the Afghanis are entitled to defend their territory against our present and future invasions of them.

Let me now bring in a third critic, who wrote me while I was putting together the material that appears above (I showed him part of it in our correspondence). He says:

"Let me first tell you that I am a longtime fan. I'm not a hostile critic. Indeed, I frequently tell my conservative friends to read [your publications].

"However, I couldn't disagree with you more about your thoughts [on this issue]. First, there can be no moral or theoretical justifications for terrorism (defined roughly as the intentional targeting of innocent civilians for political ends) consistent with libertarian principles. Therefore, your statement 'Afghans ... would be more justified in committing further terrorist acts in the U.S. than we would be in killing further innocents in that nation' is problematic. One cannot be more justified in doing something wrong than someone else you assume is doing wrong could be, except in some kind of strange scholastic sense. In other words, simply because you have suffered a greater harm than another doesn't give you a stronger claim to do something wrong itself.

"Moreover, the U.S. has not been intentionally targeting innocent civilians in Afghanistan and thus your use of the word "further" is also problematic. Unless that is that you think, that no military activity whatsoever that unintentionally harms innocents is acceptable — which is problematic on other grounds. I think the doctrine of double effect handles the problems of killing innocents during war. Second, the Afghanistan part of the current war seems entirely proper in libertarian thought.... But let me remind you also that ... pacifism is not consistent with a natural rights perspective since it assumes the right to exclude (and use force to do so if necessary) — and your position borders on pacifism."

I would like to reply to each of these three paragraphs in turn. As to the first, I have received a lot of hate mail in response to my essay on Randy Barnett. It is thus a pleasure to receive criticism from someone who can do so in a civil manner. I regard this first paragraph as supererogatory in this regard. It is nice, but unnecessary, since the remainder of the missive is completely courteous. This author is clearly a gentleman.

As to the second paragraph, with all respect, I disagree. Consider "intentional targeting of innocent civilians for political ends." But *both* sides, *both A and B*, were guilty of this outrage. Albright's blatant statement admitted no less than this. Further, no country that drops bombs from 30,000 feet (does anyone remember "shock and awe?") anywhere near civilian areas can excuse their action on the basis that it was not targeting innocents. *Both* sides acted in a manner befitting terrorists. Moreover, this writer seems to be taking the "moral equivalence" position of Murray Rothbard. I insist that my "strange scholastic sense" is a reasonable one. Not only has B, the Muslim world suffered "greater harm" in terms of sheer numbers of innocent people slaughtered, but we, A, as I can never tire of saying, *began* the conflagration. I cannot for the life of me see why this obvious fact should be ignored in any analysis purporting to be libertarian.

Now consider the third paragraph:

I agree that pacifism is not at all entailed by libertarianism. I certainly favor smiting the *guilty*. That alone deflects the charge of pacifism.

Nor do I oppose all wars, even though I full well recognize that there never was a war in which innocents were not killed. Indeed, I am on record in my response to Randy Barnett as saying "… the point must be made that it is one thing if, entirely out of the blue, an enemy attacks the U.S. Then, yes, the libertarian would have no objection to a strong defense, compatible with just war theory, and, indeed, retaliation. Our revolutionary war is one case in point." I now add this: in my view, the South was on the just side of the War Between the States. The South merely wanted to *secede* from the North; the latter was having none of this, and *compelled* the former to stay in the union, in violation of the libertarian principle of free association.

As for killing innocents in the more general case, I have an article (Block, 2011D)in the premier libertarian scholarly periodical, *The Journal of Libertarian Studies*, entitled "The human body shield," where I offer justifications, on libertarian grounds, for killing innocent people used in this manner.

Let me end on a humorous note, which handily illustrates a point I want to make. Here's an old joke: "Do you know the difference between a living room and a bathroom? No? Well, then don't come to my house."

In like manner I ask, "Do you know the difference between offense and defense? Between starting a murderous rampage, and retaliating against one, by committing another? Well, then, don't get involved too heavily in political economy.

If, entirely unprovoked, the Mexican or Canadian armies started to sweep into our country, I certainly would favor the U.S. military rolling them back, warding them off, killing them, and pursuing them to the death back to the evil lairs from which they sprang, so that they could never again launch such an attack. Our armed forces should not, in my opinion, have to wait for such an eventuality. We could act in this very aggressive manner as soon as there was a real threat, and a reasonable chance of this entirely unwarranted invasion taking place. But, we should not preemptively bomb them, on the ground that, who knows, these nations might one day want to invade us.

This reminds me of another joke. A husband and his wife are out on a rowboat. The man is fishing, and the woman is reading a book. He then swims to shore, leaving her alone. Absorbed in her reading, she doesn't notice that the boat has drifted into a non-fishing zone. The sheriff comes along, and is about to arrest her for fishing in a non-fishing zone (the fishing rods, nets, etc., are still in the boat). She protests: "But I am not fishing; as you can clearly see, I am reading a book." He responds, "But you have all the equipment necessary to fish, so I have to arrest you." Her rejoinder: "If you arrest me for fishing, I'll accuse you of rape." Incredulously he says, "But I have done no such thing." Her response: "But you have all the equipment." Precisely. The Canadians and Mexicans have "all the equipment" necessary to war against us. But they have done no such thing. Ditto for Iraq, Iran, and Afghanistan.

7.3. Roderick Long is Wrong on Randy Barnett

Why do I think of Ron Paul as a libertarian and support his candidacy for president (for purposes of the present discussion I will not distinguish between these) but do not consider Randy Barnett in this way? As Roderick Long very truly says, each of these men hold views incompatible with libertarianism. Why, then, such a sharp distinction between them on my part?

To wit, Paul in my view is mistaken in his views of abortion and immigration, while Barnett is in error on war.

There are several reasons for my judgment.

1. I regard questions of war and peace, offense and defense, as far more important to libertarianism than abortion and immigration. The essence of libertarianism is the non-aggression axiom (coupled with homesteading and property rights). I see bombing innocent children and adults as a far more serious violation of liberty than aborting fetuses, or violating the rights of people who cross national borders. If this were my only reason, I'd regard it as sufficient to distinguish between Paul and Barnett, accepting the former as a libertarian but not the latter.

2. My second reason is that I regard abortion and immigration as far more complex issues than the question of whether a person or nation is committing an offensive act of war or a defensive one. Roderick rejects this as irrelevant. I demur. Suppose we were trying to determine who is a mathematician and who is not. Candidate A does not know that 2 + 2 = 4. Candidate B knows that, but stumbles over the Pythagorean theorem. I regard the latter as far more complex than the former. I consider B more of a mathematician than A. It seems to me that if a putative libertarian (Barnett) cannot distinguish offense from defense in such a simple case as war, while Paul certainly can, even though he stumbles on the far more complex issues of abortion and immigration, then Paul is certainly more of a libertarian, or a better one. But, the difference in complexity between these two issues is so gigantic, this difference of degree is so great that it amounts to a difference in kind, that I am entirely comfortable in evaluating Paul as a libertarian, but not Barnett.

Let me try again on this point. Here are two statements to which all Austrian economists subscribe.

a. Voluntary trade is mutually beneficial in the ex ante sense

b. The Austrian Business Cycle Theory (ABCT) is correct

I regard (a) as exceedingly simple to grasp. The Austrian credentials of anyone who does not see this are nil. I regard (b) as very complex. Austrianism consists of belief in scores of such claims. If someone agreed to all such claims except for (b), I would consider him an Austrian. Heck, even an Austrian in good standing. But, if he rejected (a) but accepted everything else, I'd think he was pulling my leg, so weird would this be.

In other words, complexity is not at all irrelevant to the issues which separate Roderick and me. Indeed, it is very important.

3. My supposed argument from authority: I regard my own views on abortion and immigration to be the correct libertarian positions (if I did not, I would change them). However, in my assessment, Murray Rothbard, Hans Hoppe and Stephan Kinsella are three of the most important libertarian theoreticians in all of history. They disagree with me on at least one and I think both of these issues. Thus, I am a bit more modest in my stance on abortion and immigration than I would otherwise be. However, I know of NO eminent libertarian who thinks that our war in Iraq is defensive.

At first blush, you are of course correct in asserting that this is circular reasoning on my part. For, I readily admit it, if there were some other eminent libertarian (hey, give me a break, I don't count Randroids) who did take this view, he would be dismissed, forthwith, as a libertarian in my view. Come to think of it, I think that John Hospers takes this view. Well, scratch Hospers from the ranks not only of eminent libertarian theoreticians, but from being a libertarian at all.

And yet, how else are we to determine issues of this sort? Will you concede to me that Rothbard, Hoppe and Kinsella, completely apart from the present issues under discussion, are more deserving of the title of eminent libertarian theorist than are Barnett, Hospers and the Randroids? If so, does not your position give you pause for reconsideration?

Maybe one way to reconcile our differences is as follows. I am operating from a sort of agnostic point of view: even though I have strong opinions on abortion and immigration, I am assuming, not a God's eye point of view, but rather the position of a newcomer to libertarianism, who doesn't know which way to go on this question since libertarian leaders diverge. You, in contrast, adopt a more knowledgeable position.

Chapter 8.

Ron Paul and Military Contributions

Here is a letter sent to me by one of my readers. I quote it in full (very slightly edited for clarity, and to fill in abbreviations).

I am curious about all this 'veterans' support for Ron Paul. I am a 63-year-old veteran and belong to many vet organizations, including one from the unit I served with. The unit I was with, 1st Infantry, Black Lions, has a Yahoo based site that we communicate with each other by common emails sent through that site. The flood of outrage that was expressed by Ron Paul's statement that one of the 'American citizens' who was recently killed by a drone was denied his right to a trial flooded my email box. Honestly, I have to agree with that outrage. Does Ron suggest that we should have risked our troops by sending them in to capture this terrorist so we could give him his Miranda rights and a 'fair' trial? I just don't see the support for Ron from any of the organizations I belong to. I can say this much, those organizations are by far mostly Republican supporters and I like some of Ron Paul's ideas in other realms, however I cannot support his mind-set of the 'Golden Rule' in combat situations. In war, there is no sense of fair play. On ambush patrols, we would ideally wait for the enemy to pass our ambush site and shoot them in the back wherein, if in their death throes they squeezed their triggers, it would not be in our direction. Do you have any statistics regarding support for Ron from other generations of veterans?"

I disagree with this reader almost entirely. To take the last point first, there is no doubt that active servicemen overwhelmingly support the Ron Paul candidacy. Whether this is due to the fact that he is the only one of the five candidates presently running who is not a chicken hawk (Gingrich, Obama, Romney, Santorum), or because active duty soldiers like his policies, I cannot say. But of that fact there can be no doubt. All you need do is Google "military donations by candidate" or "military donations Ron Paul" or any other such combinations of words and you will see this for yourself.

As to their "right to a trial" I don't see why you place scare quotes around "American citizens." Does not that phrase mean something to members of the military such as yourself? According to our Constitution, which you and the president are sworn to uphold, American citizens are not to be executed without a fair trial. Do you really oppose this?

A former captain of the Air Force, Ron Paul was widely denounced for his criticism of the way Obama handled the demise of Osama bin Laden. Yes, the congressman from Texas wanted this murderer of the innocents to have a trial. We accorded this aspect of a civilized order to Nazis at the end of World War II. The Israelis dealt with Eichmann in that manner. Is Osama so much worse than these folk that he did not deserve to be heard in a court of law? We are presumably fighting for a civilized order, among other things. Well, laws, courts, trials, the presumption of innocence are all aspects of countries that are not out and out barbarians. Do you favor barbarism? As they say in the western movies, *first* we give Osama a fair trial, and *then* we hang him. (I assume in saying this that his guilt is beyond question, but I do not know this for sure; my own interests lie more in the direction of economics and libertarian theory, not historical facts, and I have not done any intensive research on this matter.)

The whole defense about water boarding is that it will help us get information about our enemies. I don't necessarily advocate this practice for bin Laden, but, why oh why was he summarily executed, before what he knows could be wrung out of him? Does that strike you as somewhat anomalous? That Captain Paul (I like that title) could wonder out loud about this does not make him the wuss and sissy you imply that he is. You don't wonder about this?

You are totally confused about Ron Paul's position on terrorists such as Osama bin Laden. A constitutionalist, Dr. Paul advocated the use of

Letters of Marque and Reprisal (see article I, Section 8, paragraph 11). These are permissions or warrants or commissions for private individuals to engage in acts that would otherwise be considered murder, or piracy or theft. Does this sound to you as if the next president of the U.S. was advocating the use of Miranda rights abroad?

As to "fair play" in war, have you ever heard of the Geneva Conventions? This does not mean that the U.S. allows the enemy to win; this does not mean that we may not shoot enemy soldiers in the back. That may be contrary to the Marques of Queensbury rules, but it is certainly acceptable in war under the Geneva Convention. What it means is that we do not aim to murder innocent civilians, women and children, as the U.S. forces have long been doing, even before Hiroshima and Nagasaki, and certainly nowadays. Mr. Paul's view on war is that we should rarely engage in it, only then in self-defense, that such an act should be declared by Congress as stipulated in the Constitution, and that we should win it quickly.

The problem with people such as yourself who take this position is that you blithely assume that those in charge of conducting these policies will resemble you in all relevant regards: they will not ever place you or your family or your friends in their gun sights. But the rights you would deny others can also be denied you and yours. Scary, huh?

Last but far from least, let us consider the "Golden Rule." According to it, one must do unto others as one would have them do unto us. If we rule out masochists who want you to beat them and therefore feel justified in beating you in accordance with this rule, this is a pretty good regulation for a civilized order. Of course, Ron Paul never ever in a million years meant this to be applied to warfare conditions as you more than imply. It would be grotesque for Ron Paul when he becomes commander in chief of the U.S. military, to order his soldiers to obey this rule during wartime when faced with the enemy. But, when not applied to wartime conditions, it is a very, very good rule. Since we would not want the Iranians to kill our women and children, we shouldn't kill theirs. Since we wouldn't want the Iraqis to set up military bases on our territory, we shouldn't set up any in theirs. Since we wouldn't want our citizens assassinated, we should not engage in such despicable acts ourselves. Since we wouldn't want foreign drones killing our residents, we shouldn't fly them over places like Pakistan.

I hope and trust you now see the candidacy of Ron Paul in at least a slightly different light. He is not at all "giving away the store." His is a counsel of peace, commercial relations with the rest of the world and prosperity. But, if anyone dare attack us, or even credibly threaten to do so, he will make every effort to protect us. He favors *defense* not *offense.* He offers the very common sense notion that the best way to protect us is not to send our soldiers all over the world, but rather to stay at home where they can engage in *defense.*

War is hell. Writing about it is depressing. So, let us end this section on foreign policy on a (somewhat) lighter note. Well sort of.

Chapter 9.

Kill All Foreigners; Kill 'em All!

Save some liberal wieners, a smattering of "progressives" and a few ungrateful pinkos, no one in the country would seriously doubt that a worldwide slaughter of foreigners would make America safer. While efforts of the heroic Bush-Obama administration to wipe out all the Arabs are certainly a good start, we must not forget that other countries in the world are evil and we've got to settle their hash, too.

Before discussing the litany, it is important to note that this article only provides a tip of the iceberg. Understanding the vital importance of a pre-emptive foreign policy, we have resolved to establish an institute to rigorously pursue this end. Heading up the International Democratic Institute for Overseas Transplantation will be a cadre of noted pro-murder libertarians, including Randy Barnett, Deroy Murdock, and Ronald Bailey. Other IDIOT Fellows will include Christopher Hitchens, Rush Limbaugh, Max Boot, Thomas Sowell, and Sean Hannity. With the institute in place to exhaustively target *all* foreign countries, do not interpret omissions as implying approval.

We do not seek world domination; to this end, we are critical of the Bush administration. We are realists and understand that we will never be able to control some insubordinates. So instead of costly bureaucracy, why not achieve control over the entire globe by eliminating every other inhabitant of it? Half measures will avail us nothing. It is time to own up to the logical implications of our present foreign policy, not cringe at them.

America must become the "terrible swift sword" of the world — a smiter of all evil and ill will. This sword, in the form of nuclear warheads, will be directed against the following evildoers (among others):

China — Not only are these people trying to industrialize, but they are hosting the Olympics. Didn't Hitler host the Olympics? By logical deduction then, the Chinese are crypto-Nazis. It's 1938 all over again; we cannot appease Hitler. What's more is that they are trying to be peaceful. Only democracies are allowed to be peaceful. Massive human rights violations obviously warrant massive human rights violations.

Canada — It is ham; there is no such thing as Canadian bacon. During our first great war, i.e. the French and Indian, they provided comfort to the enemy. Moreover, it has become exceedingly difficult to distinguish Canadians from dull, white Americans. They constitute a natural fifth column, which will one day overrun us. Better safe than sorry.

Russia — They are fooling no one with their "surrender." The breaking up of the Soviet Union was one great political ploy designed at further freezing the Cold War. While we have been navel gazing, the Soviets have been assassinating foreign nationals. It's hard not to admire the KGB, but IDIOT Fellow David Frum cautions us not to ignore "the evidence that the Russian government murdered a British citizen in the British capital with a radiological weapon." Though Frum doesn't go far enough. He says: "If we acknowledged that terrible reality, we would have to do something about it." He fails to understand that if we do the sort of thing neoconservatives are advocating for Iran, and defending for Iraq, there will be Russians who survive an invasion and conventional bombing.

Germany — One word: Hitler. As supreme enemies of liberty, Germans will never change. There are still legions of Holocaust deniers running around spouting their pernicious vitriol and singing "Du Hast." What alternative do we have other than the bomb? Allowing this anti-Semitism to continue would be unconscionable.

Vatican City — Let us not forget that the leader of this country is a theocrat, installed by elitist oligarchs. The Catholic Church is not a democratic institution and dogma is decided upon by gospel missive, not majority.

Israel — Truly a socialist country. As pro-war libertarians, we resent their socialism. The latest chapter in this sorry story is that they have adopted price controls for bread. We'll have to forcibly teach these people that free markets and private property are the last best hope for mankind.

South America — As noted political philosopher Randy Newman points out, "they stole our name" and thus a nuclear first strike is the only appropriate response to this unjust linguistic theft. If the unpatriotic have further doubts, let us not forget that we would not have cocaine, Che T-shirts, and immigrants had it not been for this horrid land.

India — It's now our turn to outsource. Why should Sanjay steal the job of Steve? Because it is more economical and conducive to a global division of labor? Because it engenders world peace? Those things are clearly anti-American. Just as the New Yorker should only purchase goods manufactured within his island or the Peorian only purchase Peorian products, so too should Americans buy American. Exportation is evil, importation, insidious.

Africa — They are continually killing each other in tribal genocidal warfare. Let us help them out, in this regard. Who says we are against foreign aid? No more people means no more genocide — we just choose to drop our foreign aid from 50,000 feet in the air in the form of tactical nuclear warheads.

Syria — This low-lying fruit of a country is ripe, but not for a picking, no, this would imply some sort of desire to govern this veritable Islamofascistan. Who are thcsc Arabs to stand against U.S. aspirations? Let us show them, in the only way these heathens will understand, what it means to mess with the good old U.S. of A.

We have the means to kill all these people; we simply lack the will.

George Bush, we implore you to accept our modest proposal! Don't label us as traitors though; you *have* made a valiant effort. But your efforts so far should only be considered the first, timid steps. This is the fundamental problem with neo-conservatism — it's a doctrine that takes too much pleasure in watching death up-close. It is true that our policy will lead to quick, painless extermination, and we can certainly understand the outrage over at *National Review*, but it is the only way. Bush can have his personal pleasure from Iraq, Iran, and Afghanistan, but this is a narrow, limited, and provincial strategy. We are the only true globalists.

Please note: this is a parody.

Part III.

Personal Liberties

Ron Paul has done yeoman work in opposing NDAA, SOPA, Guantanamo, the Patriot Act and each and every other government violation of our civil and personal liberties. He has been stalwart in upholding habeas corpus. However, if there is one violation of our personal rights that is most heavily associated with Dr. Paul in the public mind it is none of these. It is, instead, his valiant and decades-long opposition to our drug prohibition laws. This section is devoted to that fight of his.

Chapter 10.

Drug Legalization: How to Radically Lower the Number of Murders

New Orleans is now undergoing an unprecedented murder rate, even for the Big Uneasy. How can we dig our way out of this morass?

The usual suspect solutions have all been tried, have not worked in the past, and will not help us now. According to the conventional wisdom, the way to stop people from shooting at each other is to improve our public schools, promote day care, stop the drug trade with stiffer sentences, start midnight basketball leagues, bring in the social workers, promote religion, subsidize parenting skills, introduce citizenship and ethics classes in high school — the list of ineptitude goes on and on.

These "remedies" are either focused way too far in the long run to be even relevant to our critical short-run problems, or never have addressed and cannot solve such challenges, or are actually counterproductive: exacerbating murder rates, not diminishing them.

So, let us take a deep breath, open our minds, and consider something radical, way off the beaten track: let us legalize drugs, *all* of them without exception, preeminently including marijuana, cocaine, and, yes, heroin. (Legalization is to be distinguished sharply from favoring the use of these substances, something I strongly oppose.)

What does this have to do with the gigantic number of murders now afflicting New Orleans? Plenty. An inordinate amount of these episodes consists of drug dealers shooting each other in turf wars. End the prohibition, and this viciousness stops right in its tracks. Nor are these murders likely to end any time soon. Things of this sort were kept down to a dull roar before Katrina. A sort of equilibrium was attained. Every gang knew its place, at least roughly. "Property rights" on street corners and in back alleyways were semi-established. Yes, from time to time there was a bit of blood-letting, as criminals served their sentences and tried to reclaim what used to be "their" territory, or, as dealers were killed or retired, and mini-wars broke out until the new pecking order was established.

But then came the failure of the levees. "Our" dealers tried to set up shop in Houston, Memphis, Atlanta and other such refuges. The local denizens did not appreciate that one bit. Conflagrations broke out there. Then, as the Crescent City began to repopulate, heroin entrepreneurs began trickling back along with these crowds. Paradoxically, this increased crime in the temporary refuge cities from which these gangsters were emigrating, and also in New Orleans as they arrived back here. For both the egress and ingress set up jurisdictional disputes over turf, and the battle lines were drawn again and again in blood. This inflated murder rate will only recede to pre-Katrina levels, which were horrible enough in that bygone era, when post-hurricane population movement slows to previous levels. That point may not be reached for decades.

It is thus time, past time, to drain the swamps instead of following our present policy of fighting the alligators. Legalizing addictive drugs, every last one of them, will stop all this gang warfare for sure, and immediately.

Why? If marijuana, heroin, etc., were legal, it would be sold in ordinary legitimate stores such as pharmacies. These would replace the present fly-by-night murderous operators. Customers would rather purchase brand-name cocaine, replete with labels, money-back guarantees in case of defective products, as in the case of all other consumption goods. Standard business ventures have a comparative advantage over hoodlums whose only specialty resides in violence.

When alcohol was prohibited from 1920 to 1933, gangs fought it out in the streets with machine guns for the right to sell their bathtub gin. Innocent bystanders were killed in the cross fire, just as at present. Backwoods stills killed still more, with their battery acid products. Nowadays, peace reigns in this industry. Johnny Walker and Four Roses compete with each other, not with bullets, but in terms of the traditional commercial aspects of price, advertising, availability, quality, reputation, etc. The Mafia is no longer involved. No one dies, *no one*, in the creation, manufacture, wholesaling, distribution, transportation, retailing of this product. For similar reasons, the same beneficial effects will ensue when, and as soon as, we legalize drugs.

But will we not die like flies from these addictive substances once they are legalized? There is no more reason to think so than to believe that when the prohibition of booze ended, it encouraged an orgy of drunkenness. Pretty much the same people who liquored up before

1920 did so after 1933, and there is every reason to believe that drug legalization would follow the same path. Those who now abuse drugs will still likely continue to do so. Is there anyone, now, who refrains from their use simply because they are illegal? Yes, both drugs and alcohol will remain *medical problems* post-legalization, but the *crime* will be eradicated from both.

So far, I have attempted to show that the last best hope for our city in eliminating the scourge of murders presently besetting us is to legalize drugs. Why? Because a disproportionate number of these capital crimes take place between drug gangs fighting over turf, and the innocents caught in the cross fire. Legalize heroin, cocaine and marijuana, and such conflagrations will immediately cease, as they did when alcohol prohibition was ended in 1933. I now wish to consider, and reject, several objections to this very sensible plan.

1. If people drive while under the influence of drugs, the enormous increase in traffic fatalities will more than offset any saving of lives due to the elimination of murderous wars over drug turf.

Not so. Drugs can be treated in roughly the same manner as alcohol. It is legal to use the latter product, but not to drive while intoxicated. In like manner, it would no longer be a crime to erase brain cells with heroin, but it would be if you then get behind the wheel of a car.

2. This plan to legalize drugs would give a social imprimatur to abuse such substances. Children would be led to try them.

No. One cannot infer approval from mere legalization of an act or substance. Abortion, gambling, prostitution, alcohol and, homosexuality are no longer criminal offenses in civilized societies, but the attitude of society toward them is one of strict neutrality, not approval. Right now, addictive drugs have about them the lure of the forbidden; youngsters are more likely to be tempted by them. Under legalization, no drug purveyors would hang around school yards, as they now do, and try to get kids to try their deleterious wares.

3. Drug legalization would empty the city to an even greater degree than at present

There is one added benefit to New Orleans from implementing such a proposal: we will have gained for ourselves a new bouncing baby industry. Just as Las Vegas evolved from a stretch of desert into a world-class city when it was the only one to offer gambling, so will the

Big Easy surpass its previous preeminence (it was once the leading city in the entire South) when it alone offers legal drugs. This industry all by itself, will put us back on the map.

4. The state and federal courts will not allow New Orleans, all on its own, to declare itself a free enterprise zone in this regard. So, even if legalization would radically reduce our local murder rate, we will not be allowed to implement it.

Right now, like it or not, we are a tremendous burden on the rest of the state, and indeed the country. We could do far better on our own than with our palms up, begging for charity. As well, the federales owe us big. The flooding was the fault of their Army Corp of Engineers that built the porous levies. It was their FEMA that added insult to injury in Katrina's aftermath, by preventing others from rescuing us, while doing nothing much on its own in this regard. It would come with particular ill grace for them to object to a plan that would, one, stop this horrid spate of murders cold in its tracks, and two, put us back on our feet, economically speaking.

5. But is it not scurrilous to be associated with such a product? New Orleans as the drug capital of the country is something that would disgrace us.

I answer that it is far more debilitating to take on our present role as the murder capital of the country, on a per capita basis. Would you rather have blood running in the streets?

6. The Harrison Narcotics Act of 1914 was implemented for a good purpose: to save ourselves from the scourge of drugs.

Has it succeeded? To ask this question, is to answer it. People can purchase addictive substances in any major city in the country. No, this "war" has failed, like so many other such initiatives undertaken by government. The motivation behind this legislation had nothing to do with protecting the public in any case. It was pure and simple a racist anti-Chinese measure, in an attempt to criminalize them for using opium dens.

7. We are on the verge of winning the drug war. This is not the time to "cut and run."

The drug war is an utter and abysmal failure. And necessarily so. Every time a successful interdiction occurs, drug prices and profits rise, and this only strengthens the drug gangs. They are impregnable to such tactics.

New Orleanians, let us legalize drugs.! We have only to lose our title as a place where people are shot down in cold blood en masse. Let's go free enterprise. We won't be "chocolate" city; we'll be drug city instead. Safer, and a lot more prosperous.

Chapter 11.

The Libertarian Case *For* Drug Prohibition

Ok, ok, already, hold onto your horses. I have not given up on libertarianism. Nor have I finally, and completely, succumbed to Alzheimer's disease. It is just that since all of us who favor economic freedom oppose drug prohibition, the contentious part of my personality naturally looks around for reasons on the other side of this debate.

That, plus the fact that I had the unfortunate experience at a recent conference I attended of hearing a supposed libertarian "defend" drug legalization; he did so in such a manner that I didn't have to be particularly quarrelsome or defensive about libertarianism to oppose him. Moreover, the fact that this seminar was constructed in such a manner that I was not able to publicly criticize the outrageous case he offered made it all the more important that I somehow get this off my chest. You, gentle reader, will have to stand in for the audience I might have otherwise addressed.

So, what are the reasons, in general, for maintaining the status quo regarding the prohibition of addictive substances?

1. Without this law, our movies, television programming, plays, novels and other vehicles of storytelling would be much less enriched. Award-winning television series such as "Law and Order" and "The Sopranos" would be particularly hard hit by repeal. It is an exaggeration to say that programming of this ilk contains *nothing but* this motif, but not by much. Surely, at least half of the themes explored in the cops and robbers genre depend upon the fact that there is a black market in marijuana, cocaine and heroin.

2. Were addictive materials to be legalized, a whole host of jobs would be lost. (Look, I said I would give *reasons* in support of prohibition; I did not say I would give *good* ones in this regard. As far as I am concerned, there *are* no good reasons. I am willing to defend the "undefendable," but this is not undefendable.) We are talking, here, about judges, policemen, jail guards, social workers, lawyers, district attorneys, social workers, psychologists, munitions makers, pilots of small planes and boat drivers, etc. Could it be that one of the strongest reasons for the retention of this horrid law is this self-same fact? I wonder. Not, of course, that jobs are needed. That is the unfortunate

legacy of Keynes and Keynesianism. As every Austrian from Mises to Hazlitt to Rothbard has shown, it is not rational to create jobs merely for the sake of creating jobs. We could all be employed digging ditches and filling them in again, and we would starve as a result. No, the whole point of jobs is to create goods and services of *value*, and the ones that come about as a result of drug prohibition hardly qualify.

What, then, are the obnoxious reasons offered by this "libertarian" on behalf of drug legalization?

3. The present drug laws bring about a general disrespect for law and order, and this is something to be greatly regretted. But this is highly problematic from the libertarian perspective. It's likely impossible to determine how many laws there are today, with more added every day.

And, of these, how many are *good* laws, e.g., enactments compatible with the libertarian axiom of nonaggression? Well, let's see. There are laws against murder, theft, trespass, fraud, kidnapping, assault and battery, rape… I am quickly running out of examples. Well, I suppose we can pick up a few more, possibly, from the Ten Commandments; and defense of contracts from the civil law. But that is about it.

So, it is pro libertarian to promote a general respect for law? Hardly. Virtually all law is *bad* law. Only an infinitesimal percentage of all law is good law. Respecting law in general, then, is to promote evil. How, then, are we to regard favoring the repeal of drug laws on the ground that they reduce respect for law in general? Whatever else may be said about this contention, it cannot be claimed that it is compatible with libertarianism.

4. The economist goes on and on, ad nauseam, about how he needs data for public policy analysis. Without data, he never tires of telling us, it is impossible to make an informed decision as to whether or not addictive substances should be legalized.

But this is stuff and nonsense. Whether or not drugs should be prohibited by law is a matter of *normative* economics. Data, in stark contrast, is part and parcel of *positive* economics. To be sure, in some moral systems, e.g., utilitarianism, the latter is not irrelevant to the former. But for the deontological libertarian, it comes down to a matter of *rights.* Does the (adult) individual have the right to inject into his body whatever he pleases, harmful or not? And the answer is, of course he does.

It is more than passing curious that this economics professor, after recounting the necessity of data, and bewailing its absence, nevertheless takes the pro-legalization side of this debate. Perhaps the statistics are not that necessary after all.

5. According to the speaker at this conference I am criticizing, the market price of a pound of marijuana is presently about $3,000. He estimates that the total costs under legalization would be something of the order of $3 per pound. Thus, the profit (plus the black market costs, given that this market is illegal) amount to some $2,997, or 99.9% of the total.

This speaker "doesn't like" the people who are presently enjoying this differential. He favors legalization, so that they will no longer have access to these funds. He full well realizes that when and if the government legalizes this product, it will tax the stuffing out of it, just as it presently does in the cases of booze and tobacco. He offers as yet another reason for legalizing marijuana that this will, in one fell swoop, take the profits away from the present producers.

Now I full well sympathize with this professor's assessment of your typical denizen of the drug market. He is mean and vicious, fully willing and able to use violence against police, competitors, sometimes even customers. It is thanks to him and his confreres that we have a new word to describe innocent victims of drug gang warfare: "mushrooms."His product is oft-time poisonous, and the dosage uncertain. These are altogether a pretty despicable lot of people. Of course, as is well known in the libertarian community, these characteristics stem, entirely, from the illegal status of drugs. During alcohol prohibition, the proprietors were similar to today's drug dealers. Nowadays, under legalization of beer, wine and liquor, the purveyors are indistinguishable from those who manufacture cheese or chalk.

However, with whom are we comparing these very bad people? (Typical economist's joke; Question: "How's your wife?"Answer: "Compared to whom?") Answer: we are comparing them with the *government!* How many innocent people have all the drug gangs in the world murdered? Hundreds, thousands, tens of thousands? In contrast, according to Rummel (1996), governments are responsible for killing no fewer than about 170 million of their own residents and citizens in the twentieth century; we are talking noncombatants here. This economist wants data? Here is data. What can we say about the moral status of a commentator who favors a public policy (partially) on the ground that a gang responsible for a relative handful of deaths will be deprived of financial resources, and that they will be given over to a different gang of people who have killed millions?

Yes, by all means, let us legalize drugs. (I told you I'm still a libertarian). And, perhaps, our plays and movies will be less dramatic. But there will be no gain from decriminalization concerning jobs, or respect for law, or better allocation of funds from drug gang to government gang.

Part IV.

Critiques of Critics

I have criticized critics of Ron Paul in previous sections of this book, when they seemed to fall into its major sections: economics, foreign policy and personal liberty. In this section, I include my responses to some critics that didn't seem to fit neatly into any of those three categories, and/or who overlap all of them.

Chapter 12.

Stefan Molyneux

My relationship with this author is an interesting one. We had agreed to a debate, one that he aborted after changing his views 180 degrees, perhaps in response to my highly critical reaction to what I regarded as his unwarranted attack on my man, Dr. Paul. Molyneux started out with this video (http://www.youtube.com/watch?v=McNo62gpw6M&playnext=1&list=PLADDEC1E9BDF4ECE0), which I regarded as very unfair. So I wrote this criticism of his talk: "Ron Paul and the Self-Hating 'Libertarians'" (which appears below as section 12.1 of this chapter). Numerous of his followers threatened me, pleaded with me, begged me, to engage him in a debate on this matter. I was reluctant to do so, since he doesn't write his criticisms of Congressman Paul, but rather speaks them in videos. But it takes him a looooong time to say anything, and I just didn't have the patience to listen to him for hours on end (ok, ok, almost an entire hour) criticizing Ron Paul. Also, it is difficult to get direct quotes from him, for although he speaks agonizingly slowly compared with my reading speed, it is far faster than I can type. I find the experience frustrating. So I listened to about 10 minutes, all I could tolerate of this, and then wrote, I confess, a rather bitter rejoinder. In round two, Molyneux responded with this video: http://www.youtube.com/watch?v=5-j9LBCmM3c. Here, he took me to task for listening to only 10 minutes of a talk of his of almost an hour's duration.

He and I then agreed to a formal debate. We would, this time, the both of us, write our views, not merely speak them, and publish them in a refereed journal dedicated to libertarianism. We each, duly, wrote opening statements. Then, as agreed, I penned a rebuttal to his initial viewpoint, and was waiting for his critique of my own opening statement. Instead, someone else sent me this, http://www.youtube.com/watch?v=w-26c7WxaiE, which amounted to a total and complete capitulation of him to my viewpoint. To wit, he now announced himself as a supporter, no longer a critic, of

Congressman Paul. I only listened to the first few minutes of this, as is my wont; during this time, he did not credit me with changing his mind on this matter. Nor did he ever thank me, in subsequent email exchanges, for so doing. Here is another of his videos, where he defends Ron Paul against the charge of racism (http://www.youtube.com/watch?v=axN53qCJChY&feature=youtu.be). After further inquiries of mine, and entreaties to him about the status of our debate, he finally let me know that he was no longer interested in pursuing this matter with me. So, I suppose, I can at least take part credit, perhaps, for changing Molyneux from a Ron Paul critic to a supporter.

With this introduction, I now offer my opening statement supporting Ron Paul and opposing Molyneux's criticism of him, and my rebuttal to his own opening statement.

12.1. Opening the Evisceration: Ron Paul and the Self-hating 'Libertarians'

Karen Kwiatkowski (2011) wrote a magnificent blog exposing *Reason* magazine as a critics, not supporters, of libertarianism.[2] I would now like to add to her list of one "libertarian" who trashes Ron Paul. My nomination to be second on this list is Stefan Molyneux. Full disclosure: his speech attacking Dr. Paul goes on for almost an hour, and I didn't have the sitzfleisch (patience) to listen to all of it. But, in the first 10 minutes or so he criticizes Congressman Paul for, yes, wait for it, favoring the Constitution! Molyneux also correctly allows that if President Paul takes office, we "slaves" will have far fewer beatings, but claims that this is an insufficient reason for supporting him. I did indeed, until recently listening to this rant, have some respect for Molyneux (unlike for Reason magazine, which has long ago turned against libertarianism). He has authored some very persuasive material on anarcho-capitalism. But, evidently, Molyneux is one of those free market anarchists who does not really "hate the state," (see Murray Rothbard on this) certainly not enough to support one of the greatest enemies of statism the world has ever known.

We are now at a point in time where, thanks to Dr. Ron Paul, people are hearing of libertarianism to a degree that possibly never before occurred in our history. Congressman Paul's efforts in 2008 were responsible for putting our freedom philosophy in front of the American people in a gigantic, stupendous way. His present campaign is even more successful. At a time when Ron is creating libertarians wholesale, and introducing the entire world to the case for liberty, Reason and Molyneux are doing everything they can to stop this process. For shame.

I said, above, that that this list has two members. I fear there are many more, mainly beltway type "libertarians." Unhappily, these two, Reason and Molyneux, constitute just the tip of the iceberg. I can readily understand why liberals and conservatives hate Ron Paul with a purple passion. If they did not score on this litmus test in this manner, they would not be liberals or conservatives. I can even understand the case for the main stream media giving him the backs of their hands. But libertarians who oppose Ron Paul? Their stance boggles the imagination.

2Brian Doherty is an honorable exception to this general rule.

Why is it that we have so many self-hating "libertarians?" Several theories present themselves. Consider the following:

1. Inside the beltway, suck-ups realize that their very tenuous connections to Washington, D.C., power brokers will all but vanish with a Paul Administration.

2. Plain old jealousy and envy. Ron Paul has done more for libertarianism than all of his critics, put together. Indeed, the two do not even belong in the same sentence, so widely disparate has been their success in promoting liberty.

3. Ron Paul is from "flyover" country. He is not "sophisticated." He is a rube. If you look closely, he has hay on his suit. Our sophisticated libertarians thus see him as an embarrassment.

4. Congressman Paul does not look for "second-best" solutions. He is not skilled in the art of compromise. He is a man of principle. The contrast between Dr. Paul and his many critics is all too glaring.

For some libertarians, this philosophy is only a parlor game (I think of Nozick in this regard). It is a beautiful philosophy (true confession: I see it this way too.) But it has nothing to do with the real world. A Paul Administration, however, would actually *do* things: bring back the troops, save the dollar, drastically lower taxes, legalize victimless crimes. What, then, would happen to professional libertarians in such a relatively free society? Horrors, there might be fewer jobs for such presumed opponents of statism.

6. Ron Paul is too old. I'll bet that if there were a physical test between the contenders for the Republican nomination (e.g., time in the quarter-mile, number of push-ups in 3 minutes, weight-lifting, a bicycle race, something like that), Ron would outclass competitors a decade or two younger than him. But wait: this would not be a fair test. Dr. Paul was a national class athlete. Most of these others are couch potatoes. Can you picture Newt Gingrich swimming 200 yards? This picture, it wouldn't be a pretty one, puts that charge in context.

I have no idea as to whether or not these theories are true; they are only speculations on my part. Perhaps they apply to some "libertarian" opponents and critics of the Ron Paul Revolution. But, if we are to counter them, the first step would appear to be to understand them, and, perhaps, these explanations will lead others to get us that proverbial one step closer to the truth.

12.2. Continuing the Evisceration

The case for libertarians to support Ron Paul, a critique of Stephan Molyneux

I. Introduction

Ron Paul deserves better than to be attacked by so-called libertarians

I argue in this paper the following syllogism:

1. Ron Paul's 2012 campaign is putting libertarianism on the map as never before in the history of the world.

2. There are so-called libertarians who have nevertheless attacked him. Therefore,

3. These critics of Ron Paul are not really libertarians

Before elaborating on these premises, here is a bit of background. In the previous chapter, I charged that Molyneux was a "self-hating" libertarian. I confess: I did (and still do) feel more than just a little bit of animosity toward this author/speaker. I find it appalling that at a time when Ron Paul is busting his veritable gut trying to promote liberty, and doing so superlatively, relative midgets[3] such as Molyneux are carping about him, actively engaged in undermining the magnificent work for liberty in which he is involved. "For shame" I said then to Molyneux, and "for shame" I say now.

3I regard myself, too, as a "midget" compared to Ron Paul in the libertarian sweepstakes. So, in this, Molyneux and I are alike, at least in my own view.

The only version of Molyneux (2007) I had at my disposal was an hourlong speech; I had no written comments of his on this topic available to me. Nor did I have the patience to listen to more than about 10 minutes of what I regarded as balderdash.[4] My goal then, I admit it, was to put Molyneux in his place.[5]

Many of Molyneux's supporters wrote me very nice and polite[6] letters objecting to Block (2011) on the ground that I had not given Molyneux (2007) a fair shot, in that I listened to only a small part of it. In Molyneux (2011) he said something to the effect:[7] "If I were a student of Walter Block's, and I handed in a report to him about a speech of one-hour's duration, and admitted that I had only listened to some 10 minutes of it, I doubt that he would give me a good mark on this incomplete effort of mine." Nonsense. If a student of mine were listening to a presentation where the speaker in the first ten minutes took the position that the Earth is flat, or that 2+2=17, or that water runs uphill, and took one full hour to make his case, and my student turned in a paper to me rejecting any of these three theses on the basis of listening to far less than all of it, au contraire, I would *congratulate* my student for his ability to economize on time. Why waste precious resources on obvious fallacy? Yes, I do regard Molyneux's critique of Dr. Paul as roughly equivalent to one of these three claims and will attempt to make good on this charge below. In part II, I elaborate upon the syllogism introduced above. I conclude in section III.

II. The syllogism

1. Ron Paul's 2012 campaign is putting libertarianism on the map as perhaps it has never before been done in the history of the world.

4This is still my opinion of Molyneux (2007), and, no, in the intervening period, I still have not made the time to listen to his rant in its entirety.

5This goal of mine has not changed by one iota in the intervening time.

6I congratulate Molyneux on the quality of the listeners of his blogs.

7This is a paraphrase. My typing skills are not such that I can take down written remarks made at the ordinary talking speed employed by this author.

Granted, Paul's 2008 campaign cannot hold a candle to what he has accomplished, so far, in 2011, and Molyneux's critique took place during the earlier campaign. But, did Molyneux apologize for his 2007 attack on the congressman in the light of his recent far more significant accomplishments? Did he revise any of it, in view of Ron's great recent strides in converting to the libertarian philosophy not only large parts of the country, but a significant percentage of the entire world?[8] Again, he did not. Thus, I infer, he stands behind his 2007 effort. Indeed, in his 2011 blog talk, which occurs right in the midst of the Paul 2012 campaign, he has the effrontery to reiterate his complaints about Ron Paul.[9]

I am not going to document the effect that Congressman Paul has had on the hearts and minds of the public. Were I to do so, and do a thorough job of it, I would mention literally tens of thousands of radio and television interviews, op-ed pieces in the major and minor media. I cannot think that this claim would be an issue of contention between me and Molyneux. Ron Paul is introducing libertarianism to millions, maybe billions of people who have never before heard of it, and is converting a goodly portion of them to the freedom philosophy that Molyneux and I fervently share.

Doherty (2007) singles out five people he says have been instrumental in promoting liberty. They are Ayn Rand, Milton Friedman, Ludwig von Mises, Friedrich Hayek and Murray Rothbard. I have no doubt that had Doherty written a bit later, he would have included Ron Paul as a sixth member of this libertarian roll of honor. It is interesting to speculate as to which of these people made not the biggest

8The word is in that Dr. Paul's campaign has moved a significant number of Moonians and Martians to the freedom philosophy, but, unfortunately, I have been unable to document this as of yet. However, I have unleashed my several very competent research assistants on this matter, and am expecting proof of this claim any moment now.

9At least I think so. As it happens, I have not yet had the ability to actually listen to it. I imagine it would take a goodly amount of my time to do so.

contributions to libertarian theory,[10] but rather had the largest impact on the general public; that is, promulgated libertarianism farthest and widest. My gut feeling is that Ayn Rand would take first place in this sweepstakes, followed in a virtual tie by Hayek and Friedman.[11]

How does Ron Paul stack up against these illustrious five? As I see matters, he is clearly in the Ayn Rand category, and may even exceeds her impact upon the general public, although these speculations, in the absence of hard evidence, must be taken with a grain of salt. This, in spite of the efforts of the main stream media to ignore, belittle and laugh at the views of the congressman from Texas.[12] Why do I place Ron Paul ahead of Ayn Rand in terms of publicizing libertarianism? There are several reasons. Ayn specifically rejected libertarians, calling us "hippies of the right." Ron embraces libertarianism, and even ran for president on the Libertarian Party ticket in 1988.[13] She set up her own philosophy, "Objectivism"; in contrast, the philosophy of libertarianism was and is good enough for him. He is active more recently than her, and in the modern era, he commands the internet, which didn't exist during her epoch, and has been on far more radio and television shows than her. He is also a far more active public speaker than she was.

To sum up this section,. I think Doherty (2007) was right in singling out those five giants in terms of promoting liberty.[14] If he is correct, then they have contributed the most to liberty, at least in the modern day. I have made the case that Paul exceeds them all in this regard.

10Mr. Libertarian, Murray Rothbard, wins hands down in this regard

11Mises and Rothbard, too, made the greatest internal contributions to economic and free market theory. But both were relative unknowns compared to the other three insofar as being in the public spotlight is concerned.

12It might well be that the mainstream media treated Ayn Rand even more viciously.

13http://en.wikipedia.org/wiki/Ron_Paul

14I abstract here from my evaluation of how each of them stacks up against what I would consider pure libertarianism. In my view, the ratings would be Friedman, 50%; Hayek, 55%; Rand, 91%; Mises, 92%; Rothbard, 99%. How does Paul rate? He comes in at 90%, on the basis of my admittedly subjective calculations.

Thus, I conclude, Ron Paul has done more to promote liberty on a popular or widespread basis than any other human being in the history of mankind.

2. There are so-called libertarians who have nevertheless attacked him.

Why have they done this? It is difficult to ascribe motives to human action. These necessarily lie beneath the surface. Thus, my comments in this section must remain very tentative. So, I speculate, what would bring a *libertarian* to attack Ron Paul, when he is doing more to convert people to libertarianism than anyone else in our history?

A. The truth?

This of course is a primary motivation of most libertarians. Why climb Mount Everest? Because it is there. Why criticize any political leader or philosopher or economist in an area impinging upon liberty? Because they are there.

But this hardly *requires* a critique of Paul. Are there not other figures who even more

richly deserve condemnation? Let me name a few, just a few. For example, the others who are running against Ron Paul for the Republican nomination: Michelle Bachmann, Herman Cain, Newt Gingrich, John Huntsman, Gary Johnson,[15] Rick Perry, Mitt Romney, Rick Santorum. Or, some Democratic politicians, if it is politicians who raise your ire: Joe Biden, Bill Clinton, Hillary Clinton, Barack Obama, Nancy Pelosi. You say politicians are not your cup of tea? Well, then, why criticize Ron Paul? And, for sure, there are plenty of leftist scholars out there just "cruising for a bruising:": George Akerloff, David Card, Brad DeLong, Paul Ehrlich, Alan Krueger, Paul

---

15I am ambivalent about mentioning him since he is clearly the second most libertarian of all the Republican candidates for office.

Krugman, Joseph Stiglitz. There are also many right wing intellectuals, some even purporting, insolently, to be libertarians: Doug Bandow, Ben Bernanke, Tom Bethell, David Boaz, Ronald Coase, Richard Epstein, David Friedman, David Frum, Robert George, Alan Greenspan, Gregory Mankiw, Deirdre McCloskey, Jeffry Miron, Charles Murray, Richard Pipes, Robert Poole, Thomas Sowell, Abby Thernstrom, George Will, Walter Williams.

B. Product differentiation?

Yes, we libertarians want to distinguish ourselves from non-libertarians, the better to differentiate our product from theirs. But, based on the list above, there are plenty of conservatives, liberals, and, yes, even semi libertarians, from whom we can distinguish ourselves. Why pick on the one man who is doing more for liberty than all of these people put together?

C. Making a reputation

On this ground, too, Ron Paul could be in the crosshairs. Who better to put down in order to one-up oneself? If you can prove you are more of a libertarian than the congressman from the 14th District of Texas, you have indeed proven something. But there are others, surely, see list above, who more richly deserve the backs of the libertarian hand than Dr. Paul. He is, after all, not a leading theoretician, not a leading economist of our movement, not a leading intellectual, although, to be sure, for a person with a medical degree, he is near the forefront in all of these categories. But there are others even more deserving of our condemnation.

D. Self-Hatred[16]

16Full disclosure: the "Paul" in Block (2010) is of course Ron Paul. However, in my mitigation, I wrote this article in 2005, submitted it to the Journal of Libertarian Studies in 2006 and later that year it was accepted for publication. This was long before Dr. Paul began his first run for the presidency of the U.S. on the Republican ticket. Whereupon I entirely forgeot about this article. Had I realized that it would not be published until 2010, at which point, possibly, conceivably, it could have done the Paul "revolution" some harm, I would have deleted the section of Block (2010) which criticized this candidate. As it is, even in retrospect, I greatly regret this

It is not so much my contention that people such as Stefan Molyneux[17] hate themselves, as it is that deep down, they hate, well, maybe hate is the wrong word, but don't want to share and expand their supposed beloved philosophy of libertarianism with others. Perhaps they want to keep it to themselves. Maybe they prefer being a big frog in a small pool, to a relatively smaller one in a much bigger body of water. Libertarianism pre-Paul was a relatively small, intimate group. We didn't all know each other but the movement consisted of hundreds of people, maybe thousands, but not tens of thousands. Post Paul, however, we are hundreds of thousands, millions, maybe even tens of millions. Those of us such as Molyneux, who have made a small but significant contribution to the pre-Paul movement might get swept away in a much larger gathering. Who knows? I am no psychiatrist. I have never psychoanalyzed Molyneux. But I do know that making a reputation, getting at the truth, and product differentiation cannot, even all together, account for his gratuitous attack on Ron Paul. There must be something more out there, or in there, less savory, to explain such disgraceful behavior on the part of a self-claimed libertarian such as him.

3. These critics of Ron Paul are not really libertarians.

Here, we must sharply distinguish between those who believe in libertarianism, espouse it, and those who actively promote it. I will call the former parlor libertarians[18] and the latter plain old libertarians, or, for short, libertarians.

---

section of that publication. Had I known of the role Ron Paul would attain in 2007 and thereafter, I never would have written, let alone published, this section of that paper. Mea culpa.

17And Wendy McElroy (undated)

18After "parlor pinks," believers in socialism who do not actively promote this philosophy, but, rather, make a sort of game of it.

I have no reason to doubt that Molyneux is a libertarian believer. He espouses this philosophy. He does so, often, brilliantly.[19] He, even, promotes liberty in this manner, but only on a retail basis. Ron Paul, however, is doing so in a wholesale manner. Yes, Molyneux's vision is a purer version of full libertarianism than is the Congressman's. But Dr. Paul is converting people to our banner by the millions, and, perhaps, Molyneux does so by the dozens.[20] In trying to undermine Paul's success, Molyneux is thus acting in a manner that will retard these accomplishments.

My point here is that if you act objectively to tear down the efforts of those who are creating new libertarians by the bushel-full, then, while you may well be a believer in libertarianism, you are not a libertarian, for people of this ilk do all they can to *help* those who are successfully spreading the word, not undermine them.

III. Conclusion

This is a warning to libertarians; well, to believers in liberty. Sure, go ahead, try to make your reputation at the expense of mah man, Ron Paul. But, be warned: Block Power is gonna come getcha if you do. This is a war we are now engaged in. It is a war for the hearts, minds and souls of the American people, and for billions of others all around the world. Ron Paul is promoting, explaining, educating people about liberty, pretty much as well as it has ever been done on a mass basis. It is all well and good for conservatives to ignore him, to accuse him of being anti American, to maintain that our national defense will suffer if we pull troops home, etc. It is all well and good for liberals to accuse him of greed, of hating the poor, etc. We can excuse that, because these people are morally, economically, philosophically illiterate. But there

19On of my favorite speeches of his is Molyneux (2008) where is eloquently makes the case for anarcho-capitalism, or free enterprise anarchism. True, I never listed to all of it as is my wont, but the beginning of it was nothing short of brilliant and inspiring.

20An elephant, with a mouse on his back, walked over a rickety bridge, and made it sway. Whereupon the mouse piped up and said, "*We* sure made this bridge move."

is simply no excuse for *libertarians* to pile on in this effort to undermine Dr. Paul's herculean efforts. Molyneux, beware. I'm coming after you, boy. See chapter 12.3. to determine if I make good on this threat.

12.3. Concluding the Evisceration: Libertarian Goals

Molyneux opens his response on this note:

"In any discussion of the merits of political action in securing genuine human liberty, the goal is obviously to make more friends than enemies." My view, in contrast, is that the main goal is to get at the truth. However, if what Molyneux is saying is that the goal of political action is to secure converts to the libertarian philosophy, then I heartily concur. I would only add that there is no single person at present who is doing a better job of this than Congressman Paul.

Molyneux maintains that he has the "same goals" as "politically active Libertarians," to wit, "the reduction of violence, the growth of wealth and the development of a society that respects the nonaggression principle and property rights." I do not really believe that Molyneux shares these goals in reality. If he did, he would not be attempting to counter Paul's efforts to bring about just that type of society. In theory, of course, I have no doubt that he does indeed hold to these values. He just doesn't want to see them *implemented*, at least not by the likes of the only person now successfully doing so.

Molyneux states: "Criticizing any particular approach is not a rejection of the shared goal." Let us suppose that Molyneux and I are stuck in the desert with no water. I have a scheme that gets us some of this precious liquid but not perfectly well, and he has no way of getting us water at all. Instead of helping me gather some H2O, Molyneux spends part of his effort criticizing me. Would we deduce that he really wants to quench his thirst? Well, maybe, but this is by no means clear. Perhaps the best summary of his true attitude, toward both water in the desert and promoting libertarianism, is that he is ambivalent about both.

It is Molyneux's "experience that Libertarian political activists are about the hardest working, most dedicated, most generous and most committed advocates for freedom that can be imagined." That is not at all my own personal experience. As I see matters, there are many ways to promote liberty in addition to through politics. Let me list those of them that come readily to mind: academia; geographical ingathering of libertarians (free state project); generalized think tanks (Mises, Cato, IHS, FEE, some 50 state think tanks); specialized think tanks (PERC, FIRE, IJ, Acton Institute); novels (Atlas Shrugged, preeminently); TV shows (South Park); TV personalities (Stossel, Napolitano); radio shows; movies; folk songs; sea-steading; writing treatises; religion (Tom Woods, Lawrence Vance); LP; blogs (Molyneux, Gary North); bookstores (Laissez Faire books). True for all. It has been my experience, contrary to Molyneux's that there are dedicated, hard-working libertarians pursuing *all* of these avenues. Those engaged in politics do not stand out at all in my view.

Were it not for the Ron Paul phenomenon, I would be somewhat indifferent between all of these. My advice to young libertarians would be to go into whichever field is the most fun, where they felt they could be the most productive. Given, however, that at least for the present Ron Paul is doing more to convert people to libertarianism than *all* of these other options put together, it behooves us to at least acknowledge this, and, to strive mightily not to rain on his parade.

Molyneux concedes that "Ron Paul is an extremely knowledgeable and effective communicator of certain libertarian ideals, has an admirable record of consistency with those ideals within Congress, and has by far the greatest reach of any liberty activist." Why, then, light out after him, if promoting liberty is one's goal?

My debating partner makes the case that the past record of the Libertarian Party has not been stellar in attracting votes in presidential races. True, but irrelevant. The past is the past. Sunk costs are sunk. In any case, although the Libertarian Party has not made much of an impact in presidential races, it has spread the libertarian word at this level,[21] and it has done better at state and local elections.

---

21 The one exception is the candidacy of Bob Barr in 2008. He is the only flag bearer in the entire history of the LP who was clearly not a libertarian.

Molyneux makes two errors in his criticism of the Libertarian Party. First, he not incorrectly documents the case for the claim that liberty has not increased, rather, it has decreased, during the existence of this organization. From this, he mistakenly concludes that the LP has done no good.[22] He fails to address himself to the issue of contrary to fact conditionals (Hulsmann, 2003A). Suppose the Libertarian Party had never come into being. Would we be in an even *worse* position than we now are? While it is exceedingly difficult to answer such a question, it must at least be asked. In my view, the LP has done stellar work in exposing the populace to libertarianism, and we would be far worse off had they not done this important work. Second, compared to *what*?[23] It is all too easy to use the Libertarian Party as a punching bag. But what does Molyneux offer in its place? As we shall see, he is *exceedingly* coy on this matter.

Molyneux is also on shaky ground when he avers that a President Ron Paul could not make heavy inroads against statism, "since a significant majority in Congress would also need to support libertarian initiatives in order for them to have any chance of succeeding…." Not so, not so. Thanks to the recent and, not so recent, centralization of power in executive hands, the president now has *great* power. He could, for example, as head of the armed forces, pull all troops back to U.S. soil. This, in one fell swoop, would constitute a *gigantic* step toward liberty. Not only would the massive and depraved murder of innocents abroad at U.S. hands cease forthwith, this would also have great positive repercussions on our economy.

My intellectual opponent also delivers himself of the view that for success to occur, a large number of citizens would have to "be willing to give up at least some benefits, pensions and security." This is no

---

22He states: "Ancient philosophers, Enlightenment thinkers, classical liberals, Austrian economists, and modern Libertarians found no way to even reduce the speed of the growth of the State." How can this author know any such thing? Does he offer *evidence* for this claim? Of course not.

23An economist was asked, "How is your wife?" His response: "Compared to what?"

typographical error, as it is repeated several times, for example: "The public willingly takes significant personal losses as Libertarian policies are enacted" It is more than passing curious to hear a libertarian make any such concession to statism. It logically implies that government is a net *benefit* to the average person, and nothing could be further from the truth. Yes, of course, most of us would have to give up many subsidies under a Paul Administration. But the *taxes* necessary to finance these expenditures would fall as well. Which are greater, under statism: the benefits we derive from the all-loving state, or the wealth it seizes from us in the first place, in order to finance these "benefits?" It is only if, on net balance, the government creates wealth that the benefits from the state can outweigh the costs it imposes upon us. And, surely, when "Libertarian policies are enacted," there will be as a result significant personal *gains*, not losses.

Nor is it at all necessary that "The public votes in a majority of Libertarian politicians." Ron and Rand Paul between them are scaring the tar out of the powers that be, and that is only two politicians. But Molyneux avers, "There does not seem to be sufficient evidence to prove that this approach is close to working." Compared to *what*?

Not content with throwing verbal missiles at Ron Paul, Molyneux next selects as a target the *second* most successful person in promoting liberty, Ayn Rand. His first denigration of her is that the sales of Atlas did not "budge the numbers for Libertarian political candidates." Budge the numbers? There probably would not have been an LP but for her, and the hundreds of thousands of people she drew toward liberty. Imagine a world without her. Would we be better or worse off? To ask this is to answer it, despite her hatred for libertarians (hippies of the right) and her cultishness. But Molyneux is having none of this. He asks: "Did Rand's astounding and unexpected success translate into reductions in the size and power of the state? Did it even slow its growth? Obviously, it didn't reduce government but, surely, it slowed its growth, compared to the world exactly as it would have been, but with no Ayn Rand in it. What evidence does Molyneux put forth to demonstrate that Rand did *not* slow the growth of government? None, of course.

Molyneux also casts aspersions on "Murray Rothbard's plan to work with the radical Left to further the cause of smaller government?" Murray did quite a bit more than that. Rothbard inspired an entire generation of people to more finely hone their libertarianism. He brought together the strands of Austrian economics, revisionist history, and anarchist political thought into a mighty fortress of ideas. When Molyneux accomplishes one millionth of a percent of what Rothbard did, then perhaps his criticisms will carry more weight.[24]

Molyneux gives more and more evidence of his inability to consider contrary to fact conditionals. He calls into question "Ronald Reagan, a staunch minarchist with a strong knowledge of free market economics. … The Federal government grew by two thirds under his watchful eye. But would it have grown even more had Reagan's opponents (Jimmy Carter in 1980 and Walter Mondale in 1984) been in office instead? Probably, yes.[25] Arnold Schwarzenegger, was no friend of liberty, but, again, would California have been better with Gray Davis in 2003 or Phil Angelides in 2006? Says Molyneux: "Hayek won the Nobel Prize in 1974, lending enormous credibility to the Austrian school – did that help slow the growth of the state? The implication is that it did not. But, note, there is no evidence put forth to indicate this. Only that Hayek won the prize, and the state increased. But, what we are really interested in is what would have happened had he not won this prize. About this, Molyneux is eerily silent. He does not even recognize his intellectual obligation to make this case, since he seems unable to think in terms of alternatives. I am shocked, shocked, that Molyneux would include the evil monstrous traitor-to-liberty Greenspan. He might have been a thorough gold bug in his youth, but not when he took power as head of the Fed.

I shall not closely follow Molyneux in his "Sad Sprint Through The History of State-Taming." I note, only, that his inability to consider

---

24Strictly speaking, one need not have accomplished anything whatsoever to land a telling intellectual blow against one of the giants of liberty. However, it is a bit galling to witness a nonentity like Molyneux trash the likes of Paul, Rand and Rothbard.

25Reagan a minarchist, along the lines of someone like Tibor Machan? Surely, this is to jest.

alternatives shines through here, too. The heroic nineteenth century classical liberals failed; but, surely, we would have gone to hell faster had they not made their great and valiant efforts. "… the goal of the Founding Fathers was to *permanently* create the smallest government the world had ever seen." How can Molyneux know any such thing? Had they not undertaken their Herculean efforts,[26] would we have been better or worse off? Molyneux never bestirs himself to ask any such question.

True, "the U.S. government could not be controlled or constrained when it had no income tax, no Federal Reserve, no fiat currency, no electronic surveillance apparatus, no standing army, no IRS, no FBI, no CIA, no Department of Homeland Security, and no public school indoctrination. …" But would we have been better off, had we started out with these things? Hardly. Nor can I understand his belittling of the positive effects on behalf of liberty of the Internet. When I was a young lad, there was only ABC, NBC, and CBS on television, and the New York Times, the Los Angeles Times and the Washington Post held sway in print media. Libertarianism would still be confused by libertinism and librarianism if this was still the case. Thank God for the Internet, say I as a libertarian. Without it, this debate between me and Molyneux would be confined to a few souls, not the hundreds and maybe thousands of people who can witness it.

According to my debating partner, the careers of such as "the Founding Fathers, John Locke, Ludwig von Mises, Ayn Rand, Murray Rothbard, Friedrich Hayek, Carl Menger or Henry Hazlitt or countless others combined" were a failure. Again, compared to what? Would the cause of liberty be enhanced had these people never appeared, and no others like them?

We wait, in vain, for Molyneux to tell us what *has* worked in behalf of liberty; what programs *should* have been implemented in this vein, instead. There is an expression, "the perfect is the enemy of the good." Here, according to the radically pessimistic outlook of Molyneux

26Apart from slavery, of course

(nothing works) we might say, better to do something than passively acquiesce in the further diminution of our liberties. But, it is exceedingly difficult for me to accept this pessimistic outlook, particularly in the face of the miracles that Ron Paul is working every day.

I couldn't agree more with Molyneux when he says, "For political action to work – for any project to work really – it must have correctly identified the causes of the ills it is striving to remedy. Since political action has, historically, not worked, it cannot have correctly identified the true causes of State power and growth." But, again, we wait in vain for him to vouchsafe us a reason for all this dismal failure. In contrast, I think I have identified the reason it is so difficult for libertarians to promulgate our philosophy: we are hard-wired against it by evolution. It may be that we will never convince the masses of people of the benefits of freedom due to these socio-biological restraints. But, our duty and obligation as libertarians is to shine the light of liberty as far and wide as we can, and, there is no one who is doing this better than a certain ex-Air Force member from Texas.

At this point, Molyneux waxes eloquent about the failures to bring about free trade, the disappointment that Aristotle, Plato and, Alexander the Great did not bring about liberty, again without even considering whether we would be freer without their efforts or not. He then launches into a gratuitous attack on libertarian academics, presumably those who are employed by state universities, or subsidized by them. This is more than passing curious since Ron Paul has never been a university professor.

I have published exposures of the fallacy of this sort of argument elsewhere on numerous occasions,[27] so I will be brief in my refutation of it at present. Molyneux has "searched in vain for free market academics who have left their privileged positions to pursue more

---

27Block, 1972, 2002, 2004, 2006, 2007, 2008, 2009A, 2009B, 2010A, 2011A, 2011B, Block and Arakaky, 2008, Block and Barnett, 2008, D'Amico and Block, 2007. Evidently, Molyneux either does not believe in literature searches, or is too busy bashing Dr. Paul to conduct one.

consistent and inspirational teaching in the free market, through books or lectures or podcasts or videos. It is certainly possible to earn a living this way – as I and others have amply demonstrated – and the fact that free market academics reject freedom in favor of statist protectionism deals a blow to the argument that greater knowledge leads to greater virtue."

My debating partner attempts to obviate an objection to his thesis: "Alternatively, academics might argue that taking statist privileges is analogous to using public roads or water or other government services. The difference, of course, is that one cannot really live in society without using or benefiting from public roads, while one can live very well in society without becoming an academic – and teach more people thereby."

But this really will not do. What is it with the criterion of "really live in society?" This author has properly announced the *only* litmus test for a thorough going libertarian: "libertarianism is founded on two central premises – a respect for property rights, and the nonaggression principle. From whence, springs "really live in society?" It would appear that Molyneux makes up his libertarianism as he goes along, so as to support any argument he feels like making at any time. And the same applies to the goal of to "live very well." It, too, has no place in the determination of whether any given act is compatible with the philosophy I thought I shared with this writer.[28] If it is contrary to libertarian principle to utilize "public roads or water or other (such) government services," then the libertarian, if he is to be true to his own principles, should not do so. Molyneux, in effect, admits that he does indeed make use of these amenities. Therefore, based on his own determination of what it takes to be a libertarian, he may no longer use this honorific on himself.

And, as for "really live in society" and "live very well," one can do so without paying taxes, without accessing government roads or post offices, or its fiat currency, or hundreds of government services. One

28That is, libertarianism, not utilitarianism.

can become a self-sufficient hermit, if that is what is implied by being a libertarian. I have heard tell that such folk, well, maybe do not "really live in society" but at least "live very well." And if that does not suffice, one can always commit suicide, if one wants to act consistently with libertarianism, at least with the Molyneux version thereof.

His error is to grant the state far too much. Why are the roads "public roads?" This implies that the state is their proper owner. For the libertarian with even a superficial acquaintance with this philosophy, this is a logical howler. The government *stole* the money from the taxpayers in order to build these facilities. The proper owners are therefore *us*, not *them*. As for "water," according to libertarian doctrine the way to establish ownership of such amenities is to *homestead* them. Did anyone see Bush or Obama homesteading anything? The roads and water are *our* property, and it is an error of the most basic and elementary kind to cede proper ownership of them to the vicious state. We need make no apologies for using them. We do not in the slightest deviate from libertarianism in such manner, Molyneux's concession to statism to the contrary notwithstanding.

One last point, I cannot resist. In charging those of us who make use of public schools and universities with hypocrisy, Molyneux reckons without the keen insight of Rand (1957), particularly my favorite character in that book, Ragnar Danneskjold. This libertarian hero knew precisely the legitimacy with which government held property, namely, none at all. I highly recommend a perusal of this book for Molyneux.

Molyneux's ostensible reason for this gratuitous attack on libertarian academicians[29] is that an increase in education often accompanies a

---

29One wonders why Molyneux does not criticize libertarians who eat food. After all, the government subsidizes agriculture. And how about those who live in housing? Between Fannie and Freddie and HUD, the CRA and the practice of the Fed to lower interest rates, we have more residential building than would otherwise be the case. Could it be that Molyneux himself lives in a dwelling, and eats food? Ditto for automobiles, and, pretty much everything else. In fact, the government in the modern day is so heavily intertwined into the economy that it would be difficult to point to a sector into which it has not inserted its evil tentacles. Are libertarians supposed to decrease in support for liberty. True enough: the Ivy League professoriate is not exactly known for its adherence to freedom. However, Molyneux himself is an educator, of a sort. Is he not upending himself by his own petard in attacking education? Moreover, it is on the basis of his claim that education does not per se lead to liberty that he deduces that politics cannot "work."[30] Is this even worthy of sober comment? It cannot be denied that Ron Paul is educating the citizenry of the U.S., and the world too, through his books, speeches, debates, interviews, etc. This is bad? Of course, he also is awakening in the public their too often inchoate yearning for liberty, as a good *teacher* would.

According to Molyneux (footnote omitted): "There is no way to reduce the size of the state without sacrifice. People who have paid for benefits will have to accept reduced – or no – returns. People who gain benefits from state power – from farmers to teachers to lawyers to accountants to academics to financial and union executives – will have to give up at least some of those benefits." The error he commits here is that he does not consider the entire context. Hazlitt (1979, pp. 15-16) draws our attention to "the persistent tendency of men to see only the immediate effects of a given policy, or its effects only on a special group, and to neglect to inquire what the long-run effects of that policy will be not only on that special group but on all groups. It is the fallacy of overlooking secondary consequences." Yes, of course, "farmers to teachers to lawyers to accountants to academics to financial … executives"[31] will lose out, in the *first* instance. They will have to do without their government subsidies. But, in the free enterprise system, they will not have to pay the *taxes* which finance these goodies in the

---

divorce themselves from the entire economy? Let us allow Molyneux to show us the way through his personal example. McAdams characterizes this argument by Hill (2011) against Ron Paul "The Single Stupidest Attack on Ron Paul Ever." And, yet, this is *precisely* the criticism that Molyneux is launching against the congressman.

30He states: "… if education does not work, politics cannot work." It would be difficult to pack more fallacies into so few words. Molyneux, an educator, claims education doesn't "work." If education doesn't "work," what then will "work?" Shooting people? Hardly. Moreover, he says this in the face of overwhelming evidence that Ron Paul's educational efforts, via the political process, are "working" *miracles.*

31Note, I leave out unionists, who I will treat below.

first place. And, of course, what government takes away from the people is far in excess of what it gives to them. Thus, these groups will not have to "sacrifice" anything when statism is taken off of them.[32] Molyneux's economic analysis implies, amazingly, that the state is on net balance a beneficiary to the people, a strange position for a supposed anarcho-capitalist to take. As for "unionists," (Block, 2010B) they are invariably junior partners in the ruling class (Domhoff, 1967, 1971, 1998; Hoppe, 1990; Hughes, 1977; Kolko, 1963; Mises, 1978; Oppenheimer, 1975; Raico, 1977; Rockwell, 2001), and *should* lose out from a transition from statism to freedom. As concerns "those who have invested in State securities ... (if the government defaults on its debts,) ... will take a significant hit," they richly deserve such a fate, as those who aid and abet the state apparatus take on the role of criminals (Block, 2009B).

Molyneux now adds insult to injury, taking up the criticism that those such as NBC, ABC and CBS have leveled at Congressman Paul: "Ron Paul is enormously effective at directing federal money towards his own constituents, and they naturally line up at the trough to grab whatever they can. I understand the argument that Dr. Paul is only attempting to get back some of the money that the federal government has stolen from his constituents, but this seems to me more of an *ex post facto* justification than a moral argument from first principles. First of all, a good deal of the money that Ron Paul directs to his

32Perhaps the best cartoon I have ever seen that illustrates this is entitled "election cycle schematic" (http://www.russmo.com/04_11_12.html). There are four quadrants in it. In the first, a well-dressed middle-aged man points to an old woman and says: "I want corporate subsidies and incentives and I want her to pay for it. In the second, this older woman points to a man with a flag hat and says: "I want free prescriptions, and I want him to pay for it. In the third, this man with the flag hat points to a couple and says, "I want to extend the war on terrorism and I want them to pay for it. In the fourth, the couple points to the well-dressed middle-aged man (who we met in the first quadrant) and say: "We want free education for our children and we want him to pay for it." Precisely. Each member of this merry-go-round wants someone else to finance their pet project, usually benefiting themselves. They all think, along with Molyneux, that the government can create something out of nothing. None of the four, including Molyneux, realize that they are in effect stealing from each other, with a big rake-off for Washington, D.C. (It is no accident that most of the richest counties in the U.S. circle that imperial city.) All four presumably, along with Molyneux, certainly, acquiesce in the notion that if this process stops, and we embrace laissez-faire capitalism, that we as a society will *lose* out thereby. Economic illiteracy, are there no limits to your sway?

constituents has not been directly taken from them, but rather printed or borrowed from the Fed. Printed money steals largely from the poor, while borrowed money steals largely from the unborn – neither group is likely to get a lot of money from Ron Paul's political maneuverings, which mostly go to politically-connected rich folk. Secondly, Ron Paul – and presumably, anyone who votes for him for ideological reasons – knows all about the massive sacrifices needed to effectively shrink the government. If you want to credibly lead a moral crusade about sacrifice, you must first make those sacrifices yourself – it seems faintly comic for Ron Paul to demand that millions of others make sacrifices in order to shrink the power of the State, while enabling and encouraging the exact opposite behavior for his own constituents. In fact, it is distinctly possible that Ron Paul's constituents vote for him because he so consistently brings home the federal bacon, rather than out of any ideological affinity. The acid test for this would be for him to make the case for sacrifice, and see what happens to his support."

This does not seem to me to be at all "an *ex post facto* justification." Rather, it stems *directly* from libertarian first principles: return of stolen property (Rothbard, ch. 10, 13). The Texas congressman opposes *all* of these transfers of income. He votes against them in their entirety, without exception. However, if he fails to stop this process, and the government is transferring income all over the place, why shouldn't his own constituents get some of their own money back?[33] We have already seen Molyneux's error regarding "sacrifice." As concerns inflation, my debating partner is absolutely correct in maintaining that "Printed money steals largely from the poor,[34] but he neglects to note that Dr. Paul, more than anyone else in Congress, perhaps more than anyone else in the entire country, has long been inveighing against precisely this governmental outrage, with his constant barrage of attacks on the Federal Reserve System, the culprit of the piece. A curious omission on Molyneux's part.

33Molyneux here hits upon the "earmarks" criticism of Ron Paul. In his defense, see Paul (2009A) who states: "If a congressman does not submit funding requests for his district, the money is simply spent elsewhere. To eliminate all earmarks would be to further consolidate power in the already dominant executive branch and not save a penny." See also Paul (2009B).

34As well as giving rise to the (Austrian) business cycle

I will not much comment on Molyneux's anarcho-capitalist critique of the state. I largely agree with him. I only ask, how can we best and most likely rid ourselves of this pox? Surely, the answer is by creating more libertarians, who can then be converted to a more pure version of this philosophy, laissez-faire capitalist anarchism. Ron Paul is actively engaged in the first stage of this process. Stefan Molyneux, bless his heart as we say in the south, is doing his utmost to undermine this effort. Who, then, is objectively on the side of liberty?

In his section on "Incremental Validation," Molyneux asks: "For years, I have asked Libertarians to show the value of political action by infiltrating local criminal gangs and reducing their criminality. Join a group of hit men, and get them to cut their murders by 90%. Funny, very funny. What dream world is this man living in? Here, in the face of Ron Paul demonstrating "the value of political action" by publicizing the libertarian philosophy in a manner never before seen in the world, and Molyneux is busy holding his little electronic seminars poking fun at the grandmaster of libertarianism. It beggars belief. I agreed to this debate because I thought I was dealing with a rational person. Oh, well, I won't go back on my word. But, I must say, these remarks of his are just plain silly. Are we really to compare *anything* with Ron's proven success?

States Molyneux: "The Libertarian approach to gaining political power – to turn an evil institution into a virtuous gang – or at least a less evil gang – …" No, it is to acquaint millions, billions, of people with a free enterprise libertarian philosophy they never would otherwise have heard of. And, yes, it will do some good, a powerful lot of good. When the Paul Administration takes over in January 2013, the U.S. soldiers will immediately start coming home, protecting us here, where they belong. The bombs will stop dropping on innocent people in Libya, Iraq, Afghanistan, and, who knows, some half dozen other countries Obomba has decided to invade, all on his own. The drug war will stop. Thousands of innocent prisoners will be pardoned and released. The beginning of the end of the Fed will start. The minimum wage law will end, along with thousands of other regulations choking the economy. The present depression will enter the dust bin of history. What, pray tell, is so wrong with a "less evil gang?" Especially when millions of people, in the process, become acquainted with their patrimony of liberty.

Molyneux is a tiger when it comes to criticizing the attempts of others to promote liberty. He strongly avers that education is not the way to go, nor is politicking. These have not "worked," he tells us, again and again: "Abandoning the political process as the means for securing human liberty does not mean abandoning the goal of freedom – rather, it means abandoning an approach which has empirically and logically been shown to be inadequate to the task. There are other approaches to gaining and keeping the freedom from force that we most fervently desire, but as long as we continue to chase the mirage of political action, we will never find our way out of the desert."

What, then will "work?" Here, he is exceedingly coy. But, there is one small "gem" in his missive: "… as a free market educator, I have taught over 35 million 'classes,' far more than I would ever have been able to do as an academic – and the Khan Academy has been far more successful than I have, with over 80 million lessons delivered!)"

I find this preposterous, pusillanimous and self-serving. Molyneux has the audacity to reject Ron Paul's massive success in turning the world toward freedom, and to put forth his own (relatively) pathetic efforts in its stead as a pattern we should all follow.[35] To use this author's own arguments against him, if Molyneux's educational efforts are so wonderful, how come we still have the evil, murderous and monstrous state? This writer can't have it both ways. If his efforts are so great, why do we not already have the full libertarian society?

And, what has happened to his criticism of education as a means to liberty, emphatically argued all throughout his essay? Why are

35I do not denigrate Molyneux's efforts to promote liberty per se. I only do so in comparison with Ron Paul's gargantuan success. I would rate my own contributions in promoting the libertarian philosophy, also, as "pathetic" in comparison with what Congressman Paul has wrought.

Molyneux's efforts in this direction successful, but not anyone else's, not even that piker's, Ron Paul?

But wait. We so far reckon without the marvelous record of the "Khan Academy." That enterprise, surely, can bring home the bacon. But if so, why have we had no achievement of liberty as of yet? "The Khan Academy[36] is a not-for-profit educational organization, created in 2006 by Bangladeshi American educator Salman Khan, a graduate of MIT. With the stated mission of 'providing a high-quality education to anyone, anywhere', the website supplies a free online collection of more than 2,700 micro lectures via video tutorials stored on YouTube teaching Mathematics, History, Healthcare & Medicine, Finance, Physics, Chemistry, Biology, Astronomy, Economics, Cosmology and Computer Science." I cannot see the connection between most of this and liberty, but, that is probably because I am one of the "academic economists" besotted by the state apparatus. However, I did waste all too much of my precious time listening to what this "educator" had to say about fractional reserve banking.[37] It would appear that this creates a healthy economy, through the "multiplier." Unhappily, Khan seems totally unaware of the vast libertarian literature attesting to the fact that fractional reserve banking is fraudulent, and ignorant of the large Austrian literature making the case that this type of banking is instrumental in creating the business cycle.[38] So much for Khan, a faithful replicator of the type of economics taught at MIT. I shudder to contemplate his views on government bailouts, unemployment, free trade, the minimum wage or rent control, litmus tests for free market economics.[39]

36(http://en.wikipedia.org/wiki/Khan_Academy). We can immediately see the attraction of the "Academy" for Molyneux: it consists of time-consuming videos, nothing appears to be written.

37http://www.khanacademy.org/video/fractional-reserve-banking-commentary-1?playlist=Banking+and+Money; http://www.khanacademy.org/video/banking-3--fractional-reserve-banking?playlist=Banking+and+Money

38Bagus, 2003; Bagus, Howden and Block, forthcoming; Barnett and Block, 2005, 2008, 2009; Baxendale, 2010; Block, 2008; Block and Caplan, 2008; Block and Garschina, 1996; Block and Humphries, 2008; Block and Posner, 2008; Davidson, 2008; Davidson and Block, 2011; Hanke, 2008; Hoppe, 1994; Hoppe, Hulsmann and Block, 1998; Huerta de Soto, 1995, 1998, 2001, 2006, 2010; Hulsmann, 1996, 2000, 2002a, 2002b, 2003B, 2008; Murphy, 2010; North, 2009; Polleit, 2010; Reisman, 1996, 2009; Rothbard, 1975; 1990, 1991, 1993; Salerno, 2010

Chapter 13.

Wendy McElroy

13.1. Is Wendy McElroy Still a Libertarian? No; She Opposes thc Ron Paul Candidacy

At first glance, this is really a stupid question. Not only is she a libertarian, she is one of the most talented and creative and hard-working leaders of our movement. She has done yeoman work over the years on a whole host of issues, ranging from the promotion of free enterprise, to her opposition to imperialist war, covering dozens of other libertarian issues, all superlatively.

If I were to single out one of her essays, it is her paean to Murray Rothbard, Mr. libertarian himself. Here, Wendy (2008) weaves into a beautiful tapestry all of Murray's accomplishments in Austrian economics, antimilitarism, revisionist history, political activism and more. And, she does so with such great love I find myself almost next to tears as I read this, in appreciation of her absolute and magnificent brilliance. I go so far as to say that this is certainly one of the greatest appreciations of my friend and mentor Murray ever written.

No one who says things like that can be all bad. Heck, no one who says anything a half, a quarter, or a tenth as good as that should be accused of not being a libertarian. This is really very good material. I am greatly envious that she said that. I wish I had written anything half as good. But, I am grateful that she did so for, frankly, I don't have her ability to say things like that, much as I loved Murray. I go further; read this essay of hers, I implore you. You'll thank me for insisting that you do. It is a lot better than the one I'm now about to criticize.

How, then, can I call into question her libertarian credentials? I do so on the ground that she is a bitter opponent of the Ron Paul presidential

39In his analysis of credit default swaps (http://www.khanacademy.org/video/credit-default-swaps?playlist=Credit+Crisis), this educator of liberty says that only government, not private rating agencies, can be objective in discerning the creditworthiness of corporations. This is promoting liberty?

campaign, and this is the last best hope for liberty, as I see matters. I write in criticism of Wendy more in sorrow than in anger. But, there is a lot of sorrow involved, almost, but not quite verging on anger, because of her stupendous contributions to the freedom philosophy.

Before I get to the specifics, let me make a distinction. I distinguish between *being* a libertarian, and agreeing with (virtually all) libertarian principles. The former implies that you *act* so as to promote liberty. The latter means that you *agree* with these principles, and, may, perhaps, as in her case at present, *act against* them. I have no doubt that Wendy is a libertarian in the second sense. Her whole adult life gives amply testimony to that fact. She believes in the libertarian message, fervently. She defends it, brilliantly. She extends it, creatively. But, as far as *acting* so as to promote liberty, her trashing of Dr. Ron Paul's candidacy gives the lie to that. Belief is necessary, but not sufficient, for *being* a libertarian. Wendy passes the first test, but not the second.

What are the specifics of her case against the Paul campaign?

I now repeat her August 17, 2007 article, "Ron Paul or antiwar.com?" (*in italics*) along with my commentary interspersed.

Like other libertarians, I am stirred by Ron Paul's anti-war rhetoric even though I know it will not be translated into action because Paul will cease to be of significance after he is eliminated (as he will be) in the Republican primary. At that point, the millions of dollars as well as the incalculable time and energy that libertarians have donated to elect this right-wing religious conservative will disappear down the drain.

In my view, if the Ron Paul campaign stopped tomorrow (I am writing this on 12/10/11), there will be nothing much disappearing "down the drain." Au contraire, Ron has already put libertarianism on the map in a way that no one in the history of civilization has ever done. (Ayn Rand deserves to be mentioned in the same breath as Dr. Paul in terms of popularizing libertarianism, but she specifically rejected us, dismissing us as "hippies of the right." She also confused libertarianism with atheism in the minds of her libertarian converts.)

What is it with this "right-wing religious conservative" name-calling? Yes, Ron is religious, but since when has religion been rendered incompatible with the nonaggression principle of libertarianism?

"Right-wing?" "Conservative?" Is it right-wing or conservative to favor peace? To oppose the drug war? To call for a radical diminution of the government? Alright, I get it; Wendy opposes Congressman Paul. But why this inflated rhetoric? Nor will he "*cease to be of significance*" if and when he is eliminated from the Republican primary. Who knows? In that unlikely event, he may run as an independent. If New York City Mayor Michael Bloomberg and Donald Trump also launch independent campaigns, Dr. Paul has a reasonably good chance of *winning* the election in a five-man race. His supporters will not desert him. Even if not, my understanding is that his organization will long continue to promote liberty, independent of politics. Maybe then, and only then, will Dr. Paul appear in McElroy's good graces.

If you are supporting Ron Paul because of his anti-war stance, may I make a suggestion? Support the truly libertarian antiwar.com instead; this remarkable site is always desperate for donations. For years, the site has been an acknowledged and courageous leader in the broader antiwar movement, making people of other ideologies more receptive to libertarian principles and politics because they respect the commitment and damned hard work performed by the site. Unlike with Paul, your contribution will not disappear. Antiwar.com's archives and features only grow with time; its value as a resource increases with each passing day. If you care about ending the war in Iraq, please do not divert money to Ron Paul when it could be used so well by genuine libertarians who have a proven record of making a difference.

I am a warm supporter of Antiwar.com. I have contributed funds to this wonderful organization. I was even honored that they once chose to reprint one of my columns on their web site (http://antiwar.com/, 7/23/07). But, to mention this organization in the same breath as the Paul campaign, in terms of "*making people of other ideologies more receptive to libertarian principles*" is just plain silly. It is like comparing a mouse and an elephant, and by saying this I mean no disrespect to Antiwar.com. I am just remarking on the very different rate of success of the two libertarian institutions in carrying the word to people. I very much doubt that anyone associated with antiwar.com would be so rash as to claim that their success rate in promoting libertarianism is even in the same ballpark as Ron Paul's.

Remember: Ron Paul supported war in Iraq (and Kosovo, for that matter) as long as there was an official declaration; he argued this position in Congress. At that same time he asked for an official war, antiwar.com cried out against any war. I don't know if Paul is currently sincere in his antiwar rhetoric or merely an astute politician who knows there is hunger out there for peace...but I do know and trust antiwar.com.

Yes, Ron is a waffler. He keeps changing his mind. He is on all sides of every issue. He doesn't have a principled bone in his body. You can't trust him any farther than you can throw him. Paul, Gingrich and Romney are all brothers under the skin as far as continually contradicting themselves. All three of them are forever changing their tune to fit the views of their present audience.

This is about the most outrageous calumny heaped upon Congressman Paul's shoulders, and to think it could come from a *libertarian!* Well, a person who supports libertarianism. I wonder why this author does not supply a link to Dr. Paul's supposed support for wars in Iraq and Kosovo. Could it be because this is a gigantic porky, as they say in England? Yes, Ron has often said that the only legitimate way for the U.S. to go to war would be for Congress to declare it (there is that little matter of a Constitution that he is always going on and on about) but this is quite different from saying that were this put to a vote, he would have supported any such wars. The burden of proof is on this author to back up her false, malicious and, yes, libelous charge. She has not done so.

From the preceding, readers might assume that I argue against Paul because support for Ron Paul diverts money/time from causes and activities that have a lasting impact rather than one that evaporates after the faux-euphoria of political campaigning. While I do make this objection, I have several other reasons.

To argue that the Paul 2012 campaign will not have a "lasting impact" is highly problematic. He has already introduced libertarians to *billions* of people all over the world, he has inspired *millions* of people to seriously consider this philosophy, and, with his constant mention of Austrian economics, Murray N. Rothbard and Ludwig von Mises he has tuned in *hundreds of thousands* of people to sound economics. No "lasting impact?"

To be fair to Wendy McElroy, she wrote this essay on August 17, 2007, and the Ron Paul campaign of 2012 is vastly outstripping that of 2008 in terms of impact. However, that scurrilous piece of hers of 2007 is still on the web. Anyone can access it, even now. Has she apologized for this essay? Not to the best of my knowledge. Has she revised it in response to the far greater success of the Ron Paul campaign this time around? Not to the best of my knowledge. She ends her evil screed on this note: *More on this as I find time to blog...* Has she done so? Again, not to the best of my knowledge. For shame, say I.

1) The libertarian support for Paul – a candidate who cannot win because the Republicans will not nominate him – effectively guarantees that a real libertarian candidate who actually voices libertarianism will not be heard. Yes, but an LP candidate has no chance of winning, you say? Well, neither does Paul. I do not support the LP because I think electoral politics is part of society's problems not part of the solution, nevertheless, I do not dismiss the possibility that a principled LP candidate may be able to educate or raise awareness. That's always been the LP's strongest argument. But, now, instead of a libertarian candidate who cannot win, libertarians are choosing to back a right-wing conservative who cannot win. Libertarians are not even saying "put MY guy in office;" they are crying out "put THEIR guy in office because he says some of the right things." The stance doesn't make sense even to a pro-voting libertarian.

As of this writing, December 12, 2011, her statement "*Paul – a candidate who cannot win because the Republicans will not nominate him*" sounds somewhat premature. Ron is now in the "top tier," consisting of him and his two flip-flopping soul brothers, Mitt and Newt. It looks as if he can take second place in Iowa, and very likely be in the top three in New Hampshire. The debate, scheduled for tonight at Drake University will feature only six candidates: Ron and his two fellow flip-floppers, along with Bachmann, Perry and Santorum. The Cain train has derailed, and Huntsman has been dropped due to poor polling numbers. Thus, it will become more and more difficult for the mainstream media to squelch his viewpoints.

Who is this mysterious "*real libertarian candidate who actually voices libertarianism*" that we are ignoring, because Dr. Paul is hogging up the libertarian spotlight? Bob Barr? Gary Johnson? Wayne Allen Root? None of these people can hold a candle to Ron Paul in terms of adherence to libertarian principles. Enquiring minds want to know! On the other hand, there are indeed very good libertarians out there (any of the senior faculty or administration of the Mises Institute, for example), but none of these people are politicians; none of them have any chance at all of becoming president in 2013.

She says: "*I do not dismiss the possibility that a principled LP candidate may be able to educate or raise awareness. That's always been the LP's strongest argument.*" C'mon, Barr and Root were the LP's standard bearers in 2008. Neither is one one-hundredth the libertarian that Ron Paul is. Dr. Paul did indeed run for president on the Libertarian Party ticket in 1988, and received the usual 2 percent or so of the vote, without making much of a publicity splash. Now, he is absolutely amazing in terms of the bang for the buck we libertarians are getting out of him.

And what's with the repetition of the "*right-wing conservative*" charge. Does she think that if you keep repeating something, people will believe it? Well, if *right-wing conservatives* favor bringing home the troops, stopping imperialism, squelching crony capitalism (hear that, Occupiers?), getting rid of the Fed, embracing free enterprise money, radically cutting down the size of government, repealing the drug war, cutting a swath through our regulatory bureaucracy, well, then, maybe, *right-wing conservatism* isn't so bad after all.

2) By so wildly embracing a politician as their "savior," hard-line libertarians are abandoning the skepticism with which freedom-loving people must always view those who wish to assume power over the lives of others. What do they say to "power corrupts"? Maybe so, but not OUR guy? Where is the critical analysis of the terrible policies advocated by Paul, such as the use of eminent domain to facilitate the construction of wall across the U.S.-Mexico border? For that matter, where is the libertarian objection to that construction of Fortress America? It has been lost in the applause being rendered to this evangelical religious conservative who seeks power.

I do not agree with each and every opinion of Ron Paul. McElroy is a splendid libertarian theoretician. Certainly, she is right, and Ron Paul wrong, on the issue of eminent domain. There is nothing wrong with "*critical analysis*" of his positions. Speaking as a "*hard line-libertarian*" I have not at all "*abandoned the skepticism with which freedom-loving people must always view those who wish to assume power over the lives of others.*" In a previous column of mine, I awarded Ron Paul only a 95% on the libertarian scale (probably, I was too niggardly then; I now think he deserves a 97% grade). Hey, we libertarian supporters of Ron Paul are not true believers. When he errs, we are not silent about it. There is nothing wrong with criticizing everyone, me included. We can all use improvement.

But McElroy is doing more than this. She is demonizing him. She is engaged in false, malicious slander and libel against him. At a time when he is building up the libertarian movement at a pace greater than anyone else in the entire history of the world, she is busily trying to tear him down. That is not critical thinking. That is not being open-minded. That is being an objective enemy of liberty.

As for "*Fortress America*," this is just another way of saying that Dr. Paul favors a *defensive* military posture, not an *offensive* one. If I understand him correctly, the Coast Guard will become greatly enlarged under a Paul Administration, far more able to safeguard Americans in our cities and towns, instead of focusing on drug-running and smugglers (there will *be* no more of these, when drugs are legalized, and we embrace full free trade). President Paul will stop poking sticks in hornet's nests all over the world, and wondering why some of these creatures come over here and bite us; this is blowback, baby. (It is *not* because of our freedoms or our miniskirts or our rock music; according to calculations of economic freedom in the world, we are no longer even in the top ten in this regard; there are other countries that mind their own business, have mini-skirts and rock music and have not been subjected to terrorist attacks.) President Paul will make peace with the nations of the world. He will engage in free trade, cultural exchange, etc., with all of them. If this is "*Fortress America*," or, "isolationism," it is not all that bad.

3) In the frenzy that is political campaigning, libertarians are abandoning resources that have been valuable in spreading the ideas of liberty. The most recent example is the decision of LewRockwell.com to relinquish its tax-exempt status in order to advocate for Ron Paul. I differ with LRC on several important issues but I value highly the site's past contributions; especially with the economic downturn, I do not believe LRC will be able to sustain itself. I'd hate to see it die or wither... for one thing, it is one of the last living expressions of Murray Rothbard within the movement.

I will let Lew Rockwell discuss that decision of his. All I can say is that every dollar, no, every *penny* that has been donated to the Paul 2012 campaign has been a magnificent investment in liberty. Ron does not spend this money at Tiffany's. He does not spend this money on pay-offs for girlfriends. He does not spend this money on fancy cars.

He doesn't own a Rolex. He does not buy $5,000 suits. He spends *every penny* on promoting liberty, a concept that seems not to be in McElroy's ken.

I could go on ... but the foregoing objections do not touch upon my main argument against Paul. That argument: along with some fine statements about war and the free market, Paul advocates policies that are as dangerous to personal freedom as I've ever heard.

Oh yeah, as we say in Brooklyn. Name a few, lady (well, ones on which I have not already mentioned in criticism of my friend Ron Paul). Oh, wait, yes, I just realized, McElroy is right. I've just heard that Ron has changed his mind on the Patriot Act, and now supports Obama's murder of U.S. citizens abroad, and his use of drones in Pakistan, Iran and God knows where else. (For those of you who are not paying attention, this claim of mine about Ron's change of mind is tongue-in-cheek. I have to clarify things like this; assure people that I am only joking. Otherwise, I'll get complaints from people denying this.) I can't help getting giddy. When McElroy says that Paul is "*dangerous to personal freedom*" all one can do is laugh.

More on this as I find time to blog...

http://www.zetetics.com/mac/news.php?extend.946

I await, with bated breath, McElroy's return to this topic. I'm all ears, Wendy.

13.2. Is Wendy McElroy Still a Libertarian? No; She Undermines Liberty

Rational people cannot really, fully blame Rachel Maddow, Paul Krugman (2011A, 2011B), Jeffrey Sachs (2012) and their ilk for attacking Ron Paul. These are ignorant, immoral savages. They know no better. For them, the alpha and the omega are interventionism, socialism, egalitarianism and multiculturalism. No one would blame a lion, a shark, or a hurricane, for killing someone. In like manner, it would be inappropriate to condemn folks such as Maddow, Krugman and Sachs for denigrating Congressman Paul.

What then are we to say about libertarians, people with heretofore impeccable libertarian credentials, who are equally, nay, even more critical of the congressman than those "progressive" barbarians?

Before the advent of Ron Paul,[40] I thought that most libertarians were sensible and wanted, well, liberty. In the event, however, I am not quite so sure. I have had longtime libertarian friends of mine tell me that they do not support Congressman Paul's efforts because "I don't agree with his views on immigration," or, "he does not take the libertarian position on abortion," or because of those "racist newsletters" or for literally dozens of other such "reasons." My assessment of them is that a particularly low rung in libertarian hell is reserved for them. They are supposed to be promoters of liberty; at least they consider themselves in that way. Ron Paul is now converting people by the millions to our libertarian philosophy. And these "libertarians" are busy tearing him down. They know better. Or, rather, they *should* know better. They are, in effect, traitors to the philosophy they supposedly champion. Shame on them all. Some of these people have been friends of mine for years, decades. I still like and admire them for the many and important contributions they have made to our beloved libertarian philosophy. But, I cannot on that ground cease and desist from harshly criticizing them for their trashing of Ron Paul.

40Particularly in the 2012 campaign, when the mainstream media can no longer totally ignore him; they are of course still *trying* to do so, but with far less success than in 2008.

In this section I shall take to task McElroy (2007). It is a critique of Block (2007). Here are her views; my critique follows.

I have not been commenting much on Ron Paul lately because I think he will be a non-issue after the primaries and his cult status will go the way of other meteoric "pro-freedom" politicians from Henry George in the 1890s to Ross Perot in the 1990s – that is, in a downward spiral. Instead, I have been acting as a conduit for other people's commentary. In truth, my reticence also comes from finding the task of critiquing Paul to be tiresome on several levels. I was beginning to repeat myself, which is tedious to everyone … not least of all me. I am criticizing old friends, some of whom I hope to continue calling "friend" after the electoral madness has passed like a fever.

I will comment, however, on one or two aspects of Walter Block's recent article on LewRockwell.com.: An Open Letter to Libertarians On Behalf of Ron Paul, Part II. BTW, I have been on friendly terms with Walter Block for decades now and, so, I will be calling him Walter with no intended diminishment of his Dr. Block status. Walter's writing *is in italics.*

Oh well … nothing to do but launch in, I suppose.

Walter writes:, *In my view, the "Ron Paul question" constitutes a litmus test for libertarians. Simply put, the "Ron Paul question" consists of determining whether or not a person supports Dr. Paul. If so, as I see matters, he passes this test and can be constituted a libertarian; if not, his credentials are to that extent suspect.*

My response: Again, the idea that it is necessary to back a particular politician in order to be a credentialed libertarian. Thus, Walter dismisses without having to out-argue the various reasons a thorough-going libertarian might oppose Paul. Such reasons include anarchistic objections to the use of political power; non-ideological objections to electoral politics that lead you to strongly prefer a different path to liberty; your wish to support an LP candidate rather than a Republican one; and, a deep disagreement with one (or some) of Paul's significant stands (such as immigration). Every true libertarian supports Ron Paul; no true libertarian opposes him.

My reaction is threefold. *First,* to quote Sunni Maravillosa, *What happened to the understanding that liberty is, first and foremost, an individualistic idea and pursuit? How did it happen that to achieve liberty we must all unite and act as one, pulling the great lever for The One Man Fit to Rule Us All? Second,* this is a logical fallacy that is virtually identical to the one famously presented by Antony Flew as "the no true Scotsman fallacy." (In an earlier post, I presented a no true libertarian/no true Scotsman comparison.) *Third,* this is a base form of argument – or, rather, it is a way to avoid argument and substitute *quasi ad hominem* in its place. It is a pre-emptive attack upon the character of an opponent and, IMO, usually signals intellectual weakness on the part of the attacker and/or his position.

Walter goes on to describe the objections to Ron Paul of "some anarcho-capitalist libertarians" into which category I am included by name even though I am *not* an anarcho-capitalist. I do have principled objections to electoral politics, however, and I believe that is the relevant distinction being made.

In rebuttal to the rejection of electoral politics, Walter writes, *Suppose a slave master allows his slaves to choose between Overseer Goody, who has a very light and judicious touch with the whip, and Overseer Baddy, who never met a bloody back he didn't like. The slaves take up the master on his offer, and vote for Goody. Are they thereby demonstrating support for slavery, for goodness sakes? No; they are only registering a preference for Goody over Baddy.*

I will adopt the slave/master rhetoric in answering. If Walter wishes to register his preference about whom he wishes as a master, then I not only have no objection, I also have no interest. It is his body with which to genuflect or not. But Walter knows full well (or he used to) that this is not the objection offered by libertarian anarchists. A voter acts not merely to establish his own preference as master, he acts to put his preferred master in a position of unjust power over unconsenting others. It is this unconsenting "3rd party" problem from which anarchist objections arise. Walter is actively sanctioning – indeed, apparently rejoicing in – the 'transfer' of rights from unconsenting individuals into the hands of a master to whom they object but whom Walter prefers. You may well disagree with the 3rd party argument. But my point here is simply that *this* – and not the strawman Walter presents to knock down – *is the anarchist argument.*

Walter writes, *Even Spooner, who might be considered patron saint of this viewpoint, regarded voting, and, presumably, holding public office, as a defensive, not an invasive, act.*

It is impossible to comment without knowing which of Spooner's writings are being referenced. In his younger years, Spooner was a staunch supporter of the Constitution and his work was used as campaign material for the Liberty Party, which had been formed in 1840 from anti-slavery societies. In the 1850s, however, a shift in his political views was evident and that shift solidified due to the Civil War. For example, until the war, Spooner labored to integrate the principles of the Constitution with those of natural law. His pamphlet series *No Treason* abandoned that attempt with No VI of the *No Treason* series being subtitled "The Constitution of No Authority." (For more details on this shift, please see "Lysander Spooner,", an essay I wrote for *Freedom Daily.*) The later Spooner *was* quite clear about rejecting electoral politics and the authority of all elected politicians.

Walter further argues: *Every last one of the anarcho-capitalists who object to his candidacy on this ground, use the sidewalks for walking, the streets and roads for driving, U.S. currency for making purchases, post letters with the U.S. postal service, visit state libraries, museums, etc. It ill behooves so-called libertarian anarchists, who do not fully understand either of these two philosophies, to object to Ron Paul's actions, which are in this one way indistinguishable from their own.*

There is a difference of kind between walking down a sidewalk and electing someone to a position of unjust power over unconsenting others. Henry David Thoreau captured the difference well. In his pivotal work *On Civil Disobedience*, Thoreau maintained that no one had the obligation to confront, disobey or take any position whatsoever toward the state so long as his or her actions *did not injure the person or rights of an innocent 3rd party.* Otherwise, it is quite proper for a person to go about "the business of living" and deal with the state when and as it is prudent. Case in point: Although Thoreau did not like to pay taxes, nevertheless he did so when money was demanded from him to pay the salary of a teacher in his village. The tax he famously refused to pay was one that supported the Mexican American War; he refused to have his money used to harm innocent others. Assisting a politician into a position of unjust authority is a direct assault upon the rights and well-being of the innocent 3rd parties over whom he asserts his power. Walking down a sidewalk is a difference of kind, not of degree.

There is much more to Walter's article, and I could spend the rest of my evening in back-and-forth responses. But I have touched on the objections directed toward anarchists and it is getting late. If I were to continue, however, I would leave the question of "should you vote for Ron Paul?" and go on to the separate one of "is Ron Paul a Llibertarian?" My answer to the latter is not defined by anarchist theory but by a more general libertarianism. Of course, the answer to both is a resounding NO.

Block replies:

Here is now my response to Wendy (similarly, I mean no respect to her by calling my old friend by her first name).

I do not at all say "that it (is) necessary to back a particular politician in order to be a credentialed libertarian." I do not at all demand support for Ron Paul from all libertarians. I do aver that without such support, one's libertarian credentials are "suspect," but this is a very different matter. And, this suspicion can certainly be overturned, surely for libertarians who have made such magnificent contributions to our philosophy over the years, such as Wendy. I only characterize as nonlibertarian those who go out of their way to explicitly *attack* Dr. Paul, as does Wendy, unfortunately. The way I see matters, it is as if Congressman Paul is stopping a rapist, and the Wendys of the world are not only not cheering him on, but are actively attempting to undermine him. This seems incompatible with support for libertarianism, at least to me.

I certainly support "anarchistic objections to the use of political power," *if and only if* such power is used for non-libertarian ends. But the main goal of Ron Paul is to stop the mass murder of innocents of imperialistic warfare. I would use the devil himself to that end. I fail to see how it is incompatible with libertarian theory for a President Paul to "bring the troops home."

As it happens, I do indeed have "a deep disagreement with one (or some) of Paul's significant stands (such as immigration)." What can I say? I am on record as claiming for Paul "only" a 97% adherence to the libertarianism of Rothbard that I support. Immigration is part of the 3%. Give the man a break. I do not at all say that "Every true libertarian supports Ron Paul." However, I certainly do maintain that "no true libertarian opposes him." These are *very* different claims, and Wendy does not appear to recognize this.

In Wendy's interpretation of Sunni Maravillosa's "*must all unite and act as one.*" But I am not at all saying that. This is a misinterpretation. All libertarians, in my view, need be united on only one thing, the nonaggression axiom. As for support of Ron Paul, they are perfectly free to fail to support him, and can retain their full libertarian credentials, as long as they do not stab him in the back.

According to Wikipedia: "The term was advanced by philosopher Antony Flew in his 1975 book *Thinking About Thinking: Do I sincerely want to be right?*

Imagine Hamish McDonald, a Scotsman, sitting down with his *Glasgow Morning Herald* and seeing an article about how the "Brighton Sex Maniac Strikes Again." Hamish is shocked and declares that "No Scotsman would do such a thing." The next day he sits down to read his *Glasgow Morning Herald* again and this time finds an article about an Aberdeen man whose brutal actions make the Brighton sex maniac seem almost gentlemanly. This fact shows that Hamish was wrong in his opinion but is he going to admit this? Not likely. This time he says, "No *true* Scotsman would do such a thing." —Antony Flew, *Thinking About Thinking*

A simpler rendition would be:

Alice: All Scotsmen enjoy haggis.

Bob: My uncle is a Scotsman, and he doesn't like haggis!

Alice: Well, all *true* Scotsmen like haggis."

I fail to see why I am guilty of engaging in this fallacious argument. I define a libertarian as someone who wants to promote liberty, as opposed to a believer in libertarianism, who merely believes in this doctrine, but is indifferent to actually supporting it in the real world. I know that Wendy fits the latter category, but I deny she fits the former one. Why? Because Ron Paul is THE GREATEST promoter of liberty the world has ever known, certainly in terms of numbers of people he has converted to this one true faith. How can someone who really wants to promote liberty spend her efforts undermining Paul's efforts. No *true* libertarian would do this, nor would any plain old libertarian. Only a person who *believes* in libertarianism, such as Wendy, would.

Were I to use an *ad hominem* argument against Wendy, I would say something like, "She is wrong about Ron Paul because she is a woman and no female knows anything about politics" or, "she is wrong about him because she lives in Canada, and no Canadian is fit to pronounce judgement about Dr. Paul." Did I really say anything even remotely resembling such gibberish? If so, I must be losing my touch.

Wendy describes herself as having "principled objections to electoral politics." She rejects my slave-master analogy on the externalities ground that "A voter acts not merely to establish his own preference as master, he acts to put his preferred master in a position of unjust power over unconsenting others. It is this unconsenting "3rd party" problem from which anarchist objections arise." Forget about Dr. Paul's immigration policies, and other elements of his 3 percent deviations. How can bringing home the troops, lowering tax theft, stopping drug prohibitions, ending the Fed, etc., be a violation of unconsenting individuals? Any individual who does not "consent" to these reductions in the violation of the nonaggression axiom is to that extent a rights violator, and his views may certainly be ignored. For example, suppose there were an "unconsenting third party who opposed Ron's repeal of the Harrison Narcotics Act of 1917. Is Wendy seriously contending that in doing so, Ron is violating the rights of this supporter of the legal status quo? Surely, not. But I do not know how else to interpret her views on this matter. Strawman? Where?

Wendy is quite right in upbraiding me for not mentioning which Spooner (1870) piece I was referring to. It is, of course his monumental "No Treason," where he says this about voting:

"... without his consent having even been asked a man finds himself environed by a government that he cannot resist; a government that forces him to pay money, render service, and forego the exercise of many of his natural rights, under peril of weighty punishments. He sees, too, that other men practice this tyranny over him by the use of the ballot. He sees further, that, if he will but use the ballot himself, he has some chance of relieving himself from this tyranny of others, by subjecting them to his own. In short, he finds himself, without his consent, so situated that, if he uses the ballot, he may become a master; if he does not use it, he must become a slave. And he has no other alternative than these two. In self-defense, he attempts the former. ..."

All I can say is that when a political philosopher such as Spooner interprets voting as a matter of "self-defense," he can hardly be interpreted as condemning it. I just do not understand Wendy's rejection of my call upon Spooner, who we both revere, in support of my views on Ron Paul.

Wendy also rejects my criticism of her and her cohorts that they all "use the sidewalks for walking, the streets and roads for driving, U.S. currency for making purchases, post letters with the U.S. postal service, visit state libraries, museums, etc." She does so on the ground that "there is a difference of kind between walking down a sidewalk and electing someone to a position of unjust power over unconsenting others." Of course there is. But we have already rejected the contention (apart from the 3 percent issue), that Ron represents "unjust power over unconsenting others." The charge of hypocrisy (using roads, libraries, currency, etc.) was meant to deflect the oft-made claim that voting "gives sanction" to the evil state. Well, if it does (it does *not*, certainly not in the case of Ron Paul), then so do these other interactions with government. If the one should be proscribed, then so should the other. But Wendy utilizes the state in these other dimensions. Therefore, she can have no valid objection to voting, at least not on that ground.

Part V.

Strategy

This section is devoted to my suggestions for Ron Paul to better promote his candidacy. For anyone else, this would seem to be the height of presumption and nerviness. Who am I, a relative pipsqueak, to offer advice to this great man who has done more for the promotion of libertarianism than any person alive or dead? In terms of my own contribution to the cause of liberty, and his, the comparison of a mouse and an elephant would unduly reward me. Perhaps, a more correct contrast would be between the mouse and a molecule. But this is Ron Paul we are talking about. A more humbler man never walked the face of the Earth. Besides, I have been friends with the congressman from Texas for some four decades. If I can't offer free advice to Dr. Paul, then I can't do so for anyone. If that unhappy situation ever occurred, I'd simply *burst.* So, gentle reader, please excuse what might well be seen as presumption on my part. I have no doubt that my friend Ron views the contribution of my next section in precisely this light.

Chapter 14.

Advice for Ron Paul

Ron Paul is doing just fine in his campaign. He is promoting liberty at a magnificent clip. He is converting people to libertarianism en masse.

So, Congressman Paul certainly doesn't need any advice from me. Will that stop me from offering him some? Of course not. Lack of knowledge and expertise (as my critics tell me time and time again) never stopped me from mouthing off, and it won't this time either.

On the other hand, I am fully aware that in the matter of politics, the only libertarian congressman from Texas is the master, and I am but a humble student. Yet, sometimes, out of the mouths of babes come interesting thoughts. And brainstorming never hurts, even if only one out of a thousand off-the-wall ideas has any merit. So, it is in this self-effacing spirit that I offer some food for thought for the Ron Paul rEVOLution.

Send out an open letter to all other candidates for the Republican nomination, along these lines:

Dear fellow candidates for the Republican nomination:

The present format for our debates is unfair; some competitors are given way more of a chance to speak than others. Imagine if Usain Bolt were given a five-yard head start because he is expected by the judges to be the winner of the race; posit that Michael Phelps were allowed to start swimming a few seconds earlier than his competitors on this ground. The officials responsible for such outrages would be summarily fired, not to say lynched by sports fans. And yet that is *precisely* what occurs in these debates for the Republican nomination for president. These umpires, too, ought to be severely rebuked.

In order to rectify the wildly unjust situation, I suggest the following (I am open to all friendly amendments):

1. Equal time be allotted to all competitors (what could be fairer than that?)

2. Our positions on the podium be determined by lottery

3. The order in which we are asked questions be determined by a coin flip

4. Treat all candidates equally in every way, as are the runners in the 100-meter race at the starting line, and all throughout the race.

As soon as XX numbers of us sign this petition, we publicize this fact, and, agree not to be on the same stage as those who refuse to sign it.

Yours truly,

Ron Paul

This is obviously just a first draft, but, I'm sure you get my gist. Romney and Perry,[41] I expect, will at least initially refuse to sign this open letter; the others will likely do so. Perhaps those two can be embarrassed into signing it. If not, I think that Ron would benefit from allowing those two them to debate each other all by their lonesome, provided there is enough of a chance that a debate of all the signatories to this letter will actually occur on prime time TV, and be more popular. On the positive side of this suggestion, the American people, I think (well, I hope) have some sort of sense of justice and fair play. When this open letter is publicized (of course not in the mainstream media, at least at first – thank God for the internet), my hope and expectation is that there will be sufficient howls of outrage against the MSM, and Romney and Perry for not signing on (if they do not). On the other hand, there is some real danger that the MSM will jettison all other candidates, and conduct their future interviews with Perry and Romney alone, as is their heartfelt desire.

Social Security

The radical libertarian position on this institution is clear. Not only is it a Ponzi scheme, but it is a compulsory one. It ought to be ended, forthwith, and all payments stopped. What about the elderly retirees? They are the victims. They should sue those responsible for foisting this system on them, but should not collect a penny more, ever, from the long suffering taxpayer, for to do so would be to violate the rights of the innocent. (Full disclosure here; at 70 years of age, I now collect Social Security payments. I support the ending of this scheme, but am not at all about to decline my own checks for reasons mentioned.) What should be done about the perpetrators of Social Security? They should be treated roughly in the manner meted out to Bernie Madoff.

41These were the front-runners at the time. Gingrich, Santorum and Paul were all at the back of the pack.

There is of course a more moderate position, at least roughly compatible with libertarianism: end Social Security now, by not enrolling *any* new people. Allow all those on the books to either stop their payment contributions if they wish to opt out or allow them to continue, and pay retirees what they have been promised.

It has been said that "gradualism in theory is perpetuity in practice." Well, perhaps not in this case. Present enrollees and recipients will be grandfathered in, and this pernicious system will continue, for them, but, eventually it will end, starting right now. In that sense, this proposal is "gradualistic." But, in refusing to bring any young people into this Ponzi scheme, it will start to end *immediately*.

It should be emphasized, moreover, that in addition to the unsavory financial elements of this system, it tends to weaken and even break up the family. And, the family, a strong united family, is the backbone of our country. In the days before Social Security, the common practice was for middle-aged people to take care of their parents, with the full expectation that their own children would return the favor to them. But with the government thrust into this situation (whether federal or state, it matters not) these familial bonds are weakened. Even if Social Security did not constitute fraud and theft, it ought to be ended on the ground of it weakening family.

Drugs

The radical position on drugs is clear. End. The. Prohibition. Now. And, again, imprison all of those responsible for perpetrating it, as the nonviolent prisoners of this victimless crime are freed. And, while we're at it (right after ending the Fed), end the FDA. This latter institution will not even allow people who are dying to take a chance on experimental drugs. For shame.

In the free society, the FDA would be supplanted with a competitive certification industry filled with the medical and pharmaceutical equivalents of Fitch, Standard and Poor, Kosher foods, the Good Housekeeping Seal of Approval, Consumer Reports, Moodys, etc.

But, there is a moderate libertarian position open to Ron Paul as well: "Immediately upon becoming president, I will legalize marijuana, release all prisoners who are guilty of using or trafficking in, this drug." (I haven't got the foggiest notion of whether or not the president of the U.S. has this power. I don't *care* about that either. Let the politicos wrestle with that one. I am an ignoramus on these sorts of issues. My only goal here is to promote liberty. This is what *should* happen, whether it *can* or not.)

Gary Johnson

If asked to distinguish himself from the "libertarianism" of Governor Gary Johnson, Ron Paul, the next president of the U.S. (boy, I *like* the sound of that) could say the following:

"Unlike the Democratic wing of the Republican Party (Perry and Romney), we in the libertarian wing of the GOP do not relish the idea of interminably arguing back and forth over Who said What, When and Where. Rather, we focus instead on *ideas for liberty.* And in this vein, I welcome Governor Johnson to the podium. He, too, supports the Constitution, free enterprise, limited government, legalized drugs and a purely defensive foreign policy. Gary may well take some libertarian Republican votes away from me, but I am delighted that he is here at my side since he also promotes liberty."

Now, I realize that Ron will never in a million years say anything like that. He is simply too much of a gentleman to bash Perr-ney (a Perry-Romney combo that's not likely to catch on). But, I couldn't resist offering this advice to him. Also, I have no idea whether or not it would be wise to be so supportive of Johnson. I offer this one, and all these other ideas, in the spirit of brainstorming, only.

P.S. I saw Ron Paul at the Campaign for Liberty convention held in Reno (9/16/11). His speech brought tears to my eyes. I love this man. To be in the same room with him was an honor.

Chapter 15.

Seven Rules for Media Interviews: What to Do About Chris Matthews

I found it exceedingly difficult to watch Chris Matthews' interview of Ron Paul. The former would hardly allow the latter to get a word in edgewise. Matthews kept interrupting the next president of the U.S. He would barely allow him to finish a sentence. But, that's not what I want to write about. Instead, I want to discuss options for dealing with such boorish interviewers when we are next in Ron's position. What should we do when we are faced with such a situation?

1. Talk faster. Here, an attempt is made to at least get in something of substance before the inevitable next interruption occurs. But there are problems with this technique. For one thing, you can be cut off even faster. For another, you lose your "presence" when you do this. The audience will tend to dismiss you because you are being speeded up by the interviewer. I recommend against this.

2. Talk more slowly. This attempt at passive aggressiveness has something to be said for it. It makeSSSSS it crystal clear to everyone concerned exactly what is going on. I was once interviewed on Canadian television by the talk show host and former premier of British Columbia, Dave Barrett, a bully of the Matthews stripe if ever there was one. I pulled this technique on him. I hardly spoke a word in the entire 30-minute interview. The upshot: the producers apologized to me and forced Barrett to have me on his show again. This time, chastened, he acted in a more civilized manner. I sometimes think I should have refused to go on with him again, the better to underscore his barbaric behavior.

3. Keep talking. Do *not* allow yourself to be interrupted. You don't have to shout, although, if you have a booming voice this will help. In my soft voice, I just keep on going, even though the interviewer won't shut up. It is like a chicken race: who will be the first to veer away? Don't allow that to be you. Keep talking, even if what you are saying is, in extremis, reduced to nonsense syllables. Eventually, you will win, because this will make the interviewer look bad. It is his show. He

is supposedly the professional. Trust me, you will win this chicken race if you persevere.

4. Change the subject. The next time the interviewer asks you a question, say something along the following lines: "That is a very interesting question. I'd really love to answer it. However, I fear, based on recent experience, that no sooner do I get 5 words out of my mouth, you'll interrupt me, yet again. So, let's talk, instead, about your compulsive need to hog the limelight. Don't you think this interview would be more informative for your audience if you allowed me, oh, 10 full seconds to answer every question before you bully your way in, again?"

5. Counter-interrupt. When he is in the midst of asking you a question, interrupt him, to show him and the audience exactly what he is doing. I have never tried this, but, my thought is that if you engage in this behavior, your invitations to be on radio and television will decline.

6. When the Matthewses of the world interrupt your answer to a given question, and quickly pose another one, say, quietly and calmly, "I would like to fully finish my answer to your previous question." (I owe this point to Dale Holmgren). How might Matthews respond to this? One possibility is surrender on his part; he could say, "Ok, please elaborate." Then, you've won. But he might use another ploy, saying something along the following lines: "We don't have time for in-depth responses, due to time constraints. "How to reply to this? You could acquiesce. Or, you could be more assertive; claim that you'll be brief, but insist that justice to the audience can't be done with answers that are severely truncated.

7. Be a gentleman. Do exactly as Ron Paul did. Do not counter-interrupt. Allow yourself to be continually interrupted. Don't speed up or slow down your normal rate of speaking. Do not give the interviewer a lecture on good manners.

Which is best? I'm not sure. I welcome discussion on this point. I think it is good to be armed with alternative techniques and, responses. However, I'm not sure but think that Ron's response is best. Be cool. Be a gentleman. Ron, after all, is by far our best spokesman. On the other hand, we learn methodological individualism from our study of Austrian economics. In this vein, it is possible that what works best for Ron will not be the ideal response for all of the rest of us who are trying to promote liberty and rational economics, in support of Ron.

Chapter 16.

How Should Ron Paul Handle Himself on TV with Hostile Interviewers?

Ron Paul was on television with Chris Matthews. I think it was supposed to be an interview, but Matthews wouldn't allow Congressman Paul to get a word in edgewise, and continually interrupted him. I wrote this column, in an attempt to explore techniques the next president of the U.S. could have employed, and, also, I assessed how well he did in this one instance (very well indeed, in my humble opinion).

I received numerous email responses to this blog of mine. Many of them, sad to tell, were really magnificent. (I kick myself for not having thought of these really good ways of dealing with electronic bullies.) In what follows, I offer some of the very best of these letters, with commentaries from yours truly. I do this not because Ron Paul needs any advice from the likes of us. It is not for nothing that he is now libertarianism's best spokesman. If we could all be one hundredth as good as him in this sort of thing, our attempts to promote liberty would be far better than they are now. No, I offer these comments since many readers of LewRockwell.com are called upon, in our relatively more modest ways, to do public speaking, radio and television interviews, and these thoughts might well help all of us to a better job in transmitting our philosophy.

I offer these letters on an anonymous basis because several of the authors requested anonymity, and I decided to treat all of the letters the same. I have made slight edits to most, of these, for example deleting the salutations.

Author A:

We met briefly several years ago at an Austrian Scholars Conference in Auburn, though I doubt I made much of an impression.

I read with interest your LRC article about rules for interviews. I've worked in television for two decades, and accept your invitation to join in a discussion of these matters.

In my opinion, there is one absolute rule that must always be observed, and it is this: Always be a gentleman (or lady).

It is true that television did not become successful by overestimating the intelligence of its audience. But even viewers of the lowest IQ can recognize when someone is being ill-treated.

The more you can behave like someone who is in control, who can tolerate the rudeness of the host with grace and patience, the more you win. This is because your behavior speaks louder than words. Long after the talking points fade from memory, long after your irrefutable reasoned arguments are forgotten, people will remember one thing: You behaved like an adult. And they will remember that the opinions you tried to express were those of an adult, and the host behaved like a child. For better or worse, this is more persuasive to people than pure logic.

To my mind, this is the secret to Ron Paul's continuing TV success. He ALWAYS behaves like a gentleman, and therefore is always perceived as a reasonable person. Even when people might believe his views to be far outside the narrow band of mainstream opinion, his gentlemanly demeanor commands attention and respect. Believe me, people watching at home respond to this even if the host does not. It gives people pause to think: "If such a reasonable, mature man believes these things, perhaps there is something to them after all." Many times, it does not matter that he is not allowed to finish a sentence. The dignity he displays comes across sharper when it stands in contrast to the childishness of the interviewer.

Here are a few other tips for giving interviews.

- If you are invited on TV, you must accept that you are not going to be in control of the situation, you only can control your own behavior. It is their studio, their cameras, their microphones, and if they want to cut away from you and turn your microphone off, they can do so, and then take the last word. I liken it to sailing. You can only be the best captain of your ship that you can be, but what ultimately happens is up to the whimsy of the sea. Accept this, and hope for good sailing.

- If you are nervous and not accustomed to giving interviews, acknowledge this openly if you can. Paradoxically, stating that you are nervous tends to reduce the nervousness that you feel. It also garners sympathy from the audience.

- Smile as much as you can, unless it is inappropriate (obviously, you don't want to appear happy if you're being interviewed about crib death or genocide).

- Defend yourself firmly, but never appear to lose your temper. Act as if you were correcting a small child who didn't know he'd given offense. Show polite tolerance and grace, and you won't need any snide comebacks or witty retorts. Again: behavior speaks louder than words.

- And speaking of being witty, resist the urge unless you are very comfortable on TV. If you are out of your element, there is a greater chance you'll accidentally say something inappropriate that will live forever on YouTube. Remember that most of Don Imus's witticisms will be forgotten, but one crack about a basketball team will never die.

- If you want to change the subject, say "The issue is not X, it's Y." Then follow it up with a counter-question for the host. For example: "The issue is not how much credit the Fed needs to provide, the issue is how much inflation can the Fed create before it begins to ravage the economy. How do you think the housing bubble was created?"

- If the host and the producers are really determined to make you look bad, smile and jokingly say: "I'm beginning to think I walked into an ambush here." Acknowledge that you are outgunned, and you will negate the effect of your host's attack. The host may not back off, but the audience will recognize the inequity of the situation. People instinctively recognize an unfair fight, and they will turn against an attacker who presses his advantage too ruthlessly. This is true even if they were originally rooting for the host. Again, grace under pressure will be remembered far longer than salient points about policy.

You mentioned Ayn Rand in your article as being most responsible for turning people on to libertarianism. This is true, but we should remember that she did so primarily through her fictional writing, not through her appearances on TV. I suspect Paul will overtake her before he's done, because more people will see a five-minute Ron Paul TV appearance than read a 1,000-page novel.

I hope you find my comments cogent to your invitation.

Walter Block: This missive certainly has the ring of truth for me. I learned a lot from it, and I am delighted to pass this on to the

LewRockwell.com audience pretty much exactly as it was sent to me. According to the old aphorism, "a picture is worth 1,000 words." What I get from Author A is that behavior is worth 1,000 pictures.

Author B:

I watched the interview, and I have several thoughts to point out:

Relative authority position. (not sure what the proper term is) For example: if 65-year-old Chris Matthews interviews 74-year-old Congressman Paul, then Paul has much more inherent status. Just as if the now-late Walter Cronkite, at 60, interviewed a 20-year-old "nobody" the status would be with Cronkite. The dynamics of both situations are very different, and must be used to advantage during the debate.

In the Chris Matthews interview, Ron's best bet was to act the adult and take the "high road" He could have politely chided Matthews once or twice for cutting him off, elaborate on the previous question etc. When Matthews was ranting, Ron could have joked "Are you done yet?" Watch old videos of Ronald Reagan — he was a master at this.

In the other case, when the "authority figure" is the interviewer, the situation must be played differently. This is much more difficult, but you can win if the interviewer is perceived as a bully. This is like verbal judo. Take your opponents energy and use it against himself.

Hope this helps.

Walter Block: As far as I'm concerned, this helps quite a bit. In my original column, I did mention methodological individualism. This leads to the idea of "different strokes for different folks," since we are all heterogeneous, and what will work for one person will not necessarily do well for another. But, I never took the next step, as does author B, and looked at the matter in terms of differential status. A good point.

Author C:

I wanted to share another idea, inspired by your list of strategies for dealing with Chris Matthews type interviewers.

Take a stopwatch with you and time how long you're allowed to speak, while keeping it under the table, at least at first. After a few interruptions, pull out the stopwatch and bemusedly remark on how little you've been interviewed, seeing as how you've only been allowed to talk for 35 cumulative seconds or what not.

If they're wise to this and invite a speaker back for another interview, but they remain likely to bully, bring a chess timer, make it obvious and on the table that they should delimit their time speaking versus yours, as a sort of overt sharing of the stage.

Just wanted to share!

Walter Block: A very dramatic way to make the point. I once employed this technique. Not at an interview, but at a dinner table, where another libertarian attempted to draw me into a debate, well, upbraid me for all sorts of sins of commission and omission of which he thought me guilty. He has deep, booming voice, while my vocal abilities are at the very opposite end of the scale. After trying to voice a substantive reply, several times, and being shut down easily, I asked him, "Do you play chess?" He said yes. I then asked him, "Do you play with a chess clock?" That abruptly ended the very one-way "conversation." He was a bully, but he wasn't stupid. He knew that my next question would have been along the lines of, in the last 15 minutes, how much time do you think you had to express your views, and how much time did you allow me to express mine? That would have been humiliating to him.

Author D:

Dr. Paul should Domain-inate the interview, so to speak. Let me explain…

So, Dr. Paul is scheduled to appear on *Hardball*. Before the interview airs, the folks at, let's say, *Campaign for Liberty* should purchase the domain name chrismatthewsinterviewsronpaul.com. The show begins and, as expected, it's a typical *Hardball* exchange. As time runs out, Dr. Paul asks for the "last word." Matthews obliges and Dr. Paul turns to the camera and says, "For more detailed answers to all of Chris's questions, go to Chris Matthews interviews Ron Paul dot com."

What does chrismathewsinterviewsronpaul.com look like? We'd humor Mr. Matthews and transcribe his loaded questions from the interview followed by Dr. Paul's written answers. Of course, time is scarce and Dr. Paul would have to actually write some responses! Maybe you or other Austro-libertarians can volunteer some answers. This site would be an open forum for debate.

This would surely get some press and spread virally. Social Media is more effective than TV media anyway. Perhaps all of Dr. Paul's appearances can live under an umbrella site: RonPaulvsTheMedia.com. People will know that whatever misleading questions the Larry Kings or Sean Hannitys of the world ask will be dealt with properly and answered thoroughly, focusing on the root problems.

However, I'm not the target for this website (I consider myself an Austro-anarcho-libertarian). Hopefully this "stunt" would attract those that are politically and economically confused. I imagine this site would capture the libertarian spirit of Conversations with Casey. It's a weekly online Q & A that Doug Casey calls "an ongoing dialogue on the passing parade. …"

Walter Block: All I can say to this is "Wow." I'd never in a million years have thought of this one. Somehow, I can't quite see Ron Paul doing this, but you never know. In any case, this sure is a good way to promote continuity.

Author E:

Too many of these talk show hosts are unable to have a civil discussion with their guests. Bill O'Reilly is one of the worst and he is also the Village Idiot when it comes to economics, the free market, or personal freedoms. His sometimes fill-in Laura Ingraham is another who can't wait to attack some of her guests.

Glad you thought my comment worthwhile.

If I were Ron Paul, the first time I was interrupted I would say: "Chris, I had assumed the reason for inviting me to appear on your show was to interview me, ask my opinions, etc. I did not assume that the reason was so that you could interrupt me and use me as a punching bag so as I appear to be a helpless buffoon. I find it very impolite to be interrupted — I will not interrupt you. Having said that, I'm happy to be here if we can have a cordial discussion. If not, I'm also happy to leave now."

Walter Block: This author represents the tough part of the continuum of possible answers. I find this suggestion personally very gratifying. To me, it is the next best thing to punching the bully in the nose, in terms of satisfaction. But, I fear, that the person who employs this will not be invited onto too many shows. I could be wrong. Certainly, this technique should at least be part of our possible repertoire, to use, perhaps, when desperate.

Author F:

I saw the interview in question and thought Ron Paul handled it relatively well. I watch the Matthews' show often, and he treated Paul better than most. It is unfortunate that the majority of the media interviewers engage in this conduct due to the time constraints placed on them by the networks but also because they seem to have big egos. The exception has been NPR and public TV which is (relatively) commercial-free and seemingly more fair minded and objective.

Perhaps Mr. Paul should have said: I had assumed, since you invited me to be on your show, you were interested in what I had to say, yet you constantly interrupt my replies. I have not interrupted you once, please allow me to answer your questions or respond.

I once saw an interview on O'Reilly with a spokesman from the Ayn Rand Institute. It was an extreme display of this sort of behavior but what can one expect from a jackass like Bill O'Reilly?

Walter Block: Another tough-minded response. This is at the opposite end of the spectrum from the technique I mentioned I employed with Dave Barrett in my original column. There, I was almost entirely passive, allowing him to stomp all over me, so to speak. I think it is good that we all become acquainted with as wide a range of possible responses as possible.

Author G:

All the listed strategies have their advantages, but really which one to use depends on the temperament of the person being interviewed. Some people could pull off the blunt, hostile reaction very effectively while others couldn't. Really the absolute best reaction to a typical left-wing brat would be a back-handed slap to the face followed by a stream of threats and obscenities, but the consequences would prove to be counterproductive. Most people would probably do best adopting your approach. That's a very effective way of simply robbing the interviewer of credibility and making him lose the moral high ground completely. After all, a decent, moral person on a program of the sort you are describing isn't there to change the minds of the sort of audience that would watch that show. He is there simply to provide a punching bag for the interviewer. Therefore, anything that turns the tables on the interviewer and reveals him as a petty, leftist tyrant is probably the most positive thing that could possibly happen on such a program. It's just show business. Refuse to play your allotted role the best way that you can.

Walter Block: This letter is certainly supportive of my contention regarding the heterogeneity of libertarian interviewees. Anything that can "rob the interviewer of credibility and make him lose the moral high ground" is worth considering.

Author H:

I read this piece with great interest. I have often wondered what I would do in a similar situation, should I ever have the dubious honor of being interviewed on radio or television. I, too, bristle at the treatment given to guests on radio or TV shows, especially if they are of the opposite political persuasion. Conservative talk show hosts are as guilty of this as liberal ones.

My idea is a combination of a couple of yours. Since one would have to know, going in, that hosts engage in this behavior, my strategy would be to ignore their interruptions and go right on answering their question, and continue in that vein until they stop interrupting or I finished making my point. I think this would take a Herculean effort on the guest's part, simply because the hosts would probably start throwing out outrageous charges and statements just to get you to react. The temptation to respond would be almost unbearable.

Of course, one always runs the risk, with this strategy, of appearing to dodge questions, and the host would not hesitate to insinuate that you are doing just that. But, I would think that fair-minded individuals would be able to see through that tactic.

I know that bombast gets ratings, but I would think that it is also just as likely that a host could get ratings, and a reputation for fairness, by simply letting the guest make his or her points and let the audience decide. If the guest really is a nutcase, their answers would confirm it without the host exercising an editing function.

Walter Block: Aha, support for my "keep talking at all costs" modus operandi. This, too, is located on the harsh side of the continuum, and perhaps should only be used as a last resort.

Here is an overall comment on all of this. Confession: I never really paid too much attention to this sort of thing in my career. I probably should have done more in this direction. My focus has always been on the substantive dimensions of the argument; to make sure I understood the libertarian or Austrian perspective, and could articulate it when called upon to do so, at least to the best of my ability. My initial response to the Matthews interview of Congressman Paul is that the latter should have taken the most aggressive stance possible: keep talking, upbraid him for interrupting, walk out in a huff, etc. I had the same thought when Anderson Cooper wouldn't allow Ron Paul to speak more than a minute or two during the 2008 campaign. But, upon further reflection, I am not sure but that Ron's response wasn't the best of all possible choices, certainly for his own temperament. You can't argue with success. Dr. Paul has been *the* most successful politician ever, to get out the libertarian word. I think it unlikely that this is in spite of his presentation style.

My hope, here, is not that Ron Paul will greatly benefit from these musings. He doesn't need our help all that much. However, it is likely that the Paul campaign of 2012 will inspire dozens, hundreds of libertarians to seek political office, whether in the Republican or Libertarian party, it matters not. Perhaps these thoughts will be of aid to them.

Chapter 17.

To Accept Matching Funds, or Not to Accept Matching Funds?

Should Ron Paul apply for, or accept, matching funds from the government for his political campaign? Would he be justified in doing so? Or, more generally, what is the libertarian position on anyone accepting any monies from the state for whatever reason?

Many libertarians argue that all such financing should be strictly eschewed. For is not government in general, and the U.S. version of this curious institution in particular, an organization simply incompatible with libertarian principles? Yes, this cannot be denied. Governments necessarily tax their victims, that is, rob them. They also prevent others from supplying supposedly quintessential "governmental" services in competition with them, for example, army, police and adjudication offerings.

Further, the state receives all of its money from only three sources, all of which are entirely illegitimate: taxes, inflation and borrowing. Tax levies are blatant and outright theft. If you do not believe this, try not paying them and see what happens to you. Governmental printing of money, whether directly through the printing press or indirectly via fractional reserve banking, is nothing less than counterfeiting, a form of fraud, which is equivalent to theft. And, as for borrowing, anyone who lends money to the state apparatus is complicit in its evil doings. When libertarianism supplants present institutional arrangements, these bonds will not be repaid.

Given that this is the case, accepting money from the government, it is argued, is indistinguishable from accepting stolen goods or merchandise. Perhaps this ought to be a crime, severely punished by some future libertarian Nuremberg court.

But wait; there are difficulties here. For the modern state is so involved in the lives of its citizens that it is the rare individual who does not accept *some* form of government largesse, whether in the form of money payments, services, or goods of one type or another.

For example, while not everyone goes to a public school or teaches there, it is the rare individual who does not: walk on statist sidewalks, drive on public roads, carry currency in his pocket, avail himself of the services of governmental libraries, museums, parks, stadiums, etc. Which of us has not entered the premises of the motor vehicle bureau, sued someone in court, posted a letter, attempted to attain a passport, or interacted with government in any of the thousand and one other ways it touches upon our lives? And this is to say nothing of seeking government permissions for commercial purposes, accepting Social Security payments, voting, taking an air flight (where we are "protected" by the security apparatus).

If it is per se illegitimate for a libertarian to accept anything of value from this evil institution, then there are very few people who act fully compatibly with this philosophy: maybe a hermit or two. The implication here is that *we are all* guilty of the crime of statism; under a regime of full, complete and impartial justice, we would *all* be in jail.

The error in this thinking, I suggest, stems from failing to view government as precisely the moral monstrosity it is. There is one fictional character who did not make this mistake: Ragnar Danneskjold, one of the heroes of Ayn Rand's *Atlas Shrugged*. He knew full well and so should we, that the state is a thief, and should forthwith be relieved of its ill-gotten gains. Yes, one justification for using roads, a regulated bank, the post office, a public library or park, is that the money to build and administer these amenities was mulcted from the taxpayers, and therefore in utilizing them one is "only getting one's money back." I go further, however. Even if someone came from Mars yesterday, and thus paid not a single iota in taxes in the past, he would *still* be justified in taking government wealth.

Why is this, if the Martian libertarian cannot rely upon the argument that he is merely reclaiming his (or his parents') stolen wealth? This is because the state as thief simply has no right to this booty. Better that any nonstatist possess this wealth than the thieving state. Yes, of course, there will arise the question of whether and to whom and how these monies are to be returned to their rightful owners, but this complication cannot be allowed to get in the way of appreciating the primordial moral fact that the state has no legitimate claim to this wealth.

May *anyone* properly seize state wealth in this perspective? No. *Only* nonstatists may legitimately do so. Not Halliburton nor Bechtel; not

Hillary nor Rudy. They are all supporters of statism. They are all members in good standing in the ruling class. But Ron, and also the average guy in the street, may do so. They have no blood on their hands. Indeed, it is a positive mitzvah for people of this sort to relieve the government of its stolen property.

Would Ron be *wise* to accept government matching funds? No, despite the fact that he would be *justified* in doing so. This would be a gigantic pragmatic mistake. First of all, these monies come replete with all sorts of strings attached. My admittedly imperfect assessment of this situation is that the gains would not be worth these costs. Second, and more important, there are very few libertarians who agree with me on this analysis. Most take the position that it is illegitimate to accept funding from the government. Why should Ron split his supporters at this particular point in time, and on such a complicated issue? Third, and most important, one of the major benefits of Ron's candidacy is that so many, many people are now hearing about libertarianism for the first and only time from one of the best and most attractive spokesmen for this philosophy we have ever had. For him to accept government matching funds would confuse the message in the minds of these newcomers. This is a complex enough issue as to be divisive within the libertarian community; very few of those we now hope to attract to the movement for liberty will be able to appreciate the deontological points sketched out above.

Let us conclude by now directly addressing the questions posed at the outset. Should Ron accept government matching funds? He would be very unwise to do so, despite the fact that there is nothing in the libertarian legal philosophy that would be violated by such an action. Should the rest of us stop availing ourselves of government "services?" Not at all. The problem is not when the government returns wealth to us; the rights violation occurs when the state seizes *our* income.

Chapter 18.

Open letters on behalf of Ron Paul

In the 2008 campaign, I participated in an "open letter to Ron Paul" effort. Part of the impetus for this initiative was to actually give advice to the man. He is so unassuming that many of us thought, correctly, that he would accept counsel from his well-wishers, such as me, even though he was and isn the master of the craft, and we mere dilettantes, if I can speak in this way not only about myself but also those others involved in this "open letter" effort. But another part of this movement was, frankly, to give aid to each other, and to make up in some small way for the strong tendency of the main stream media to all but ignore Dr. Paul's efforts.

18.1 Open Letter to Ron Paul

Dear Ron:

Please excuse me; I can't help it. As the Jewish Mother of the libertarian movement, I just have to give advice to all members of it, you included. Here, then, is some advice. You'd better take it. I have weapons of mass destruction for those of "mine kinder" who refuse to obey me: chicken soup to pour over your head, nagging, whining, etc. I give you fair warning: I am a world-class nudge.

1. You are asked, ad nauseam, if you lose the Republican nomination, will you back the winner? You reply, quite reasonably that you gladly will, but only if that person changes his views on foreign policy, free enterprise, etc. I wonder what would happen if journalists asked Rudy, Mitt, Fred, Mike, John what would they do if you win it: would they back you? I expect they would all lie and say they would. But, the truth is that they would support Hillary, Obama or Edwards instead of you. After all, the views of the present Republican poll leaders are far closer to those of the present Democratic poll leaders than they are to yours.

2. Here's an answer to those, libertarians amongst them, who say you are not "cool" enough to become president, you are too much of an "isolationist" (I know, I know, they can't tell the difference between an

isolationist and a noninterventionist), you lack international experience, exposure, you'll be dismissed by the rest of the world as a redneck hick Texan. To me, the most interesting part of this survey shows how the Israelis would vote for Republican candidates. Hint: they vote for the same person who currently receives the most donations from members of the U.S. military. So, let us hear no more about how a Paul presidency would be bad for Israel. True, this is a rather small sample. But bias in sampling never stops the mainstream media (MSM); why should it deter us?

3. Tom Tancredo (when he was still running) and Fred Thompson started "money bombs" of their own, based on your success. To say the very least, they do not do anywhere as well as you (understatement of the century). This reminds me of the movie *Mondo Cane*, which depicted the "cargo cult." That refers to Stone Age people who saw planes landing on runways, and disgorging cargo. So, they built runways in the middle of the jungle, and even seeded them with planes made out of wood they had whittled, so as to entice real planes to land and disgorge cargo. I guess what I'm trying to say is that Tancredo and Thompson are still living in the Stone Age in terms of their understanding of what's going on in terms of fundraising. They haven't got a clue that the secret of your success has nothing to do with "money bombs" or "charisma" or "expert fundraisers," etc. Rather, it concerns, solely, your brilliant message about freedom, liberty, less government, nonintervention, sound money, etc.

4. Ron Paul as Nazi. When I first began to give public lectures on rent control (the topic of my Ph.D. dissertation) in the early 1970s, I was ready for all sorts of technical, mathematical, statistical, theoretical questions. Do you know what the media kept asking me about, instead? Am I a landlord? Am I in the pay of landlords? Do I *know* any landlords? Nothing much has changed in the intervening decades. Instead of focusing on your message, they are trying to Nazi-bait you, of all things. I don't really know what to do about this. But, lack of knowledge never stopped me before, why should it now? So, let me speculate. One tack is to equate Nazism and Communism. One is national socialism, the other is international socialism. You oppose both. If anything, you incline toward the latter, since you are an internationalist (that ought to confuse them, if nothing else). They are *equally* bad. No, wait, here you can incline on the Nazi side, since the Communists have murdered more people, far more people. (Maybe not a good idea; I'm just thinking out loud, here; give me a break.)

Another tack to take is to support the moral equivalence of the two. The mainstream media sees dangers in only one direction, not both. When Britain's Prince Harry wore a swastika, they went ape. This is evil, this is an abomination. Well, yes, of course, it is. But, seemingly every fifth kid on college campuses wears a Che Guevara T-shirt, or one depicting a hammer and sickle, and no one in the MSM says word one about it.

Happily, this smear is so far from the truth that it has no chance to take hold. As my friend Michael Edelstein says: "Ron Paul as a Nazi symp is akin to claiming Hitler was a closet pacifist." Indeed, I am surprised at the *New York Times*; can they not do any better than that? Perhaps the best response, Ron, is a good old ad hominem attack: any newspaper that *still* has not apologized for its journalist Walter Duranty's reports that things were fine in the Soviet Union during its terror famine cannot and should not be taken seriously.

5. Tim Russert. You did brilliantly in this interview. The problem you faced, of course, was that before "machine gun mouth" Russert allowed you to answer one question, he was asking a second; and, while you were just beginning to wrestle with that one, a third was in the offing. Your style in these contexts, if I may characterize it thusly, is one of politeness, supreme courtesy. Indeed, good manners, respect and graciousness fairly exude out of you. I think that is one good tack to take, and, maybe, you should stick to it, given that it comes so naturally to you. But, there are others. In order of increasing pushiness (I don't like to brag, but I am nothing if not an expert in this particular field) are the following responses:

A. Please allow me to answer your first question before breaking off and trying to answer a second, and then a third, all at the same time. B. I am sure your audience will get more out of this interview if you allow me to answer a question. C. Please do not continually interrupt me; it is impolite. D. Ignore his follow-up questions, and tell him you are going to keep doing this, until you answer the first few questions to your satisfaction. As I say, your style may well be the best for you, but, in the interests of notifying others of us who will also be called upon to take up roles of this sort in behalf of libertarianism, I thought I would at least mention other possible responses.

6. Sean Hannity. Again, you were magnificent in this harrowing experience. I'm sure the non-committed audience was with you, vis-à-vis this boor. Whereas Russert would confine himself to questions,

Hannity would “ask” you something, and, as soon as the first word was out of your mouth, would presume to lecture you and “educate” you about the issues of the day. With him, again, you were unerringly polite. I think you have a courtesy gene in you. Well, I don't. Here are some of the tacks I’ve taken (I confess, with far less success than you have had, but I mention them one, to get them off my chest, and two, in the hope that a discussion of them will help some of us).

A. Ask, who is the interviewer, and who is the interviewee? B. Keep talking no matter what. Don’t let him interrupt you. Do NOT pause for breath; heck, you’re a world class athlete, you ought to be able to outlast that windbag in a contest of lung power. Get used to the idea that the two of you will both be speaking for a minute or two. Practice this with one of your staffers. The problem here is that you will both come off as jerks. Probably, this will hurt you more than him. Heck, dare I say it, I don't really care about his career, although the sooner he is off the air the better for rational discourse. I offer you these options in case you may ever choose to use them. But, knowing you, I think you'll stick with your style, and, as I say, I am not at all sure yours is not the best way to go for you, and, maybe, for all the rest of us, too.

6. Gold. Strictly speaking, you do NOT favor the gold standard. Rather, you favor free market money: any monetary medium chosen by market participants. The only reason you mention gold at all is that whenever people were “free to choose" (the title of a book written by an opponent of the gold standard, Milton Friedman), as a historical fact they chose gold (and sometimes silver). But, if in the future, under the sort of free enterprise system you will promote as president of the United States, if the market settled on copper or platinum, or, indeed, anything else, you would have no quarrel with that outcome. This is a complex issue to bring up in the 30-second sound bites you are often accorded, but I thought you might find some time to emphasize this point.

7. Ron, please get more bodyguards. I don’t care how many you now have, get some MORE. Now that your candidacy is taking off, the powers that be can no longer ignore you. Other people who wanted to, and did, shake up the power structure were assassinated: Martin Luther King, Jr., the Kennedy brothers, Malcolm X. Compared to yours, though, their programs advocated only marginal changes. There are lots of weirdoes and nuts running loose. BE CAREFUL out there.

8. Ron, previously, I wrote a piece asking economists not to vote for you. Here's another reason I "oppose" your candidacy: I just can't get much writing done (apart from writing about you, that is). In the early days of your candidacy, I would Google you, and reading all the stories about you would take, what, an hour or so a day? But then things gradually escalated. Nowadays, if I read every day for 24 hours daily, I still couldn't read everything written about you. My problem is that I'm so enthralled with what you're doing that I can't seem to keep away from doing just that. Nor am I the only Austro-libertarian with a Ron Paul addiction. You're not only ruining my productivity, but, if I can speak for the entire movement for a moment, you are doing this to all of us. Ron, if Murray were still around, I have no doubt that he'd be doing the same thing. Although I am a devout atheist, I just know Murray is up there somewhere, cackling away at a thousand miles per hour with glee. God bless you, you are doing the Lord's work, so to speak.

Best regards,

Walter

18.2. Open Letter to Ron Paul, Part II

By Walter Block, David Bergland, and Jordan Bullock

Dear Ron:

Here is some more free advice:

1. Next time Fox News or any other such "unbiased" forum excludes you from a debate, DON'T ASK to be included. Instead, use this as a publicity opportunity. In the debate, you only get to answer, oh, 3 or 4 questions for 30 seconds each (we're exaggerating by a bit, but not by much). Instead, give a speech and hold a press conference either right before, or right after the "debate," (dare we suggest *during* it?) for the entire length of time of their "debate." Let's see who is laughing loudest after that.

Earlier, during the first few debates, we would not have suggested any such thing. You were relatively unknown then, and needed the exposure those "debates" offered. Now, however, we feel that your candidacy is strong enough to make this tactic the optimal one. Those five intellectual, creative and moral midgets, Rudy, Mitt, Fred, John and Mike, need you for respectability far more than you need them. On the other hand, we do not suggest you pull a "Fred Thompson" and spurn future debates. To do that would be to make too much of a good thing.

On the other hand, there are well-intended and committed Ron Paul supporters who are taking an entirely different tack: threatening to boycott the sponsors of Fox if they do not renege on their decision to exclude you from this upcoming debate. We realize that decisions on strategy involve difficult and complex empirical considerations. We may well be wrong, and the boycotters right. It is difficult to determine, given that there are no praxeological axioms supporting either response nor any possible controlled experiments. Nevertheless, it is our considered judgment that you are now in a strong enough position to thumb your nose at those who would exclude you. On the other hand, these two tactics are not incompatible with one another. *Both* may be engaged in as far as we are concerned.

2. Here are a couple of tactics you might consider using with aggressive interviewers. Some like to rattle off a series of questions in one breath, each of which requires a substantial answer. For some reason, it is usually the lefties who use this tactic. Others will ask a

question then interrupt you in the first sentence of your response to argue with you. With the former, mentally count the questions as they tumble out. Then say: "You have asked me six questions. Which one would you like me to answer.?" Audiences like that, recognizing the questioner's cheap trick for what it is. With the latter, adopt the practice of waiting several seconds after the question. Usually the questioner will then say something like: "Are you going to answer?" Then you can reply: "I just wanted to make sure you were finished. I wouldn't want to interrupt you; that would be rude." That will always be fun, and often effective.

3. The setting: RP describes what, as president, he would do with regard to Iran, Pakistan, Israel or some other hypothetical conflict. Q (incredulously): So, you're saying you'd do NOTHING? A (RP): Sure I'd do nothing. In fact, I think we oughta be doing a lot more "nothing" overseas. Nothing, that is, with guns, missiles, ships, planes and bombs. Instead, we ought to be doing PLENTY of talking with people in other countries, trading with them, engaging in artistic and cultural exchanges, etc.

Q (somewhat hopeful): So if you don't win the Republican nomination, will you run as an Independent or 3rd Party candidate?

A: Look, this question is a bit of a trap. If I swear I won't, and I don't get the Republican nomination, I either disappoint and disenfranchise a lot of voters, or I'll break my word and run anyway. If I say I WILL continue, I'll shoot my bid for the Republican nomination in the foot. Right now, I'm focused on winning the Republican nomination and not considering other avenues. Ask me again, if I don't win.

Q (continual questions about Lincoln, the Civil War, the Civil Rights Act, et al).

A: I'm a busy person. I'm focused on winning a campaign at the moment. I'd be happy to come on the show sometime when I'm not campaigning to discuss these issues at length, but right now I'd appreciate if we could stick to the real campaign issues rather than discuss history.

Ron, we think you started to follow the last suggestion on Morning Joe the other day, but you let them bait you back into the history discussion. Your comments on the subject were right on the money, but why discuss events of 1861 when there are real threats to the country going on right now?

But wait, there's more to be said on this matter. Ron, the next time someone tries to digress, tell them this: If you are so intent on discussing these issues RIGHT NOW, here's the contact information for my friend and trusted advisor Tom DiLorenzo. He is a world-class economic historian, and the world's leading expert on Abraham Lincoln. He is the author of this best-selling book on the issue, *The Real Lincoln*, which I highly recommend to you and your researchers, who have sadly mislead you. By the way, there WAS no "Civil War" in 1861. A civil war implies that there are two forces fighting each other for the control of the territory and people under the jurisdiction of both. There WERE civil wars in Spain in 1936, and in Russia in 1917. What occurred in the U.S. in 1861 was, instead, a war over Southern Secession.

This is what Abraham Lincoln had to say about the matter: "My paramount object in this struggle is to save the Union, and is not either to save or to destroy slavery. If I could save the Union without freeing any slave I would do it, and if I could save it by freeing all the slaves I would do it; and if I could save it by freeing some and leaving others alone I would also do that...."

And Lincoln's First Inaugural Address contains these words: "... I have no purpose, directly or indirectly, to interfere with the institution of slavery in the States where it exists. I believe I have no lawful right to do so, and I have no inclination to do so."

If these quotes don't stop your interrogators in their tracks, just repeat them. And once again if need be.

18.3. Open Letter to Ron Paul, Part III

Dear Ron:

Re your application of the Golden Rule to foreign policy, and getting booed for it. You should keep doing this. You should "double down" on this. You should bring it up at every debate, whether or not you are asked about it. Whether or not you get booed about this again, you should say something along the following lines:

The Golden Rule is one of the basis elements of Christianity. I find you people despicable who are booing me for invoking the Golden Rule, for trying to apply it everywhere, EVEN to foreign policy. You are not only not Christian, you are anti-Christian. Please, do not vote for me. I don't want your votes. Go vote for one of the other four candidates for president, Romney, Obama, Gingrich or Santorum. They, all four of them, reject the Golden Rule. I only want the votes of people who support the Golden Rule. I trust that there are more than enough of those good people to put me into the White House.You people who boo the Golden Rule ought to be ashamed of yourselves.

Here are some more ideas for you

1. Perhaps THE most powerful short, 15 second, political advert EVER made was the one that Johnson used against Goldwater. A little girl was picking a flower. Along came a nuclear bomb with that famous cloud, and the scene ended. Ron, you could use this against Obama, and/or all three remaining contenders. How better to illustrate your differences in foreign policy?

2. Ron, you should offer a challenge to Obama and/ or all three remaining contenders: "I challenge you to a pentathlon. It will consist of a bike ride of one mile, a 100-meter freestyle swim, a 200-meter running race, 10 frames of bowling and 10 shots from the free-throw line in basketball. Needless to say, these specifics can be changed to suit you better.

If any of these people take you up on this challenge, well and good. I don't expect that any will. But, in making this challenge, you will establish you competitiveness, you good health, and undermine criticisms that you are too old to be president.

Newt made a challenge to debate with Obama: he would allow the latter to use the teleprompter. Well, Ron you could make a similar offer to fatso Newt: you'll spot him 10 percen of the time; for example, Ron, you will give Newt a 10-meter lead in the swim or 20 meters in the run, etc.

This challenge could be made at a press conference, or at an upcoming debate when and if someone brings up your age, or in an advert. Why not use this particular strength of yours to your advantage?

In one of the debates, you jokingly mentioned you would enter a 25-mile bike race with any of your three Republican competitors in the Texas heat. That was a good start. What I have in mind here is a much more formal challenge. Even if none of them take you up on it, getting this in front of the mainstream media, and hopefully, accurately to the people (ha, ha) ought to allay concerns about your age.

VI. Publicity

The essays in this section are an attempt to do two things. One, promote publicity for Congressman Ron Paul. Here, the interpretation of articles discussing his likely pick for vice president, or Supreme Court nominees, is mainly an attempt to publicize his campaign. By discussing these choices, the goal is to make it more likely that he will one day be faced with actually making them, from the vantage point of the White House. But there is a second agenda as well: to help with the transition period. If Dr. Paul becomes our next president, he will indeed need to pick a vice president, and, perhaps, some replacements on the Supreme Court. If so, then, perhaps, these essays will be of some help to him and his staff.

Chapter 19

Ron Paul *Can* Triumph

If Ron Paul can somehow win the presidential nomination of the Republican Party, he will have an excellent chance of beating Barack Obama in November 2012. He will, of course, face great obstacles in the Republican primaries, but, if he can overcome them, it ought to be downhill after that.

Why will the congressman from Texas have a good shot at beating a sitting president during (non-declared) war time?

Paul can out-left Obama on foreign policy and personal liberties, and thus make gigantic inroads on the latter's base, while at the same time maintain his right-wing credentials on economics.

Not only has Obama not fully withdrawn the U.S. from Iraq as promised, he has involved us in yet another undeclared war in Libya. He has expanded the hostilities from Afghanistan to Pakistan, utilizing drone strikes. He has presided over the murder of dozens of Yemenis, none of whom posed any threat to our shores. He has allowed torture for the WikiLeaker, and on U.S. territory. Obama is responsible for the biggest military spending in the history of the world, has bailed out fat cats from Wall Street to Detroit, and still has not closed down our torture chamber in Cuba, again as promised. Ron Paul, in contrast, opposes corporate welfare, and would not only exit, and forthwith, from Iraq, Afghanistan, Libya, but would do so for hundreds (yes, *hundreds*) of other nations ranging from Germany to Japan to vast parts of South America, Asia, and Africa. What on earth are we still doing in all these faraway places, the left wing of the Democratic Party might well ask?

A Paul Administration would hack away heavily at the previously sacrosanct military budget, radically tackling our financial crisis without any need to raise our debt ceiling once again. In contrast, it will be the same old, same old, from Obama. The deficits will continue to be monetized by the Fed, creating inflation, and thus exacerbating poverty (Isn't the left supposed to be against poverty?) and further decreasing the value of the sinking dollar.

Another area in which Obama's base will actually prefer Paulian policy is drug legalization. Disproportionate numbers of young black men are now in jail for engaging in this victimless crime, and all too many others of them have perished from violence due to prohibition (Aren't "progressives" supposed to favor the black community?). Have we learned nothing from our dire experience with the prohibition of alcohol? The country to the south of us is unraveling at a ferocious pace due to these selfsame drug laws, and we ourselves cannot much longer remain immune from the whirlwind this legislation has created.

Of course, Paul's policies on eliminating U.S. imperialism abroad and saving us from the scourge of drug prohibition at home will not resonate too well with the conservative Republicans, who are pretty rabid in the wrong direction on both issues. And, while Representative Paul has made great strides in denigrating the central planning Fed and promoting the 100 percent gold-backed dollar as a method of quelling the business cycle with its heightened unemployment and bankruptcies, it cannot be said that this is at all acceptable to the party faithful on either side of the aisle. (Do both the left and the right favor our current depression?)

Dr. Paul is particularly vulnerable on the question of Israel, in the view of some people. He wants to end so-called "foreign aid" (more accurately and less pejoratively translated into "government-to-government transfers of funds," which does not at all imply program benefits). But this would mean that the only functioning democracy in the Middle East would have its financial support taken away from it. However, U.S. transfers of funds to Israel's enemies in the Arab world vastly outweigh that given to this country alone. This home of the Jewish people would have less money (private donations would of course be unaffected) from the U.S. government absolutely, but relative to its enemies it would actually gain. As well, these funds render the Israeli economy less efficient than would otherwise be the case. These points have recently been appreciated by the Jerusalem Institute for Market Studies. For more on why Ron Paul should be greatly appreciated by the Jewish community.

Social Security, too, is a sacred cow amongst the Republicans. So much for their adherence to the philosophy of free enterprise. But this is actually a vast left-wing conspiracy (FDR inaugurated it). Bernie

Madoff just went to prison for something very much along these Ponzi-scheme lines. The idea behind this "third rail" of American politics is that people are too stupid to save for their old age, and the state must force them to do so, for their own good. But if the electorate is that deranged, how can we allow them to vote at all, let alone to expect them to mark their ballot boxes wisely. And, how is it that they are so wise so as to elect politicians who will then correct these errors of theirs? No, this policy rends asunder family ties between the younger and older generations, and is not needed. Just because some few will act in a silly manner is no reason to forcibly victimize all of us with the Ponzi scheme. Ron will end this sacred cow, but the Republicans, to say nothing of the Democrats, will not like it one bit.

But at least this statesman from Texas is not a socialist like Romney with his medical plan for Massachusetts which anticipated Obama's compulsory support for the health insurance industry. Dr. Paul would rely, instead, on a truly free market in medicine to drive prices down to reasonable levels, as this system has done in all other industries that have been left relatively free. Capitalism works for everything else, why not health care? Nor is Congressman Paul a theocratic imperialist as is Mike Huckabee, nor is he a lightweight of the order of Sarah Palin, nor is he a flake like Donald Trump, whose main accomplishment in politics is to force Obama to release his birth certificate. So, will Ron win the Republican nomination, and then go on to victory in the next election?

All we can say for sure is that the next political cycle is likely to be fought over ideas and philosophies, not personalities as in the past, if Paul gets the nod from the Republicans.

Chapter 20.

Ron Paul Can't Win? BS

The latest entry into this sweepstakes is the War Street Journal (1/20/12). They opine of Dr. Paul "He knows he can't win, but he wants to use his delegates to hold the Republican Party hostage to his views on national security and presidential power."

How come no one in the mainstream media says that Donald Trump can't win? That Michelle Bachmann can't win? That Rick Perry can't win? That Jon Huntsman can't win? That Herman Cain can't win? That Mitt Romney can't win? That Newt Gingrich can't win? That Rick Santorum can't win?

Why is it that ONLY Ron Paul can't win? Lookit, when there are almost a dozen initial candidates, all but one of them "can't win."

Let me assure the War Street Journal: Not only CAN Ron Paul win, not only does he WANT to win, but, stick this in your pipe and smoke it, he WILL win.

Arguendo, it is entirely possible that "Ron Paul didn't win Iowa. He didn't win New Hampshire. He won't win here on Saturday, and he won't win Florida. The Texas congressman will not likely be the first choice for Republican nominee in a single U.S. state." However, if he keeps coming in second and third, and no one else wins all the contested states, he might well amass enough delegates to win. So far, Santorum won in Iowa, Romney in New Hampshire, and if Gingrich takes South Carolina, this scenario looks as if it has some legs.

But, the main reason Congressman Paul is not taking first place is the incessant media chatter that Obama will beat him; he is not "electable." However, at least so far, only Paul and Romney tie Obama. When this begins to percolate through the electorate, we will see not only second- and third-place showings, but some wins for liberty as well.

Chapter 21.

President Ron Paul's Likely Supreme Court Nominations

Who will President Ron Paul nominate for any Supreme Court vacancies that occur during his first administration, 2012-2016?

Before we get down to specifics, here are a few introductory remarks.

First off, we must deal with some objections.

One objection is that it is extremely unlikely that Dr. Paul will become president, in the view of some. Why, then, waste time ruminating about his Supreme Court appointments, when he will not ever be called upon to make any such decisions. Yes, it is not likely that he will be chosen by the Republican Party for a face-off with President Obama. To win the Republication nomination may not be in the cards. However, if he does, he has far more than a good chance of beating Barack Obama in November. And, when this finally dawns on the rank and file Republicans, he may well win the first-round race against Romney and company. So, who knows? If the congressman from Texas can somehow utilize the fact that even nowadays he does better in projected races against the incumbent than most of his primary competition, he might yet become the Republican standard bearer.

Here is another objection. According to Lew Rockwell, Ron Paul is of the opinion that there is no mandate that a Supreme Court judge be a lawyer, that clerks can supply needed technical knowledge, and that he would like to see, say, an economist on the court. Despite this, there is still a justification for the present essay. For one thing, Ron Paul will certainly not *exclude* people from consideration just because they chose to become lawyers. Thus, the lists compiled below will still be of help to him, since he will undoubtedly want to begin his search in the widest reasonable manner possible. Second, I hate to say this, but the congressman from Texas is a *politician*. That means, among other things, that he will have to *compromise* from time to time. Now, of course, it is not within Dr. Paul's DNA to be deflected from libertarian *principle*. It is not for nothing that he is known, near and wide, as "Dr. No." But, there is nothing at all in the entire corpus of libertarian law that would preclude him from selecting an attorney for this purpose. Suppose that Congress will not support any of Ron's nominations to the Supreme Court who are not members of this profession. Then, the next president of the United States, I imagine, will face a stark choice: leave unfilled seats on the highest court in the land, or, compromise with his stated openness to appoint an economist. Under these conditions, I will stake my bottom dollar that our man will give way, and appoint a lawyer to the bench, provided of course, he can find one, see below, who otherwise fits the bill.

Here is a second reason for seriously considering the scenario of Dr. Paul appointing one or more Supreme Court judges. Primary candidates are judged by the electorate on the basis of many considerations. Foreign policy, domestic programs, plans for the economy, views on civil liberties and personal freedom, etc. But, surely, one of the criteria is, wait for it, possible appointments to the Supreme Court of the United States. If only for that reason it behooves us to consider his possible choices in this regard.

A third justification for our present deliberations is the sheer *joy* of doing so. How many times in the entire history of the universe has it been even a remote possibility that a libertarian president could actually appoint libertarian judges to the Supreme Court? Would that Murray Rothbard were alive on this day?. He would have been jumping with glee. If there is no other reason for contemplating this situation, this one alone would surely suffice.

But there is one more as well. It is important that we recognize libertarian legal scholars, and that they become aware of one another, so as to better and more efficiently promote liberty. Even if Ron Paul were not a serious candidate for the presidency of the U.S., these speculations would still be worthwhile on that account alone.

Okay, already. We have justified, or at least attempted to do so, this initiative. How shall we now proceed with the specifics?

First, we shall limit our considerations to those with a law degree. In my judgment, there are indeed numerous scholars without this credential (foremost among them at present, Hans Hoppe, and, surely, in the previous generation, Murray Rothbard) who have made important contributions to legal theory of the sort that Congressman Paul would appreciate. However, we are already going pretty far out on the proverbial limb merely to posit a Paul Administration (true confession, here; I really like the sound of that), one that could actually accomplish something important in the face of a Congress to say the least, is unlikely in the extreme to fully support him. (Although, when he beats Obama, he will find that his coattails have vastly expanded.) Why risk total incredulity by supposing Ron to nominate someone without a law degree, when there are many worthwhile candidates with this credential?

What kind of legal theorist is Congressman Paul likely to nominate for the Supreme Court? Obviously, one who supports his limited government, private property, economic and personal freedom and constitutional philosophy.

Right off the bat this eliminates from consideration several lawyers who are conservatives, not libertarians. For example, Richard Posner. Erudite, brilliant, even, certainly vastly productive in terms of his published output, this economist-lawyer-philosopher is an enemy of private property rights, not a supporter. We can also strike off our list Randy Barnett who is, paradoxically, in many, many ways, a libertarian. He has made numerous original contributions to our understanding of libertarian law. However, Randy Barnett is a warmonger, and that alone ought to remove him from consideration. Roger Pilon, too, must be struck off the list. I hate to add yet one more person to the list of libertarians unlikely in the extreme to be appointed by Ron Paul, well, for anything, but we cannot ignore Ilya Somin either.

Further, there are several people who would otherwise qualify, but for their advanced ages, or infirmities. Henry Manne and Gordon Tullock come to mind in this regard. Both have law degrees, and have made signal contributions to free market jurisprudence, on at least some issues. (I wish the late Bernie Siegan were still alive; he would fit in well in this category). However, surely, Ron would want to appoint a younger man, someone in his forties or fifties, or even thirties, if he could find someone with a strong track record at that early age.

Alright, alright already, we are all on pins and needles to find out not who Dr. Paul will not nominate, but who he will. So, cough up some names already, impatient readers will likely demand at this point.

My first nomination is of course Andrew Napolitano. As an ex-judge, surely he has an inside track. I hesitate to mention him in this context because I see him more as a vice-presidential candidate than a potential Supreme Court judge. But, if Dr. Paul chooses someone else for that position, it is hard to imagine a better nomination than Andrew.

There is also a sitting judge, U.S. Federal District Court of New Orleans, Martin Feldman, who is a personal friend of Judge Napolitano. Marty, who on October 12, 1983, was appointed United States District Judge for the Eastern District of Louisiana by President Reagan, is justly famous for lifting President Obama's ban on deep water oil drilling in the Gulf of Mexico. One trouble with Judge Feldman for this purpose is that he is closer to the end of his career than to the beginning of it.

Alex Kozinski is Chief Judge of the United States Court of Appeals for the Ninth Circuit. His rulings have at least a slight libertarian bent. This makes him a natural for consideration. The only problem with his candidacy is that he was born in 1950, and thus will be 62 when Ron Paul is sworn in. Not too old, surely, but, at least, on the borderline.

Another good candidate is Richard Epstein. This longtime University of Chicago now NYU professor of law is widely respected in the field, even by some on the other side of the aisle. I cannot bring myself to agree with everything he has written, but I am sure that Congressman Paul will be a big-tent-enough president to stretch all the way to the "libertarianism" of Richard Epstein. In my own view, Epstein occupies ground near the border between libertarianism and classical liberalism, just on the good side of this line in the sand. Were he a solid libertarian, I would not have written so much criticism of his publications.

My next suggestion is a dark horse candidate as far as the legal profession is concerned. He has fewer publications in prestigious law reviews than does the man mentioned above. However, as far as the libertarian movement is concerned, I regard Stephan Kinsella as our leading legal theoretician. Whenever I am puzzled by arcane libertarian legal theory, it is to Stephan that I first turn. He has elevated our understanding of private property rights, and punishment theory, and his contributions to the issue of patents and copyrights have been nothing short of magnificent.

I single out one last person for particular mention because he is so young. Although there are other legal scholars on my master list below who are as youthful as Jacob Huebert, his accomplishments at such a young age make him quite remarkable.

There are many other worthwhile candidates for a Paul Administration to consider. I list them in alphabetical order, below. All of them qualify under the criteria I have set out. However, I myself am only a dabbler when it comes to my understanding of this field. So, gentle reader, I ask for your help. If I have inadvertently left out anyone who belongs on this list (or less likely, have included anyone who should not be on it), please let me know. I intend to make good any errors of omission or commission I may have committed in the permanent version of this essay that will remain on LewRockwell.com.

Here, without any further ado, is my stab at a comprehensive list of libertarian legal theorists. For purposes of comprehensiveness, I include some names I do not think would be good candidates.

It will be up to President Paul's team to go over this list, and others like it, with a fine-tooth comb. Hopefully, this compilation will serve as a good starting point for that process.

Paul Aubert, Daren Bakst, Randy Barnett, William Barnett II, Jeffrey Barr, Scott Bauer, Joe Becker, Shana Black, Clint Bolick, Don Boudreaux, Scott Bullock, Gary Chartier, Carrie Ann Citren, Dick Clark, Mila Cobanov-Vecore, Jeff Deist, John Denson, David Dieteman, Brad Edmonds, Richard Epstein, Marty Feldman, Deanna Forbush French, Kurt Gerry, David Gruning, John Hasnas, Jared Hausmann, Jule Herbert, Jacob Hornberger, Jacob Huebert, Lee Iglody, Stephan Kinsella, Manuel S. Klausner, Thomas Lambert, Bart Lee, George Leef, Glen Lenihan, Dan Levine, Robert Levy, Floy Lilly, Geoffrey Manne, Henry Manne, David Mayer, Bob McGee, Todd McMullan, William Mellor, Andrew Morriss, Andrew Napolitano, Nadia Nedzel, Clark Neily, James Ostrowski, R. J. Peltz, Stewart Rhodes, Roger Roots, Clay Rossi, Noah D. Rubins, Matt Saltzman, Butler Shaffer, Norman Singleton, Brad Smith, Jeff Snyder, John Sotirakis, Maurice Thompson, Patrick Tinsley, Gordon Tullock, Jim Viator, Marc Victor, Eugene Volokh, Roy Whitehead, Joshua Wright.

Here are some more names that have come to me in response to my queries; but I am less sure of these than others: Jonathan Adler, J. Michael Altman, Steve Bainbridge, Stuart Benjamin, Adam Clanton, Ronald Coffey, George Dent, Eric Gookin, Gene Healy, Christine Hurt, Stavros Katsios, Russell Korobkin, David Mayer, David Post, Glenn Reynolds, Ron Rychlak, Sukrit Sabhlok, Emmanouil Savoidakis, Ilya Shapiro, Keith Sharfman, Bill Sjostrom, Justin Skidmore, Brad Smith, Gordon Smith, R. Ben Sperry, Maria Topakitzian, Fred Tung, Bryan Dean Wilson.

Here are the names I am now adding, thanks to the responses of the first publication of this essay: Janice Rogers Brown, Lloyd Cohen, Steven Eagle Robert Fast, Bruce Fein, Kevin Gutzman (I had over a dozen letters objecting to my not including this name in my first draft, way more than for anyone else; so, this omission was by far my biggest error in the previous version of this essay), Thomas Hazlett, Christopher Horner, Sam Kazman, Michael Krauss, Jonathan R. Macey, Kevin A. McCabe, Todd Ptak, Paul Sherman, W. Randall Stroud, Jonathan Turley, Edwin Vieira, Jr., Patrick Wood, Todd Zywicki.

I am delighted that many of our libertarian students at Loyola University New Orleans went off to law school for their graduate education, since I arrived there in 2001, and are now attorneys:

Max Chiz, Dreda Culpepper, Tiffany Fleming, Jamie Ianelli, Emily Kott, Christie LaPorte, Mike Lloyd, Joe Morrel, Michael O'Brian, Greg Rome, Brandon Thibodeaux, Katherine Wingfield.

Who knows, maybe one day some of them will be considered for the Supreme Court by a Rand Paul Administration.

Do foreigners count? That is, may Ron nominate one of them to our Supreme Court? I have no idea. But, if he can, here are some possibilities:

Martin Fronek, Remigijus Šimašius, Lithuania; Avril Allen, Walter Boytinck, Kelly Connell, Derek From, Gary Mah, Andrei Mincov, Stephen Paine, Daniel Roncani, Tom Ross, Chris Schafer, Karen Selick, Mike Sporer, Canada; Frank van Dun, Belgium.

None of these people have given me their names, or permission to use them in this context. Many were gathered from questionnaires. My intention in listing these names is to be as inclusive as possible. I do so based on the maxim that it is easier to erase names that do not belong here, than to add those who do. I have purposefully erred, if I have, in the direction of inclusiveness. Since I am not a lawyer by profession, I am not as aware as I might be about the libertarian qualifications of all the people I have mentioned. I shall leave this for others to sort out. There are several people I have mentioned who might not consider themselves libertarians. Their inclusion is then my assessment, not theirs.

I thank Stephan Kinsella and Lew Rockwell for helpful comments on an earlier version of this chapter.

Chapter 22.

Ron Paul's Vice-Presidential Choices

22.1 The Vice-Presidential Sweepstakes, Part I

by Walter Block and Steve Berger

Politico has focused on the vice presidential sweepstakes, and who are we to demur? Of course, this organization does not mention Congressman Ron Paul as a viable candidate, and, on this, we agree. Dr. Paul will, instead, become president of the United States in 2012, so he will just not be available to be anyone else's vice president.

However, he will need one of these for himself, and that is the subject of our present deliberations. Who will Ron Paul choose? Who should he choose? In order to make these deliberations easier for the incoming administration, we venture forth with our own opinions on this crucial matter of the day. Accordingly, we list several possibilities, with our comments about each, some of them snarky, attached. So as to not prejudice anyone, we list these choices in alphabetical order.

Michele Bachmann. No one who takes Mises's books to the beach for some light reading can be entirely ruled out of these sweepstakes, and Congressman Bachmann, say what negative you will of her otherwise, qualifies for serious consideration, at least on this one ground. Of course, it is extremely unlikely she has done any such thing. However, merely for mentioning Mises's name in a positive context, she deserves some kudos, and mention on this list. On other issues, her candidacy is not at all attractive. For example, she is a bloodthirsty warmonger, pretty much of the same ilk as all other candidates for the Republican nomination.

Mitch Daniels, governor of Indiana, was early on mentioned as a potential presidential candidate based on his turnaround of state finances in Indiana, his forthright, no-nonsense style of leadership and his frequently voiced opposition to crony capitalism, including a June, 2010 *Wall Street Journal* op-ed. The State of Indiana was a lonely holdout in the Chrysler bond reorganization and quite vocal in its opposition to Obama's arbitrary and capricious cram-down of senior bondholders to the benefit of the auto unions. As governor, he also privatized the Indiana state toll road so that should be dear to libertarian hearts. Unfortunately Mitch Daniels' record on Iraq when he was Director of Office of Management and Budget (OMB) under Bush isn't compelling.

Doug French, the president of the Mises Institute, and a former banker (and former football player as well), is a long shot. He is the "favorite son" of no particular state, having spent time in Nevada getting his master's degree under the tutelage of Murray N. Rothbard, playing college football in Kansas and now residing in Alabama. He would, then, be unlikely to be selected as vice president by any of the ordinary Republican candidates. However, we are now discussing the choices of Congressman Ron Paul, someone likely to judge a VP candidate on his merits. And, here, there is little question: under a French presidency, we would have peace abroad and economic tranquility at home. That is to say, Mr. French would faithfully follow the Ron Paul philosophy.

Jim Grant, former Barron's columnist, founder and editor of Grant's Interest Rate Observer, author of Money of the Mind, a history of credit booms and busts in the United States, and a frequent guest on Bloomberg and CNBC, is well-known for his florid and witty literary style and trenchant criticism of the Federal Reserve and Keynesian economic policies. Jim is an ardent backer of hard money and is admired by legions of investors for his intellectual honesty and wit. He would be a compelling proponent for a return to free market money and for repeal of the Dodd-Frank financial strangulation bill.

Gary Johnson. It is too bad that the former governor of New Mexico as of the time of this writing has not been able to enter into the debates. If he did so, then there would be, not one, but two libertarians on stage at these important events. On the other hand, we know Ron Paul, and Gary Johnson is no Ron Paul. He is more of a "beltway" or Reason Magazine or Cato libertarian than a real one. He is far better than the neocons on foreign policy, but does not call for a purely defensive stance for our military. He wants to legalize drugs, but only some of them; he did not pardon any victimless criminals when he could have as governor. He favors the legalization of prostitution, but not based on a matter of rights; merely utilitarianism. He urges reform of the Fed, not abolition. Go down the entire list: he is pretty good on most issues from a libertarian point of view, but doesn't hit the bull's eye on any of them.

Andrew Napolitano. The judge has a print and electronic record a mile long. And, he keeps hitting home runs; no Gary Johnson, he. Judge Napolitano is a charismatic, telegenic presence who is always willing to stand up to the Fox News neo-nuts who clamor for war mongering and Wall Street bailouts. With a Paul/Napolitano ticket, the Republicans would finally have a team that has read, understood, and would *honor* the original intent of the Constitution. This includes reducing the power of the imperial presidency, engaging in wars for only self-defense purposes, ensuring that Congress declares them, freeing up the economy and promoting personal liberty and responsibility. In any one-on-one debate, Napolitano would overwhelm Biden.

Rand Paul. There have been father and son presidents in the past. The Adamses and the Bushes come to mind. Well, let's forget the latter duo, please. There has never been a father-son pair running for president and vice president at the same time, however. Well, there is thus a case for breaking that particular pattern. A Paul-Paul Republican ticket would be unique, and attract global attention on that ground alone. It would certainly lay to rest any fears about Ron Paul's age; should he, God forbid, perish in office, there would be another Paul immediately ready to step into the breach. (Not that this is a reasonable fear: A former track runner, Congressman Paul could run rings around any of them. However, we make a concession here: if there was a pie-eating contest, our money would be on Newt Gingrich). One more reason for a Rand Paul vice-presidential run: think of how that would upset the Republican hierarchy. On the other hand, this senator from Kentucky recently voted *in favor* of sanctions against Iran. This one error does not disqualify him, but it certainly constitutes a black mark against him.

Lew Rockwell. A former advisor to Ron Paul, Lew Rockwell would make an excellent running mate for the congressman from Texas. Lew is knowledgeable, and passionate about a peaceful foreign policy, economic freedom, and personal liberty. Thus, he fully mirrors the Ron Paul philosophy. There is, however, one drawback to Mr. Rockwell as vice president, and it is a serious one. If he went off to Washington, D.C., in this capacity, who would run LewRockwell.Com? The present authors look with dismay at the prospect of this blog being run by anyone else. Nevertheless, if there were a button we could push that would install Lew as VP, we would blister our thumbs pushing that button.

Tom Sowell. If taking high elective office were a matter of promoting personal liberties and economics freedom, Professor Sowell would be our man. Not only has he made the libertarian case as far as economics and personal rights are concerned, he has been widely, and unfairly criticized for doing do. "Oreo cookie" is only a relatively polite manner in which he has been castigated. However, there is a lacuna in the Sowell curriculum vitae: foreign policy. He is a war hawk, and thus does not deserve space on any Paul ticket. However, his contributions have been so important and insightful in economics and personal freedom, that he deserves an honorable mention on this list.

Jon Stewart. The acclaimed host of The Daily Show on Comedy Central, he recently excoriated the mainstream media for ignoring Ron Paul's success in the August Iowa straw poll, and Ron has been a frequent and well-received guest on his show. Jon is America's preeminent political satirist, and his shows and publications reveal a striking independence of political thought. To those who exclaim 'how can we recommend a comedian for high office?' We would respond: Better a comedian than an actor, bodybuilder, attorney, deranged neo-nut or community organizer who never held a "real" job. His sense of humor and satire would quickly pierce through the absurdity of the welfare/warfare state and crony capitalism. Further, what better mode of defusing international tensions than having Jon give a monologue at a G7 meeting? Imagine how much damage we would have been spared if only HL Mencken had been put in high office. Since Mr. Stewart is a big-government liberal, he is not a serious candidate for running mate for Congressman Paul. However, his hilarious attack on the mainstream media for ignoring Dr. Paul after the Ames Straw poll merits him mention on this list.

John Stossel. Say what you will about this man, he is no Jon Stewart when it comes to political philosophy. Stossel is the equal of Stewart as far as performing brilliantly on television, but unlike the latter, he is a staunch libertarian (well, a bit too much tied in to the Cato-Reason crowd). For years, Stossel has been a one-man-band undermining the nanny state's interferences with consumer welfare. Of course he has not been elected to political office. But that should not be an insuperable barrier for a man with strong libertarian beliefs. Who would the libertarians rather trust with the reins of the state apparatus? John Stossel, or Rick Perry/ Mitt Romney? We rest our case.

22.2. The Vice-Presidential Sweepstakes, Part II

By Walter Block and Steve Berger

Who should Ron Paul choose for vice president, when he wins the Republican nomination for president? The present authors have already taken one hack at this crucial question of the day, and are now back for round two. Again we mention several possibilities, so as to ease the way for the Ron Paul team on that day they must make this decision. Here are the additional possibilities, as we see them.

Herman Cain. Ron Paul would never in a million years choose this man because he is black, so as to defend against the charge that he is a racist. He need not do so. Dr. Paul is just about the most color blind man we know in U.S. politics, slurs to the contrary notwithstanding. In the view of the Congressman from Texas, "Racism is simply an ugly form of collectivism, the mindset that views humans strictly as members of groups rather than individuals. Racists believe that all individuals who share superficial physical characteristics are alike: as collectivists, racists think only in terms of groups. By encouraging Americans to adopt a group mentality, the advocates of so-called 'diversity' actually perpetuate racism. Their obsession with racial group identity is inherently racist. The true antidote to racism is liberty. Liberty means having a limited, constitutional government devoted to the protection of individual rights rather than group claims. Liberty means free-market capitalism, which rewards individual achievement and competence, not skin color, gender, or ethnicity." So, what are the merits and demerits of placing Mr. Cain on the Ron Paul ticket? On the plus side, he is a successful businessman, very articulate, even charismatic. He is pretty good on economic issues, albeit a bit too soft on unions for our taste. Unfortunately, his foreign policy planks are not at all compatible with Ron Paul's emphasis on defense, not offense. Cain makes no such distinction on his website, and this is a crucial oversight.

Dennis Kucinich. He is a Democrat. Dr. Paul is a Republican. Have we lost our minds? No. (Well, at least not for this reason.) Congressman Kucinich is an ally of Congressman Paul's at least insofar as foreign policy is concerned, and that is no small achievement for a member of *either* party. However, unfortunately, while Kucinich is excellent on war and peace, and is not so bad on personal liberties, he is a big-government liberal when it comes to economics. Thus, no sale, here.

However, he does deserve mention in our compilation for his support of Dr. No on a very important public policy.

Karen Kwiatkowski. She is a retired U.S. Air Force Lieutenant Colonel and a regular contributor to LewRockwell.com. She is currently running for the 6th District of Virginia House seat. Her place on the ticket would underscore, ever the more, that of all Republican candidates for president, Ron Paul not only receives the most donations from members of the U.S. military, he garners more from this source *than all of the others put together.* If her presence on the ticket will not banish forever the calumny that Dr. Paul is "weak" on defense, then nothing will. If Hillary is Obama's VP choice in 2012, Colonel Kwiatkowski's presence on the Paul team will help counteract that perceived benefit. However, Congressman Paul will *not* choose her for that reason. He will do so, if he does, because he trusts Karen Kwiatkowski to promote liberty, freedom, and constitutionalism. Can you imagine the magnificent thrashing Karen wouldwill give Hillary in a vice-presidential debate!?!

Lewis Lehrman. He is co-author with Ron Paul on the book, The Case for Gold. Needless to say, Mr. Lehrman is sound as a bell on monetary questions, crucial for understanding the present plight of the American economy. In 1981, he ran for governor of New York State, losing by only a few percentage point to Mario Cuomo. He was a fellow member with Ron Paul of the U.S. Gold Commission; the two co-authored its minority report. Ron knows and trusts Lewis. The two would make a great team.

Rick Perry. He is a blowhard, doesn't have a freedom-oriented bone in his body, was recently, ugh, a Democrat, and a strong supporter for, double ugh, Al Gore. However, fair is fair. No one who dumps on the Fed can be all bad. He characterized Ben Bernanke as "treasonous." While Ron Paul does not employ such language and prefers to criticize ideas, not people, Perry deserves inclusion on this list of possibles for his stalwart condemnation of the Fed. Of course, a Paul-Perry ticket would not be exactly geographically "balanced," but that would not stop Dr. Paul from choosing Governor Perry as his running mate, if the latter were worthy. But, alas, he is not worthy.

Peter Schiff. The CEO of Euro Pacific Capital, he is an esteemed investor and outspoken advocate for hard money, free markets and the end of crony capitalism. He is author of primers on investing and economics and is an accomplished Austrian economist (as is Ron

Paul). Amidst great and raucous laughter, Schiff flashed early warning signs of the housing and subprime mortgage bubbles that brought America's financial system to its knees. Peter Schiff continues to sound the alarm bells on sovereign debt bubbles, the perils of central banking and Keynesian fiscal policies. In 2010, Peter ran for U.S. Senate from the state of Connecticut. He was a formidable debater and continues to make frequent guest appearances on CNBC and Bloomberg. Peter didn't fall far from the tree. His heroic father, Irwin Schiff, is a noted tax protester, who challenged the constitutionality of the federal income tax and is serving a 13-year federal sentence for tax crimes. Bush the younger waged an unconstitutional, immoral war on Iraq to avenge the "failures" of Bush the elder to trample Saddam. By contrast, Peter can be expected to wage a moral, constitutional war to validate the efforts of his father to unmask the illegitimacy of the IRS, yet another project of Ron Pauls'. For his extremely bearish views on the U.S. economy, Mr. Schiff has earned the title, Dr. Doom. Can you imagine the combination of Dr. No and Dr. Doom? This would give rise to the slogan: "No Doom with the Paul-Schiff team."

Jesse Ventura. He was elected governor of Minnesota as an independent on a budget of only $300,000. He is a staunch Ron Paulite on economics, personal liberty, and, most important, foreign policy. He has been an outspoken critic of government propaganda and deception in war. His recent book is all about the government's biggest lies. Ventura, along with Ron Paul himself, is that rare breed of politician willing to be outspoken and candid regardless of political consequences. He would be like a breath of fresh air on the Ron Paul ticket.

Walter Williams. If we were considering the criteria of adherence to economic liberty and individual personal freedom, there are few people more qualified to be Ron Paul's running mate than Williams. A black man like his mentor and friend Thomas Sowell, Williams has taken quite a bit of unfair criticism for being a "traitor" to his race, since he favors laissez-faire capitalism and private property rights. Again, like Sowell, he has done more than practically anyone else on the globe to expose the idiocy, immorality and inefficiency of our affirmative action industry. However, and this is a big however, Prof. Williams "parts company" with Ron Paul over foreign policy. Therefore, although he richly deserves mention in this compilation, we would reject him as a leading candidate for VP on the Ron Paul ticket.

The lead author of this essay is particularly proud that Williams is one of his co-authors.

Tom Woods. He would be an excellent choice. An avid Catholic, he would "balance" Congressman Paul's Protestantism. More to the point, Woods is "solid" on every conceivable libertarian issue, likely even more so than Dr. Paul himself. Although a relatively young man, phenomenally productive Dr. Woods (Ph.D. from Columbia in history) has published 11 books and is the editor of five others, enough, more than enough, for an illustrious entire career. We doubt that his parents gave him "Charisma" as a middle name, but in failing to do so, they missed a bet. Tom Woods is perhaps the most charismatic public speaker on the planet, putting Barack (teleprompter) Obama to shame. A dark horse candidate? Yes. But a worthy one. A very worthy one. The present authors would sleep a lot easier each night with Tom Woods in the position of vice president.

Honorable mention:

There were numerous letters sent to us in response to our first attempt to shed light on this important decision. Many suggested names we had not included in our first go around, including some of the above. Also among them were almost all of the senior fellows of the Mises Institute. In addition, the following people were mentioned, and we pass them along in alphabetical order without comment, except for one case: Jim DeMint, William Grigg, Richard Mack, Fred Reed, Paul Craig Roberts (not a supporter of full free trade and thus highly problematic), Lawrence Vance and Jack Wheeler. Certainly, these names should all be placed at least on the Ron Paul team's initial list.

Chapter 23.

The 2008 campaign

The following five chapters were originally written in 2007, and thus apply, mainly, to the 2008 campaign. But, without that initial effort, my thought is that Ron Paul would not be doing as magnificently as he is now doing. Thus, even though this material might be seen by some as out of date, I think that it is part of the historical record of the greatest promotion of the ideas of liberty, ever, and thus worth preserving.

23.1 Ron Paul Can Too Win

Here are some arguments, to be refuted, criticizing Ron Paul's chances of being elected.

1. There's more to life than winning. Even if the congressman from Texas doesn't win this time, still, he is spreading the libertarian message like pretty much NO ONE else before him. (Yes, Ayn Rand, Murray Rothbard and Ludwig von Mises popularized libertarianism, but none of them did so in the political sphere). Our refusal to support him can't help this campaign. I would think that as a libertarian, we would want to help this effort, whether Dr. Paul wins or not. We should all get behind him as strongly as we can. This is perhaps the best opportunity in a long while to introduce libertarianism to the wider public.

2. Barry Goldwater didn't "win," even though he got the Republican nomination. But, he set the groundwork for Ronald Reagan, who did win, later on. Even if Ron Paul doesn't win, if he does well he can set things up for the next libertarian candidate who can potentially attract masses of people to the libertarian message, and then perhaps even "win." We can all help with this initiative. (I'm not a fan of either Goldwater or Reagan, since I don't regard either as libertarians; I'm only using them as an example to illustrate the point.)

3. Don't be sure Ron can't win. No one, right before the fall of the Berlin Wall, or of the U.S.S.R., thought that either of these things

would happen, not even the "experts." No one now thinks Ron can win....

4. Here's the case for Dr. Paul winning the Republican nomination. The Iraqi "police action" deteriorates even further. Ron is the ONLY Republican candidate who will be no Johnny-come-lately to the anti-war position. Mitt Romney changes his mind on this, but is dismissed as the waffler he is. The others split the pro-Iraqi war Republican vote. One by one they fall out. (Even at this early date, Ron Paul already has more money in the bank than John McCain. Strange, it turns out that the one congressman who demands fiscal responsibility of this august body is also the only candidate who is responsible with his own money.) Ron sticks it out until the bitter end. He doesn't need as much money as the others, since his supporters are very committed to him. Let's say, finally, it is Ron vs. Giuliani. Then, a new scandal erupts (Rudy did drugs, was divorced even more than we think he was, harassed even more innocent businessmen, whatever). Dr. Paul wins the Republican nomination.

In their defense, it cannot be denied, the other Republican candidates will say that the war was not a bad idea but it was badly executed, "and here's how things will be different when I am president." But the American people are not infinitely stupid -- even Bryan Caplan (2007) does not go that far. They have already heard this sort of thing hundreds of times. By the time the primaries are over and the convention begins, they will have heard it even more. Eventually, enough of them will tire of it, particularly as the body bags mount up.

5. Here's the case for Dr. Ron Paul winning the overall election, against whoever the Democrats nominate. Now Ron faces, say, a Hillary-Obama ticket. He kicks their butt, again, over the deteriorating Iraqi war situation. There is no way these war-mongering chameleons will be able to attain the mantle of isolationist foreign policy. With a country heartily sick of U.S. Imperialism, the Republicans hold their noses and vote for Ron against the Hated Hillary. The Democrats desert in droves over the war. It is a super "keep clean for Gene" (McCarthy) scenario. Likely? No. Impossible? Not at all. Ron Paul will actually have a better chance in the general election than in the primaries, much like Rudy.

6. Can't happen? Give me some odds on a bet. (According to some polls, the odds against Ron winning are 200-1). I'm willing to put up

$1 against the $200 of all suckers, sorry, I meant takers, that my favorite Texas congressman will win.

Libertarians should be relatively happy with either Thompson or Giuliani, in comparison to any Democrat.

Well, maybe this applies to some "libertarians" who believe in pre-emptive war as "defense" and who are weak, to boot, on economic and personal liberties issues. But for real libertarians, the non-aggression principle is and must ever be foremost. That means a strong *defense*, but *not* maintaining our stance as policemen of the world. The Thompsons and Giulianis of the world support our present system in which U.S. soldiers are posted in hundreds of other countries as trip wires. Whenever there is a local conflagration, we are involved. This is *defense*?

We might as well bomb all of New York, since the monster responsible for the Oklahoma City bombing, Timothy McVeigh, came from that state, as attack Afghanistan since there was support for the 9/11 monstrosity in that country. A majority of the slaughterers of the innocent on that day (fifteen out of the nineteen) were born in Saudi Arabia; should we unleash weapons of mass destruction on the entire citizenry of that country?

George Washington's "Farewell Address" was very libertarian in terms of how we should relate to other nations. He said: "The great rule of conduct for us in regard to foreign nations is in extending our commercial relations, to have with them as little political connection as possible." Thomas Jefferson called for: "Peace, commerce, and honest friendship with all nations, entangling alliances with none." Said John Quincy Adams: "America . . . goes not abroad seeking monsters to destroy… We favor the freedom of all nations, but will fight, only, to protect our own."

As to domestic policy, Dr. Ron Paul wants to wipe all victimless crimes off the books; can the same be said of Thompson and Giuliani? To ask this is to answer it. And, as far as economic liberty is concerned, none of the other Republican candidates even deserve to be mentioned in the same breath as Ron.

Libertarians shouldn't be voting for ANYONE, Ron Paul included, since this goes against their principles.

Stuff and nonsense.

If a slave master allows his property to vote between a harsh and a more humane overseer, we are to blame slaves for choosing the latter? This is a perversion of libertarianism.

Murray N. Rothbard was interviewed on this matter by the New Banner in 1972. Yet, apart from the date, and the mention of the presidential candidates of that day, so fresh is his voice he could well have been talking about Dr. Ron Paul, his good friend and confidant.

NEW BANNER: "Some libertarians have recommended anti-voting activities during the 1972 election. Do you agree with this tactic?"

ROTHBARD: "I'm interested to talk about that. This is the classical anarchist position; there is no doubt about that. The classical anarchist position is that nobody should vote, because if you vote you are participating in a state apparatus. Or, if you do vote you should write in your own name; I don't think that there is anything wrong with this tactic in the sense that if there really were a nationwide movement — if 5 million people, let's say, pledged not to vote. I think it would be very useful. On the other hand, I don't think voting is a real problem. I don't think it's immoral to vote, in contrast to the anti-voting people.

"Lysander Spooner, the patron saint of individualist anarchism, had a very effective attack on this idea. The thing is, if you really believe that by voting you are giving your sanction to the state, then, you see, you are really adopting the democratic theorist's position. You would be adopting the position of the democratic enemy, so to speak, who says that the state is really voluntary because the masses are supporting it by participating in elections. In other words, you're really the other side of the coin of supporting the policy of democracy — that the public is really behind it and that it is all voluntary. And so the anti-voting people are really saying the same thing.

"I don't think this is true, because as Spooner said, people are being placed in a coercive position. They are surrounded by a coercive system; they are surrounded by the state. The state, however, allows you a limited choice — there's no question about the fact that the choice is limited. Since you are in this coercive situation, there is no reason why you shouldn't try to make use of it if you think it will make a difference to your liberty or possessions. So by voting you can't say that this is a moral choice, a fully voluntary choice, on the part of the public. It's not a fully voluntary situation. It's a situation where you are surrounded by the whole state, which you can't vote out of existence. For example, we can't vote the presidency out of existence — unfortunately, it would be great if we could, but since we can't, why not make use of the vote if there is a difference at all between the two people. And it is almost inevitable that there will be a difference, incidentally, because just praxeologically or in a natural law sense, every two persons or every two groups of people will be slightly different, at least. So in that case, why not make use of it? I don't see that it's immoral to participate in the election provided that you go into it with your eyes open — provided that you don't think that either Nixon or Muskie is the greatest libertarian since Richard Cobden — which many people, of course, talk themselves into before they go out and vote.

"The second part of my answer is that I don't think that voting is really the question. I really don't care about whether people vote or not. To me the important thing is, who do you support? Who do you hope will win the election? You can be a non-voter and say "I don't want to sanction the state" and not vote, but on election night who do you hope the rest of the voters, the rest of the suckers out there who are voting, who do you hope they'll elect? And it's important, because I think that there is a difference. The presidency, unfortunately, is of extreme importance. It will be running or directing our lives greatly for four years. So, I see no reason why we shouldn't endorse, or support, or attack one candidate more than the other candidate. I really don't agree at all with the non-voting position in that sense, because the non-voter is not only saying we shouldn't vote: he is also saying that we shouldn't endorse anybody. Will Robert LeFevre, one of the spokesmen of the non-voting approach, will he, deep in his heart on election night, have any kind of preference at all as the votes come in? Will he cheer slightly or groan more as whoever wins? I don't see how anybody could fail to have a preference, because it will affect all of us."

If Ron Paul, somehow, wins, he should immediately abdicate, since it is inconsistent with libertarianism to act as president of the U.S.

First of all, there is such a thing as limited government libertarianism, or minarchism. Although I myself am a staunch anarcho-capitalist, I know and respect the other position. Indeed, it is my opinion that the overwhelming majority of people (properly) calling themselves libertarians (I am otherwise a big-tent libertarian, but I personally find no room in our movement for the so called pro-war "libertarians" in the present context) fall into the former, not the latter, category. In this view, there *are* legitimate functions of government, namely protection of person and property, and to this end there are three, but only three, legitimate institutions: armies, to keep foreign enemies at bay, *not* to initiate attacks on them on the grounds that one day they *might* attack us; police, to quell domestic rights violators, *not* to arrest people for engaging in victimless "crimes;" and courts, to distinguish between those who perpetrate aggression and those who are their targets. As long as Dr. Paul pared down the swollen U.S. bureaucracy to match these ends, he would be acting in a manner compatible with our libertarian philosophy.

But, second, I go further. I maintain that it would be licit even for an anarcho-capitalist to take on the role of president of a country, any country. I know full well that power corrupts, and that absolute power corrupts absolutely, and that this office in the U.S. veers toward the latter. Nevertheless, it is not a logical necessity for this to occur. As long as the president limits himself to tearing down illegitimate power, he can be acting in accord not only with minarchism, but also with free market anarchism. Yes, there are very few people I would trust with such awesome responsibilities. Ron Paul is one of them.

I wish to thank the following for help with this article: Max Chiz, Ross Kaminsky, Max Raskin.

23.2 Why Not Ron Paul?

In what follows, there is a correspondence between me and a friend of mine who works at a libertarian think tank. This friend of mine, I will call him B to preserve his anonymity, recently gave a speech at Loyola University. The formal commentator for this speech was a Loyola colleague of mine, a professor in the law school, who I will call A. B gave what I thought was a magnificent talk on property rights and environmentalism, from a free market, limited government point of view. A offered what I consider a highly competent and interesting response, but from an anti-private property perspective. As a result of my attendance at this exchange, I challenged A to a debate. I copied B on this offer to A. The correspondence to be seen below consists of several letters between me and B that ensued as a result of my letter to A. This entire correspondence took place on October 26, 2007. I have inserted all material that appears in parentheses () in order to preserve anonymity. The time of day of the various letters does not fully match, due to time-zone differentials.

Letter I

From: Walter Block

Sent: Friday, October 26, 2007 8:00 AM

To: A

Dear A:

I was fascinated with your response to B's presentation the other day at the law school.

I wonder whether you would be interested in debating me at an upcoming economics club meeting, some Tuesday at noon next semester. I am copying the officers of the econ club on this, as well as B. Based on the comments I heard from you, topics over which we have sharp differences of opinion include the following:

can property rights save the environment?

property rights in general

socialism vs capitalism

the civil rights revolution: free association vs anti-racial discrimination laws the right to discriminate on the basis of sex

statism vs anarchism

the Kelo case

Ronald Coase

As an alternative, if you are interested, we could hold this debate under the aegis of the law school. Even better: how's about a home and away series? One debate at the law school, and a follow-up one for the econ club, or vice versa?

Best regards,

Walter

Letter II

From: B

Sent: Friday, October 26, 2007 9:10 AM

To: Walter Block

Subject: RE: debate

Still defending the Undefendable are you, Walter?! I allude to your discrimination suggestions (above). You'll find my own politically incorrect views on the subject here: (deleted by Walter Block, to preserve B's anonymity)

Good seeing you again.

Letter III

From: Walter Block

Sent: Friday, October 26, 2007 12:29 PM

To: B

Subject: RE: debate

Dear B:

Great seeing you again, too. I really enjoyed your presentation. I'm envious, too. I could never give an hour lecture not only with no notes, but without, even, hardly a pause for breath. Masterful.

Please, when you next come to NO, give me as much advance notice as possible. I'll try to snag you for a piggyback lecture to my own econ students, or at least be free to have dinner with you.

Just out of curiosity, why is (your think tank) supporting, of all people, (X, a candidate for the Republican nomination for president)? Why not our guy, Ron Paul?

Best regards,

Walter

Letter IV

From: B

Sent: Friday, October 26, 2007 10:33 AM

To: Walter Block

Subject: RE: debate

Thanks, Walter. (My Institute), technically, doesn't support or oppose anyone or anything. As for the people here, my sense is that they may be all over the place in this election, and for good reason: no one out there really excites.

Letter V

From: Walter Block [mailto:walterblock@cba.loyno.edu]

Sent: Friday, October 26, 2007 12:40 PM

To: B

Subject: RE: debate

That piques my curiosity. Why doesn't Ron Paul "excite?" He certainly excites me. On a scale of 0 to 100 where the latter is the most libertarian, Ron is at least a 90. No other candidate, of either party, in my view, gets above 20, and that's stretching it.

Letter VI

From: B

Sent: Friday, October 26, 2007 11:12 AM

To: Walter Block

Subject: RE: debate

I don't know his positions well, but even if he were a "100 percenter," he's not going to make it. That's politics, unfortunately.

Letter VII

From: Walter Block [mailto:walterblock@cba.loyno.edu]

Sent: Friday, October 26, 2007 1:45 PM

To: B

Subject: RE: debate

Ron was once given a 200-1 chance of winning. I have a $1 bet on that basis with Bryan Caplan. Later on, he became a 16-1 odds against candidate. I have a bet with Bill Barnett at those odds. He now has 6-1 odds against. Care to bet me $6 for anyone else against my $1 on Ron?

All of the four "leading" Republican candidates have grave problems as far as the nomination is concerned. Giuliani has had 3 marriages, his kids hate him, he publicly humiliated his second wife, he dressed up in drag for a gay parade, and he's weak from a Republican perspective in terms of abortion, gun control. The Christian right has already threatened to bolt if Jailiani gets the nomination. Romney is MORMON, for goodness sakes. Enough said. But, I'll say more. He's a flip-flopper, taking "conservative" positions now that are very different than when he was governor of Taxachussetts. Fred Thompson has all the charisma of yesterday's hamburger. Without being fed lines by scriptwriters, he's a bust. Also, he is married to a very beautiful young wife, several decades younger than him. Virtually no Republican woman of middle-aged years is going to vote for him. McCain is a joke. He has demonstrated that he can't handle money. People are waiting for him to burst like Howard Dean. They fear that his experience in Vietnam will render him unfit to be president, harsh as this sounds, indeed, is. In these statements, I am not talking about right or wrong. Most of these things are irrelevant to libertarianism. I'm confining myself solely to electability among Republicans.

No, no, Ron's best competitor, in my view, will be Mike Huckabee. He has had only one wife, and she is of long duration. He has a record of espousing conservative (well, neo-con) principles. But, he raised only a paltry $1million in the third quarter of 2007. Still, I see Huckabee as Ron's biggest competition. My biggest fear is that Ron is doing such a magnificent job in promoting liberty that he'll be assassinated.

In contrast to the presently leading candidates, Ron has had one and the same wife for some 50 years. When the Christian right discovers him, he'll get a big boost. They agree on guns, abortion and immigration (on the latter two, I happen to disagree with Ron). The mainstream media try to paint Ron as a Libertarian, not a Republican. Nonsense; he is both. Of course, he is a libertarian, but he is ALSO a Republican;, a Taft Republican. Happily, one of the early elections will take place in New Hampshire, chock full of Free State Project libertarians.

Further, and TERRIBLY important, Ron is the ONLY Republican who can beat Hillary. He'll "steal" many antiwar democrats from her. As a doctor, he'll kick her butt on socialized medicine. The reason Ron is now so low in the polls is that most people simply haven't yet HEARD of him. When they do, WATCH OUT! When Republicans come to realize that only Ron can beat Hillary, there will be no stopping the publicity for the free society.

But none of this is entirely relevant to your Institute's non-support for Ron. Let us stipulate that you are right, I am wrong, and that Ron's candidacy will not succeed. But, still, he's got almost $6 million in the bank. Soon, he'll start an advertising campaign. This will have the effect of massively promoting liberty, even more than so far. In fact, I would say that Ron has ALREADY promoted liberty to the average person better than anyone in history. Ayn Rand only comes in second, in my opinion. Ron will next week be on the Jay Leno show for goodness sake. Even the NY Times now writes about him without calling him a wieeirdo. And this is only the tip of the veritable iceberg. I tell you B, when his campaign first started, I used to hungrily search for mention of Ron. I can no longer do that. To keep up with the publicity he is now garnering, I'd have to devote my full-time efforts to this one task. Ron is a one-man band of publicity for liberty. I am appalled that (your Institute) takes the stance on him that it does. In my view, Ron is a sort of litmus test for libertarianism. So far, (your think tank) is failing this test. Can you not talk Ron up with X and Y and your other colleagues?

Letter VIII

From: B

Sent: Friday, October 26, 2007 12:07 PM

To: Walter Block

Subject: RE: debate

I'll pass this on here, Walter. What are you bucking for, Treasury secretary?

Letter IX

From: Walter Block

Sent: Friday, October 26, 2007 2:12 PM

To: B

Subject: RE: debate

I'm open to offers from President Ron. I'd take treasury, labor, commerce, the fed, education, the BLM, etc. I guarantee that if I got any of these positions, those departments would be ended within 6 months. Then, I'd go back to academia, after my one-semester break. But, don't you agree with me that even if Ron doesn't become president, he is still doing great work for our cause?

Some other reasons his poll numbers are now so low (although rising): he never gets his fair share of time during those Republican debates. Usually, he gets the least of all the candidates. Those biased polls go to registered Republicans who previously voted in primaries who have land phones. This leaves out a lot of Ron's supporters.

Letter X

From: B
Sent: Friday, October 26, 2007 6:10 PM
To: Walter Block
Subject: RE: debate
Agreed, and agreed.

Chapter 24.

Open Letters

So far, two people have published open letters on LewRockwell.com addressed to various voting communities on behalf of Ron Paul, making the case that they should support his candidacy for president of the United States. They are my own "An Open Letter to the Jewish Community on Behalf of Ron Paul" and "An Open Letter to the Protestant Community on Behalf of Ron Paul" by Laurence M. Vance.

24.1. An Open Letter About Open Letters

Why is this a good idea?

For one thing, any publication, whatsoever, that mentions the name of a certain Republican congressman from Texas is a wonderful thing; even if they are critical. Ignoring Ron is just about the worst thing that can happen in this regard, as the mainstream media has so far tried (not too successfully) to do. But letters in this series I envision would certainly be positive; which is of course even better, far better.

For another, it is simply not enough to make the general libertarian case for Dr. Paul's election: support for free enterprise and private property rights, an immediate pullout from Iraq, return to the Constitution, an end to fiat currency untied to a commodity money that creates inflation and the business cycle, cessation of the "war on drugs," etc. This is of course magnificent; but we need to do more.

This is because there are a lot of people who view the election not from this general perspective of the public good, but rather on the basis of their own more narrow interests. Forget whether or not this is a good thing; it is part of reality that we supporters of Ron need to take into account. This is why I was led to start things off in this regard with my "An Open Letter to the Jewish Community on Behalf of Ron Paul." Previously I had written several other essays in support of Dr. Paul, and had joined the group Jews for Ron Paul. As a result, I was barraged with letters from Jewish people, and others, too, saying, in effect, that, yes, Ron was a good libertarian, but his policies of no military interventionism abroad and an end to foreign aid, would be a disaster for Israel. Many of these people were reluctant to vote for him on this one ground.

In my view, this sort of thinking is by no means limited to my co-religionists; rather, it is pervasive. To wit, I regard Laurence M. Vance's contribution, directed to Protestants in general and to Baptists in particular, as crucially important. These people, also, while perhaps attracted by Ron Paul's overall stance, needed to be reassured on issues specifically important to them. Not only should they be made aware that Ron agrees with them on issues of concern to them (e.g., abortion) but also that Ron is a libertarian, not a libertine: while he favors the elimination of laws prohibiting addictive drugs, he actually *opposes* their use. He would not incarcerate people for engaging in "adult" behavior on a voluntary basis, but as his own life eloquently attests, this is not at all an aspect of what he sees as the good society.

The reason I am writing this "Open Letter" is to encourage other Ron Paul supporters to write additional "Open Letters" of this sort. To wit, we need:

- "An Open Letter to the Catholic Community on Behalf of Ron Paul"
- "An Open Letter to the Hindu Community on Behalf of Ron Paul"
- "An Open Letter to the Muslim Community on Behalf of Ron Paul"
- "An Open Letter to the Mormon Community on Behalf of Ron Paul"
- "An Open Letter to the Buddhist Community on Behalf of Ron Paul"
- "An Open Letter to the Sikh Community on Behalf of Ron Paul"

I am not enough of an expert in many of these religions to even begin to know what to say to their followers. But I am sure experts in the relevant faiths will know far better than I about such matters. Nor do the writers have to be practitioners of these religions, although, other things equal, this would certainly be preferable. All that is needed is *expertise*, ability to connect Ron Paul's program with these religious perspectives.

However, allow me to mention some possibly salient points. (Lack of knowledge has never stopped me before in any of my writings, as my critics often point out; why should it do so now?)

For Catholics, the following points might be mentioned: Ron's views are fully compatible with Catholic just war theory, with their views on abortion, and also that the philosophy of the 16th-century school of Salamanca, started mainly by Dominican and Jesuit priests, is entirely consistent with Ron's economic views. For example, for the Salamancans, the just price was the market price; the just interest rate was the market interest rate.

For Mormons, a straight shooter like Ron Paul can be relied upon to carry out the overlap between their philosophy and his to a much greater degree than even Mitt Romney, who flip-flops, and then flip-flops once again. Wouldn't it be great if Ron could beat Mitt in Utah? But this won't happen unless someone can spell out the specifics of these commonalities in detail.

For Hindus, Muslims, Buddhists, Sikhs and others: a Ron Paul Administration can be relied upon to stay out of your personal business, and also to remove troops from your homeland countries, wherever they are.

As I say, it is very important to link Dr. Paul's platform with such groups. However, the "trouble" with open letters to Jews, Protestants, Catholics and other religious communities on behalf of Ron, is that there are only so many religions, and people are members of many other categories that need to be addressed as well in this manner.

For example, this idea could be expanded to include not just religions, but occupations. Now, not every pursuit can be covered; for example, there is nothing Ron says that is narrowly pertinent to waitresses or plumbers. These would have to be covered on the basis of his general program. But, there *are* professions on which Ron speaks, specifically. For example,

- A doctor could support his opposition to socialized medicine
- A lawyer could support him on habeas corpus, the Patriot Act, the elimination of anti-trust
- An economist could support him on gold? The Fed? The IRS? his entire domestic program?

- A businessman (a Hank Reardon, not the Wesley Mouch-types who are all too prevalent) could wax eloquent about Ron's views on deregulation, lower taxes
- A historian could support his foreign policy

Then there are the "man bites dog" twists:

- Tenants against rent control
- Teachers against the department of education
- Accountants against the IRS
- Farmers against farm subsidies
- Medical researchers against the National Institute of Health
- Astronomers against NASA
- Bankers against the Fed

These are particularly efficacious. When a landlord association opposes rent control, it is dismissed as the pleadings of special and selfish interests. But when a tenant does so, on the basis of basic economic understandings (e.g., Hazlitt's *Economics in One Lesson*) it is much more difficult to ignore.

But we have not yet fully scratched the surface. There are other special-interest groups:

- Someone, a black person preferably but not necessarily, could demonstrate that the state is not exactly the best friend of this community; he could do worse than mention Walter Williams' book *The State Against Blacks*.
- Someone, a homosexual preferably but not necessarily, should make the case that gays would do better under a President Paul than any other
- Someone, a woman ideally but not necessarily, might show just how politically incorrect a Paul Administration would be, and that it is mainstream feminism that has been responsible for the plight of females

Then, there are *our* own "special-interest" groups:

- A member of NORML could support Ron on drug legalization
- A hard money advocate could support him on gold
- A member of the National Rifle Association could promote Ron's views on gun control
- A (free market) environmentalist could demonstrate how Ron's championing of private property rights would promote ecological values

Let me conclude: the "problem" with Ron Paul is that he does not trim his sails by one iota to conform to those of any particular audience of his. What you see is what you get, with him. The message is the *same* wherever he goes. But we also need tailoring to specific narrow interests. Even if Ron wanted to do this (happily he does not), no one man can be an expert in each of these narrow fields. So, it is up to his supporters, who among us comprise expertise in all of these callings, to make the case for compatibility between Ron's message and their own more limited concerns.

Nor should these "Open Letters" be limited to one to a customer. As long as there is no serious overlap, for example, there could be some *half-dozen* such missives for each of them: for Catholics, for doctors, for blacks, etc. My fervent hope is that this call of mine for one, two, many "Open Letters" will be met with a plethora of such essays. If so, and they are of sufficiently high quality, they will be published on LewRockwell.com. Perhaps Lew will even organize a special section for them under his rubric, the "Ron Paul File." Who knows: there is always the possibility of a book publication of such missives. If so, I would certainly volunteer to edit such a compilation.

24.2 An Open Letter to Libertarians On Behalf of Ron Paul, Part II

The present article is part of the Open Letter Series on behalf of Ron Paul.

True confession time. This idea of mine for a series of Open Letters in support of Ron Paul came about as the result of the following conversation I had with Lew Rockwell a few weeks ago:

Walter: Wouldn't it be great if Murray were alive now, witnessing the Ron Paul phenomenon? Murray would be so pleased, he'd be jumping up and down with glee. We'd have to peel him off the ceiling

Lew: Yes, Murray would be writing articles on Ron for LRC, one per day.

Walter: Well, I'm no Murray. I've met Murray, and I can assure you I am no Murray. I am simply not capable of writing one article per day on LRC about Ron or anything else, certainly not while continuing with my other work, and not even otherwise, as Murray could do. However, I am perhaps capable of doing this once a week, or, if not, then once per month. Perhaps I can make up for this shortfall by inducing others to help me with this labor of love.

The present article is a follow-up on David Gordon's brilliant Open Letter to Libertarians on Behalf of Ron Paul.

In my view, the "Ron Paul question" constitutes a litmus test for libertarians. Simply put, the "Ron Paul question" consists of determining whether or not a person supports Dr. Paul. If so, as I see matters, he passes this test and can be constituted a libertarian; if not, his credentials are to that extent suspect.

So, who is failing this exam?

Some anarcho-capitalist libertarians

First of all, let us consider the anarcho libertarians who oppose voting on principle, and, worse, taking on elected political office.

David's response to their objection to Congressman Paul is brilliant:

"However good his program, though, isn't Ron Paul attempting to become head of the criminal gang that constitutes the state? To come to grips with this question, we need to ask, why is the state a criminal gang? As Franz Oppenheimer, Albert Jay Nock, and Murray Rothbard have explained, the state is not a productive organization. To the contrary, it seizes property from the productive members of society. Given this understanding, we can see that the objection against Ron Paul fails completely. His proposals are all efforts to curtail the exactions of the state, not to continue or extend them. The objectors count both political supporters and opponents of state power as 'statists.' Apparently, by participating in the electoral process, regardless of the program one advocates, one incurs some sort of pollution."

In my view, this is definitive; David has rendered the proponents of this view figuratively lying on the ground on their backs. But, as I am a firm believer of kicking people in the crotch when they are down, let me add the following:

If it is wrong to be part of a criminal gang calling itself the state (Spooner), it is not also improper to cooperate with it in any way; to avail oneself of its benefits, lest one give one's imprimatur to this evil institution? If so, then it would be impermissible on libertarian grounds to become an employee of the government. Dr. Paul's actions are therefore incompatible with our libertarian principles, not only for running for President, but also for being a (10-term) congressman. I, too, am not without guilt in this regard. Previously, I taught at (was an employee of) a state university. At present, I am employed by a private university, but one that accepts money from the government. But more: all of us, me, Ron, every last one of the anarcho-capitalists who object to his candidacy on this ground, use the sidewalks for walking, the streets and roads for driving, U.S. currency for making purchases, post letters with the U.S. postal service, visit state libraries, museums, etc. It ill behooves so-called libertarian anarchists, who do not fully understand either of these two philosophies, to object to Ron Paul's actions, which are in this one way indistinguishable from their own.

The correct libertarian anarchist position, as I see matters, is that the state is of course evil. Therefore, anyone who decreases its power is on the side of the angels. Mr. Paul certainly fits this bill; his critics do not, no matter how tightly they wrap themselves in the black flag.

Those who err in this regard include Wendy McElroy, Carl Watner and Sunni Maravillosa.

Then there are those libertarians who oppose Congressman Paul's stance on immigration and abortion.

(Full disclosure here: I agree with the critics, not with Ron, on these two matters. However, I do not at all conclude from this fact that Dr. Paul is unworthy of my support. Very much to the contrary, I yield to no man as far as enthusiasm for his candidacy is concerned.)

We libertarians are a fractious bunch. What else do you expect from a group of very bright, committed and opinionated people? We cannot and do not all agree with one another on all germane issues. Every dog should get at least one bite. Or, to mix metaphors, organizing libertarians is like herding cats. However, there are issues, and then there are issues. Now, if Ron Paul were to support drug prohibition, or the War on Iraq, or the Fed, or public education, even I would be disconcerted, and mightily so. Why? Because these are as near to settled issues among libertarians as any issues can be.

However, immigration and abortion are *highly unsettled* issues in our community. I regard Murray Rothbard, Hans Hermann Hoppe and Stephan Kinsella as three of the most gifted libertarian theoreticians that have ever graced our movement. All three disagree with me and Paul's critics on these two matters. As I stated here, when expert libertarian philosophers disagree with each other, it is a bit much to declare *either side* anti- or non-libertarian. It is therefore highly improper to castigate Dr. Paul for taking a position on immigration and abortion incompatible with libertarianism, *no matter how much, nor how fervently, we disagree with Paul, Hoppe, Rothbard and Kinsella on these two issues*, as I do.

Perhaps an analogy may be of use in this context. When physicists are not of one mind on a problem (is matter a wave or a particle) it is altogether too harsh to castigate an engineer from taking either side. When doctors cannot agree on a diagnosis, nurses cannot be expected to come to an unambiguous conclusion either. When economists cannot agree to an assessment of the business cycle, then bankers cannot be held responsible. I go further: when experts in *any* field are at hammer and tongs with each other, then laymen are free to take any position on the issue, without being called down for it as in violation of principles. Well, libertarian theoreticians are the experts on the niceties of free enterprise and capitalism. Libertarian politicians are but laymen; they are charged, merely, with implementing the policies implied by private property rights and the non-aggression axiom.

Thus, it is exceedingly unfair to criticize Congressman Paul for taking an "unlibertarian" position on immigration and abortion: these are *unsettled* issues among the ranks of the experts.

The people who err in this regard include Steve Horwitz and Peter Boettke.

Roderick Long's Randy Barnett challenge

This philosopher states: "Imagine, for example, that instead of Ron Paul it's Randy Barnett who's running for president. Paul and Barnett have a lot in common; they're both fairly thoroughgoing libertarians, they're both enthusiasts for the Constitution, and they both take some positions that many libertarians regard as deviations.

"… Yet the argument that they have offered on behalf of Paul would seem to apply equally well to Barnett: 'Even if you think Barnett is wrong on some particular issues, he's still *far, far more libertarian* than any of the other candidates, so why not support him?'"

But this attempt to cram Randy Barnett down the throats of those of us who support Ron Paul, despite his deviations, fails.

There are several reasons here. First, as stated above, immigration and abortion are unsettled issues amongst libertarians. We have to be able to tolerate some degree of uncertainty, of ambiguity, in our perspective. I defy Roderick Long or anyone else for that matter to cite acknowledged leaders of our intellectual movement, such as Rothbard, Hoppe and Kinsella, who favor the U.S. role in the Iraq war.

Second, the issue of what is a threat, what is coercion, is very *central* to libertarianism, and relatively straightforward. According to that old joke, if you can't tell the difference between a living room and a bathroom, then "don't come to my house." If you can't tell the difference between aggression and defense, then don't get into political economy. Randy Barnett fails this test dismally, while Ron Paul passes with flying colors. Indeed, to place the two of them in the same sentence in this regard is highly problematic. What can we say about anyone who seriously maintains that the U.S. invasion is justified on grounds of defense against attack from Iraqis? At the very least, it cannot be seriously maintained that they are libertarians at all in any meaningful sense.

In sharp contrast, abortion and immigration are highly complex issues, as the voluminous scholarly literature on them eloquently attests. Nor are they at all at the very core of our libertarian philosophy; rather, they are *implications* of it.

Long is absolutely correct in claiming that those of us who support Ron Paul "owe" scholars such as he "an explanation of why the two cases differ." But I think we have herein supplied it.

Ron has no chance; he is not a serious candidate.

The mainstream media (MSM) which has somehow been put in charge of determining such matters, claims that Ron Paul has no chance of being elected. Therefore, support for him constitutes a "wasted vote." And we should *believe* this? The MSM has a reputation for fair dealing? They are unbiased? The editorial section of the New York Times is the fountainhead of wisdom, good sense, justice and economic sophistication?

Au contraire. The polls are replete with error. They focus on people with, of all things, land-based telephones. They seek the opinion of those who voted in previous Republican primaries. They do not even *try* to measure the *intensity* with which voters regard candidates. Needless to say, all of these phenomena underestimate Congressman Paul's true chances of winning.

One problem with the polls is that the American electorate is *still* not fully familiar with Congressman Paul. When this changes, then watch out. For he is the *only* candidate on the Republican side to oppose the U.S. intervention in Iraq (the only Democrats who agree with Ron on this are Dennis Kucinich and Mike Gravel), a viewpoint held by a *majority* of the American people. And this is not a mere matter of who is "winning" over there. No, it goes much deeper than that. The voters are heartily sick of the U.S. as the policeman of the world, with its hundreds of foreign military bases.

Moreover, buying into this doctrine is a self-fulfilling prophecy: if we acquiesce to a sufficient degree, it will thereby be rendered true to that extent. It is a recipe for disaster, in other words. No, we must reject this counsel of defeatism. We must realize that Ron's chances depend upon *us*: our commitment, our monetary contributions, our willingness to publish on his behalf, to pound the pavements, to "be clean for Ron." (Remember being "clean for Gene" McCarthy in 1968).

As well, the people making this prediction have no great record for accuracy. Why should we believe them? They may be sure that Dr. Paul will not win, but they have not the foggiest notion of who will emerge victorious. The nomination for the Republican Party this time around is in a state of flux. There are at least six candidates who are front-runners: Giuliani, Romney, Huckabee, Thompson, McCain and Paul. Is it not suspicious that the pundits well know that the latter cannot win, but cannot name the victor with any certainty at all?

Justin Raimondo, author and editorial director of Antiwar.com, quite properly rejects this argument. In his view, the conventional wisdom that rejects Ron Paul as a serious candidate has been wrong before; spectacularly so. Why should we give them credence now? They erred on weapons of mass destruction; with regard to the "welcome" we would receive as we invaded Iraq. None of them predicted the rise of Obama, the fall of Hillary, the rise of Huckabee, the fall of Fred Thompson. With experts like these…

So far, I have considered, and rejected, what I consider serious arguments against Dr. Paul's candidacy for president. I do not agree with them, but I acknowledge they are reasonable, coherent. I now move to a series of objections I do not at all regard in this way. Rather, they are silly, or vicious, or irresponsible or all of the above.

Ron isn't cool

It pains me to even have to mention this "argument," but there are actually people out there who oppose Dr. Paul because of his dress, his behavior, his demeanor, his personal lifestyle.

What are the specifics? According to Brink Lindsay, a scholar at the quasi libertarian Cato Institute:

"Though Paul defines himself as a libertarian and attributes the dedication of his young supporters to libertarian positions — such as allowing people to opt out of Social Security and Medicare — many libertarian pundits say Paul isn't in sync with younger, more 'modern' libertarians.

"He's sort of an old-style, old-right libertarian candidate," explained Lindsey. Paul departs from younger libertarians with his opposition to abortion rights and free trade agreements, for example, Lindsey said."

This sort of trash has been forcefully taken to task by several libertarians. Raimondo, states:

"What Lindsay, who enthusiastically supported the Iraq war, doesn't say — or isn't quoted as saying — is that he hates Paul's old right and quintessentially libertarian opposition to our foreign policy of global interventionism. Senor Lindsay and his fellow 'modern' libertarians have made their peace with the Empire. As long as they can take drugs, abort fetuses, … he and his Beltway buddies have no problem with the U.S. rampaging over half the earth, regime-changing and taking out 'rogue' states at will. As long as it's a 'free market' empire, they're all in favor of it."

And Tom DiLorenzo, author and economics professor, also gives this nonsense the back of his hand:

"But the 'Beltway liberventionists' tend to be totalitarian-minded and childishly intolerant of this live-and-let-live philosophy. They display a venomous hatred toward those of us who choose to largely ignore these issues but would never stand in the way of anyone who wanted to pursue them. They insist that all libertarians be champions of feminism, gay rights, and, apparently, even health club membership. They remind me of the campus leftists who keep informing me that I must not only tolerate all possible varieties of sexual diversity but 'celebrate' it. ('Celebrate Diversity' has been the multiculturalist credo of higher education for about 15 years now)."

Fred Thompson is the real libertarian candidate.

I had better buttress this with more than just a few citations. Otherwise no real libertarian would for a moment believe me when I say I am not making this up.

Here is Cato's Michael Tanner:

"With former Tennessee Senator Fred Thompson creeping ever closer to a formal announcement that he will run for president, it is worth asking whether he is the genuine small-government conservative that has been missing from the top tier of the Republican field (with all due apologies to Ron Paul). A preliminary look at his record suggests that while he is not quite the second coming of Barry Goldwater or Ronald Reagan, he may be much better on most issues than the alternatives.

"During his eight years in the Senate, Thompson had a solid record as a fiscal conservative. The National Taxpayers Union gives him the third highest marks of any candidate (trailing only Paul and Rep. Tom Tancredo). While he sponsored or cosponsored legislation over the course of his career that would have resulted in a net increase in federal spending of $3.1 billion, that is the smallest increase among the contenders. (By comparison, John McCain would have increased spending by $36.9 billion). He generally shared McCain's opposition to pork barrel spending and earmarks, and voted against the 2002 farm bill. He voted for the Bush tax cuts and has generally been solid in support of tax reduction.

"He has been a consistent supporter of entitlement reform, voting to means-test Medicare and supporting personal accounts for Social Security.

"His record on free trade is solid. In the past he has been supportive of comprehensive immigration reform, but has been critical of the current bill, shifting toward a 'control the borders first' position. Still, he has not been Tancredo-like in his anti-immigration statements.

"On federalism, there may be no better candidate. His Senate record is replete with examples of his being the lone opponent of legislation that he thought undercut federalist principles. He took this position even on legislation that was otherwise supported by conservatives. He opposes federal action to prohibit gay marriage on federalist grounds, although he supports state bans. One blight on this record is his vote in favor of No Child Left Behind."

More from Michael Tanner:

"The Republican debate in California last night showed that the field of candidates still lacks a Reagan-style small-government conservative among the top tier of candidates. The candidates invoked Reagan's name at least 19 times, but one had to go all the way down to Rep. Ron Paul's quixotic campaign before someone reflected Reagan's commitment to limited government. None of the major candidates made a serious call to limit the size, scope, and power of government. While they talked about cutting spending in the abstract, none of them could identify a single government program they would eliminate. On the other hand, from alternative fuels to a national ID card to government regulation of health care, they seemed all too happy to embrace bigger government.

"There's still a long way to go," Tanner concludes, "before any of these candidates can lay claim to the Reagan legacy."

But Justin Raimondo is having none of this. He states:

"Never mind that the Reagan administration's commitment to limited government was purely rhetorical, and that it never did anything to actually roll back the state: after all, the Cato-ites live and work in Washington, D.C., where partisan myths are sonorously uttered and routinely believed. However, this business about "all the way down" clearly denotes the attitude that Rep. Paul is beneath notice, and certainly doesn't deserve to be taken seriously by the notoriously haughty Deep Thinkers over at Cato. (Say, aren't these the same folks who are now telling us that twenty-five years of libertarian activism and scholarship have led to the growth of government, and 'this isn't as bad as it seems?')"

Here is a horror from Chris Edwards, another Cato-ite, entitled "Frederalism:"

"What about presidential candidate Ron Paul? Paul is certainly a strong believer in the 10th Amendment, but he has been mainly occupied by the war in Iraq and hasn't focused his campaign on cutting domestic spending.

"That's why I'm pleased that Fred Thompson has thrown his hat into the ring. Thompson has been talking and writing about his belief in federalism. In a recent speech, he argued that 'centralized government is not the solution to all our problems … this was among the great insights of 1787, and it is just as vital in 2007.'"

But Tom DiLorenzo's rejection of this arrant nonsense is definitive. According to DiLorenzo, in his essay, Phony Federalism: "Thompson supports the war in Iraq and almost all of the gross civil-liberties abuses championed by his fellow neo-cons. But he has included in his political rhetoric a few statements about cutting government spending, and that is apparently enough to generate great enthusiasm for him at Cato."

Nor is DiLorenzo finished with Edwards and Cato: "The Cato Institute, on the other hand, is known for championing the cause of giving even *more* power to the federal judiciary under the mistaken belief that our black-robed deities can somehow be transformed into libertarians (like Fred Thompson, for instance?! Or perhaps Iraq war/Bush regime apologist Randy Barnett?). Roger Pilon is the best-known Cato scholar who has made this argument, and the Institute has published several books by Clint Bolick that make the same case for giving more power to the central government's judiciary. This is how to return to federalism?"[42]

42I would like to thank Kay Wosewick for research assistance with regard to some of this material

Part VII.

Defenses of Ron Paul on grounds of religion

Chapter 25.

Anti-Semitism: Response to Alan Dershowitz

Alan M. Dershowitz, who needs no introduction here or anywhere else for that matter, has written in the *Jerusalem Post* (1/7/12) what I consider a slanderous attack on Ron Paul for the latter's supposed racism and anti-Semitism. Well, let me just say that this Harvard Law professor is likely to be nominated for the Supreme Court by Obama (all the more reason we need to work even harder to elect the congressman from Texas). Dershowitz's calumny is entitled "Why Anti-Semitism Is Moving Toward the Mainstream" and was published electronically on January 3, 2012. Most of this article deals with his claim that the following people are anti-Semitic: Brian Leiter, John Mearsheimer, Gilad Atzmon and Richard Falk. These people, Dershowitz charges, are guilty of enabling these "classic anti-Semitic tropes —'the Jews' control the world and are to blame for everything that goes wrong, including the financial crisis; 'The Jews killed Christian children in order to use the blood to bake Matzo; the Holocaust never happened — (to become) acceptable and legitimate subjects for academic and political discussion.'"

First, I object, strenuously, to Dershowitz's besmirching of Ron Paul's name merely by linking him with these "classic anti-Semitic tropes." By writing about Dr. Paul in an article that even mentions these things constitutes guilt by association. Further, why is the Texas congressman coupled with these other people? Cannot Dershowitz bring himself to attack Dr. Paul on his own? As far as the evidence indicates, Congressman Paul is as knowledgeable of and supportive of the views of Brian Leiter, John Mearsheimer, Gilad Atzmon and Richard Falk as he is of Aerosmith, the Rolling Stones and Kelly Clarkson.

Second, Dershowitz and I have very different views as to what constitutes "acceptable and legitimate subjects for academic and political discussion." If he had his druthers, these "tropes" would be banned from any and all discussion at universities, if I understand him correctly. In my view, *nothing at all* should be precluded as a legitimate subject for analysis in such places, and, indeed, anywhere else. And here I include such issues as whether or not the Earth is flat, whether or not 2+2 really equals four, whether or not triangles have 180 degrees, whether or not the Pythagorean theorem is true, whether or not demand curves slope in a downward direction, along with the "tropes" against which Dershowitz inveighs (I join him on the specifics of this, of course). Let me repeat that *nothing at all*, should be precluded as a legitimate area of inquiry, at least at a university devoted to free inquiry. The entire concept of academic freedom lies in precarious balance between Dershowitz and me on this issue. I follow in this regard the teachings of John Stuart Mill in his essay, "On Liberty" who states:

"Even in natural philosophy, there is always some other explanation possible of the same facts; some geocentric theory instead of heliocentric, some phlogiston instead of oxygen; and it has to be shown why that other theory cannot be the true one: and until this is shown, and until we know how it is shown, we do not understand the grounds of our opinion. But when we turn to subjects infinitely more complicated, to morals, religion, politics, social relations, and the business of life, three-fourths of the arguments for every disputed opinion consist in dispelling the appearances which favour some opinion different from it. The greatest orator, save one, of antiquity, has left it on record that he always studied his adversary's case with as great, if not with still greater, intensity than even his own. What Cicero practised as the means of forensic success, requires to be imitated by all who study any subject in order to arrive at the truth. He who knows only his own side of the case, knows little of that. His reasons may be good, and no one may have been able to refute them. But if he is equally unable to refute the reasons on the opposite side; if he does not so much as know what they are, he has no ground for preferring either opinion. The rational position for him would be suspension of judgment, and unless he contents himself with that, he is either led by authority, or adopts, like the generality of the world, the side to which he feels most inclination. Nor is it enough that he should hear the arguments of adversaries from his own teachers, presented as they state them, and accompanied by what they offer as refutations. That is not the way to do justice to the arguments, or bring them into real contact with his own mind. He must be able to hear them from persons who actually believe them; who defend them in earnest, and do their very utmost for them. He must know them in their most plausible and persuasive form; he must feel the whole force of the difficulty which the true view of the subject has to encounter and dispose of; else he will never really possess himself of the portion of truth which meets and removes that difficulty. Ninety-nine in a hundred of what are called educated men are in this condition; even of those who can argue fluently for their opinions. Their conclusion may be true, but it might be false for anything they know: they have never thrown themselves into the mental position of those who think differently from them, and considered what such persons may have to say; and consequently they do not, in any proper sense of the word, know the doctrine which they themselves profess."

Please excuse me for quoting Mill at such great length. I do so because I find it quite disgraceful that an academic at one of our nation's most prestigious universities wishes to limit free speech in, of all places, institutions of higher learning.

With this introduction, I now proceed to examine Dershowitz's case against Paul on the grounds of anti-Semitism and racism. (I quote his remarks in *italics;* my responses are preceded by these arrows: <<)

The same can be said of Ron Paul, who everyone has heard of.

<< Dershowitz is placing the congressman from Texas in the same category as the aforementioned Brian Leiter, John Mearsheimer, Gilad Atzmon and Richard Falk. He has no warrant to do any such thing.

Paul has, according to the New York Times*, refused to "disavow" the "support" of "white supremacists, survivalists and anti-Zionists who have rallied behind his candidacy." (These "anti-Zionists" believe that "Zionists"– Jews – control the world, were responsible for the bombing of the Oklahoma federal building, and caused the economic downturn, because "most of the leaders involved in the federal and international banking system are Jews.")*

<< Why anyone should trust the *New York Times* on *any* issue is beyond me. This is the very same yellow journalist rag that published Walter Duranty's numerous reports to the effect that all was well in the Soviet Union during the times of Lenin when he was murdering millions of innocent people. For this one episode alone, that newspaper should have been run out of town on a rail. To use the *Times* as a source for the criticism of *anyone* constitutes a per se *support* for that person. Nor does Dershowitz link to this very imperfect source of inaccurate information.

<< Ron Paul did indeed refuse to "disavow" the "support" of "white supremacists, survivalists and anti-Zionists who have rallied behind his candidacy." Dr. Paul has stated again and again that "*they* support *him; he* does not support *them.*"

<< According to this source, "The Paul campaign suggests he will put the money to better use than Black would if it were returned, and Black acknowledges he knows Paul doesn't share his views on race." (The "Black" here is Don Black of West Palm Beach, who runs a Web site called Stormfront). But is it not *true* that the money will be better spent in behalf of promoting liberty by Ron Paul than it otherwise would have been by these racists? What is so wrong with using the money donated by evil people for good purposes? Said Jesse Benton, Ron Paul's spokesman: "If someone of a small-minded ideology sends money, it's his loss. First, it's $500 less for Black to use on whatever it is he does. Then, it's $500 more for Dr. Paul to use to protect the individual rights of all Americans."

<< So the *facts*, even as reported by the disreputable and unreliable *New York Times,* undermine Dershowitz's claim.

<< Does not Dershowitz recognize a man of *principle*, or a *principled* act when he sees one? I suppose not. The typical politician when given a donation from such unsavory sources either returns the money, or donates it to a noncontroversial charity, such as for cancer research. Does Dershowitz really think that Paul needs the stinking, lousy $500 that much? Does this college professor really think that the congressman wants that vast amount of money so that he can show his support for such disreputable lowlifes? Don't they require *brains* before they give you a tenured faculty position at Harvard?

He allowed his "Ron Paul survival report" to espouse David Duke-type racism and anti-Semitism for years during the 1990s, claiming he was unaware that they were being promoted under his name. Edward H. Crane, the founder of the libertarian CATO Institute, has said, "I wish Ron would condemn those fringe things that float around" his campaign, but he refuses to reject the support of these anti-Semites who form a significant part of his base. The New York Times has criticized Paul for his failure to "convincingly repudiate racist remarks that were published under his name for years—or the enthusiastic support he is getting from racist groups," including those that espouse "anti-Semitism and far-right paranoia."

<< Dershowitz has not done his homework. If he wants to make any of these smears stick, he has to go way beyond merely reiterating them. These charges have been made again and again (google Ron Paul and racist, or Ron Paul and anti-Semite and you will find *thousands* of such entries.) The sum total of the offensive lines in all of those years of newsletter publication amounts to less than a dozen lines. My two favorite refutations of the nonsensical charge of racism on this ground are these: "Bombs and drones may break human bones but only 'insensitive' words can truly hurt us," by Will Grigg, and also this one: "Ron Paul is vilified for missing a few paragraphs out of hundreds of

newsletters by people who pass 2,000-page bills without reading a single word," by Hosanna Myers.

<< Dershowitz, go back to the drawing boards. Do your homework; read this material I have already provided for you, you lazy rascal. I assume you will remain unconvinced by all this evidence. You will still see Dr. Paul as a racist and an anti-Semite. But, if you *read* this material, you can do a *better* job of falsely vilifying him. Get to work. Enquiring minds want to know what lies you will make up about him after you are thus better prepared. And I, personally, stand ready to refute you once again, should you ever care to do a workmanlike job. As it is, your critique is a shonda for the goyim. What kind of Yiddishe cup writes inferior material like this? Surely, you can perpetrate evil more effectively than this?

<< As for Ed Crane's "wish (that) Ron would condemn those fringe things that float around" his campaign, Dr. Paul already *has.* Again and again. Is no one listening? He has *continually* disavowed these statements, and their support for these ideas that he finds abhorrent. Dershowitz and the *New York Times* might consider CATO to be a libertarian Institute, but this is strictly an inside-the-beltway perspective. In my own assessment, they are at best semi-libertarian. (It is not easy for me to determine who is speaking in this paragraph, Crane or Dershowitz; if I have inadvertently assigned a viewpoint to one of them that belongs to the other, it is due to this difficulty.)

Even now, Paul continues to accept contributions from Holocaust deniers, from those who blame the Jews for everything and from other bigots, thus lending some degree of legitimacy to their hateful views.

<< We have already dealt with these charges. Does Dershowitz have so little to say against Paul that he has to be so repetitive? Maybe this response will stick: One need not lend any legitimacy to a group by reducing the amount of money with which they have at their disposal so as to spread their hateful programs.

When Nazi anti-Semitism began to achieve mainstream legitimacy in Germany and Austria in the 1930's, it was not because Hitler, Goebbels and Goering were espousing it. Their repulsive views had been known for years. It was because non Nazis—especially prominent academics, politicians and artists—were refusing to condemn anti-Semitism and those who espoused it.

<< Dr. Ron Paul has been condemning anti-Semitism from morning until night. He has been doing this pretty much every day on the campaign trail. The mainstream media's attempts to mischaracterize his views on these matters, to obfuscate them, to ignore them, have been an utter failure. As have been your attempts to do the same thing.

It has been said that "all that is necessary for the triumph of evil is that good men do nothing." Leiter and Paul may or may not be good men, but they are guilty of more than merely doing nothing. They are, by their actions, helping to legitimate (sic) *the oldest of bigotries. Shame on them!*

<< Shame on *you*, Dershowitz, for trying to drag a good man through the mud. And shame on you too, for doing such a pathetic job of it. I've got some advice for you, Harvard professor: stick to your day job. Your attempts to denigrate the next president of the United States are a dismal failure. Good man Ron Paul has been promoting personal liberty, economic freedom, Constitutionalism, and an anti-imperialist foreign policy. He is awakening the entire country, no, the entire *world*, to this message. He has been using the Golden Rule; asking Americans how *we* would like it if some other country did to us what the U.S. has long been doing to them. That is the action of a man you are trying to paint as hopelessly immoral? Give it a rest.

<< Why continually attempt to beat up on Dr. Paul for his supposed racism and anti-Semitism? It is because the enemies of a free society, such as you, Dershowitz, cannot lay a glove on this future POTUS in terms of any of his substantive programs. You and they know full well that the horrendous wars (on drugs, on foreign countries that have no

chance at all of invading us) disproportionately negatively impact black and brown people. You and they know full well that Obama is vulnerable on the economy. There is an aphorism in the profession of law that Dershowitz is applying here: "If you can't win on the facts, try the law; if you can't win on the law, try the facts. If you can't win on either ground, scream, hurl garbage at the other side, engage in libel, etc. This is exactly what Dershowitz has done in his unwarranted, unsubstantiated, improper attack on Congressman Paul.

Also see this as a refutation of Dershowitz's thesis: Block, Walter E. 2012. "Endorsement for Ron Paul." January 1; http://www.lewrockwell.com/blog/lewrw/archives/102702.html video

Chapter 26.

Is Ron Paul an Anti-Semite? No

Gay people, it is said, have a radar system (gaydar) which enables them to discern anti homosexual bigotry, even when it is not in your face; when it is not apparent to all. African-Americans rely on blackdar, which, similarly, presumably allows members of this community to ferret out racism no matter where it appears, no matter how well-hidden. Some of them even see this malady within their own race, and characterize such people as "Oreo cookies."

In like manner, many of us chosen people are supposed to be able to peer deeply into the souls of the goyim to determine if and to what degree anti-Semitism lurks. I don't like to brag, but (in all such sentences, the reader is advised to ignore everything that appears before the word "but") my Jewdar abilities are second to none. I'll pit them against any other Jew no matter how finely tuned are his abilities in this regard.

I have known Ron Paul for some four decades ever since the 1970s, when he and I would attend many of the same conferences on gold and free enterprise. I have had dinner with him on more than one occasion. I have spoken to Ron on a one-to-one basis numerous times. We have, and had, many friends in common (e.g., Murray Rothbard and Lew Rockwell, among others), and I have had many chances to see Congressman Paul interact within this smaller circle of people. I can say with absolute confidence, based on these experiences and my own finely honed jewdar, that Dr. Paul does not have a single solitary anti-Semitic bone in his entire body.

This of course is not the opinion of many of my co-religionists, even those within the Republican party. Just google "Ron Paul" and "Jews" and you'll get hundreds if not thousands of entries. These fellow members of my tribe are sadly and tragically mistaken. They ought to go visit the Jewdar repairman, because their abilities in this regard are off kilter, way off. Particularly egregious was the decision of the Republican Jewish Coalition to exclude Dr. Paul from its Victory 2008 Republican Jewish Coalition Candidates Forum. Jews are supposed to be "people of the book." Which means, if it means anything, that they are to be open to what appears in books, namely, ideas. By not permitting themselves to even hear the thoughts of the only libertarian running for the office of president at that time, they give the lie to this appellation.

What is their reasoning? Why do they characterize perhaps the least anti-Semitic non-Jew in the history of politics in this manner? Simple. Ron Paul opposes foreign "aid" (scare quotes around this last word in homage to the career of Peter Bauer, who did more than anyone else to demonstrate that this is a pejorative; it is by no means true that "government-to-government transfers of funds" – his characterization of this process – is in any way beneficial). The congressman from Texas knows full well that foreign "aid" *harms* recipients, amounts to a theft from Americans, and has no Constitutional warrant. And, since he is a principled man, he makes no exceptions in this regard. He would cut off the spigot for *all* foreign countries, including Israel.

Jews who look at this superficially see this even-handed policy as anti-Semitic, to their eternal shame. It is nothing of the sort. Our laws against murder and rape make no exceptions for ethnic or religious groups. *All* people must abide by them. If a Jew commits one of these heinous crimes, he will be charged, along with any others who do so. According to the "logic" of those who charge Ron Paul with anti-Semitism for his opposition to foreign "aid," anyone who applies laws against murder or rape would fit this bill as well. When the emotions are in the ascendency, logic flies right out the window. Here, this congressman from Texas applies a principle across the board, to all, equally, and he is condemned as an anti-Semite because he refuses to make an exception for anyone? C'mon, give me a break. This is a shonda (a disgrace) to Talmudic study, which is one of the main foundations of Jewish thought, and prides itself on the depth of its reasoning.

In a previous article, I defended Dr. Paul against these outrageous charges. Please read that essay as an antidote to these scurrilous claims made against him. Before I get to the main point I want to make today, I briefly take note of the fact that according to the latest round of Wikileaks, at least insofar as reported in the *New York Times* (they always tell the truth and nothing but the truth about all the news that's fit to print, so we can believe them on this), the U.S. government has been spying on Israel. Note to my fellow Jews: Ron Paul is not now the president of the U.S. Therefore, this anti-Semitic act *cannot* be blamed on him. Instead, the responsibility for this anti-Semitic act (well, anti-Israel act) must fall on the present leader of "the free world," Barack Hussein Obama (non anti-Semite?) However, I strongly suspect that this policy was not begun by the present occupant of the White House. I expect that it has been undertaken at the direction of an entire series of "anti-Semitic" presidents, stretching back, perhaps, to the creation of the Jewish state in 1948.

Now, at last, I arrive at the main topic for the present essay. My fear is that the larger Jewish community will not trust the assessment of Dr. Paul's foreign policy as it affects Israel, based on the Jewdar of a boy born in Brooklyn who has never so much as set foot in that country. So, I want to acquaint you not only with some Israeli voices in general, but with those whose Zionist credentials are impeccable. (I am greatly indebted to Michael Makovi of Jerusalem, Israel, for sending me this material.)

Op-Ed: Ron Paul Should be the Zionist Choice for U.S. President

Published: 15/11/07, 10:04 PM

He opposes U.S. foreign aid to Israel

Shmuel Ben-Gad

Shmuel Ben-Gad is a librarian at George Washington University in Washington, D.C., a registered Republican and an overseas member of Manhigut Yehudit. The views expressed are his own.

Since the Six Day War, U.S. presidents and presidential candidates have tended to speak of the U.S. and Israel as great friends and allies. They have also tended to favor the shrinking of Israel's borders. This has reached a low point under the Bush administration, which is the first one to explicitly make its policy the establishment of an Arab state in Judea, Samaria and Gaza. Thus, the U.S. alliance with Israel has been a decidedly mixed blessing.

Israel receives military and financial assistance, and also some diplomatic support at the United Nations, but the U.S. puts pressure on Israel to surrender parts of the homeland. Even worse, this relationship seems to foster a mentality of dependence amongst many Israelis who, it seems, cannot imagine Israel defying the United States in any major way.

In the upcoming presidential election, however, there is a chance to change this dramatically, by electing Congressman Ron Paul, a candidate for the Republican presidential nomination. Dr. Paul favors a non-interventionist foreign policy. He has written:

"Yet, while we call ourselves a strong ally of the Israeli people, we send billions in foreign aid every year to some Muslim states that many Israelis regard as enemies. From the Israeli point of view, many of the same Islamic nations we fund with our tax dollars want to destroy the Jewish state. Many average Israelis and American Jews see America as hypocritically hedging its bets.... It is time to challenge the notion that it is our job to broker peace in the Middle East and every other troubled region across the globe.... 'Peace plans' imposed by outsiders or the U.N. cause resentment and seldom produce lasting peace....The fatal conceit lies in believing America can impose geopolitical solutions wherever it chooses."

In this, Dr. Paul is hearkening back to what George Washington counseled in his famous farewell address: "The great rule of conduct for us in regard to foreign nations is, in extending our commercial relations, to have with them as little political connection as possible."

The Republican Jewish Coalition (a fervent supporter of the Bush administration, which it claims is a great friend of Israel) refused to invite Dr. Paul to its candidates forum because he opposes aid to Israel. But, as we can see, Dr. Paul's position is based upon a principled, modest, non-interventionist foreign policy – not upon anti-Zionism. Indeed, in a way, his foreign policy is mirrored by his small government domestic policy. Both recognize there are real limits to what a government can usefully do.

It is true that Israel is a small state in a highly dangerous neighborhood, but it is an economically and technologically vibrant country – even more so recently, as the shackles of socialism have been somewhat loosened. Cutting the apron strings to the U.S. would, I think, make Israel become more maturely self-confident, because it would be more self-reliant.

A Ron Paul presidency would be healthy for Israel in yet another way. Dr. Paul is opposed to organizations like the United Nations and the International Criminal Court that dilute national sovereignty. If the United States, in a Paul administration, withdrew from the U.N. and similar institutions, imagine what a blow this would deliver to their power and prestige. I find it a thrilling prospect. Maybe Israel would have a wise enough government to follow suit.

Dr. Paul's position is based upon a principled, modest, non-interventionist foreign policy – not upon anti-Zionism.

Now, I do not support Ron Paul only for Zionist reasons, nor do I think U.S. pressure is the primary cause for the current politically and culturally debilitated conditions of Israel. The primary cause, in my opinion, is the self-debasement of the Hebrew nation both in the homeland and abroad. This manifested itself most severely in the Israeli government's expulsion of Jews from Gaza and northern Samaria, and in the almost total lack of opposition that greeted this from the Jewish Diaspora.

It seems to me a Ron Paul presidency would be good for Israel and for the United States. Its foreign policy noninterventionism and its concern to protect national sovereignty would provide Israel with a greater impetus to increase its own independence and sense of national honor. I hope American Zionists will resist the immediate, meretricious attractions of American financial assistance for Israel. Ron Paul would both end this infantilizing, and even corrupting, aid and respect Israel's national sovereignty.

Taking the long and deep view, Ron Paul should be the Zionist choice.

Israeli Economists Agree with Rand Paul: End Foreign Aid

Written by Daniel Sayani

The New American

Monday, 07 February 2011

The question of foreign aid is one that has pitted economists against politicians, special interest groups, and foreign policy demagogues for decades. No stranger to this controversy is Kentucky Senator Rand Paul, who like his father, Texas Representative Ron Paul (both Republicans), has proposed ending U.S. foreign aid to all countries, including Israel, a decision that has earned the scorn of numerous groups on both the Left and the Right.

However, one critical aspect of the debate that has been neglected from public discourse on the topic – and that Sen. Paul may be unaware of – is the opposition of numerous Jewish and Israeli economists and religious Zionist groups to Israeli foreign aid. Like

Sen. Paul, these figures believe that foreign aid is an affront against Israeli liberty and sovereignty, as well as a drain on the development of numerous sectors of the Israeli economy, such as the weapons and biotechnology industries.

Individuals including Israeli economists Ran Dagoni, Yoel Bainerman, and Alvin Rabushka, the late Rabbi Meir Kahane, as well as groups including the Jewish Task Force, the Zionist Freedom Alliance, and the Manhigut Yehudit faction of the Likud Party have long advocated for an end to U.S. foreign aid to Israel. These groups insist that Israel must develop her own economic strength and move towards more free-market economic reforms as a means of boosting national prosperity and strength.

Even Israeli Prime Minister Benjamin Netanyahu has stated that foreign aid may do more harm than good, and proposed efforts to wean Israel off of American military aid payments.

It becomes clear, therefore, that Sen. Paul's proposal to cut foreign aid is one which is not without support from innovative Israeli and Jewish thinkers on the issue.

Manhigut Yehudit (Hebrew for "Jewish Leadership") is considered the most right-wing and the largest sector within the Likud Central Committee. It is committed to Israeli safety, territorial integrity, and the promotion of privatization reforms and traditional Torah values. According to co-founder Shmuel Sackett, its long-term goal is to "perfect the world in the Kingdom of the Almighty."

Chief among the group's priorities is "a modern and open economy based on Jewish Values," and this entails, for the group, "No financial aid from foreign countries." As a result of this, Manhigut Yehudit member Shmuel Ben-Gad, also librarian at George Washington University, in 2007 wrote an editorial in *Israel National News* actually endorsing Ron Paul, saying he should be "the Zionist choice for President."

The U.S. puts pressure on Israel to surrender parts of the homeland. Even worse, this relationship seems to foster a mentality of dependence amongst many Israelis who, it seems, cannot imagine Israel defying the United States in any major way.

In the upcoming presidential election, however, there is a chance to change this dramatically, by electing Congressman Ron Paul, a candidate for the Republican presidential nomination. Dr. Paul favors a non-interventionist foreign policy.

Dr. Paul's position is based upon a principled, modest, non-interventionist foreign policy – not upon anti-Zionism. Indeed, in a way, his foreign policy is mirrored by his small-government domestic policy. Both recognize there are real limits to what a government can usefully do.

Cutting the apron strings to the U.S. would, I think, make Israel become more maturely self-confident, because it would be more self-reliant. Ron Paul would both end this infantilizing, and even corrupting, aid and respect Israel's national sovereignty.

In a similar argument, Rabbi Meir Kahane also advocated for an end to American foreign aid for Israel. He was the founder and leader of the Jewish Defense League, and is considered by many to be the first victim of al-Qaeda on American soil, as he was assassinated in cold blood by convicted terrorist El Sayyid Nosair, who was also involved in the 1993 World Trade Center bombings. He also led the right-wing Kach Party in Israel until his death, and once stated that foreign aid "turns Israel into a junkie looking for her fix." In his 1990 essay "Isolation," he said the following about foreign aid, framing it in religious terms the Biblical notion of a Chosen Nation:

Exile has turned the Jew of faith into one who trembles before the man of the dust. Unless we become of might and faith, and unless we ignore both the money and the honey of the United States and their empty threats and condemnation, we stand no chance. We must be a self-reliant, set-apart, and fearless nation doing the Will of the Almighty.

Likewise, the Jewish Task Force (JTF), a group committed to Kahane's ideology, states among its principles a commitment to:

An immediate end to all U.S. foreign aid, even to a genuine friend and ally like Israel, which is harmed rather than helped by her counterproductive dependency on America's addictive welfare handouts.

Echoing this stance is L' Herut Tzion (Hebrew for "Zionist Freedom Alliance"), a group committed to the ideology of Zev Jabotinsky, father of Revolutionary Zionism, also known as Revisionist Zionism. Jabotinsky was a fierce anti-communist, and opposed all forms of statism, which he labeled "Communo-Fascism." His disciples in the Zionist Freedom Alliance also believe that foreign aid is an affront against Israeli sovereignty, and thus oppose it on ideological grounds.

The group's founder, Yehuda HaKohen, also directs "Zionists for Ron Paul," and has also endorsed Ron Paul for president in a radio interview with *Israel National News*. In addition to advocating for Israeli territorial integrity, the group supports American and Israeli withdrawal from the United Nations, and is steadfastly opposed to foreign aid for Israel, saying the following:

In addition to having no constitutional basis and being an unnecessary burden on the American taxpayer, United States foreign aid has also impaired the national sovereignty of the State of Israel. The aid prevents the Jewish state from adopting economic reforms that would make her self-reliant and it creates a mindset of dependency among the Israeli people. A nation cannot be both dependent and independent. ZFA calls upon the government of Israel to stop behaving like the leaders of a vassal state and begin working towards the realization of true political and economic freedom. We also advise the U.S. government to completely end foreign aid to all nations and to concentrate instead on rebuilding the American economy.

This is a sentiment that is corroborated by numerous economists and academicians.

In the September 1995 issue of the *Middle East Quarterly*, economist Joel Bainerman authored an analysis entitled, "End American Aid to Israel?: Yes, It Does Harm." Bainerman outlines a sound economic argument for opposing aid:

Arnon Gafny, who served as governor of the Bank of Israel from 1976-1981, points out that foreign aid has caused Israel to suffer from what economists call the "Dutch Disease," a generous but temporary gift (such as oil or external aid) that brings short-term benefits but impairs a country's long-term competitiveness.

It is very difficult to prove that a rich country's bestowing bilateral aid on a poorer one actually helps the poorer economy.

Ezra Sohar, author of *Israel's Dilemma: Why Israel Is Falling Apart and How to Put It Back Together*, notes that the lion's share of U.S. aid to Israel in the 1970s consisted of loans to purchase military equipment. "The end result should have been known from the start," says Sohar. "There is logic in borrowing to build a factory with the anticipation of repaying the loan out of profits. But in the case of armaments, it is obvious that there cannot be any profits."

Likewise, Hoover Institution Fellow Alvin Rabushka says that aid to Israel hurts Israelis:

Free money is the scourge of Israel's economy. It is the difference between a free, prosperous Israel and a statist, dependent Israel. Before U.S. aid began flowing, Israel's economic performance rivaled that of the high-growth Asian Tigers. Since then, Israel's growth rate has fallen by more than half.

An article published most recently in response to the hoopla over Sen. Paul's announcement also articulates this belief. Ran Dagoni, in the Israeli business publication, *Globes* wrote:

The time has come to bid goodbye to the military aid that the U.S. extends to Israel, that generous package (currently worth $3 billion) that enables the Israeli taxpayer to share the cost of procuring equipment for the IDF with the U.S. taxpayer. Israel should itself initiate the process of detachment from the Washington breast. It should be done gradually, on terms that will enable Israel to wean itself off this intoxicating milk, before the Americans take action, on their terms. Israel won't collapse.

Both the younger and elder Paul, as well as those opposing foreign aid in general, to Israel and all other countries, are also in the good company of none other than Benjamin Netanyahu himself. In 1996, he addressed Congress and declared his intention for an end to foreign aid, according to the *Harvard Israel Review*:

For their part, the members of Congress gave Netanyahu a rousing welcome, applauding him 14 times, including a standing ovation when he promised to reduce Israel's reliance on the $3.2 billion in aid the United States provides the Jewish state each year.

In his promise to eventually seek less aid from the United States, the prime minister significantly did not mention any amount that might be reduced, nor did he give a timetable for achieving Israel's "economic independence." The day before, at a White House news conference, he said the reduced aid policy would be "pursued over the course of the coming 10 years." In the next four years, we are going to begin the long-term process of gradually reducing the level of your generous economic assistance," Netanyahu said. "We are committed to turning Israel's economy into a free market of goods and ideas, which is the only way to bring true independence."

"I believe that we can now say that Israel has reached childhood's end, that it has matured enough to begin approaching a state of self-reliance.... We are going to achieve economic independence." In stating this goal, Netanyahu had two major projects in mind: ending U.S. economic aid to Israel and reforming the Israeli economy into "a free market of goods and ideas."

This sentiment was echoed earlier by Zalman Shoval, former Israeli Ambassador to the United States and a leading figure within the Likud Party. Shoval, in 1992, told an American audience that Israel should suggest through its own initiative that the United States gradually phase out civilian economic aid.

Sen. Paul and his father are not without precedent in their proposals to cut foreign aid. Perhaps without their knowing it, they are fulfilling the policy desires of a cadre of right-wing Zionist and Jewish leaders, including Ambassador Shoval, Prime Minister Netanyahu, Rabbi Kahane, and leading economists, such as Bainerman, Rabushka, Sohar, and Dagoni.

Chapter 27.

Response to the Republican Jewish Coalition on not inviting Ron Paul

The Republican Jewish Coalition bars Ron Paul from their presidential debate, saying he is too "misguided and extreme."

According to the website of the RJC, "seven of the top Republican presidential candidates (will) gather next week at a forum hosted by the Republican Jewish Coalition." They do not condescend to name Ron Paul as the one top candidate who will be shunned by this group, but their spokesman elsewhere makes this clear: "He's just so far outside of the mainstream of the Republican party and this organization," Brooks said. Inviting Paul to attend would be "like inviting Barack Obama to speak."

Outside of the Republican Party mainstream? No, not at all. Rather, Congressman Paul's seven competitors, all invited by the RJC, are the ones outside of the Republican mainstream, at least if this includes people like Robert Taft and Howard Buffett. States Taft: "It follows that except as such policies may ultimately protect our own security, we have no primary interest as a national policy to improve conditions or material welfare in other parts of the world or to change other forms of government. Certainly we should not engage in war to achieve such purposes." No, it is not Ron Paul who is out of step with (at least this kind of) Republicanism. It is, rather, the seven dwarfs (Romney, Gingrich, Cain, Bachmann, Perry, Huntsman and Santorum) who are marching to a non-Republican drummer (actually, a neo-con drummer, comprised mainly of ex-commies, Trotskyites and Democrats).

Is Dr. Paul "far outside of the mainstream of … this organization?" Well, that depends upon what are the goals of the RJC. Here is its mission statement: "We seek to foster and enhance ties between the American Jewish community and Republican decision makers. We work to sensitize Republican leadership in government and the party to the concerns and issues of the Jewish community, while articulating and advocating Republican ideas and policies within the Jewish community. We are committed to building a strong, effective and respected Jewish Republican voice in Washington and across the country." And here is its position on Israel: "We fully embrace a pro-Israel foreign policy. The RJC is a Jewish organization; we recognize and support the importance of Israel as a Jewish state to Jews and non-Jews worldwide. As the only democracy in the Middle East, Israel shares our values and is a bulwark against the forces of repression and anti-human rights regimes. It is our obligation to ally with other nations who share our fundamental values – there are few enough of them – especially those who are willing to stand up and fight for those values. Israel is our only ally that has never asked for American blood to be shed in her defense." I could not find anything on their website discussing anti-Semitism, but I think I may take it as a given that the RJC opposes this scourge.

So, to repeat, is Dr. Paul "far outside of the mainstream of … this (RJC) organization?" I think not. Congressman Paul, a U.S. Air Force veteran, the only non-chicken-hawk of the group of seven (apart from Perry), fully embraces "a pro-Israel foreign policy." Is it the *same* policy as that of the other contenders for the Republican nomination? Of course not; otherwise, he, too, would have been welcomed by the RJC to their "debate." But it is a *different* "pro-Israel foreign policy." How so?

For one thing, Ron Paul espouses a policy of ending all U.S. transfers of funds to foreign nations; since the Arab countries, all together, receive far more than Israel, although this "hurts" (read Peter T. Bauer for an explanation of these scare quotes) Israel absolutely, it *helps* that country *relative* to its enemies. Jews are supposed to have great intelligence, and they do. But sufficient to grasp this admittedly complicated point? Evidently, not enough of this intellectual ability has percolated down into the membership and leadership of the RJC. I wonder; given their obtuseness, are they real Jews? Surely, Israel's absolute power to impose its will is as nothing compared to its power *relative* to that of its enemies.

For another thing, the representative of the 14th congressional district of Texas favors Israeli sovereignty, unlike the other candidates for the Republican nomination for president, and, presumably, the RJC. This means that Ron Paul trusts the population and leadership of Israel to defend itself more than he trusts the population and leadership of the U.S. for this vital task. Under a Paul Administration, Israel will no longer have to ask U.S. permission before it sneezes. More to the point, before it erects buildings wherever it wants to, before it bombs installations it deems hazardous to its national health, before it negotiates with bordering peoples (e.g., Obama's claim that the 1967 borders must serve as a jumping-off point for any subsequent treaty between Israel and its neighbors.) Had a noninterventionist of the Paul stripe been in charge of U.S. policy in the 1950s, the land of Greater Israel would now include the entire Sinai Peninsula.

But what about Iran? Of all the candidates for the Republican nomination, Ron Paul, alone, has seen all this before, with Iraq. The neo- whipped up public sentiment for that disaster, and are now attempting to satisfy their blood lust yet again. How many countries has Iran actually invaded in the last epoch? None. They want to kill every Jew in Israel? Why, then, have they not started with the Jewish community of Tehran? Is bombing innocent men, women and children in Iran really the best way to safeguard Israel? Or will poking yet more sticks into more hornet's nests only achieve blowback against Israel and the U.S. as well? The U.S. and the Soviet Union endured several decades of Mutual Assured Destruction. Would it not be better for the Israelis to go through a MAD period like this with Iran, when and if the latter gets a nuclear device? Are these ideas, for goodness sakes, *not even worth discussing?*

Is Ron Paul an anti-Semite? To even ask this question is to insult this good man. I am of a Jewish background and I have known Dr. Paul for more decades than either of us would be happy to admit. I have had numerous discussions with him, I have broken bread with him on more than a few occasions, and have attended many conferences with him. I tell you, my "nose" for this sort of thing is as a good as any other Jew's, and never have I encountered even the slightest whiff of anything of this sort in my long association with Ron. My friends Murray Sabrin and David Gordon have had similar experiences with this member of the House of Representatives, and fully share my assessment. There could hardly be an organization Jews for Ron Paul if there was a scintilla of doubt about Dr. Paul on this matter. Want some more evidence? The two economists who are the favorites of the next president of the U.S. are the Jewish intellectuals Murray N. Rothbard and Ludwig von Mises. Ron Paul never tires of citing them when he discusses not only economic subjects such as money, the business cycle, unemployment, Austrian economics, but also, ethics, liberty, freedom. These two are his greatest intellectual and moral influences. Can anyone imagine a real anti-Semite befriending the likes of me, Gordon and Sabrin, welcoming an organization of Jews dedicated to supporting him, and mentioning two prominent Jews as his prime mentors?

But, let us assume, arguendo, that it is indeed true that, as charged, Ron Paul is wildly outside of the mainstream of the Republican party, and, perhaps even more important, holds views that counter by 180 degrees those of the RJC. (In case any members of the RJC do not understand the concept of "arguendo," this does not mean I stipulate these points to be true. As a matter of fact, I sharply disagree with them. Arguendo means, "for the sake of argument." So, I am now *assuming* the RJC charges against Dr. Paul to be true.) Does it even then logically follow that you, the RJC, are wise or even justified in excluding him from your debate?

It does not.

Here are several reasons. Given that the goal of the RJC is to reduce the chances of Ron Paul becoming the next president of the U.S., the *last* thing it needs is for him to garner more publicity. But its decision to exclude him has already given him an additional and gargantuan amount of press coverage. Thanks to the RJC, more precious ink and electronic time will be given to this man than had he been invited. (Hey, he could have been limited to 89 seconds; there is precedent for that sort of thing. No, maybe, give him two or three minutes; that attempt to shut him up didn't really work.) And not only that, Ron is now an underdog, as a non-invitee. People root for underdogs. It wouldn't surprise me if more people voted for him because of this snub. If the goal is to squelch him, it has already backfired. Is there a renegade cabal of Ron Paul supporters deep within the bowels of the RJC who concocted this exclusion idea so as to *promote* his candidacy? Naw, couldn't be. Conspiracy theories, by definition, must all be wrong.

In chess, every time you make a move, you're supposed to ask yourself, "If I do this, what will my opponent do in response?" Well, how will the Paul campaign react to this insult? Take it lying down? Not bloody likely. Dr. Paul might schedule a press conference, where he gives a major speech on how his policies will actually *help* Israel, and thus demonstrate that he is the very opposite of an anti-Semite. He might schedule this event right before or after, maybe even *during* your phony "debate." Very likely, the contrast between his creative ideas for the protection of Israel and the tired old shopworn bumper sticker "thoughts" of the other seven (let's throw more money at Israel, let's bomb Iran back to the Stone Age) will draw attention away from your event and toward his.

Then, there is the issue of anti-Semitism. Have you people lost your minds? Do you not realize that there are *real* anti-Semites out there, just looking for an excuse in support of their views? Why strengthen *them*, for goodness sake? They will use this as yet another bit of "evidence" demonstrating the perfidy and unfairness of our co-religionists.

Further, suppose, for argument's sake, that Ron Paul becomes the next president of the United States. (Mathematically, the odds of this occurring are one in sixteen, or 6 percent: there are 8 Republican candidates; let us award each of them a 12% chance; then, take half of that, given that the Democratic candidate also has a 50 percent shot at winning.) Of course, if Ron Paul loses the Republican nomination and runs as an Independent or on the Libertarian Party ticket, and New York City Mayor Bloomberg also launches a foray, then Paul's chances rise to 25 percent; e.g., a one in four chance, based on the admittedly unrealistic mathematical assumptions I am now making). Do you really want it on record that an important part of the Jewish community gave a gratuitous slap in the face to the man who might lead the country for four years?

We Jews are supposed to be people of the book. This means, if it means anything, that we are supposed to be open to *ideas.* Your decision to exclude Paul is a disgrace to this precious tradition. It is a shonda for the goyim.

The RJC of course has a *right* to invite anyone it wants to its functions. This is not censorship; that only occurs when the government prevents free speech. But, it is unwise, unfair, unjust and immoral. It trashes our reputation for lighting a light to the nations. So, I implore you, in the name of Judaism, safety for Israel, protecting our community against anti-Semitism; reconsider. It is not too late. Ron Paul is gentleman enough, I think, to accept an invitation from you, even a belated one.

Chapter 28.

Response to a Jewish Opponent of Ron Paul

Aaron Biterman posted his list of "Top 25 Reasons to Oppose RON PAUL's 2012 Campaign."

I repeat his list below, exactly as it appeared on the web site Jewish Libertarians on 12/7/11, interspersed with my commentary (<<) on each of his objections. I have no idea whether his first or 25th reason is the most important, but I follow the order of these reasons that Mr. Biterman set out in his missive.

25) Jon Huntsman

<< It is greatly to his credit that Huntsman turned down the invitation to debate from "moderator" Donald Trump. And, of course, Ron Paul did so, too. Heck, even "Mr. Principled" Mitt Romney turned up his nose at this "debate." However, Huntsman is a weather socialist, and has supported the poisonous individual health care mandate, along with his spiritual and moral counterparts, Romney, Gingrich and Obama. Huntsman does not deserve to be mentioned in the same breath, at least from a libertarian perspective, as Ron Paul. That Biterman would place him above the congressman from Texas indicates that his own libertarian credentials are hanging by a thread.

24) Gary Johnson

<< Former New Mexico governor Gary Johnson is an excellent candidate. On a scale of libertarianism, I would award him a passing grade of 65 (Romney, Gingrich, Santorum, Bachmann, Huntsman and Perry all clock in at less than 5 out of 100. Ron, in my view, hits the 95 level.) When asked, at one of the few debates he joined, who he would pick as his vice president, Gary Johnson chose Ron Paul. No one can be all bad who articulates such a thought. Indeed, in my own publications about who Ron should pick as his veep, Gary Johnson was prominently mentioned. This is what my co-author and I said about him then, and I stand by it now: "Gary Johnson. It is too bad that the former governor of New Mexico as of the time of this writing has not been able to enter into the debates. If he did so, then there would be not one but two libertarians on stage at these important events. On the other hand, we know Ron Paul, and Gary Johnson is no Ron Paul. He is more of a 'beltway' or *Reason* magazine libertarian than a real

one. He is better than the neo-cons on foreign policy, but does not call for a purely defensive stance for our military. He wants to legalize drugs, but only some of them; he did not pardon any victimless criminals when he could have. He favors the legalization of prostitution, not based on rights; merely on the basis of utilitarianism. He urges reform of the Fed, not abolition. Go down the entire list: he is pretty good on most issues from a libertarian point of view, but doesn't hit the bull's-eye on any of them."

23) The Libertarian Party

<<I am a fan of the Libertarian Party. I ran for office under its auspices in 1972. I have been an active member of it (well, except for the debacle of Bob Barr in 2008 when I quit in protest) since its founding in 1971. I have spoken often at its conventions. I am a card-carrying member of the LP. My expectation is that if Ron wants to make a third party run, which he now denies, 99% of the Libertarian Party members would vote to nominate him. If Ron Paul wins the Republican nomination for president, I have no doubt that the LP will support him as their standard bearer, too, and do everything they can to see him beat Obama. But, the Libertarian Party usually polls some 1-3 percent of the electorate, and is brutally ignored by the mainstream media. Also, unhappily, the LP scheduled its convention in 2012 before the one to be held by the Republicans.

How does that compare with the inroads Ron Paul is now making into the consciousness of the American electorate? To ask this is to answer it. Ron, even though all too often ignored by the mainstream media, is still burning up the airwaves and dominating the editorial pages of the major newspapers and magazines. Anyone who refuses to support Ron Paul on the ground that the Libertarian Party exists is surely smoking some controlled substances. Lots of them.

22) Paul claims to support free trade, but the truth is otherwise (find Paul's Cato ratings).

<< Ron Paul subscribes to the Murray Rothbard-Milton Friedman-Hong Kong-Singapore view of free trade; inaugurate a policy of full free trade, no barriers, with all countries of the world. He opposes "fair trade," "managed trade," customs unions, and treaties such as NAFTA, CAFTA, etc. He wants a unilateral declaration of free trade with all

nations, whether or not they reciprocate. Would that the Cato Institute adopt such a strong principled viewpoint. When an inside the beltway "libertarian" organization such as the Cato Institute is proposed as the rating agency for Ron Paul, we are all in trouble.

21) Paul endorsed the Constitution Party nominee for president in 2008; have you read the Constitution Party platform?

<< The Libertarian Party platform, although egregiously watered down from the days that Murray Rothbard was active in this organization, is still far superior to that of the Constitution Party. Here, I agree with Biterman. However, a case can be made that Chuck Baldwin, the Constitution Party's nominee that year, was more libertarian than Bob Barr. So, Ron is to be blamed for supporting the man, and not the party platform? That seems to be more than just a bit harsh.

20) Paul's campaign team consists of folks who have spent considerable time working for Pat Buchanan, Pat Robertson, the Christian Coalition, the Family Research Council, and various other unsavory causes.

<< It is time for an economics joke. Economist A asks economist B, "How is your wife?" Comes the reply from B: "Compared to what?" Yes, the two men mentioned, and the two organizations, each have "unsavory" (e.g., nonlibertarian) elements). But compared to *what?* In 2008, the Libertarian Party, favored by Biterman, nominated Bob Barr as president, and Wayne Allyn Root as vice president. Barr is a drug warrior and Root is a war monger. Neither was much of a libertarian. I would place Barr and Root in roughly the same political economic category as Buchanan and Robertson and rate the LP, for nominating these two nonlibertarians in 2008, in a similar manner to the Christian Coalition and the Family Research Council. No, worse. At least the latter two did not claim to be libertarian, and thus did not engage in outright fraud.

But suppose Biterman manages to evade these comparisons. Let us stipulate, arguendo, that Buchanan and Robertson, the CC and the FRC, are horrid people and organizations. Just because someone worked for them in the past does not mean they were infected by these nonlibertarians. I know Ron Paul, and I know he would not knowingly associate with nonlibertarians in his campaign. I fully expect that when Dr. Paul is sworn in to office in January 2013, he will bring with him to Washington people who will eliminate unnecessary departments, end the Fed, help him bring home the troops, shut down U.S. military bases in foreign lands, etc. Does Biterman really doubt this? No. These are precisely the reasons why that "libertarian" *opposes* Ron Paul.

19) Where is the campaign money being spent? Who is benefiting from the donations? Who is getting rich? These questions remain unanswered.

<< What is the source of Biterman's income? How does he spend his money? Who benefits from Biterman's largesse? These questions remain unanswered. Biterman, ever hear of privacy? Why is this information any of Biterman's business? It is not. However, the Paul campaign complies with all sorts of intrusive questions such as these because it is required to do so by law.

18) Paul was the economic advisor of Pat Buchanan's 1992 presidential campaign

<<So was Murray N. Rothbard, for a time, until he could no longer abide Buchanan's protectionism. Is Pat Buchanan some sort of boogeyman, the mere mention of whose name is supposed to send us running for the hills? Buchanan had, unfortunately, only some libertarian elements in his philosophy. Biterman champions the Libertarian Party but Barr and Root are no more libertarian than Buchanan.

17) Paul says Gaza is filled with "Concentration Camps."

<< There are concentration camps, and then there are concentration camps. The meaning that most people ascribe to this phrase is Nazi concentration camps, where millions of people perished. But never in a million years did Dr. Paul mean to refer to Gaza in any such context. What, then, are the other meanings of this phrase? One such definition reads as follows: "The term *concentration camp* refers to a camp in which people are detained or confined, usually under harsh conditions and without regard to legal norms of arrest and imprisonment." Under this definition, concentration camps were used by the British in South Africa and the Spanish in Cuba, long before Hitler. They were used, too, by the U.S., for Japanese-Americans during World War II. None of these other "concentration camps" are to be mentioned in the same breath as the one organized by the Nazis.

I regard this of all Biterman's 25 points as the one that rankles the most within the Jewish community, particularly among Israelis. But, I contend, when these people hear of this statement by Congressman Paul, they think, only and solely of *Nazi* concentration camps, for which there is absolutely no comparison. But how does Gaza stack up against the U.S. internment camps (concentration camps) utilized against Japanese-Americans? I maintain that while of course there are differences, the two are in the same or at least similar "ball parks." Also, it is possible that Congressman Paul misspoke, had a slip of the tongue (which of us can say that this never occurred to us?).

Do I regret that my friend Ron Paul used this particular phrase in that interview? I do. Well, at least without mentioning that he had more in mind the U.S. – Japanese-American internment camps rather than anything even resembling the Nazi case. But distinctions of this sort are difficult to make in three-minute interviews.

Nor must we lose sight of the fact that in this short interview Dr. Paul made the following very important points: He would change our Mideast policy with the goal of preventing these problems in the first place. He assigns blame to both parties. He says that Washington should mind its own business; that people in Gaza know that *our* weapons are used against them and blame us as well as Israel; and that we can't afford to intervene any longer.

But, stipulate that Congressman Paul erred in this regard. No one should oppose *any* candidate for one single mistake. We all have slips of the tongue, and bad days (Barack Obama once mis-counted the number of states in our union, claiming there were 57 of them, not 50.

16) Paul's "We the People Act" would forbid federal courts from adjudicating "any claim involving the laws, regulations, or policies of any state or unit of local government relating to the free exercise or establishment of religion,", i.e., it would remove all federal remedies for allegations of state violations of religious freedom.

<<Ron Paul is a federalist, like many of our founding fathers. He sees the major enemy of our freedom as an out-of-control *federal* government. He believes that placing greater reliance on the 50 states will better ensure our liberty. So, of course, he wants to trim the sails of the federal government, and give the states more control. His reasoning is that if one state violates rights, it is far easier to deal with than when Washington D.C. does so. This is a reason to oppose his

candidacy? Does not Biterman take cognizance of the concept of "voting with the feet?" Does he not realize that it is far easier to move from one locality to another, than from one country to another?

15) Paul says church-state separation has no constitutional basis.

<< Does Biterman point out the constitutional basis for church separation? He does not. He merely mentions this as a reason to oppose the Paul candidacy as if it is obvious. Is Biterman a member of the mainstream media? Isn't there a rule that only members of the MSM are allowed to do this? I am an economist, not a constitutional scholar, so I really can't delve deeply into this question. However, it appears to me as an outsider that the burden of proof rests with this author, and not only has he not fulfilled it, he does not realize that it is incumbent upon him to do so.

14) Paul would be age 78 at the start of his first term.

<< True. But Dr. Paul was a national class track athlete when he was in college. He is a *young* 76, right now. I have no doubt that with any athletic competition between the Republican candidates (running, swimming, biking, etc.), the congressman from Texas would acquit himself very well. Hey, Biterman *opposes* Paul. This should be an argument *for* his candidacy. For if Paul has a short life expectancy, Biterman ought to *rejoice* in this, not complain about it. If Paul wins, according to this "logic," he will soon be gone in any case.

13) Anyone (including you) can vote "no" on legislation in Congress.

<< Frankly, I don't understand this objection. He refers to Paul's congressional voting record. Either he is being critical of the entire record or he thought he could be clever without being clear or thorough. And I don't get the "anyone."

12) Paul has no executive experience: how will he perform?

<<Obama had no executive experience before becoming president either. So what? In any case, I know *exactly* how President Paul will perform, and so does everyone else who has not been Rip Van Winkling it through this campaign. He will cut taxes and pull the troops home to a *defensive (not offensive)* position; he will cut spending by one *trillion* dollars in his first year. He will end, not mend, the Fed. He will rescue the U.S. dollar with a gold standard. He will no

longer allow the federal government to run roughshod over state decisions to allow (medical) marijuana.

11) Paul is the choice of various notable conspiracy theorists, 9/11 truthers, and anti-Semites – and refuses to distance himself from these endorsements.

<< *They* support *him; he* doesn't support *them.* He "distances" himself from them all right: by saying he doesn't agree with them. By the way, are *all* conspiracy theories false? Is not a one of them true? That seems to be the underlying premise of this objection, but, as usual, it is not spelled out, certainly not defended.

10) Paul posed for a photo with KKK Grand Wizard Don Black after refusing to return $500 from Black in 2008.

<< Dr. Paul takes pictures with tens of thousands of people. At the end of every speech he gives, people line up by the hundreds for a quick picture with him. Does anyone really think that Ron Paul can recognize everyone who asks to have a five-second audience with him for a picture-taking? As for giving money back, under which conditions will justice better be served: The congressman is plus $500, and the anti-Semite at zero; or, the Congressman ends up with zero funds from this episode, and the anti-Semite has the $500? Does Biterman favor enriching anti-Semites?

9) Paul supports the Defense of Marriage Act, voted for a sodomy law for D.C. in 1981, and voted against adoptions for gays in D.C. in 1999.

<<Ron Paul's votes on these matters have more to do with his espousal of federalism than with these substantive issues. Ronald Reagan was once so incensed at the rent controls of New York City that he thought seriously of using the weight of the federal government to right this obvious local wrong. Ron Paul is more of a federalist than that, and Reagan was, too. This, too, is a contentious issue amongst libertarians, and, as far as I am concerned, politicians get a bye when the libertarian community is unsettled on a given law or public policy.

8) Paul supports the repeal of birthright citizenship, part of his platform of "common sense" immigration reforms.

<< I disagree with Ron Paul on immigration. However, there are leading libertarians (Murray N. Rothbard, Hans-Hermann Hoppe) who

espouse the Paul position on this question. When there are leading libertarian theoreticians on both sides of an issue, it is a bit much to make such an issue a litmus test for politicians. This issue, as far as I am concerned, is part of the 5% where Ron Paul diverges from libertarianism. So, go, sue him. No one is perfect. And for this, we libertarians are supposed to jettison Ron Paul? And for whom? Mitt Romney? Newt Gingrich? It is to laugh.

7) Paul signed a pro-life pledge from the Susan B. Anthony List, which involves the federal government in the issue of abortion, contrary to his rhetoric.

<< The weasel word, here, is "involves." Of course this pledge "involves" the federal government. Congressman Paul's "rhetoric" is to enable each of the states to determine these issues. Now, who is it do you think that will do this "allowing"? Why, the federal government of course; nowadays, it does most of the allowing and disallowing in our society. So, Dr. Paul's signing of this pledge is not at all incompatible with his states' rights rhetoric. It is rather disingenuous of Biterman to make this charge. Did he not think that any Ron Paul supporter would look into it?

6) Paul is among the most vocal opponents of equal protection under the law in Congress.

<<Why no link to any support for this charge? As it stands, it is a criticism without any foundation at all. Or is it Biterman's view that Dr. Paul must prove himself innocent, rather than this critic demonstrating his flaw, thus turning on its head the usual, civilized assumption of innocent until proven guilty? What does it mean to oppose equal protection of all citizens? Does it mean that a politician wants to violate the rights of the downtrodden? If so, the very opposite is the case. The war on drugs disproportionately and negatively impacts the black community. Dr. Paul has bitterly opposed it, thus helping to better protect this segment of our populace. But, it is difficult to defend the next president of the U.S. on this point, since our critic is so unclear.

5) Paul is among the most vocal opponents of Israel in Congress.

<< Nonsense on stilts. Dr. Paul is the best friend that Israel has in the entire Congress. He is among the few that favors Israeli independence. He speaks out in favor of the sovereignty of this country. U.S. foreign

"aid" to Israel's enemies is a multiple of what that country receives. Ending that program thus redounds to the *benefit* of Israel. Paul was the only one to oppose the U.S. Congress's condemnation of Israel's attack on the Iraqi nuclear facility at Osirak.

4) Paul is among the most vocal defenders of earmarks in Congress.

<<Earmarked funds are thus already consigned for expenditure. Ron Paul violates no libertarian axiom in attempting to divert some of them to his constituents who have paid for them through taxes. Earmarks also increase government transparency, surely a goal to be desired by libertarians. By the phrase "among the most" is a rather improper way of quantifying anything. Biterman should do his homework, if he wants to make these charges stick.

3) Paul has the arrogance to want to redefine human life itself.

<< Yes, what "arrogance" on the part of an Ob-Gyn who has delivered some 4,000 babies. Who is Dr. Paul to define life as beginning at conception? Why, everyone knows, they just *know,* that life really begins at birth. Therefore, such horrors as partial-birth abortion are entirely justified. I mean, the *effrontery* of the man! Here, I must agree with Biterman; Ron Paul is an arrogant would-be dictator, wanting to save the "lives" of mere bits of protoplasm, of no more moral importance than a cyst.

On a more serious note, this is part and parcel of what it means to be pro life. It is entirely legitimate for a libertarian to disagree with Dr. Paul on this issue. The libertarian community, as in the case of the population at large, is greatly divided on this issue. Thus, to make this into some sort of litmus test for libertarians is improper.

As it happens, I disagree with Dr. Paul on this issue. I am neither pro-life nor pro-choice. I adopt a third alternative, the evictionist position (Block and Whitehead, 2005). But, do I oppose Congressman Paul's campaign since he does not agree with me on this stupendously complicated issue, about which the greatest minds in libertarianism can come to no consensus? Of course not. I'm no Biterman.

Let me end this depressing section on a lighter note. Question: Do you know when the fetus is viable in the Jewish tradition? Answer: When it graduates from medical school.

2) His mean-spirited cult of supporters

<<Well, I suppose I'm one of them. I worship the very ground upon which Ron Paul treads. (Where's the Kool-Aid?) I'm meaner than a rattlesnake. Every other supporter of this congressman from Texas is just like me in this regard. Nasty as the day is long.

Hey, a silly objection deserves a silly response.

1) The racist Ron Paul newsletters, which Paul admitted writing in his 1996 Congressional campaign (Dallas Morning News, May 1996)

<< This old charge has been answered, and answered and answered once again. Only a mean-spirited cultist would bring it up again at this late date.

Walter Block thanks the following people for valuable feedback on an earlier version of this article: Thomas Nash, Lew Rockwell. All remaining errors are of course his own responsibility.

Chapter 29.

To the Jewish Community on Behalf of Ron Paul: A Love Letter

Ron Paul favors the elimination of foreign aid to Israel. Many Jews, even those who favor free enterprise, individual rights and peace, thus oppose the most libertarian candidate ever to run for the Republican nomination for president. This enmity goes so far as to account for his being barred from the Republican Jewish Coalition's candidates' forum. There is no doubt that this action was taken out of fear that if Congressman Paul's policies are put into effect, they will be harmful to Israel.

At first blush, this seems reasonable enough. The U.S. gives lots of money to thc Israeli government for use by its military, and if this were totally eliminated, it is not unwarranted to think that Israel would thereby be weakened.

However, I contend that there are several good reasons to doubt this popular belief. Consider the following.

Relative statistics

Dr. Paul by no means would single out the single country of Israel for an elimination of foreign aid. Much to the contrary, his is a thorough plan that would end this pernicious program for *all* countries. Indeed, *each and every* nation on the face of the Earth that had been receiving U.S. tax dollars would be told that their ride on this particular gravy train had ended. Would this hurt Israel? Of course, at least in dollar terms (see below for the argument that foreign aid actually *hurts* the economies of the recipient countries). But, it would also harm every other recipient as well (I am still positing, arguendo, that foreign "aid" benefits recipient countries). In order to determine whether or not Israel would be better off or not, one must make a *relativistic* judgment. That is, will Israel lose more or less than its enemies?

The facts for a recent year appear below. Here are the top 16 recipients of U.S. foreign aid for 2005:

1. Israel	$2.58 billion
2. Egypt	$1.84 billion

3. Afghanistan	$0.98 billion
4. Pakistan	$0.70 billion
5. Colombia	$0.57 billion
6. Sudan	$0.50 billion
7. Jordan	$0.48 billion
8. Uganda	$0.25 billion
9. Kenya	$0.24 billion
10. Ethiopia	$0.19 billion
11. South Africa	$0.19 billion
12. Peru	$0.19 billion
13. Indonesia	$0.18 billion
14. Bolivia	$0.18 billion
15. Nigeria	$0.18 billion
16. Zambia	$0.18 billion

Israel, as can be expected, is right at the top of this list. It would lose $2.58 billion, under President Paul's administration (I have to confess that I really like the sound of that phrase. I think I'll repeat it: President Paul's administration. Perhaps this sounds even better: President Ron Paul's administration. Or maybe this: The Administration of President Ron Paul? Okay, okay, back to business, now.) However, let us add up the amounts received by only these few countries, all of them mainly populated by either Muslims and/or Arabs:

2. Egypt	$1.84 billion
3. Afghanistan	$0.98 billion
4. Pakistan	$0.70 billion
6. Sudan	$0.50 billion
7. Jordan	$0.48 billion

If we do so, we arrive at the figure of $4.5 billion. So, yes, Israel will lose $2.58 billion, but its enemies, both actual and potential, are out of pocket a far larger $4.5 billion. If we sum up the amounts received by *all* countries which harbor anti-Semites, we reach a much higher figure. If we define this broadly enough, this might well include just about every other nation on Earth. No matter what statistics we consider, Israel is relatively *strengthened* by the Ron Paul policy on foreign aid. It loses, but its actual and potential enemies lose *more.* Thus, it becomes relatively stronger. Note, also, that these figures do not include the vast amounts currently spent by the U.S. on and in Iraq and the Palestinian territories, certainly no friends of Israel.

Private giving

There is nothing, *nothing at all*, in Ron Paul's program that would even in the slightest interfere with private foreign charitable giving. In other words, Jews in the U.S., and non-Jewish American supporters of Israel, would be just as free as at present, to donate to this country. In fact, there is every reason to suppose that these private gifts to Israel would increase, not decrease. For one thing, with the slight (foreign aid comprises only in the neighborhood of 1% of GDP) reduction in taxes this would imply (in a Ron Paul administration, such savings would be funneled into lower taxation, not into other programs; did I mention that I really like the sound of that phrase, a Ron Paul administration?) more disposable income for all. Since Jews are often in higher income brackets than the average person, and we presently suffer under a progressive income tax (which, by the way, would also be ended by President Paul) the largest donors to Israel would have even more income at their disposal. Then, too, this community might be so upset at this action of President Paul (I really like the way that phrase rolls off the tongue; ah, the sheer alliteration!), that they would donate additional monies.

Foreign aid weakens the economy

If we learn anything from Peter Bauer, it is that government-to-government transfers of income do not constitute foreign "aid." Very much to the contrary, they typically amount to foreign *detriment*. Much of the money goes to the three Ms: monuments, Mercedes and machine guns. The first need not be in the form of a statue of the leader: it could also take the form of a mill that produces steel at a multiple of the price available on world markets. The second includes not only automobiles, but also, invariably, engorged Swiss bank accounts. And the third is usually utilized by Third World dictators to keep the citizenry in thrall. Then, too, while foreign "aid" is a small part of the donor's economy, it accounts for a large percentage of the recipients' economy. Instead of the best and brightest of their young people aiming at careers that can help economic development (doctors, engineers, entrepreneurs), they engage in training that will help them divert some of the boodle to themselves, and their relatives and friends (civil servants, lawyers, bureaucrats).

In Israel, the main negative implication of U.S. largesse has been promotion of socialism. Had our country not been financially supporting a heavily unionized and socialized economy in Israel, these policies would likely have never been as large as they were, and would have diminished much sooner. There are strong empirical illustrations attesting to the correlation between size of government and economic regulations, on the one hand, and attenuation of the economy on the other (see Gwartney, et.al., 1996. For a non-empirical treatment of this phenomenon, see Smith, 1776).

That is, without U.S. "aid" to Israel, the economy of the latter would have been stronger. But a richer country is usually a safer country. One of the effects of Dr. Paul's policy, then, would be the *strengthening* of the Israeli economy.

The U.S. handcuffs Israeli policy

Because of its monetary transfers to Israel, the U.S. is in a position to dictate policy to its client state. Sometimes, perhaps, this is in the best interests of the nation of Israel. At least, it does not constitute a logical contradiction to entertain such a notion. But there are numerous cases where the U.S. has obviously handcuffed the Israelis, not to the benefit of the latter, at least as the Israelis saw their own best interest.

Perhaps the most famous example of this phenomenon is when Eisenhower forced the British, French and Israelis to pull back from their invasion of the Suez Canal in 1956.

According to one historian: "President Eisenhower of the United States pressured Britain, France and Israel into agreeing to a cease-fire and eventual withdrawal from Egypt." Forget about the rights and wrongs of the matter; they do not concern us. My point is that it is extremely difficult to interpret this little episode as being in the best interests of the security of the state of Israel.

A more recent case in point took place when Condoleezza Rice forced the Israelis to postpone the bombing of a possible nuclear facility in Syria. This was done in the context when the Israelis certainly saw *quick action* as being in their national interest. According to a news report:

"A mysterious Israeli military strike on a suspected nuclear site in Syria last month was opposed by Condoleezza Rice, the American secretary of state, because she feared it would destabilize the region, according to a report this weekend.

"Rice persuaded the Israelis to delay their operation. …"

Say what you will about these two events, which are only the tip of a very large iceberg, it cannot be denied that they constitute a serious drawback to the safety of Israel, at least in terms of how the Israelis themselves see their own best interest. Needless to say, this sort of interference would come to a halt under a Ron Paul presidency.

Then, there is the issue of "proportionality." When rockets come in from Gaza and elsewhere, Israel is warned by the U.S. to be "proportional" in its response. I wonder whether the U.S. would be "proportional" with regard to rockets coming in from Mexico or Canada and killing its residents?

Guarantor

Forget about the money, at least for a moment. The U.S. also provides Israel with a guarantee: any country trying to overrun Israel will have to deal with the armed might of the U.S. Iran, the member of the "evil axis" du jour, had better watch out.

But just how good are U.S. guarantees? As but one example you can ask the Vietnamese, who supported the U.S. incursion into their country, all about that.

Would an Israel completely untied to the apron strings of the U.S. be able to take care of itself? There seems little doubt that not only would Israel be able to defend itself, it would be *more* able to do so without the U.S. continually orchestrating matters in a paternalistic manner.

How about in the face of nuclear-armed Iran? An Israel able to operate on its own, without a by your leave from Uncle Sam, might be *better able* to prevent just such an occurrence. If not, that nation has its own nuclear weapons at its disposal. If the U.S. and the U.S.S.R. could endure decades of cold war, with only Mutual Assured Destruction keeping the "peace," it may well be that Israel and its Arab neighbors will have to go through the same process. At the very least, this present tossing of missiles from Gaza over to Israel would have to come to an end; it would be far too dangerous in a Middle Eastern MAD. Without the U.S. in the neighborhood, the major Muslim/Arab powers such as Iran, Egypt and Syria would never tolerate such risky acts.

Having given several reasons for doubting that Ron Paul's program would harm Israel, let us move on to a conclusion.

Perhaps, if Ron wanted to help Israel vis-à-vis its enemies, The U.S. would *end* government-to-government transfers of income to that country, and double or triple it to every other nation, particularly to its most vociferous enemies. With the poison of foreign "aid" applied to its enemies, but *not* to Israel, the latter might become even the more strengthened relative to them. This is an interesting speculation. But this is *not* part of Ron Paul's program. For one thing, there is nothing in the Constitution allowing, let alone requiring, such a policy. (Ron really ought to give a free copy of this document to his Republican debating partners.) For another, it is highly incompatible with libertarian prohibitions against stealing.

The action of the Republican Jewish Coalition in barring Ron Paul from their debate was a disgrace. We Jews are supposed to be the people of the book. That is, open to intellectual dialogue. How is it possible to reconcile this with a refusal to hear out one of the Republican candidates for the presidency. I urge all Jewish Republicans and libertarians to express their dissatisfaction with this act, and to join Jews for Ron Paul.

Note the narrow scope of this article. I am *not* engaged in any discussion of shoulds or oughts. I take no position, whatsoever, on whether Eisenhower was *justified* in forcing an end to the Suez crisis, nor whether Condoleezza Rice was *justified* in postponing the Israeli bombing of possible Syrian nuclear installations. I am addressing myself solely to the narrow question of whether Ron Paul's plan to eliminate all foreign aid will likely help or hurt Israel. The mainstream Jewish community fervently believes the latter. And this to such a degree that they have acted disgracefully by barring Dr. Paul from their debate. With leaders like that, the Jewish community in the U.S. hardly needs enemies.

Chapter 30.

Response to the Love Letter and a Reply

Among the many letters I received in response to the previous chapter was one from a former student of mine with whom I am still on very good, personal terms. He is an orthodox Jew and a highly intelligent professional man, who has lived in Israel for a number of years now.

In what follows is a correspondence between the two of us, in response to my Chapter 29. I will identify his words by FS, for former student, and my own by WB.

FS: Well, I've now read up on Ron Paul. Thanks for your article about why Jews should support him. I've read quite a few other items and blogs on Congressman Paul. I can see why you support him from a libertarian point of view, and as a libertarian myself, I have some sympathies there, too. From a Jewish point of view, however, which is how I usually view a candidate, I could not see myself supporting him and here are some of my reasons:

Iran. I read what Dr. Paul wrote in the Congressional record on Iran. He would not be in favor of taking out their nuclear sites. But this country is an existential threat to Israel and analogous to that against the Jews from Hitler in the 1930s. Whether the Iranian threat is imminent or not isn't too relevant. Iran is led by a bunch of Hitler clones who want to destroy the Jewish people in general and Israel in particular. For the U.S. to ignore this in the push for "non-interventionism" is no different, in effect, from the views of Father Coughlin and Henry Ford toward Jews in the 1930s.

WB: Right now, under present arrangements, Israel must seek U.S. *permission* in order to deal with Iran. Surely, that is not a good position for a supposedly sovereign nation to be in. Paul is not in favor of the U.S. taking out Iranian nuclear sites. Whether Israel does so or not, he regards as none of his business. And, by extension, not the business of the U.S. government. That is, under a Paul Administration, Israel would not have to have any go-ahead from what many consider an Arab-oriented state department before it took whatever action it decided upon against Iran.

FS: Aid to Israel: I actually agree that Israel would be better off without U.S. "aid," especially if it would get the U.S. off Israel's back.

Since 1993 and the Oslo Accords, this has been quite a thorn in Israel's side and has led to several disasters, with more likely to come. But there already is a candidate who wants the U.S. to lay off Israel and stop the pressure heaped on the "vassal state." His name is Rudy Giuliani. That is one reason I support Rudy.

WB: Rudy would continue to boss Israel around, despite what he now says. He has flip-flopped so much, you can't trust *anything* he says. According to this bit of folk wisdom, "He who pays the piper calls the tune." Surely, this would apply to Rudy, or any U.S. president, given that the U.S. continues its relationship with Israel as patron to client state. Israel would be far better off with a Ron who can be trusted to keep his mitts off Israel, than a Rudy who promises continued foreign "aid" and an unbelievable hands-off policy.

FS: The Israel Lobby. Paul has said (I'm paraphrasing because I don't remember the exact quote) that AIPAC is the best example of a "bad lobby" that we have. In other words, they are the bad guys in American foreign policy. He didn't say that about the Saudi lobby or the oil lobby. He singled out Israel. He never took back that comment.

WB: Paul opposes *all* lobbies that call for the mulcting of the U.S. taxpayer, not just AIPAC. Ron Paul is an equal opportunity hater of *all* attempts to promote U.S. interventionism abroad. Of course, AIPAC is just about the most successful of these. "Singling out" Israel sounds like anti-Semitism, so I'll reply to that below.

It is untrue, moreover, to assert that Ron Paul has singled out the Israeli lobby. He has *also* condemned the Saudi lobby.

Not only does Congressman Paul not single out Jews (AIPAC) for condemnation, he is also on record as singling out Israel for *support.* For example, consider this: "During the Lebanon war last year, he spoke against a House resolution condemning attacks on Israel and supporting Israel's right to defend itself. He warned that the resolution could lead to an escalation of the war."

FS: Anti-Semites. While I'm sure Paul is not an anti-Semite (and you are someone I can trust to vouch for that), he is supported monetarily and editorially by some of the biggest anti-Semitic people and groups. He doesn't seem to disavow them, which is a big problem. He didn't return that $500 from that neo-Nazi. If you don't disavow them, then you are welcoming their support, even indirectly. It seems that the Holocaust-denying industry is rallying around him. Am I wrong?

WB: As a Jew, I can vouch for Ron as a non-anti-Semite. I've known him for four decades, personally. I never experienced even a whiff of anything like that. But this is not just me. There is now an organized group, Jews for Ron Paul, who feel about him as I do. They would hardly join if they thought this charge had any merit whatsoever.

Ron's view on accepting money from such groups is that "they support us, we do not support them." That seems eminently reasonable to me.

I think that people who make this charge are "singling out" Ron. Other candidates get money from all sorts of nefarious sources. The Democrats are supported by unions. I regard unions as worse than criminal gangs. Is there anyone asking the Democrats to return union money?

What about taking government money? Ron refuses, on principle. (I disagree with his stand on this matter.) The other candidates, all of them, in both parties, would happily and enthusiastically take government money for their campaigns if they thought it would help them financially. Is there anyone asking any candidate to return government money?

The Communists support the Democrats. Is there anyone asking the Democrats to return this money? When Prince Harry of the U.K. wore a swastika, everyone went ballistic. And, rightly so. But, half the kids in the U.S. wear T-shirts that support Communists (Che Guevara is the most popular, but there are plenty of others). No one bats an eyelash. Why the vast difference in popular response? The Communists are International socialists. The Nazis are National socialists. Apart from that "vast" difference, they are just about the same: mass murdering scum, the both of them.

Wait, there is one more difference: the Nazis are avowedly anti-Semitic, the Communists are not. But so what? They are both evil, pure evil. Actually, according to Courtois, Conquest and Rummel, the Communists killed far more innocent people than the Nazis. To tell a political candidate like Ron that he can accept money from Communist groups, but not Nazis, is surely to commit a moral blunder.

We must "never forget" that it was the U.S. which overthrew Mossadegh in the 1950s, then undermined the Shah in the 1970s, bringing the mullahs into power in Iran. Engaging in contrary to fact history is a risky endeavor, but had the U.S. not done this, it is entirely possible that Israel would not now be facing its present threat from Iran. Congressman Ron Paul, a Taft Republican, would never in a million years be guilty of any such external meddling. No, for that, you would need a Rudy, or a Hillary.

Here is Ron in his own words on Israel: "Yet, while we call ourselves a strong ally of the Israeli people, we send billions in foreign aid every year to some Muslim states that many Israelis regard as enemies. From the Israeli point of view, many of the same Islamic nations we fund with our tax dollars want to destroy the Jewish state." Are these the words of an anti-Semite or an Israel hater? Hardly.

Walter Block wishes to acknowledge the help of an anonymous Israeli citizen in writing this essay.

Chapter 31.

May Catholics Vote for Ron Paul? I'll Give You One Guess

For whom should Catholics vote in the Republican primary? Who should they support this November? If this community stands by its principles, there is an overwhelming case for favoring Congressman Paul.

Pro life

Dr. Paul has delivered 4,000 babies. Early in his medical career, he was shocked at the inhumane way our society treats these youngest members of our species. He was particularly horrified by partial-birth abortions. This obstetrician-gynecologist is just about the staunchest pro-life advocate this side of the pope himself. Romney has waffled on this issue, as he has on pretty much every question, and the less we say about Obama's views on this matter, the better. Paul's dedication humans is not limited to babies. He opposes the death penalty, and his anti-imperialism war positions are perfectly congruent with his pro-life philosophy.

Subsidiarity

This is the doctrine in Catholic social thought that supports decentralization. Other things equal, preference ought to be given to the lowest level of organization possible: first, the individual and the family, then the community, the church and other voluntary groups, followed by the city and, the state, and, in rare instances, the national government or a world body. As far as this doctrine is concerned, the name of this man should really be Ron Subsidiarity Paul. Does he not insist that Congress (a lower level of government), alone, not the more powerful president, should declare war, as stipulated in the U.S. Constitution? Does he not wish to undermine Roe v. Wade by allowing each of the 50 states to decide this matter, rather than the federal government? Does he not follow the same policy with regard to ending our insane (and racist) war against drugs?

What about subsidiarity between the private sector and the government? What follows is a more controversial interpretation of this principle of Catholicism, but I would venture to say that the state is always a higher level of organization than is any purely private actor, no matter how large, at least assuming away the phenomenon of crony capitalism or economic fascism. For, when there is a confrontation between even the lowest level of government, say, at the village level, and a very large corporation, for instance, Wal-Mart, the former must always prevail, since it has the police power. Just as in bridge where the lowest trump card exceeds in power the highest nontrump card, so does the local sheriff have more pure power, hence authority, hence higher standing in the subsidiarity sweepstakes, than does the CEO of the most powerful corporation in the nation.

Solidarity

This aspect of Catholic social teaching has been defined as "We are one human family, whatever our national, racial, ethnic, economic, and ideological differences. We are our brothers' and sisters' keepers, wherever they may be. Loving our neighbor has global dimensions…" Who does this sound like? Obama? Gingrich? Romney? Santorum? Of course not. When you want to bomb innocent people to smithereens, it is hardly compatible with "loving our neighbor." With regard to our brothers and sisters in Iran, these four candidates do not want to "take anything off the table." This means they are actually contemplating nuking Iran. Ron Paul accuses the four of them of taking *one* thing "off the table" and that is negotiations. Actually, *talking* to the Iranians. Obviously, he is the only one with even a scintilla of solidarity for our fellow human beings.

Preferential option for the poor

Congressman Paul favors the free enterprise system. Laissez faire capitalism (the very *opposite* of crony bail-out-the-fat-cats capitalism), is the last best hope for the poor. There can be few who have done more to alleviate poverty than Bill Gates, Ray Kroc and Wal-Mart. Adam Smith's invisible hand said it best: under a small government limited to protecting rights, people are led by their self-interest to promote the public good, which, preeminently, involves enriching the poor.

Just war doctrine

Let us consider just two elements of this magnificent philosophy:

- War as a last resort. All nonviolent options must be exhausted before the use of force can be justified.

- Self-defense against an armed attack is always considered to be a just cause

Have Iraq, Afghanistan, Iran and Libya actually attacked us? Of course not. No self-defense there. The moral monstrosity of 9-11 was perpetrated mainly by *Saudis*; 'twas blow-back from prior U.S. invasions. How can stationing U.S. troops in 130 different countries be reconciled with Catholic just war theory?, asks Paul.

Golden Rule

The rule, "do unto others as you would have them do to you," while not quintessentially Catholic, is certainly included, and given an important place, in this religious tradition. Congressman Paul is forever voicing such sentiments as, How would *we* like it if *they* did to us (bombing innocent women and children, invading other countries, stationing our military bases there) what *we* are doing to *them?*. If this way of analyzing the world does not fit in with the Catholic tradition, then nothing does. In sharp contrast, the other candidates for the Republican Party's nomination for president claim that the reason *they* hate us is because of our freedoms and liberties. Nonsense on a stick. We are not all that free, as it happens. In any case, this sort of Golden Rule thinking is a Ron Paul refrain, and very consonant with Catholicism.

Objections:

Ron Paul, with his "states' rights" philosophy, supports rights-violations as long as they are perpetrated by the 50 states. Nonsense. The 14th Amendment to the U.S. Constitution imposes the Bill of Rights on the latter.

Paul's anti-war stance would leave our country defenseless. Nonsense. He opposes *imperialism,* not self-defense. His policies would leave us *safer.* Our military would not seek foreign monsters to destroy, but would rather be stationed on our shores, the better to *protect* us. When we stop poking sticks at foreign hornet's nests, fewer of them will come here to bite us.

Those racist newsletters of his from the 1980s disqualify Ron Paul from higher office. He has apologized and disavowed them until he is blue in the face. He didn't write the offensive material and he didn't edit it; he only published it. Do Murdoch or Sulzberger read every word in their publications? Hosanna Myers states, "Ron Paul is vilified for missing a few paragraphs out of hundreds of newsletters by people who pass 2,000-page bills without reading a single word." Paul is the least racist candidate for the presidency of the U.S., and this includes Obama.! Foreign and drug wars disproportionately kill and/or incarcerate young black men, and only he has opposed this injustice.

Paul is out of step with yet another vital doctrine of the Catholic Church, a motto of my own Loyola University New Orleans: "social justice." No. There are *numerous* scholars/pundits, with impeccable progressive, leftist, socialistic and liberal credentials, who favor his anti-war, anti-drug law, anti-bailouts over crony capitalist policies vis-à-vis Obama, Romney, Gingrich and Santorum. These commentators are second to none in their support for social justice.

VIII.

Defenses of Ron Paul on other grounds

Chapter 32.

Nicholas Lemann of the *New Yorker*

Nicholas Lemann of the *New Yorker* wrote in January 2012 a particularly ill-mannered, nasty and ignorant dismissal of Ron Paul and his campaign for the presidency. I shall subject his vicious screed to a line-by-line criticism. I will do so emulating Henry Hazlitt's intensive response to Keynes' General Theory. Why should I spend so much time on such unimportant drivel as this, written by an author of no particular distinction? I'm not sure. It is by far not the worst of the smears about Congressman Paul. There are more objectionable pieces out there. Maybe it is because I am originally from New York City, and I used to regularly read the *New Yorker*. Maybe it is because, as I write, the returns are coming in from Iowa. I really don't know. All I'm aware of is that this *New Yorker* essay really stuck in my craw, and the only way I know how to alleviate these feelings of helplessness at the unfairness of it all is to write about it. That's my way of kicking butt. So, here goes. (My comments are in italics, following these marks <<.)

Comment: Enemy of the State by Nicholas Lemann January 9, 2012

For the past six months or so, the Republican-primary electorate has

had a polite, patient, reliable, steadily employed suitor chatting with Mom and Dad in the parlor, while a series of more exciting but less appropriate rivals have come knocking at the back door. Mitt Romney will probably win in the end, but each of his serially surging competitors enjoys more immediate access to some essential region of the Republican soul. Herman Cain is the tough, no-bullshit businessman, Rick Santorum the devout pro-lifer, Rick Perry the hyper-masculine cowboy, Michele Bachmann the evangelical populist, Newt Gingrich the swashbuckling geostrategist.

<<So far, so good. No real criticisms, yet. I didn't much like that crack about "Mitt Romney will probably win in the end," *but I am nothing if not generous; so I'll not pounce, yet. But, I can't resist. Why, in 2012, still mention Cain? He dropped out of the race in December of 2011.*

It seems fitting that the final surge should belong to Ron Paul, who speaks most directly to one of his party's deepest emotions: hostility to government. At seventy-six, Paul has aged perfectly into his personality. He's a white-haired, wide-eyed prophet – it's easy to imagine him in white robes, instead of a business suit – who must rail against the outrages he has witnessed. To a pinched, stressed, war-weary, declinist nation, he offers the clearest program of any of the candidates. Five federal departments gone in Year One. Ten percent of the federal workforce laid off. Income tax abolished, along with the I.R.S. regulations and social programs repealed. No more foreign wars; no more foreign aid; not even very much foreign policy.

<< Ron is not "hostile to government." He does not reject the state per se. He is not an anarchist. Rather, he rejects excessive government; out of control government; large government; unconstitutional government. Congressman Paul supports a limited role for government. That business of "Ten percent of the federal workforce laid off" sounds as if it would increase unemployment. The very opposite is the case. How can this be? It is due to the fact that we should only count a job as real "employment" when the worker actually creates goods and services that people want. Call that "positive employment." But, suppose, as Keynes famously mentioned, workers only dug holes and filled them up again, and at the end of the day we the people had no more toys and food than we had at the beginning. Call this "neutral employment." It doesn't reduce poverty, but it doesn't increase it either. Now consider the scenario where goods and services actually fall as a result of a given "job." That would be in our lexicon "negative employment." How could this be? Simple. The employment slot consists not of creating anything nor of coming out even, but of preventing other people from working, or reducing their productivity. These are the kinds of government jobs Dr. Paul would eliminate. So, paradoxically, by doing so, we will have more real goods and services with fewer workers toiling away. That is not unemployment; that is an increase in productivity. Those workers who are fired will be able to find "positive employment," provided, of course, that we follow Austrian Business Cycle Theory, and allow the market to throw off the present depression; more about this below.

Especially to the self-selected group that comes to the Iowa

Republican caucuses, Paul's positions are pulse quickening. If you are anti-tax, Paul has that sentiment nailed more than any other candidate. If you are anti-war, Paul is right there with you. If you fear for your personal freedoms, Paul has you covered. And if you want a sweeping philosophy, deeply grounded in fundamental texts (Hayek, von Mises, Rothbard), Paul is your man. Nobody has a better claim to be a protest candidate. He's the only one who has ever run for office from a third party. He's not about passing bills; he's about root-and-branch change. His popularity, even if it's temporary, demonstrates that all politics isn't necessarily local – that big ideas can exert a pull on voters, too.

<<Dr. Paul is not "anti-tax." He opposes the income tax, but would not eliminate all taxation. Nevertheless, this is a pretty good paragraph. I especially appreciate the author's mention of Rothbard. All too often mention in the mainstream media of the "fundamental texts" written by Austrian authors is limited to Mises and Hayek. I regard Rothbard as far more important in this context than Hayek, and, roughly equal to Mises.

Paul's baseline obsession is with currency: President Nixon's decision, forty years ago, to take the United States off the gold standard is what brought him into politics. His hatred of the Federal Reserve Board is related to a mistrust of currencies managed by governments. Underlying everything is, of course, a larger mistrust – the sense that in some hushed Washington conference room highly consequential arrangements are being made that will help a few privileged insiders and hurt ordinary Americans. Although Paul has spent most of his life directly benefitting from one or another federal payroll or program, starting when he served in the Air Force, he isn't just striking a pose when he describes government as the enemy of freedom. He means it.

<<Congressman Paul is not "obsessed" with the gold standard. He is concerned. He is pretty level-headed about this. If there is any "obsession" going on in the race for the presidency of the U.S. in 2012, it is on the part of all the other candidates, and it has nothing to do with monetary policy. Rather, it concerns blowing up hundreds of thousands of innocent people abroad who are citizens of countries that have never attacked us, and are incapable of invading us, in any case. Another error: Nixon only closed the gold window for foreigners in 1971. FDR gets the blame for a far bigger step away from gold in

1933 when he prohibited the use of it for money on the part of U.S. citizens. Nor does the congressman "hate" the Fed. Dr. Paul is not much of a hater. He sees this institution as a destabilizing force in the economy, leading from depression to inflation and back. Yes, of course, the good doctor 'mistrusts ... currencies managed by governments," and with very good reason. Nor can it be denied that these "arrangements ... help a few privileged insiders and hurt ordinary Americans." Lemann sees Paul as "benefitting" from his military service. This is more than passing curious. Presumably, this New Yorker author, then, would interpret the non-service of all those chicken-hawk armchair generals running for the presidency as somehow more noble. They, at least, didn't "benefit" from their contribution to the Army, Navy, Marines or Air force. And, yes, the Texan certainly "means it" when he sees not "government," but rather out-of-control government, as the "enemy of freedom."

The other candidates ignored Paul until he looked like a serious threat, and then they began attacking him. He doesn't care whether Iran has nuclear weapons. He wouldn't have killed Osama bin Laden. He's the only Republican candidate who is not an ardent supporter of Israel. He suggests that the 9/11 attacks were comeuppance for our misguided interventionism, and doesn't think they justified a declaration of war. He has given at least silent assent to full-on paranoia and racism among his supporters. Gingrich has declared Paul's views to be "totally outside the mainstream of virtually every decent American."

<<It is a blatant and outright lie to say that Dr. Paul "doesn't care whether Iran has nuclear weapons." He cares very much. Why? Because such devices are necessarily invasive. They cannot be pinpointed at the guilty. Ron Paul stands against any country wielding them. But, he maintains that there is zero chance of Iran using this ordnance against our country, and that therefore that situation is none of our business, a concept alien to the thoughts of our mainstream media. He would, too, have presided over the execution of bin Laden, if a court decreed that verdict (although he now opposes the death penalty as unfair to black people). He would want this murderer to be treated in roughly the same manner as were the high-ranking Nazis at the end of World War II; e.g., the Nuremberg trials. What is so bloody awful about treating bin Laden in that manner? By the way, the entire point of water-boarding and other such torture is to gain information. Why then was bin Laden summarily killed before he could speak about what he knew? Dr. Ron Paul most certainly is "an ardent supporter of

Israel." He thinks that this can best be done, however, by respecting their sovereignty, not by treating them as a naughty child. He opposes giving massive amounts of foreign aid to all nations, certainly including the enemies of Israel. This, the congressman from Texas argues, will be to the relative benefit of the latter. By allowing Israel to attain her sovereignty and thus control over her own fate, she will be in a far better position to protect herself. Ron Paul doesn't only "suggest" that the "9/11 attacks were comeuppance for our misguided interventionism," he demonstrates the truth of this claim. I note that this New Yorker author contents himself by merely listing this litany of complaints, as if they were God's given truth. He doesn't bestir himself to defend these charges against the counter evidence that has been put forth. He acts as if there could not possibly be anything to be said in Dr. Paul's defense. This applies, too, to Lemann's correct statement that in Paul's view, the horrid events of 9/11 did not justify "a declaration of war." Against whom? Should we have warred against Saudi Arabia, since 15 of the 19 terrorists responsible for this despicable act emanated from that country? One might as well declare war against New York State since Timothy McVeigh was born there. No, instead, statesman Paul favored the use of Letters of Marque and Reprisal, which would enable us to pinpoint our reaction on the guilty parties. But why utilize the Constitution, when instead we can inaugurate undeclared wars against innocent people, and use this sorry episode to export "democracy" at the point of a gun? I won't dignify yet another linkage of Dr. Paul and "racism" with a response, but I will say that "Gingrich" and "decent American" do not belong in the same sentence.

Yet what is and isn't part of the mainstream is something that political campaigns determine. And the truth is that Paul's vision reveals – with candor and specificity – what the G.O.P.'s rhetorical hostility to government would mean if it were rigorously put into practice. A minimal state, without welfare provisions for the unemployed. A quarter of a million federal workers – as a first installment – joining those unemployed. Foreign policy and national defense reduced to a few ballistic-missile submarines. The civil-rights legislation of the 1960s repealed as so much unwarranted government intrusion. As for the financial crisis, Paul would have countenanced no regulation that might have prevented it, no government stabilization of the financial system after it happened, and no special help for working people hurt by it. This is where the logic of government-shrinking leads.

<<Unemployment insurance increases unemployment, and lengthens its duration. Whenever you subsidize anything, you get more of it. UI subsidizes unemployment. You stating it isn't undisputed proof. National defense would not be "reduced." With President Paul at the helm, it would be increased, and vastly so. Instead of poking sticks in hornet's nests all over the world, and then wondering why some of them come back here to bite us. -- hint: it is not because of our freedoms – Under a Paul administration, our soldiers and sailors would come back to our shores to protect us. Think in terms of a gigantic and powerful Coast Guard, with of course, more "ballistic-missile submarines," if President Paul thought them necessary. He would have additional funds to do so, if soldiers were pulled out of not only Iraq and Afghanistan but from all over the world. What is the U.S. military doing in Germany and Japan for goodness sake? Did we not conclude wars with those two countries a while ago? Ron Paul fervently supports those aspects of the Civil Rights Act of 1964 that ended Jim Crow legislation with its government mandated discrimination. However, he opposes those elements that violated private property rights, another phrase seemingly not in the lexicon of sophisticated New Yorker writers. Dr. Paul opposes "... regulation that might have prevented ... the financial crisis?" Why, 'twas the Fed, and onerous regulations emanating from Fannie, Freddie, HUD, etc., that caused it in the first place. Congressman Paul is against "... government stabilization of the financial system after it happened?" That was precisely what FDR did in the 1930s, and that only increased the severity and duration of the Great Depression. It would appear that Obama is channeling this hero of his, and is emulating him to the greatest degree possible. In contrast, no one ever hears of the depression of 1921, when the "magic of the market" was allowed to bring back the economy after only a short disturbance. Our future president does not see the need for "...special help for working people?" The nonworking people of this country don't need any "help" from the government. What they most need is to get this institution off their backs. The unemployment rate is so high because of the minimum-wage law, out-of-control unions, and the fear of Obama-care in the offing. Employers are not adding to their payrolls, in part, because they don't know the full extent of their financial responsibilities for any new hires under new socialized medicine.

Even if Paul wins in Iowa, his campaign will almost surely falter; don't count on seeing him deliver a prime-time address at the Republican National Convention. Still, Paul's brief heyday will – like the Tea Party, itself a rather Pauline affair – have an effect, on both parties. For the Republicans, the question is whether Paul's enumeration of the minimal-state particulars will entrench the appeal of government-bashing or serve, instead, as a vaccine that protects the party against taking politically disastrous stands in the future. Would a President Romney be able to operate under the rules that applied to Ronald Reagan and the two Bushes – as long as you say you're for limited government, you can expand government freely as the need arises – or would the lingering effect of Paul's campaign curtail his options?

<< *If the powers that be within the Republican Party had their 'druthers, Ron Paul would never get within a million miles of a podium at the Republican National Convention, or anywhere else for that matter. However, if they have any sense, they will smile and invite him to deliver a prime-time address there. Why? So as to decrease the likelihood that he will run as a third party candidate. So that at least some of his followers will vote for tweedle dum or tweedle dummer, the winner of the Republican primaries, if it is not him. But it is quite premature to assume that Dr. Paul's campaign will "falter." His money-raising "bombs" will finance his continued run until November. His army of inspired followers will get many more chances to demonstrate their enthusiasm. Even if the media continues to ignore him (they had threatened to ignore the entire state of Iowa, had he won their caucus election), a close third-place finish there gives him plenty of momentum for New Hampshire. When Gingrich was the front-runner, Ron Paul advertisements (remember "serial flip-flopper") brought down that worthy. The Paul campaign will now demonstrate that both Romney and Santorum are big-government, left-liberal, flip-flopping, chicken-hawk war-mongers.*

For the Democrats, Paul presents a different problem. In politics, there's the small set of issues that draw public attention and then there's everything else – ninety-five percent of what happens in Washington. When anti-government rhetoric meets big issues like war and economic disaster, it's usually good for the Democrats, because they can make the argument for action without being hypocritical. On the small issues, though, the triumph of anti-government rhetoric has been a real impediment for President Obama. It gives the Republicans a justification to oppose, by rote, every appointment and every expenditure, which helps make their belief in public-sector inefficiency self-fulfilling but otherwise doesn't do anybody much good.

<<*"For the Democrats, Paul presents a ... (gigantic) ... problem." If and when he becomes the Republican standard bearer (take that, Hannity, Trump, Fox News, O'Reilly, Gingrich), he will roll right over Obama. I give Paul only a fifty percent chance to get that far, but a ninety percent chance of winning the presidency if he does. Why? Because Paul appeals to that "old right" Taft wing of the Republican Party that values peace and defense rather than offense. He will couple that with Independents and Democrats sick of all the wars, all the death. He will have a field- day exposing the gigantic gap between Obama's promises and his actual policies. He will garner the votes of people who oppose Obama's militarism, SOPA, NDAA, drug policies, unemployment, the list goes on and on. There are numerous pundits with impeccable leftist, progressive, and socialist (it is hard to keep up with these people, they keep changing their name so much) credentials, who are seriously supporting Ron Paul, or at least contemplating doing so. Obama will be both out left-flanked and out right-flanked.*

Right now, it must be tempting for Obama to let Ron Paul's moment play out as long as possible: it usefully draws attention to the less seemly aspects of Republican political culture. But silence doesn't solve the problem of day-to-day, full-bore Republican resistance. Obama would do well to take Paul's success as an opportunity to engage in a debate about fundamentals. He'll have an easier time governing in practice if he can defend governance in principle.

<<*A debate? Without a teleprompter for Obama? Paul will make mincemeat out of him.*

Chapter 33.

Those Beltway "Libertarians"

Alexander McCobin wrote me as follows:

Walter,

I just read your recent blog post on LRC that claims "*Reason* is anti-libertarian" and goes on to recommend people shouldn't give money to *Reason*, which is, in essence, a way of saying you don't think *Reason* should exist. I have to say, I was surprised and disappointed by the post given our past conversations when you expressed a strong desire for the libertarian movement to avoid infighting and work together to advance liberty. What's more, when we last spoke, you said that your criticism of other libertarians was meant to advance the search for truth and was done with a sense of respect for those you criticized. I am having a difficult time interpreting a post like this as either overcoming infighting within the liberty movement or written with respect for *Reason* or Bob Poole, in particular.

On a different note, I also think your criticism of Poole's article is wrong. There is a difference between promoting libertarianism as a philosophy and promoting liberty as a cause for a freer society. I think it both poor strategy and unprincipled to say that we should only promote libertarianism as a philosophy at the expense of liberty by requiring people to make decisions and judgments using the same philosophical rationale as us. If we want more people to support the cause of liberty and make a difference in the world, we need to use persuasive techniques and analysis that goes beyond quoting our favorite libertarian figures. Just because "[i]t could have been written by any mainstream urban analyst" does not mean it is not advancing liberty. In many ways, because its analysis is not indebted specifically to libertarian figures, it can appeal to more individuals and shows that liberty is a sound position simply on face.

Sincerely & For Liberty,

Alexander

Alexander McCobin
Co-Founder & Executive Director
Students For Liberty
www.StudentsForLiberty.org
www.PoliticalConferences.org
www.facebook.com/StudentsForLiberty

The present essay is an attempt to reply to this critic of mine.

I answer McCobin under three headings.

First, Katherine Mangu-Ward. If this *Reason* editor was really a *libertarian* who thought Ron Paul has a poor chance of becoming president of the U.S. (not a totally unreasonable stance) she could have praised him to the skies, and then said something along the lines that there simply aren't enough libertarians in the populace to give him a win in 2012. She could have gone on to say that if any person could create enough libertarians for this purpose, and has *almost* done so, it would be the very Ob-Gyn from Texas under discussion. Did Mangu-Ward do that? Did she even come close? Not at all. Instead, she stated that even Ron Paul knows that he won't be president, and that explains his supposed lack of coverage. Her proof? Dr. Paul "has no plan for becoming president." But that is a blatant falsehood. His plan, reiterated over and over again, is peace with foreign nations (pull the troops home), economic freedom at home via a sound money policy? (no Fed), limited government (eliminate some half-dozen federal departments plus HUD), lower taxes (no IRS), personal liberties (end the drug war), and Constitutionalism. How did Miss Mangu-Ward ever get to be a political commentator for *Reason* and not be acquainted with these basics of his plan for becoming president? We either have to conclude that Miss Mangu-Ward is very stupid, which I do not believe for a moment, or something far worse. More evidence in this regard: Mangu-Ward extols the candidacy of Gary Johnson, a libertarian lightweight with far less of a chance of becoming president than Ron Paul. If the likelihood of being elected is so important, how can her support for Johnson be explained?

Liz Trotta, no libertarian she, was by far more sensible. No eye rolling at Congressman Paul's expense for her. Instead, a fair assessment: that the congressman from Texas was tapping into something important, a new interest in liberty, and tiredness with all of those wars, none of which are defensive. Indeed, a fair-minded commentator who didn't know better might well have concluded that Trotta was the libertarian, not Mangu-Ward. I listened to that Trotta/Mangu-Ward tape again before responding to Alexander McCobin, and, let me tell you, it really made my blood boil at *Reason* for unleashing this woman upon the public. She was just so totally *unfair* to the man who is now promoting liberty to a greater extent, perhaps, than any individual in the history of the world. She would fit in fine at a place like CNN, ABC, PBS, NBC, CBS, the New York Times, etc. Has *Reason* fired this virago for her attempted trashing of Ron Paul, and thus diverted her career toward a more appropriate employer? No, they have not. Have they even publicly upbraided her? Alas, no. Instead, they issued a mealy mouthed semi apology, semi explanation, along the lines of upholding diversity of opinion. Diversity of opinion on a periodical supposedly devoted to promoting liberty? Well, yes, perhaps, on a complicated issue where eminent libertarians cannot agree. But the contribution of Ron Paul to promoting liberty, surely, cannot be considered one of these.

I had no difficulty, then, when I wrote this critique, in concluding that *Reason* is not a libertarian organization on this basis, nor do I now, Alexander McCobin's views to the contrary notwithstanding. In fact, in reconsidering this episode, I am far more sure of my ground than before.

Second, Bob Poole. He is, if anything, guilty of far more a serious breach of libertarian propriety than is Mangu-Ward. He is a veteran, presumably of our movement; she, far younger than he, is a mere beginner. We can be far more justified in excusing an error made by an apprentice, than by a supposed master of the craft.

Bob Poole has for many years now been an efficiency expert for the

state, not a libertarian. In the specific issue under debate, Poole takes the position that government should not subsidize high-speed rail. Well and good. For a libertarian, that is surely a no brainer. But *why* not? Is it based on the libertarian case that such government subsidies are predicated on compulsory taxes (or unjust government land grant subsidies) which are incompatible with libertarianism? Not at all. Instead, Poole's opposition stems from cost considerations, passenger miles, population densities, etc. This is not a libertarian argument at all. Indeed, if cost considerations and population densities were the only relevant consideration, then private enterprise should not invest in these amenities either. In contrast, the libertarian view on the matter, the *only* libertarian view on the matter, is that private individuals should be free to invest their hard-earned money in whatever economic areas they wish, and the free market with its profit and loss considerations will properly settle the issue of whether or not this was a wise decision. When *Reason* was begun, all its well-wishers hoped for the day when its spokesmen would have the ear of the readers of a periodical such as USA Today, where Poole published his statist screed, so as to be able to promote liberty far and wide. To think that the day has finally come upon us, where people like Poole are given a national podium, and for them to promote not free enterprise, but pretty much its very opposite. Oh, how the gods must be laughing at our feeble attempts to promote liberty.

But McCobin is not at all happy with these critical comments of mine on Poole. Instead, he takes the not unreasonable position that we should not try to force every jot and tittle of our own philosophy down the throats of others, only its main focus. For example, if I am a deontologist, and reject government subsidies to high-speed rail because they violate rights, and Poole is a utilitarian, and opposes them on the ground that population densities simply will not support such investments, then it is improper for me to criticize Poole for leading us to liberty via a slightly different route than my own. This at least, is how I understand McCobin's objection. If my interpretation is correct, his point fails. For Poole is not opposing government subsidies to high-speed rail solely on utilitarian grounds. As he concedes, there are *some* areas where such investments would actually be justified. For example, Boston-NYC-Washington, D.C. and San Francisco-L.A. Here, Poole's analysis does not support the libertarian solution at all.

McCobin also accuses me of demanding that Poole "quot(e) … our favorite libertarian figures." But I made no such demand; I wonder from whence this charge springs? My critic further avers: "Just because '[i]t could have been written by any mainstream urban analyst' does not mean it is not advancing liberty." Nonsense. Mainstream urban analysts are without exception supporters of urban socialism, central planning for cities, etc. To say that Poole's analysis is indistinguishable from theirs is to clearly assert that this author is one of theirs, not ours.

Third, should *Reason* exist at all? McCobin interprets my remarks in precisely this way: "You (Block) go … on to recommend people shouldn't give money to *Reason*, which is, in essence, a way of saying you don't think *Reason* should exist." Certainly, my critique of this organization is compatible with a desire that they close shop, but it does not at all logically imply any such thing. Indeed when I wrote my critique of Mangu-Ward and Poole, I did not have that in mind at all. I was hoping, first, that these two would see the error of their ways, apologize for their mistakes, resolve to take a more libertarian path in future, etc. Failing that, I would have welcomed *Reason* firing whichever of these two remained adamant in their error. It is only if *Reason* stood behind both of these miscreants that I would even contemplate this more radical solution. But I would have done so only reluctantly. *Reason* magazine and Foundation have been in business since 1978. They have done many, many good things over the years. It would be a crying shame if such an organization were to come to an end. However, I am not closed-minded. Now that McCobin has raised the issue, I am willing to at least contemplate the demise of this organization, even though, frankly, I did not really have any such thing in mind previously.

At the outset, I think it would be difficult to make the case for *Reason* closing its doors. I am guided in this, as I am on so many other things, by Murray Rothbard, who was a "big tent" libertarian. Many are the times I have heard Murray say, "Every dog gets one bite." What Murray meant by this is that if a person deviated from plumb line libertarianism on one or even a few important issues, he was still a libertarian. Surely, the peccadilloes of Mangu-Ward and Poole, and even *Reason*'s refusal to upbraid them, would not rise to the level necessary to consider them non-libertarian. Of course, you can only take this so far. When an organization becomes guilty of "a train of abuses and usurpations" then perhaps it is time to consider whether they belong in the movement at all, big tent as it is. Then, we might well consider alternatives.

So, would the libertarian movement be better or worse off if the *Reason* enterprise came to a halt? In part, this depends upon where the money that otherwise would have accrued to them would go instead. If to the Brookings Institution, American Enterprise and Hoover Institutes, or Heritage Foundation, well, then, better *Reason* than those other worthies. Sure, *Reason* is a son of a bitch, but at least they are *our* son of a bitch. On the other hand, if these monies went, instead, to the Independent Institute, or to Antiwar.com, or to the Mises Institute, or to the Ron Paul campaign, then we have pretty much of a no brainer. These latter groups have been stalwart undeviating supporters of liberty for decades. On the other, other hand, if Brookings, AEI, Hoover, etc., were financially strengthened at the expense of *Reason*, at least no one would be able to use that old charge, "Well, even libertarian *Reason* concedes…." Friedman and Hayek, bless their souls, have been used as a stick with which to beat up on libertarians for lo these many years in such a manner. With no *Reason* in existence, at least we might be spared this stab in the back.

Do the two episodes of Poole and Mangu-Ward, heinous as they both were, rise, or rather fall to the level where libertarians should seriously consider cutting *Reason* off at the knees and encouraging its dissolution. Of course not. These are only two Rothbardian "bites," after all. However, thanks to McCobin's challenge, I have done a bit of research, and come up with a horrendous list of many other "bites." Read them and cringe. On the basis of all of them, and I have been assured by my researchers that even all of these comprise, merely the tip of the veritable iceberg, I say, down with *Reason*. This organization has been doing its level best to undermine liberty, from a supposed libertarian point of view, for years. Libertarians, do please send your contributions elsewhere. Here is the evidence upon which I base such a conclusion:

Kinsella on Poole on the TSA; Klein on Poole on Buckley; Vance on Poole on McCain/Bush; Gregory on *Reason* on inflation; Woods on *Reason* on Ron Paul; Rockwell on *Reason*; Kwiatkowski on *Reason* on Ron Paul; Parfitt on *Reason*; Kinsella on *Reason* on IP; Rockwell on *Reason* on Libertarian Heroes; Kinsella on *Reason* on rights of patients; Mortellaro on organ donations; Wicks on Rand Paul and slavery; Raimondo on *Reason* and Ron Paul. I thank Skyler Collins and Dick Clark for providing me with this bibliographical information.

Chapter 34.
Ron Paul and the election of 2012

Many mainstream critics were calling for Ron Paul to drop out of the race for the Republication nomination, on the ground that he has so far been very unsuccessful. He has not won any state race. But how *is* Ron Paul doing so far in the election of 2012? One way to look at this is via the table below:

Results for U.S. Presidential Primaries

	State	Gingrich	Paul	Romney	Santorum
02/07	CO	12.8%	11.8%	34.9%	40.3%
02/07	MO	-	12.2%	25.3%	55.2%
02/07	MN	10.8%	27.1%	16.9%	45.0%
02/04	NV	21.1%	18.8%	50.1%	10.0%
01/31	FL	31.9%	7.0%	46.4%	13.3%
01/21	SC	40.4%	13.0%	27.8%	17.0%
01/10	NH	9.4%	22.9%	39.3%	9.4%
01/03	IA	13.3%	21.4%	24.5%	24.6%

Source: AP

Here, it does not look as if the Congressman from Texas is doing all that well. No outright winner. A string of thirds and fourths. Is he about to be tailed out of the election? Is he about to be turfed off by the mainstream media that would like nothing better? Not a bit of it.

Let us greatly simplify the electoral statistics mentioned above concerning the results of the Republican Presidential Primaries. We now consider not the actual votes, but, merely, the places taken by the four remaining candidates. Then, the table would be greatly simplified, and look like this:

State Candidate

	Gingrich	Paul	Romney	Santorum
Colorado	3	4	3	1
Missouri	(4)	3	2	1
Minnesota	4	2	3	1
Nevada	2	3	1	4
Florida	2	4	1	3
New Hampshire	3	2	1	4
Iowa	4	3	2	1
South Carolina	1	4	2	3
Total	23	25	15	18

About this new way of looking at the matter, a few comments.

The lowest ranking is of course the best. Based on these very rough statistics Romney is now in winning position with a score of 15, Santorum places second with 18, Gingrich shows at third with 23, and Paul brings up the rear of the pack with 25.

I had to insert a ranking of fourth for Gingrich in Missouri, because he was not on the ballot there. However, there are several other states for which neither Gingrich nor Santorum qualify for ballot status, such as Virginia. Only Paul and Romney will contest these states. Thus, I will in future award Gingrich and Santorum with a 3rd and 4th "place" in each of these cases (I will give the third place nod to whoever is leading in the polls at the time). So, while Paul is now in fourth or last place, the prognostication for future improvement, at least vis a vis these two candidates, is positive. On the basis of this consideration I offer a prediction: the last two candidates standing will be Paul and Romney. (Well, it is actually more of a hope than a predication, but who knows.)

A question immediately arises: is Paul even keeping "touch" with the pack? Is he in the race, or is he so far behind at this early date that he is not even part of the story? It is difficult, on the basis of these simplified statistics, to draw any such conclusion much as the main stream media would like to do. Yes, the duo of Romney and Santorum are now showing some space between them on the one hand, and Gingrich and Paul on the other, but, unless we are willing to stipulate that Gingrich, too, has lost contact with the leaders, the same cannot be said about Paul, either. For there are only *two* "points" separating the third and fourth place holders. This is important, given the cries from the mainstream media likely to occur to the effect that Paul is just confusing matters, and should drop out of the race. No, he is *in* it, *all* the way in it, and *in* it to *stay.* If there is an argument for him leaving, it applies to Gingrich as well. Here is my second predication: one of the four candidates will drop out before Tampa, and it will not be Paul. I suspect it will be Gingrich, or, possibly, Santorum.

It is important to appreciate the fact that it is still early days in this horse race. So far, we have only heard from eight states, and there are 50 of them (not 57, as maintained by Obama).

But, so far, the other three candidates have each won, outright, in at least one race. The same cannot be said for Paul. Alas, 'tis true. However, this is by no means necessary for success. There are many NCAA track meets where the team that wins the grand prize never succeeds in placing *any* of its runners at the very top. Their team victory is fashioned on the basis of many second, third, and even fourth and fifth place finishes. Ron, a Pennsylvania state champion in the 200 meter sprint, should know this full well, as he has taken part in many such types of track meets. It is entirely possible for Dr. Paul to never reach the top perch on the podium, and nevertheless register the best result, amass the most delegate votes. So far, he has registered two second place finishes in eight tries. If he steps up his game just a little bit, and emulates this a bit more, he does not need the winner's circle for success, although that of course would be nice.

And, each of his three opponents has Achilles' heels. Indeed, the all have the same identical weakness. Namely, they are all weather vanes. Each of them, when attacking the other two for "flip-flopping," are entirely correct. Indeed, this is one of the rare occasions where I agree with all three of them, when they criticize the other two on this ground. Well, they are all statist warmongers too, but why be critical?

It cannot be denied that Congressman Paul, too, has "weaknesses." Why, this maniac favors freedom across the board, without fear or favor. He, idiotically, wants to apply the Golden Rule, hold on, wait for it, you had better be sitting down when you read these next few words, to *foreigners.* He got booed for saying this in the South Carolina debate by a bunch of chicken hawks, but numerous members of our armed forces support this basic element of Judeo Christianity. So much so that they donate more money to him than to all of his four competitors (I include Obama, here), *put together.* I just can't *wait* until these soldiers hold their march in favor of Dr. Paul. Stupidly, he wants to End the Fed, HUD, Fannie, Freddie, the sources of our present great prosperity, as everyone in the mainstream media knows full well. He doesn't think too highly of the Department of Education, which is responsible in part for our present high student scores; he must be against education per se! What a horrible person he is. Brainlessly, he wants to end our war on drugs, and put these substances on some sort of par with alcohol. Hey, you can't get any more dim-witted than that. Why, millions of (disproportionately black) innocent prisoners who never engaged in any violent acts would be freed if this jerk had his way. So, yes, he, too, has his weaknesses. But, hopefully, as more and more people hear his views, these will be converted to strengths.

But he also has his strengths, even at present. He is what we call in sports, a "winner." He has won 12 elections in his congressional district, amongst the voters who know him best. In contrast, in sharp contrast, the other three are "losers." Santorum lost badly in his Pennsylvania race for the Senate, as did Romney vis a vis Ted Kennedy for the Massachusetts senate seat. And, the less we say about Gingrich's being booted out of congress on morals charges, to say nothing of his personal life, the better. This man's middle name must be "loser."

Onward and upward for Ron Paul!

Here is an update on this table, now organized according to alphabetical order (as of 4/30/12).

When this new information is incorporated into the analysis, the results look like this:

Jurisdiction

Candidate	Gingrich	Paul	Romney	Santorum
Alabama	2	4	3	1
Alaska	4	3	1	2
Arizona	3	4	1	2
Colorado	3	4	2	1
Connecticut	3	3	1	4
Delaware	2	3	1	4
Florida	2	4	1	3
Georgia	1	4	2	3
Hawaii	4	3	1	2
Idaho	4	3	1	2
Iowa	4	3	2	1
Illinois	4	3	1	2
Kansas	3	4	2	1
Louisiana	3	4	2	1
Maine	4	2	1	3
Maryland	3	4	1	2
Massachusetts	4	3	1	2
Michigan	4	3	1	2
Minnesota	4	2	3	1
Mississippi	2	4	3	1
Missouri	(4)	3	2	1
Nevada	2	3	1	4
New Hampshire	3	2	1	4
New York	3	2	1	4
North Dakota	4	2	3	1
Ohio	3	4	1	2
Oklahoma	3	4	2	1
Pennsylvania	4	3	1	2
Puerto Rico	3	4	1	2
Rhode Island	3	2	1	4
South Carolina	1	4	2	3
Tennessee	3	4	2	1
Vermont	4	2	1	3
Virginia	(4)	2	(3)	1
Virgin Islands	4	1	2	3
Washington	4	2	3	1
Washington DC	3	2	1	4
Wisconsin	4	3	1	2
Wyoming	4	3	1	2

Total	126	118	57	89

A splendid result. Ron Paul actually beats Newt Gingrich! Ta da! Dr. Paul is closer to Santorum (only 29 "points" separate them) than is the latter from Romney (32 "points.") Of course, another, far better, way to look at this is in terms of not votes, nor places, but, rather, *delegates.* And here Ron Paul comes into his own.

Chapter 35.

Is Ron Paul Out of Date? No.

There is a segment of the electorate that greets Congressman Paul's continual harking back to the Constitution, and to the wisdom of the Founding Fathers, as follows: Sure, those were good ideas, *then*; but nowadays, things are far more complicated. We lived a relatively simple, bucolic life as a nation in the late eighteenth and early nineteenth centuries. We traveled by horse and buggy, at best. There was no television, no computers, no al-Qaeda, no cars, no weapons of mass destruction; there was far less poverty, crime, juvenile delinquency, divorce, etc. Dr. Paul's ideas are two centuries out of date. Nowadays, due to the complexity of modern society, his type of limited-government free enterprise system simply cannot suffice. Congressman Paul should wake up to the fact that wc arc now living in the twenty-first century. An old fuddy-duddy who is continually looking back to the past cannot possibly be a good presidential candidate in 2012.

There is much wrong with this negative assessment of Ron Paul's limited-government philosophy. I shall address these "he is out of date" criticisms under three headings: foreign policy, civil liberties and economics.

1. Foreign policy

In the early days of our nation, we were protected by *four* oceans: the Atlantic, the Pacific, the Arctic and the Gulf of Mexico. Even if we made mistakes engaged in "entangling alliances" and searched for "monsters to destroy" abroad, these bodies of water served as a buffer. Yes, the sailing ships could come get us, but that would take a long time; we could see them coming long before they got here.

Nowadays, modern technology has rendered the preventative function of these bodies of water pretty much inoperable. So, any mistakes we make are likely to be met with faster and more effective blowback, e.g., 9/11. If George Washington's advice to be noninterventionists was right during his day, it is even more correct at present.

Similarly, if there were a "terra-ist" in, say, the year 1799 who had it in for us, he would come to our shores armed with a sword, or a musket. At worst, he could murder few people. Nowadays, this is simply not the case. It thus behooves us to be *more* cautious with our foreign policy in the modern era.

Terrorists do not put us in the crosshairs because we have rock music, mini-skirts and freedom. Many other countries that have not been attacked exhibit the first two; as for the third, the U.S. is no longer among the freest of nations. According to one source (Gwartney, et. al, 2011), we are ranked tenth, with Hong Kong first, Singapore second, New Zealand third, Switzerland fourth, Australia fifth, Canada sixth, Chile seventh, the U.K. eighth, and Mauritius ninth. Rather, we have been recently targeted by murderous killers because of what we have *done*: we have been poking sticks in hornet's nests in *every* corner of the globe. Then, our mainstream media register shock and horror when some of these insects come here and bite us. In contrast, in the early days of our republic we pretty much minded our own business, and did not have these horrid events befall us.

According to Dorothy Rabinowitz, Dr. Paul is "the best-known American propagandist for our enemies." Not at all. Dr. Paul, as a physician knows full well that he cannot cure any medical problem until he is clear as to its underlying cause. As a presidential candidate he is fully cognizant of the fact that he cannot stop an outbreak of attacks on our country and our people unless he fully understands their genesis. And, how can this be accomplished? For Ron Paul as doctor, this involves the stethoscope, the X-ray machine, the thermometer, blood-pressure measurement devices, the CATScan and the MRI. For Paul, it requires, at least, *listening* to what they have to say when they explain why they have attacked us. It necessitates *reading* what the intelligence community of our country has to say about blowback.

2. Civil liberties

We did not have a drug war until the Harrison Narcotics Act of 1914. Before that time, these drugs were a medical crisis, only. Afterward, the medical challenges became exacerbated, and an entire new host of problems ensued. Black people are about 14 percent of our population, but account for some 63 percent of the prisoners in jail for drug crimes. Numerous deaths have also been attributed to these vicious laws as well. There are strong parallels with alcohol. During Prohibition, this drug, also, created havoc in our society, needless deaths due to fighting over territory, and poisonings due to "bathtub gin."

Yes, Ron Paul "wishes to turn back the clock" to a previous era, here too. But earlier does not necessarily mean worse. Would anyone seriously like to turn the clock *forward* and reinstitute alcohol prohibition? Of course not. And, yet, anything that can be said in criticism of alcohol can probably be said, or worse, of narcotics. Both are dangerous substances; but more people die of the former than the latter. The prohibition of *each* of them leads to deaths. Libertarians oppose allowing children to have access to either of them, but if we cannot trust *adults* to make decisions about them, how can we justify giving them the right to vote?

In like manner, Congressman Paul opposes the Patriot Act and NDAA and SOPA because they trash the Constitution and violate our basic civil rights. Here, too, he prefers an earlier epoch to a later one, because he is not at all concerned with dates, but rather with *rights*.

3. Economics

Yes, our present day economy comprised of one third of a billion Americans, and billions of other people across the globe, is far more complicated than the one over which the founding fathers presided. But this is not an argument in favor of more regulations, it is an argument *against* them. For, the more complex an economy, the more it needs to rely on the "magic of the market," not on central direction. If there is any case for a centrally planned economy, it applies, not at present, but 300 years ago, when matters were far simpler, and thus socialistic planning could not, paradoxically, be quite as deleterious.

At the beginning of our Republic, some 98 percent of the people were farmers. They didn't need price signals *as much as* modern entrepreneurs do. They could pretty much judge the best way of engaging in human action based on tradition. Grandpa planted such and such, and so did dad, so the way was clear for the present farmer. But in an epoch where automobiles supplant horses and buggies, computers take the place of typewriters and telephones, etc., when there are millions, maybe billions of prices, not merely a few tens of thousands, it is *imperative* that economic freedom and private property rights coordinate economic activity. Yes, the Jamestown colony almost died out due to socialism. I am *not* advocating any such system, for *any* time. But I do insist that the simpler an economy, paradoxically, the *less* harm that price controls and socialism can do.

In like manner, it is also paradoxical that if you must have governmental interferences with the economy, it will hurt fewer people, and less seriously, if this is confined to luxury goods. If price controls and central planning are imposed on diamonds, jewelry and Rolls Royces, users of these goods will be dis-accommodated. But they will not perish. However, if these dirigisme initiatives apply to milk, bread, meat, apples, etc., many people will die, particularly the poor. Yet, it is the rare socialist-fascist who advocates a government takeover of luxury goods. Rather, these economic illiterates target things like housing (rent control) and food. They make a mistake akin to the one made by those who think that since our economy is now more complicated than ages ago, it needs more tender loving care by government, inc.

Let us conclude.

It is not at all the case that newer is necessarily better than older. Murray N. Rothbard has characterized this as the Whig fallacy. Yes, certainly, in many arenas, we have made great progress. Transportation, communication, medical practice, all readily come to mind. But it cannot be denied that in other areas, we have retrogressed. We no longer have the technology or the skills to manufacture Stradivarius quality violins. Although this is of course subjective, I and many others would argue that modern music is vastly inferior to that of Bach, Mozart and Handel. And so it is with our Founding Fathers (apart from slavery, of course). Their foreign policy was arguably better than that of Bush and Obama. Just because it is historical, does not render it fallacious, as critics of Ron Paul all too often "argue." Similarly, Congressman Ron Paul sees our drug policies pre-1914 as far more humane and beneficial than our present drug war. Noting he is living in the past is not sufficient to prove him wrong. No, these things have to be argued out on their merits. It is simply fallacious to maintain that since this policy was once tried and then rejected, (with the Harrison Narcotics Act of 1914), it is inferior to present-day practices. As far as economics is concerned, the move from Carl Menger, Ludwig von Mises and Murray N. Rothbard to the likes of Paul Krugman, Joseph Stiglitz and Ben Bernanke was one of retrogression, not progress. By going "forward," we have lost, not gained.

Chapter 36

Michael Tomasky of the *Daily Beast*

Michael Tomasky wrote a severe criticism of presidential candidate Ron Paul. In every way, except one, it would scarcely rise (fall?) to the level where it needs to be smacked down in the present compilation. And in what way does this otherwise very pedestrian, undistinguished, critique rise above (ok, fall below) the other tens of thousands of brickbats launched against Dr. Paul? It's flowery language. Say what you will about Tomasky, and I intend to fully give him the back of my hand, but you have to admit that anyone who calls Dr. Paul a "batty old reactionary," to say nothing of "pestilential little locust," and who characterizes Paul's supporters as the "Hipster Caucus" has certainly distinguished himself in the name-calling sweepstakes. I don't know about you, but as far as I'm concerned, this leaves "poo-poo head," "do-do" and "your mother has a mustache and wears army boots" back in the dust.

What, then, are the specifics of this particular indictment? (I won't even mention his tired reiteration of the racism-newsletters issue, as this charge has already reared its ugly head, along with the refutation).

Tomasky sneers that the Paul campaign "would be likely to fade pretty quickly." This statement was made right before the Iowa caucus vote, when there were nine candidates for the Republication nomination. Ron Paul, then, was pretty much lost in the crowd. At the time of this writing, there are only three competitors besides the Texas congressman: Gingrich, Romney and Santorum. So much for "fading fast."

Our author next tries the "Kingmaker in Republican politics" ploy. When will these people learn that yes, kingmaker is good, contributor to the party platform is, too, but that Ron Paul, delegate-hunter extraordinaire, is in this race to *win.*

Next up in the batter's box is the implication that the only reason Dr. Paul is anti-war is to garner votes. Does Tomasky think that the only veteran of the armed services is a weather vane like Mitt, Rick and Newt, always and forever willing to trim his sails to prevailing opinion? Evidently, this author does not realize that Paul has *consistently* held his defense-not-offense views on the military for lo these many *decades*. If anything, Ron Paul has probably lost more votes than he has gained by taking this courageous stance year in and year out.

Tomasky also avers as in "infrequently discusses negative side to (Paul's) foreign-policy views that sometimes American powers actually helps do good things. We need look only as far back as Libya." Given the present chaos in that country, this is a particularly inept example to buttress this critique. But there is a *reason* the positive side of U.S. imperialism is so rarely discussed: it does not exist! With the Muslim Brotherhood taking over Libya, this episode is certainly no exception. Exhibit "A" in the argument is of course the "Greatest Generation's" victory over the abomination that was Hitler and Nazi Germany. But there is the likelihood that had the U.S. not intervened in World War I, the Fuhrer would have ended up a house painter, and there would not have been any World War II.

What are we to make of the unwarranted claim that "there are a million and one things the United States does every day in terms of global development and mitigating disease and hunger." We cannot make too much of this. Of course, if you throw vast amounts of money at something, there are bound to be *some* successes. But as Peter Bauer (1981, 1982, 1984, 1991) has demonstrated again and again, compulsory government-to-government transfers of funds have propped up third world dictators, promoted stultifying socialism and impoverished the already poverty-stricken people of Africa, Asia and South America.

It is stuff and nonsense to think the reason the U.S. government grew into a gargantuan monster is "because dishonest and immoral and cheap and corner-cutting shysters in the private sector did things that ripped people off, made them sick, killed them, rendered them unequal citizens, and someone had to step in."

Of course there will always be Enrons and Madoffs (who the SEC failed to stop). There are outlaws in every walk of life, certainly including business, but also in academia, religion and, yes, we dare say so, politics. But even freshman economics students are a bit too sophisticated to swallow pap like that, claiming that the central government is the be-all of all that is good in society. They know full well that an important explanation for the rise of the state is that producers are politically more concentrated than consumers. The big corporations get subsidies from government that cost the average person only a few dollars. The former thus have an incentive to exploit the latter. It is no accident that some of the richest counties in the entire country are clustered around Washington, D.C., the home of vast transfers of wealth from the many poor and middle class members to the wealthy one-percenters. It is not at all the case that the state grew because only government bureaucrats could stop cheating businessmen. Kolko (1963), Paul (2010), Rothbard (1963), Friedman (1962) and other revisionist historians have amply demonstrated that the Fed, the USDA, the FDA, the SEC, the AMA, Fannie, Freddie, HUD and several of the departments that President Paul will dump into the dustbin of history have functioned *not* to help the poor to resist the depredations of large corporations, but as an effort of the crony capitalists to escape marketplace competition and certification that would have far better promoted the public good.

Tomasky's last riposte is this: "… if someone gets beaten to a pulp on the street simply for being who he is, don't go knocking on Paul's door, as he'll be nowhere to be found, hate-crimes laws being a threat to the freedom of the hater and all." Yeah, yeah. How do hate-crime laws help protect innocent victims? We already have laws on the books prohibiting mayhem, assault and battery, rape, murder, theft, kidnapping, car-jacking, etc. Why is it better from the point of view of justice to tack on additional penalties if the perpetrators of these crimes "hate" their victims? Don't *all* criminals in some sense "hate" the victim's who'se lives they ruin? If criminal penalties are presently too low, such that additional years of prison need to be tacked on for criminals to "hate," why not up the ante for *all* malefactors? And, suppose A "hates" B with a purple passion, but never lifts a finger against him. Should A be considered a criminal merely for "hating?" If so, apart from a few Mother Teresas and Ron Pauls, we will all be in jail. Does not Tomasky "hate" Ron Paul? As it happens, Dr. Paul is one of the least hateful people on the planet. Every Republican debate demonstrates this again and again.

When it comes to protecting victims from criminal behavior, moreover, Ron Paul's proposals to legalize drugs will do more for innocent people than all the hate-crime legislation put together. And this is something Gingrich, Romney and Santorum refuse to go along with. (Both the present president and his immediate predecessor admitted to using prohibited drugs. According to the law they both support, both of them ought to have served jail sentences). Innocent people, disproportionately black, are incarcerated for committing these victimless "crimes" and suffer a disproportionate number of murders when gangs fight it out over turf. Tomasky, unfortunately, does not see how repeal of this legislation will reduce real crime.

Part IX

Explanations of the Ron Paul Philosophy: Libertarianism

Chapter 37.
Ron Paul: Far Right or Far Left?

http://lewrockwell.com/block/block192.html

"If you want government to intervene domestically, you're a liberal. If you want government to intervene overseas, you're a conservative. If you want government to intervene everywhere, you're a moderate. If you don't want government to intervene anywhere, you're an extremist."
~ Joseph Sobran

Dick Morris accuses Ron Paul of being far left. This Fox News analyst and Republican strategist claims that Congressman Paul stakes out a position to the left of Obama. He states: "Ron Paul remains terrifying. He is really the ultimate liberal in the race. He wants to legalize drugs, repeal the Patriot Act, slash our military spending, pull out of Afghanistan. … On these issues, he's way, way to the left of Obama. What makes him a conservative is hard to tell. But, whatever he is, he would be a disaster as the Republican candidate."

On the other hand, the *New York Times* maintains that Dr. Paul is far right, in bed with neo-Nazis, white racists and others of this ilk. Mainstream media stories or reports have linked the congressman representing the 14th district of Texas, specifically, with "The American Free Press, which markets books like 'The Invention of the Jewish People' and 'March of the Titans: A History of the White Race,'" with "Don Black, director of the white nationalist Web site Stormfront," with "Far-right groups like the Militia of Montana," with "white supremacists, survivalists and anti-Zionists," with "the nether region of American politics," with 'the John Birch Society," with "David Duke, the founder of the National Association for the Advancement of White People," and with "Holocaust denier Willis A. Carto."

So which is it? Is the highly respected (in neocon circles) Dick Morris to be believed, in which case Dr. Paul is an extreme leftie, practically a commie? And he is not the only one to make this charge. In the view of the *Washington Post*, Ron Paul has "the foreign policy views of Jeremiah Wright." Or should we take seriously the *New York Times* according to which this gentleman is a far rightie, practically a fascist? It is important that we be clear on the question of whether Ron Paul is an extreme right- or left-winger, since the mainstream media seem fixated on one or the other of these accusations. Sometimes, both. As the *Times* also avers, he occupies "the nether region of American politics, where the far right and the far left sometimes converge."

My short answer is, "None of these criticisms are true." Dr. Paul is neither of the far right, nor of the far left, nor do these two ever converge.

For a more thorough reply to this question, we need to reconsider, and reject, the entire left-right spectrum, on the basis of which either of these labels are placed on people.

What is this left-right spectrum? In order to see it, one must draw a line on a piece of paper, thus, and label the left side of it "Left," and the right side of it "Right." To wit, see figure 1:

Left  Right

Figure 1

Then, one must fill it in with various people and organizations. The idea is that the further to the left (right) are a person's or an entity's views, then the further to the left (right) it is placed on this scale. For example, we know that Hitler was an extreme right winger, and Stalin an extreme left winger, so we place each of these murderers at the appropriate extreme end of this spectrum: Hitler to the right, and Stalin on the left. It is uncontroversial that Senator Bernie Sanders is a strong leftist, and Senator Rand Paul a moderate-strong rightist, so we place each of them nearer to the center of the diagram, the former nearer to Stalin, and the latter nearer to Hitler. No one would object to placing feminism on the left and the National Rifle Association on the right, so each of them takes an appropriate position (see figure 2):

Stalin Sanders Feminists NRA Rand Paul Hitler

Left Right

Figure 2

How do others place? Well, John Boehner is a mild rightist, while Nancy Pelosi is a mild leftist. Our present Communist Party is far to the left, but not as far as Stalin, while the neo-Nazis are far to the right, but not as far as Hitler (both have been defanged, a bit). Similarly, Fox News is on the right, while CNN can be placed on the left. Another left-right pair consists of Martin Luther King and Malcolm X. When we incorporate these new entrants, our spectrum looks like this (see figure 3):

Stalin Sanders Feminists NRA Rand Paul Hitler

Left Right

Commie King CNN Pelosi Boehner Fox Mal X NeoNazi

Figure 3

Our spectrum is getting pretty crowded now, so we will not add any more people or organizations to it. However, a few comments at this point may be advisable. One can see even at this level of roughness that we do not have a precise measurement, such as inches, or degrees Fahrenheit. And, not only that, there might be quarrels on the left between placing entrants in this order: Stalin, Commies, King, Sanders, CNN, Feminists, Pelosi. Some might argue that feminists are "leftier" than King, or Sanders. Similarly, on the right, it might well be maintained that Fox and Malcolm X should switch positions. Or that the NRA is to the right of Fox.

But this problem is as nothing as to the next. This can be illustrated when we introduce our next two, and last entrants: Mother Teresa and John Brown. Where do we place the former? Well, she was no moderate, so she cannot occupy space in the middle. Is she a right winger? Do not be silly. So, the only slot to assign her is on the extreme left, cheek by jowl with her political ally, Stalin. Say what? If there is anything true, it is that Mother Teresa and Joseph Stalin do not belong on the same planet. A case can be made that they should not even be mentioned in the same sentence. One of them devoted his life to murdering innocent people, the other to caring for them. Two greater opposites would be hard to imagine.

And the same holds true for John Brown and his supposed soul mate, Adolph Hitler. Brown was a deeply religious man, one might even say an early conservative evangelical, who hated slavery with a purple passion. Unlike other abolitionists, he thought that violent methods were justified against the organization that supported this "curious institution," namely, the U.S.A., and thus attacked a government fort in an attempt to end slavery. Malcolm X, during his most racist days, allowed that John Brown would have been the only white man welcomed into his Nation of Islam organization.

(If you don't like John Brown as an example of a "good" right winger, try Bill Gates. He is clearly in the 1 percent of wealth owners; heck, he is one of the richest men on the globe. Gates earned all of his money in the private sector. He was unfairly attacked by the big government anti-trust regulators. Or, so as to feature a female matching Mother Teresa on the left, there is Ayn Rand, another very wealthy person who earned all of her income in the marketplace, through the voluntary payments from those who purchased her many best-selling books. She venerated private property rights, free enterprise and capitalism.)

Let us now return to our left-right spectrum, considering only these four people (see figure 4).

Figure 4

This diagram does violence to political economic reality in several ways. First of all, there was not a "dime's worth of difference" between our Nazi and our Communist. Both were cruel, inhumane, mass murderers. Yes, their rhetoric was slightly different, but their deeds were for the most part indistinguishable. (Stalin killed about double the number of people that Hitler did: 20 million versus 11 million, according to the best estimates.) Both were socialists. One was a national socialist, the other an international socialist, but both were avowed socialists. (It is amazing that when Prince Harry wore a swastika, the mainstream media went apoplectic; but, seemingly, every third kid on most college campuses wears a Che Guevara T-shirt, and no one objects.) In any fair assessment of Guevara or Stalin on the one side and Hitler on the other, they were soul mates. Twins. And, yet, according to the left-right spectrum, they are as far apart from each other as it is possible to be.

Next, consider the Stalin-Mother Teresa relationship. This, too, is a gargantuan anomaly. There is nothing, nothing at all that the two of them have in common. They are polar opposites on the basis of any criterion anyone could mention. And yet, on the basis of the left-right spectrum, they are twins. So much the worse for this way of measuring, or evaluating, political positions.

Matters do not improve very much at all when we consider the third combination, Mother Teresa and John Brown. In some sense, they were very different. One gave life, the other took it. But Brown attacked only soldiers guilty of upholding the inhuman system of slavery. In a sense then, an important sense, they were both on the side of the angels. Each was doing the Lord's work, properly understood. And, yet, we find them at opposite ends of the spectrum, when they belong much closer together.

As for the last pairing, yes, both Brown and Hitler took lives. But there the resemblance ends. The former did so in order to end slavery; the latter as part and parcel of the slave system he favored, organized and promoted.

If the left-right spectrum makes no sense as a shorthand political economic heuristic, what can we put in its place? Some people use the Nolan Chart, but this too has grave shortcomings: it measures only economic freedom and civil liberties, thus ignoring the third leg of the three-legged stool of political economy: foreign policy.

A better way to look at this issue is with the help of a two-dimensional cross. In figure 5, we maintain the left-right spectrum as the unimportant part of the cross, and superimpose on it a vertical line, which we label "good" at the top and "bad" at the bottom:

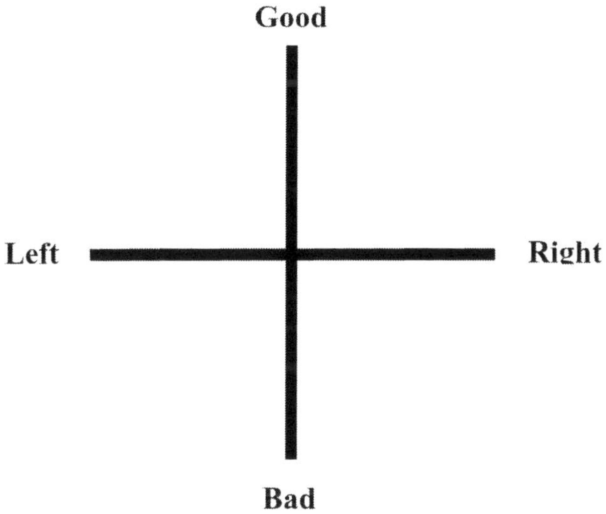

Figure 5

What is our criterion for good? It is adherence to the libertarian nonaggression principle (NAP), combined with property rights based on initial homesteading and legitimate voluntary title transfers afterward: trade, gifts, inheritance, gambling, etc. And for bad? Acting incompatibly with the NAP.

Now, let us fill in the names of the four main characters in our little play (see figure 6):

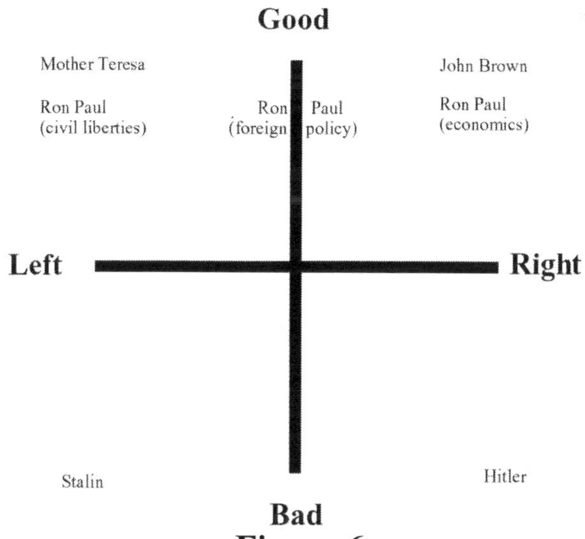

Figure 6

Note that Mother Teresa and John Brown are equally good, as we have depicted them, because they are equally high up on the good axis.

Brown used violence, but it was in behalf of the NAP, not incompatible with it. They represent different rhetoric, hence their opposite positions on the relatively unimportant left-right axis, which we still retain. Mother Teresa is *very* far removed from her fellow leftist, Stalin, as is Brown from his fellow rightist, Hitler. And Stalin and Hitler are at the very bottom of the good-bad axis, as they should be, but far apart in terms of relatively unimportant style and idiom, as was also the actual case.

It cannot be emphasized enough how unimportant is the left-right spectrum. According to it, a violin is right wing, and a guitar is left wing; beads and scruffy clothing are leftish, and tuxedos are rightish; rock and rap music belong to the former category, while symphonic offerings to the latter. Why? Because the first of these pairs are culturally associated with the one group, while the latter members of these pairs with the other. Silly, yes. Unimportant, yes. But, maintaining this left-right axis in our cross does at least enable us to make sense of political economic reality.

Let us now return to Ron Paul's place in this mathematical space. Where does he fit in? Well, it depends upon whether we are talking economics, civil liberties or foreign policy. It is easy to place Dr. Paul as far as economic policy is concerned: right near where John Brown appears in Figure 6. Why? Who knows? Culture? History? But to favor free enterprise, limited government, and private property rights is to be a right winger. (Where does crony capitalism or economic fascism appear? This system features a veneer of markets, but is of course not the real thing. So it finds its place somewhere above where Hitler holds forth in Figure 6.)

It is also noncontroversial where to place Ron Paul with regard to civil liberties. His deep, bitter and consistent opposition to the drug war, to the Patriot Act, to killing U.S. citizens without a trial, entitles him to real estate right near where Mother Teresa appears in Figure 6. Insofar as these considerations are concerned, Congressman Paul could be a card-carrying member of the ACLU – if the latter were more consistent with its own supposed philosophy.

What about foreign policy? Is Dick Morris correct in labeling Ron Paul to the left of Barack Obama on foreign policy? Well, yes and no. Yes, in the sense that there is a strong anti-war element on the left, which did indeed oppose Bush's interventionistic wars. Shame on them for not equally opposing Obama's indistinguishable imperialistic foreign policy (libertarians are the only ones to oppose both, equally.) But no, given that there is also a strong old-right tradition of opposing offensive, in contrast to defensive war making (this is a distinction seemingly beyond the ken of Ron Paul's competitors for the Republican nomination.) This is the old right of Taft, Boren, Rothbard and others. So, where to place Congressman Paul in terms of foreign policy? Right up there at the top, halfway between Mother Teresa and John Brown, neither right nor left, because of this virtual tie.

Much as it pains me to agree with Yahoo.com on anything, given that they have been bitter and unceasing critics of Dr. Paul, I must in all fairness agree with Yahoo when they say of Ron Paul, "On the campaign trail, he reaches out to Tea Party supporters on the right and Occupy Wall Street supporters on the left." Such an insight is very compatible with where we have placed him on our political cross-spectrum. This is precisely why he will badly beat President Obama for the presidency in November 2012, if he can but win the Republican nomination: Dr. Paul will out left Obama on civil liberties, out right him on economics, and win the votes of all those sick and tired of our endless wars; and this includes preeminently the military, plus many independents, and disaffected Democrats and Republicans to boot.

Do the right and the left "converge" as the *New York Times* suggests? Not a bit of it. If we utilize the cross analysis, we can see that left and right are relatively unimportant. They convey style, not substance. As we have seen, the real indication of political economic reality is the north-south axis. And here, there is no "convergence," neither at the top nor the bottom. Style and rhetorical differences divide people both at the top and bottom of our chart. And, our man Ron perches at the very pinnacle on all three criteria: economics, foreign affairs, and personal liberties.

Is there any sense at all to be made of the left-right distinction? Yes, if we break things down into these three constituent elements. For example, on economics, conservatives on the right are slightly more in favor of free enterprise than are liberals (they now characterize themselves as "progressives;"; it is hard to keep track of what they want us to call them) on the left. When it comes to civil and personal liberties, this is reversed. Insofar as foreign policy is concerned, in my judgment there is a rough tie; both have very many bad elements, and a few good ones. If this distinction is applied not holus bolus to everything, but to one of these elements at a time, then there is some limited coherence to the left-right distinction.

Now for the $64,000 question: where oh where do we place Obama and his Republican opponents for the presidential nomination? Rather than attempting to distinguish between: Mitt Romney, Newt Gingrich, Michelle Bachmann, Jon Huntsman, Rick Perry and, Rick Santorum, I will consider an amalgamation of them all. There is not that much difference, after all, between any of them. For good measure, I'll toss in some of the Republican candidates from 2008 who are no longer running now, such as Fred Thompson, Rudy Giuliani, Mike Huckabee and the eventual winner, John McCain. Again, these are all birds of a feather. What have you got when we consider them all together? Why, the Republican Establishment, or RE (Note, I do not include Gary Johnson here; I consider him quite a few cuts above the rest, apart from Ron Paul, of course. In a previous writing, I claimed that Ron Paul earns a 97% on the good-bad scale, Gary Johnson weighs in at 65%, and the REs perch below the line in figures 5-7, at 10%). So, how does Obama stack up against RE?

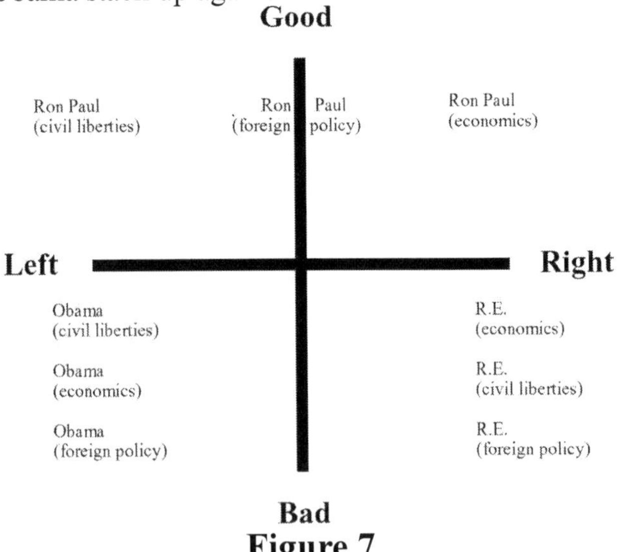

Figure 7

In my view, Obama is slightly better than RE on civil liberties. I know all about the present president's support for the Patriot Act, NDAA and SOPA. But, I insist, RE would be even worse, at least if we are to believe half the rhetoric from this season's Republican debates. On the other hand, RE is somewhat to be preferred on economic issues. Both Obama and RE are died-in-the-wool interventionist fascists, pretty much equally so, but the former includes quite a dollop of egalitarianism and pro-unionism that is less emphasized amongst the latter. Similarly, I place Obama higher than RE on foreign policy. With McCain at the till, I fear, we would have already used nuclear weapons on Iran, something that Dr. Paul's present opponents, I think, are frothing at the mouth to do. (I supported Obama over McCain in the last election for this very reason.) Happily, Obama has so far not done so. This is why, if there were only two choices open to me, the present president of the U.S. and any of the REs, I would support the former in 2012.

Let me conclude by addressing the issue of whether Ron Paul is in bed with invidious members of the hard right, the people and groups mentioned by the *New York Times* at the beginning of this column, because he accepts their endorsements and their money. Or, as Dick Morris charges, Ron is really in the clutches of people to the left of Barack Obama, insofar as drug and foreign policy are concerned.

Reason Magazine asks: "Is Ron Paul Responsible for His Supporters' Views?" Unfortunately, and unsurprisingly, it reaches no conclusion in its editorial on this crucial topic.

What does Congressmen Paul say on this matter? Here, a spokesman of his avers in his behalf: "If people hold views that the candidate doesn't agree with, and they give to us, that's their loss."

Here, Dr. Paul himself states: "If they want to endorse me, they're endorsing what I do or say – it has nothing to do with endorsing what they say..." And again "I'll go to anybody who I think I can convert to change their viewpoints. ... I'm always looking at converting people to look at liberty the way I do."

Ron Paul will go to the very gates of Hell (left Communist or right Fascist, it matters not) and try to convert the Devil himself to the freedom philosophy. As far as I am concerned, this is an altogether virtuous stance to adopt.

Chapter 38

May a Libertarian Take Money From the Government?

This chapter takes the form of responding to a letter from one of my readers.

Prof. Block,

First of all, I want to say what a huge fan and follower of your work I am. Of all the contributors to LRC and the LVM Institute, I look forward to your articles the most, and *Defending the Undefendable* is a truly entertaining and insightful work.

I have a question that I hope you might find the time to answer. Next fall, I will be starting an Assistant Professor appointment at the University of A in the Department of B. I understand that while possibly less-than-ideal, the anarcho-libertarian academic can justify employment at a State university because academia is a profession that has been monopolized by the state and therefore we make do given our circumstances, much like when we use government roads. As Murray Rothbard said, it's not necessary for us to become martyrs. My question, as a young faculty member on a tenure track at a research university, what is the anarcho-libertarian position on state research grants? Obviously, we cannot lobby the state to increase funding for these, but since they exist anyway, may we pursue them and still remain consistent libertarians? (I am assuming that any technology developed would not be directly used to perpetrate aggression, but for basic science and technologies that could lead to higher production, safety, better standards of living for all.) My plan is to pursue every opportunity possible to work with private industry, and ideally not take a penny from the State, but this may not be a successful strategy.

I would very much like to hear your opinion on this issue and I thank you in advance for any time you may give to respond.

Regards,

Professor C

Dear Professor C:

Thanks for allowing me to address you (anonymously, for obvious reasons) in this public setting. I wanted to do so, instead of replying to you alone, since I get many, many letters from people on this very question, or closely related issues. And, for every letter of this sort I get, there are probably dozens of others who either do not take jobs they would relish, or do so, and feel guilty about this since they think they are violating libertarian principles. This letter, then, although addressed to you, applies to all the others as well. Hopefully, at least some of them will find solace from what I am about to say.

1. It is only a libertarian, and a thoughtful one at that, such as you are, who would ever think to ask a question like this. This issue would never in a million years arise on the left, or even the right. They both believe in statism. In contrast, we libertarians support the non-aggression principle (NAP) and thus are quite properly leery of having anything to do with the government (the prime violator of the NAP), and, certainly, to take money from the state is to be involved with it. So, this question in and of itself is a great credit to you.

2. This question most often is articulated by academics such as you. As libertarians, we do not want to contradict our principles. (In contrast, the leftie egalitarians are happy hypocrites; they preach equality, and yet run around with two eyes, when they could have donated one of them to a blind person; and so are the chicken-hawk generals on the right, who would like the U.S. to invade *every* country on the planet, and, maybe, some on Mars, too, and yet do not volunteer for the military.) In a sense, libertarianism is simple: just keep your mitts to yourself, don't steal, rape, murder, etc. But, being true to the NAP is difficult when the state has its tentacles in virtually every aspect of life. The state violates rights with a vengeance, and it is difficult to lead a normal life without being ensnared in its web.

3. My take on this is that it is a positive virtue to relieve the government of its ill-gotten gains. Suppose Z steals an apple from Y and then X comes along and takes this fruit away from Z. Did X do anything wrong? Did he act incompatibly with the NAP? Is X no longer a libertarian? Of course not. Very much to the contrary, X did something entirely compatible with our philosophy. Certainly, all libertarian theories of private property rights, of punishment, would agree that of all people in the world, Z is the absolutely *least* deserving of this foodstuff. Now, it might be nice, it might be virtuous, for X to

return the apple to Y. Indeed, this was precisely the relationship between Ragnar Danneskjold (X) and Hank Reardon (Y) in Ayn Rand's magnificent and monumental novel, Atlas Shrugged. The government (Z) stole from Reardon (and of course others) and Ragnar was just returning these stolen goods to Hank, the victim. But, Ragnar's behavior constituted a double or two-stage act. First, he grabbed gold from the government; then, and only then, did he return it to Hank. But, if a double act is to be licit, then each and every part of it must be, too. Two wrongs cannot make a right, and neither can one right and one wrong. So, I deduce, it was entirely proper for Danneskjold to relieve the evil government depicted in *Atlas* of its stolen property, even if he did not give a penny of it to Reardon. Taking money from a thief is an unadulterated good deed. Returning it to victims is virtuous, too, but it is supererogatory: it is not needed to convert the first part of this double-stage act into righteousness; the first part is good in and of itself.!

4. If you take statist money, and I have, suppose someone else asks you for it, on the ground that the government stole his money, and you should return to him what you took from them. Well, first off, you wouldn't owe him all of it; you could keep a sizable portion of it as a salvage payment (the private law of the sea judges in medieval times commonly awarded the rescuer of a boat at sea one-third of the value of the vessel). As for the rest of it, the person requesting money from you must come with clean hands himself. He cannot be anything but a libertarian; if he is not, he is a supporter of this theft in the first place. He is thus in cahoots with this criminal gang. And, if he is a libertarian, he will fully realize that you are the first homesteader of this wealth, and thus its proper owner. If he wants some, too, as is his right, he should go to the same place as you did, and seize it from the same bad guys.

5. I have in my time been "guilty" of accepting subsidies from the state. I shop for food in supermarkets, and eat even more of it in restaurants. I therefore indirectly avail myself of agricultural subsidies (I full well realize that farm goods would be cheaper in the fully free society, but, still, given our lack of economic freedom, there may well be a subsidy in it for me from dining.) I have U.S. fiat fractional reserve bank currency in my wallet and use it, too, even though as a libertarian I favor free market (e.g., gold or silver) money. I use streets, sidewalks, roads and highways, brought to me courtesy of our least favorite institution. I went to public schools as a student, and taught at

a few of them as a faculty member. I had a New York State Regents' Scholarship, and I'm not giving back a penny of it to the government. I use public libraries, art galleries and museums, shamelessly. I avail myself of the services of statist parks: Central Park in New York City, Stanley Park in Vancouver, Canada, and Audubon Park when in New Orleans, and others besides. And when I do so, I give off with a little smirk of satisfaction for a job well done. Please, as the Jewish Mother of the libertarian movement, I absolve all you kinder regarding the guilt you may have accepting these and other such subsidies. Go out there, and proudly get everything you can from the government. Hold your head high; you are doing a mitzvah!

6. Which organizations may properly accept government subsidies? May the typical private university do so? My answer is no: while there may be a few free enterprise professors on staff, typically in the economics department, virtually all of the rest are hand in glove with the state, supporting its depredations. For example, it is very rare indeed that there will be even one freedom oriented professor in American higher education in departments such as sociology, anthropology, philosophy, law, political science, history, religion, literature, to say nothing of multicultural departments such as feminist, black and queer studies. In my experience, the majority of the faculty, even at business colleges, are critics of the free enterprise system, not supporters.

7. Now, at long last, let me reply to the specific points you make. I don't think that the "anarcho-libertarian academic can justify employment at a State university because academia is a profession that has been monopolized by the state." First of all, the government has not fully monopolized education. There are, after all, numerous fully private institutions of learning. There are many, many ostensibly private universities that are only partially subsidized by government. The government, moreover, has not fully monopolized information flows: there are many alternatives to its Post Office. Yet, it is entirely justified for libertarians to avail themselves of snail mail. You are quite right: Murray Rothbard truly said that it's not necessary for us to become martyrs. Libertarianism does not at all require any such thing.

I have no objection, at all, to your plan of pursuing "every opportunity possible to work with private industry." But, realize that if you do, you will not be awarded any libertarian brownie points at all for helping to relieve the government of its plunder. Please understand me: I certainly don't oppose private industry (under present institutional arrangements, there's very little of that out there, except for a few mom-and-pop operations). It should not at all be an "ideal … not take a penny from the State," at least not for the libertarian. No, no, no, a thousand times no, it is a *virtue* to take money away from this illicit organization, and way more than a penny, too.

8. But wait! If you cooperate with the government in this manner, can you not be properly accused of "aiding and abetting" an evil institution? Well, yes, sort of. If you take money from the state, you are indeed giving it your imprimatur, or "sanction" as the Randians would say. And, indeed, you are helping the government in the ex ante sense, in that both parties always and ever, and necessarily so, benefit from any voluntary exchange, and, here, you are both agreeing: you to accept the funds, they to give them to you.

However, you are not promoting statism any more by taking their money than by carrying around their cash, patronizing their libraries or streets, etc. And, too, while you are of course benefiting them in the ex ante sense, you are certainly not doing so in the ex post sense. That is, they are giving you the money in the hope that by doing so, they can better promote statism than by the use of it in any other way. But you, by your actual actions, will not be doing any such thing. Now, I am not at all knowledgeable about your own specialty, B. So, I cannot say how this will play out in your field. So, let me talk about my own. I have previously taught economics at several public colleges and universities. What the powers that be would have liked me to teach was moderate neoclassicism; the doctrine of market failure, according to which while free enterprise does indeed function well under the conditions of perfect competition, in the real world these conditions are often not met, and thus there is an important role for the government to engage in anti-trust, welfare policies, to enact pro-union legislation, tariff barriers, etc. As you can imagine, while I did indeed acquaint my students with these claims (not to have done so would have left them helpless, and would have been to cheat them), I have also pointed out serious, nay, fatal, flaws in this analytic framework. So, when the libertarian Nuremberg trials begin for me, and I shall indeed be in the dock for consorting with the enemy in this manner, I fully expect that I will be exonerated. But what about the Marxist, socialist, mixed economy or interventionist professor? Will he also be found innocent by the libertarian jury? Not at all. In contrast to me, he really did “aid and abet” the evil state, by promoting its doctrines, inculcating them among the youth.

What of your field, B? Let us posit that it is impossible for you to promote liberty in it. If you do your job (if not, you’ll quickly be fired so your question is all but moot), you cannot promote liberty, since your calling is too orthogonal to freedom for that purpose. Here’s a suggestion for you; if you still feel guilty about becoming enmeshed in statist finance (feelings I strongly urge you to squelch), and have no way to promote liberty (as I do in economics), then how about the following. Take a hefty part of your salary (net not gross), say 5 percent or even 10 percent, and donate it to an organization that promotes freedom in a spectacular manner. Hint, hint: I can think of no better group than the Mises Institute, and/or, at least in the short term, a contribution to Ron Paul.

9. To conclude. Enough of pure theory. Let us now get down to practical reality. It is entirely legal under the present laws of the land for you to apply for, and receive, wealth from the government of the sort you describe, so all of this talk of “theft” is beside the point from the pragmatic perspective. I urge you to apply for all of the grants you possibly can. Murray Rothbard said that a man’s contribution to society is proportional to the profits he earns. I say in a similar vein, the more money you take from the coffers of the state, the better libertarian you are.

Chapter 39

Ron Paul and Liberty

If Ron Paul had won the Ames Iowa poll, the mainstream media would have dismissed the entire exercise as unimportant. If he had come in at, oh, 6th place, they would have used this as evidence that he is incompetent, not in the first rank of Republican candidates, can't get out the vote, the American people had rejected his candidacy, etc. So, when Congressman Paul took a magnificent second place, only 1 percent behind the winner, I said to myself, hot diggity dog; the MSM can't ignore him now. They cannot dismiss this entire result because then they would have to also deprecate Michele Bachmann's win, and that they will not do. They now MUST give Dr. Paul his due credit, since he finished in a close second to her. They will be forced to discuss his ideas: bring the troops home, get rid of the Fed, drastically reduce taxes, eliminate a slew of illicit federal departments, legalize drugs and other victimless crimes, stop foreign "aid," save the American dollar via 100-percent gold backing, etc.

Silly me. That shows how much I know. Instead, the talking heads are now tooting this line: "The three front-runners are Mitt Romney, Rick Perry and Michele Bachmann." In their view, these are the major candidates, and all the others are also-rans. Why Mitt Romney? Well, he looks presidential, and he has a good chance with the tea partiers despite his Romney-care health policy in Massachusetts, oh so similar to Obama-care. Why Rick Perry? Well, he's the governor of Texas, the second biggest state, isn't he? And this despite the fact that he has not yet won anything in the presidential sweepstakes. Why Michele Bachmann? This is because, of course, she just won the Ames Iowa poll. Notice any name missing from all of this? I'll give you a hint: this is the guy who came in SECOND, 1 percent behind "major candidate" Bachmann in this recent election. There used to be among the beltway "Austro-libertarians" a campaign to promote and study Austrian economics without "You Know Who" (Ludwig von Mises, of course). There is now a campaign among the major media to analyze the Republican presidential process without uttering the name of "You Know Who" (Ron Paul, of course).

What can be done about this? Well, keep sending in those cards and letters; keep protesting; keep writing those emails to these self-appointed judges. Vote for Ron Paul. And, most of all, let us all pledge to donate as much as we can to all of the upcoming Ron Paul money bombs.

There are some otherwise excellent libertarians who hold their noses at the political process. They think it is somehow incompatible with the nonaggression principle, the foundation of our philosophy. Voting just gives "them" sanction, these people think. Well, if so, then libertarians should not use fiat currency to transact grocery purchases, travel on government roads, attend concerts at public theaters, patronize public libraries, parks, museums, teach in, or attend, any public university, or even private one that is subsidized. They should also not eat food, since the government is heavily involved in subsidizing some of it. They should not live in houses, since the statists have heavily involved themselves with building materials. They should eschew … the list goes on and on, and includes every jot and tittle of the economy, so heavily ensconced in it is the state apparatus.

The point is, the modern government is so heavily engaged in ALL facets of our lives. If we really didn't want to give "sanction" to them, and wanted, also, to be logically consistent, we could not operate in modern society at all. We would have to either go off to live in a self-sufficient farm, or commit suicide. Hey, we don't want to lose our souls, do we?

Some libertarians say that we have a choice regarding whether or not to vote, to support Dr. Paul, whereas we have no choice with regard to any of these other things. Nonsense. Human action always includes choice. We are engaging in human action all over the place. Self-sufficient farming, and/or suicide ARE choices! This attitude of libertarians is very self-destructive. It prevents us from supporting Ron Paul to the extent that would otherwise be the case.

I suggest a remedy for this sort of irrational thinking. It is Murray Rothbard's (1977) "Do you hate the state?" While you're at it, read this other excellent piece by the same author, about my man Hector (Rothbard, 1961). If we really see our political leaders as the gangsters most of them are (there are but a few honorable exceptions to this general rule, certainly including in the modern day You Know Who, and his son, the junior senator from Kentucky), we will reject this utter nonsense that to engage with them in any way is to be false to libertarianism. If we don't engage them, in many, many ways, certainly including voting, how will we ever rid ourselves of this pestilence? If we don't support the greatest advocate of libertarianism now active on behalf of the cause of liberty (hint: You Know Who), we lose the best opportunity we now have to promote this philosophy.

Part X. Interviews

In this section, there are three interviews. None of them started out being about Ron Paul. So, I didn't contemplate including them in this book. But, I must have the congressman from Texas "on the brain" or something, because I managed to insert him into each of these interviews. I sometimes think that if someone mentions frogs, or spaghetti, or pretty much anything else in the universe, I will find a way to bring the discussion back to Dr. Paul. I wonder if he likes to eat frogs' legs, or that Italian dish. Probably, the frog and spaghetti industries would do better under free enterprise. Probably, there is a U.S. department charged with the administering of these products that Mr. Paul will disband when he gets to Washington, D.C. In any case, enjoy these interviews, and see if you agree with my contention that I did not adventitiously smuggle in Ron Paul into my responses to these questions where he did not belong.

The first two of these interviews, from Taiwan and Iran, respectively, were conducted by people with imperfect command of the English language. I did not try to edit their questions, as their intent was perfectly clear to me (and I am sure this will hold for the reader as well), even though sometimes phrased awkwardly. Well, their English is a lot better than my Chinese, or Farsi, which are non-existent.

Chapter 40.

Taiwan

1. While capitalist and socialist value systems seem to have both collapsed in the recent financial crisis, what kind of values should the young people believe in? How shall we act?

There are actually not one but two capitalist systems; ditto for socialism. Only one of each, has failed. Young people should follow both successful scenarios, and avoid the other two. What are the four varieties?

Let us take capitalism first. There are actually two categories here. One is laissez-faire capitalism. Under this system of free enterprise, if government exists at all, it is strictly limited to protecting persons, property rights and contracts against fraudsters and marauders, whether domestic or foreign. This system consists, only and solely, for voluntary acts such as buying, selling, renting, lending, borrowing, barter. All such acts are necessarily mutually beneficial, otherwise contracting parties would simply not agree to them. That being the case, free markets necessarily enhance human welfare, since this system consists of nothing but mutually beneficial acts. Young people, and old ones too, should embrace this system.

The other type of capitalism is state monopoly corporate capitalism, or crony capitalism, or economic fascism (you don't need knee-high boots, or mustaches, or goose-stepping, or swastikas for this). Here, while there is a veneer of private property, the government engages in bail-outs, subsidies, and protections for its favored special interests, and minute rules and regulations for them, too. The state intervenes throughout the economy with central banks, orders, price controls and myriad other rights violations. People of all ages should steer clear of this pernicious system, which is indeed collapsing all over the world.

What of socialism? There are two varieties in this case, also. Both give lip service to the notion of "from each according to his ability, to each according to his need," but one of these implements this on a voluntary basis, the other coercively.

What are some examples of voluntary socialism? They are the nunnery, convent, kibbutz (when run on donations from members), commune, collective, syndical, cooperative, monastery, abbey, priory, friary, religious community, the family. Charitable and other religious organizations are included in this category. These groups are often undermined by both coercive capitalism and compulsory socialism, but when left alone to their own devices they often serve admirably, and should serve as an example to us all. (Workers' communes, collectives, cooperatives and syndicals often do not function as well as corporations and businesses led by entrepreneurs, but that is a mere matter of efficiency, not justice.)

What is coercive socialism? This is a system where government owns the means of production through seizure of private property; where virtually all work for the state since they are prohibited from setting up on their own. Examples in the modern day are North Korea and Cuba, and in the last century the U.S.S.R., China, East Germany and other Russian satellites, plus many of the newly liberated African nations and others with five-year plans such as India. In western democracies, this philosophy is exhibited in socialized medicine, socialized retirement Ponzi schemes such as Social Security in the U.S., which compels membership, state owned roads and highways, public housing and (partial) nationalizations such as the Detroit auto companies.

Socialism of this sort has always been an economic disaster, wherever and whenever it has been tried (see Mises' 1922 book *Socialism* on this). It is a vicious and immoral system, since people are compelled to join it against their will. (Were it not compulsory, it would be part of the voluntary socialist system; it would then be compatible with justice, albeit economically inefficient.) People of all ages should reject this system.

2. We believe that the key to the bright future of European

younger generations is the awareness that individuals should make more choices by themselves, and the government should have less control. What do you think?

I entirely and enthusiastically agree with this assessment. That is why I say that the real battle is *not* between left and right, between socialism and capitalism. Rather, the real antagonists are voluntary socialism and voluntary capitalism on the good side, and coercive socialism and coercive capitalism on the bad side. The former two, *both* of them, allow scope for individual choice. The latter two, without exception, control people against their will.

3. However, to be responsible for oneself means to take more risks. In this era of high uncertainty, is that good for us?

I do not agree that to be responsible for oneself necessarily means to take more risks. The purchase of insurance on the free market is a way of reducing risk. Surely, all those who do so are not, certainly not for that reason, irresponsible. Becoming a teacher, doctor, nurse, plumber, electrician or carpenter are presumably less risky occupations than that of speculator, land developer or, prospector, and yet practitioners of both sets of occupations can be equally responsible for themselves. No, self-responsibility lies in other directions. It consists of embracing freedom, whether of the socialist or capitalist variety.

Yes, we do indeed live in an era of high uncertainty. But this is solely due to government involvement in the economy. In the U.S., the Federal Reserve System deserves a lot of the blame for creating what Robert Higgs (1987, 2004) calls "regime uncertainty." Its inflationist policy of artificially reducing interest rates has played havoc with the economy, creating vast unemployment, the highest level since the Great Depression of the 1930s.

4. It is more difficult for the young people to find a good job after the financial storm. Don't you think the government and the current situation should be responsible for youth unemployment? Is it totally one's own responsibility to be jobless? Do you think the market

economy can solve the problem?

Of course the market system can solve our present depression. It was caused by governmental mismanagement. And now, further statist interference is exacerbating and prolonging it. If free enterprise were allowed, no one would be trying to save the housing and auto industries which were overdeveloped with low-interest-rate policies. HUD, Fannie and Freddie led to the mortgage crisis. Under free enterprise, housing prices would no longer be propped up; they would be allowed to fall so that this sector of the economy could once again be integrated with other economic activity. Wages would not be artificially boosted with support for union demands and the minimum-wage law. The gold standard, or whichever commodity money won out in the competitive struggle would be adopted. The Fed would be disbanded. There was no economic debacle in 1921 (Woods, 2009) because the government of the day adopted a more laissez-faire hands-off policy, allowing the "magic of the market" to do its thing.

Yes, the government *is* responsible not only for youth but overall unemployment. However, their policies of bailing out the unemployed though unemployment insurance and welfare payments only prolong the agony. The more you pay people who are unemployed, other things equal, the greater the duration of their joblessness.

5. Following the questions above, many technology companies are replacing workers with direct hires overseas. Take Apple for example. Apple employs 43,000 people in the United States and 20,000 overseas. Many more people work for Apple's contractors: an additional 700,000 people engineer, build and assemble iPads, iPhones and Apple's other products. But almost none of them work in the United States.

We know the United States has a tradition to stand for free market, which resulted in huge job opportunities created overseas, not at home. Some think that is a flaw in capitalism, what is your opinion?

Outsourcing, hiring foreign workers to do jobs that could have been done in the U.S. occurs for both healthy and unhealthy reasons. It is important to distinguish between them. The unhealthy reason is U.S. unionism. Organized labor has been powerful enough to raise their wages above productivity levels, acting like a tapeworm, creating bankruptcy for firms unfortunate enough to be afflicted by them. Semi-skilled shop floor workers in Detroit were mulcting their employers for some $70 per hour. If this factor were eliminated (all extant unions are nothing but criminal gangs; not only their leadership, but all of their members too, ought to be jailed) there would be less corporate outsourcing to other countries.

But even under a regime of full economic freedom in labor markets, there would still be plenty of international trade and investment. This is due to specialization and the division of labor, that holds true not only domestically, but throughout the entire world as well. The U.S. has a comparative advantage in some goods and services while other countries can outcompete us in different items. If we want to cure poverty, enhance wealth, grow the global economy, we have to eliminate all governmental interferences with free trade: tariffs, quotas, so-called "fair trade," etc.

There is thus absolutely nothing untoward about Apple employing tens of thousands of workers abroad. As far as I am concerned, if this corporation fired every last American employee in a successful attempt to maximize profits, and located its entire operation in another country, that would still inure to the benefit of Americans. Residents of our country would now own an even more valuable operation than when it was located here. And we would then be able to purchase its products even more cheaply under these assumptions. When the Japanese purchased Rockefeller Center, did this hurt their economy, assuming, contrary to fact, that the value of this real estate did not later decline? Of course not. So, why should successful American ventures abroad hurt us?

President Obama is now bragging about "insourcing." This is the setting up of companies within our borders that otherwise would have been located elsewhere. If this is part and parcel of the market process, well and good. But if it is a violation of our comparative advantage, it impoverishes us. Investments elsewhere are not the source of our unemployment. This stems, rather, from misallocative effects of the Fed, and statist propping up of wages and other prices.

The Smoot-Hawley tariff of the 1930s knocked an already teetering world economy into a deeper abyss. My fear is that present widespread economic illiteracy will allow governments to replicate this awful policy in the near future. Free trade, full free trade with no interferences at all, is the last best hope for the planet's economy, as it always is. Free trade is not a "flaw" in capitalism. It is, rather, the very jewel in its crown.

6. After the financial crisis, the people of Taiwan were of the mind that "the big government" would help solve youth unemployment by means of distributing unemployment subsidies and increasing public sector workers. What is your opinion? In addition to these ways, is there anything else the government can do?

Youth unemployment is greater than joblessness for adults by a factor of three to four. This is due almost entirely to the pernicious minimum-wage law. Subsidies for unemployment will not solve this problem; they will worsen it. The more you pay for something, anything, including unemployment, the more of it you get, other things equal. Increasing public sector hires is exactly the wrong way to go, unless we want to embrace coercive socialism-fascism.

In order to see why the minimum-wage law is such a disaster for the employment of young people, we must take a step back and ask what determines wage levels in the first place. The answer is, productivity (more exactly, marginal revenue productivity, but we need not go into that at this time). Suppose a teenager can add to his employer's bottom line to the tune of $5 per hour; that is his productivity level. What will his wage be? It cannot be higher than that amount; if it is, his boss will lose money on the deal, and be forced into bankruptcy if he makes this his general practice. For example, if this youthful worker is paid $8 per hour, the firms will lose $8-$5 = $3 per hour. Can this teen's wage be below his productivity level of $5? Again, no, at least not in equilibrium. Suppose that this wage is initially set at $1 per hour. Can this long endure? No. For at this level, the firm is earning $5 (productivity) - $1 (wage) = $4 (profit). If the young person does not leave, seeking a better situation, some other employer will come along and bid this worker away from this present job slot. What will this competitor offer? If he is a profit maximizer, he will dangle $1.01, earning a profit of $3.99. But then a third person will come along with a bid of $1.02, yielding $3.98 in profit. Where will this upward process end? In equilibrium, if we ignore the transactions costs of finding such underpaid workers, it can only be at $5, where no profits are earned.

Now, we introduce the minimum-wage law. It stipulates a payment of $7 per hour. If the young worker is hired, the business loses $5 (productivity) - $7 (wage) = -$2. The firm will simply not make an employment offer to the teen. No wonder young people all around the world are precluded from employment, from the banlieues of France to the slums of Newark. There are hordes of young people in many other countries, all of them unemployable because of laws of this type.

If the minimum wage is such an utter disaster, why do we have it on the law books of many nations? A small part of the reason is economic illiteracy. People are either ignorant of economics, or miseducated in it. This legislation *sounds* like a good idea. Its adherents say it will raise wages, and who could be against that? A larger part of the explanation is unionism. When organized labor demands a wage increase, the firm is tempted to substitute relatively cheaper factors of production for this now more expensive one. For example, a lot of unskilled, youthful labor can replace more highly-skilled, adult) workers. But that is the *last* thing desired by the unionists. In the old days, organized labor would indulge in hate speech, call these young replacements “scabs” and try to physically intimidate them. But the teens could fight back. A far more efficient way of ridding themselves of this unwanted competition would be to price them out of the market. Pass a law mandating a wage so high for them (compared to their relatively low level of productivity) that employers would lose all incentive to hire them, even in the face of increased pay for union members. And this law? The minimum-wage law, of course. End this evil legislation, and the special problem of teen unemployment would disappear.

7. We think the young generation is more stressed financially than ever. One of the reasons is, the social welfare system in Europe, Japan and Taiwan, which forces the young people to contribute (e.g., the national health insurance program, the labor insurance, and the national pension fund in Taiwan). The young generation must support the medical expenditures of the seriously sick and the living of the elderly and retired. As a result, the young cannot freely use every cent they earn by themselves. What do you think?

I entirely agree with this assessment. The elderly are more politically organized than are youngsters. More of the former vote in elections than the latter. The old people are a very powerful special interest group.

In the free society, no one is forced to pay anyone else's bills. Compulsory hearth services, compulsory unemployment insurance, compulsory pension systems amount to no more and no less than organized theft, from the weak to the powerful. Unfortunately for the newcomers to the labor market, they are in the former group.

8. The figures for 2010 show that 115 million Europeans, or almost a quarter of the EU's population, live in households with less than the poverty level; 20 countries recorded a higher rate of poverty and risk of social exclusion among young people than among the general population. Moreover, the World Economic Forum recently issued a report that says greater income disparity and fiscal imbalances are the most likely threats to global prosperity in the next decade. What is your idea to deal with "greater income disparity"? How should we solve "fiscal imbalance"? Many governments are pitching a "Robin Hood Tax," which is receiving growing support. Is that right?

Many government programs as we have just seen forcibly transfer money from the relatively poor to the relatively rich. In the free society, all such compulsory transfers, whether from poor to rich or rich to poor, whether from the old to the young or from the young to the old, would be summarily ended. Would there be income inequality in a regime of economic freedom? Of course there would be, and every penny of it would be entirely justified. Income disparity, apart from luck, is due to differences in skills. In order to see why Robin

Hood Taxes are always and ever unfair, consider this consideration. If we really opposed any and all inequalities, and had the technical ability to do so, we would not be content with any Robin Hood Tax. Rather, we would transfer the skills from those who had too much of them, to those who had too little. Think of two people, A and B. The former has an IQ of 150, the latter, 50. We could, if we had an IQ transfer machine, force both of them into it, pull the switch, and then both would come out of it with identical IQs of 100. This is the "logic" of the Robin Hood Tax. Why take mere money from the one and give it to the other when we can transfer the underlying abilities that allow incomes to diverge (IQ in this case) from the one to the other? If it is morally repugnant to engage in forced transfers of IQ points, this applies, too, to taking money from the one and giving it to the other. To take a more realistic case, should we compel people with two eyes to give one of them to those without any? Of course not. How, then, to justify the Robin Hood Tax? It cannot be done.

9. The overall situation is many governments tend to play "big governments." The relationship and interaction between people and government is gradually changing. Shall we take back the rights corroded by the government? If yes, how could we take them back? What is your most direct suggestion to the young people?

How can the people take back their long-lost rights from overwhelming and overweening gigantic governments? I have but one suggestion. Support Ron Paul! If you live in the U.S. vote for him and contribute money to his campaign. If you live elsewhere, do the latter.

Why? Because Ron Paul is now the last best hope for a free society, and not only in the U.S. He will return imperialist troops to America from some 900 military installations in about 130 different countries. In one fell swoop, he will thus free up both Americans and peoples all over the planet. He will, if elected president, end all U.S. trade interferences. This, too, alone, will greatly enrich us all. He will end the Fed (Paul, 2010), a source of great economic instability. When the U.S. sneezes, the rest of the world catches a cold. Well, the Fed is the world's greatest sneeze machine. Its demise will energize the economies of all nations on the surface of the Earth. A President Ron Paul will greatly streamline the U.S. government. This, alone, will help cure poverty worldwide.

Here is one last suggestion for all young people. Immerse yourselves in Austrian economics, the economics of Menger, Mises, Hayek and

Rothbard. The Austrian School (named for the birth place of the founders of this philosophy), is the preeminent free market school of economic thought.

Chapter 41.

Iran

1. Upon the recent events like economic crisis, recession, people losing homes, increasing unemployment and Wall Street Occupy Movement, how do you analyze the next election?

Reza, I fear you are very accurate in your assessment. The United States is now indeed in an economic crisis. I am not sure of whether to call it a recession or a depression. Certainly, it is the biggest economic crisis since the Great Depression of the 1930s. Unemployment is very high, and underestimated by false government figures. Young black men in particular are suffering from astronomical unemployment rates. The Occupy Movement knows that there is something seriously wrong with U.S. society, but is incapable of distinguishing between crony capitalism, where favored businesses are subsidized and bailed out by government, and laissez-faire capitalism, where government is limited to defense of person and property right and contract. My analysis of the election of 2012 is that if Ron Paul becomes the next president, not only will the U.S. head into a peaceful and prosperous epoch, but so will the entire world follow us in this direction. If any of the other four win, we will have no change from present horrid conditions, both economically and militarily.

2. Do these problems arise from socialist wants?

Reza, I define socialism as excessive government ownership, and fascism as excessive government rules, regulations and control of the economy. So I interpret your question as asking about socialism-fascism, or, Big Government. I then answer, yes, these problems do indeed arise from excessive government. The unemployment problem can be best explained by Austrian Economics, the views of Mises, Hayek, Rothbard, and, yes, Ron Paul. Here, the Fed artificially lowered interest rates, which led entrepreneurs to misallocate resources in the direction of roundabout investments (housing and automobiles). HUD, Fannie and Freddie exacerbated matters regarding over-building of residential units. The result is both high unemployment and a housing crisis, where many homeowners now find themselves "under water:": their mortgages are greater than the value of their houses. Instead of allowing the free enterprise system to bring us out of this morass, the Obama Administration is propping up wages and housing prices, thus lengthening and worsening the crisis. We had a similar bust in 1921, but the Harding Administration allowed the market to work, and this recession was short and shallow. Only a President Paul would follow a laissez-faire policy and allow us to benefit from the "magic of the market."

3. How do these events provoke the feeling of voters?

Reza, the electorate is profoundly unhappy with the political status quo. But, they are not supporting Ron Paul in droves, as they should be doing, as would be in their best interest. Why not? To a great degree, this is due to the mainstream media. They have made fun of Ron Paul, they have smeared him, they have tried to ignore him, and, at least in my own view, he has been victimized by the Republicans in terms of voter fraud, most recently in our state of Maine. But, Dr. Paul plows on despite these obstructions, gathering more and more very enthusiastic adherents.

4. Is it possible that a socialist can win the election?

Yes, it is all too possible. Right now, there are only five major candidates for the office of president: Barack Obama, New Gingrich, Mitt Romney, Rick Santorum and Ron Paul. The first four are all socialists – advocates of big-government spending and involvement in the economy to varying degrees. Both Obama and Romney favor a version of socialized medicine: forcing people to pay for health insurance whether they wish to do so or not. Gingrich has rarely met a government program he doesn't like, and is now ranting about renewing our space program, setting up a moon base at the cost of trillions of dollars. Santorum voted for the "bridge to nowhere" and as a senator from Pennsylvania had a record as a big spender. Only Ron Paul stands apart from this socialist philosophy.

5. Can Obama and his semi-socialist slogans impress people and absorb their vote again?

Obama is a brilliant orator. Unfortunately, many voters are indeed all too likely to be taken in by his mellifluous voice, his wonderful timing as a speaker and, his enthusiasm. In contrast, I must admit, Ron Paul is not as good a public speaker. On the other hand, when it comes to substance, I must reverse my evaluation of these two candidates. President Obama probably never had an original thought in his entire life; he mouths leftist shibboleths in bumper-sticker style. He depends to a great degree upon a teleprompter that feeds him his lines. In sharp contrast, Congressman Paul is an original thinker, and has made profound contributions to the theory of foreign policy, and to economics, particularly as regards the Federal Reserve System. In 2009 I hosted him at Loyola University New Orleans. He spoke from the podium without notes for about 70 minutes straight. This was a magnificent display of extemporaneous speech-giving.

6. Is the next presidential election for social democrats or liberal democrats?

The next election will be between a socialist-fascist imperialist warmonger and an advocate of peace, a strong defense (not an offense), free enterprise, and limited government, if Ron Paul wins the Republican nomination. Otherwise, it will be between two socialist-fascist imperialist warmongers, with very little substantive differences between them.

7. Tell us about the current economic status of America and people and the impact of the economy on these elections.

I hate to say this, but the election is not now the top news story, despite how crucially important it is for the well-being of the masses. Rating much higher were the Super Bowl (a football game where the Giants beat the Patriots), the successful athletic doings of Jeremy Lin, a Harvard graduate Asian-American member of the New York Knicks basketball team who was spurned by all the experts, and events of local interest such as Mardi Gras in my home city of New Orleans. However, the impact of the economy on the elections will be very important, in my estimation. This is in accordance with the popular slogan, "It's the economy, stupid." Quite possibly any of the Republicans, including Ron Paul, will be favored against President Obama in November, unless the economy improves significantly.

8. Last, what should be the economic program of the next state? On what challenges should the next state focus?

The next administration should cut taxes and spending significantly, reduce the deficit, say, by $1 trillion in the first year, eliminate government departments, the Fed, regulations, ownership and control over the economy, bring all the troops home where they can defend the country, instead of attacking others that have not even threatened us, let alone have any power to defeat us, legalize drugs, etc. Come to think of it, this sounds rather like the Ron Paul platform.

Chapter 42.

Lara-Murphy

Lara-Murphy Report: How did you discover Austrian economics?

Walter Block: Through Murray N. Rothbard. I was introduced to Murray by Larry Moss and his roommate, Jerry Woloz. My introduction to Murray was solely based on my interest in libertarianism; I had at that time not even heard of the Austrian School of Economics. I was then a graduate student at Columbia University, and was a minarchist libertarian, thanks to Ayn Rand and Nathaniel Brandon, my first mentors of the freedom philosophy, and the two books they urged me to read: Atlas Shrugged and Economics in one Lesson. That conversion took me several months. In contrast, Murray converted me to anarcho-capitalism in about 10 minutes, using Hazlitt-type arguments on me regarding defense, police, law, etc. But my conversion to Austrian economics took a lot longer. I had an investment in mainstream economics from my Ph.D. program, and was loath to give up the neoclassical school. I was a devotee of the logical positivist philosophy, according to which a statement was either empirical, about the real world, in which case it could only be tentatively known, or it could be apodictic, absolutely known for sure, in which case it was not about the real world at all, but was only a tautology. It took me several years to see, and agree with the Austrian praxeological insight that there were statements about the real world that were nevertheless impossible to deny. For example synthetic a priori statements like there is a tendency for prices of identical goods to be the same, when there is voluntary trade, both parties gain welfare in the ex ante sense, etc. To show you the state I was in when I first began discussing Austrian economics with Murray, and with my then-mentor, Walter Grinder, I saw a picture of Ludwig von Mises on Murray's wall. I objected to this, since Mises was not an anarchist. Murray just smiled at me. I'm lucky that he was that gentle with me.

LMR: Your lecturing and writing style is decidedly "in your face," in the sense that you are sometimes intentionally provocative to force your opponent to consider the argument. Can you discuss why you use this approach, and how you think it has served you over the years?

WB: Moi? In your face? Surely you jest! Am I not known far and wide as Walter Moderate Block? Ok, ok, here I go again, getting in *your* face now. I do indeed confess to using reductios ad absurdum. I guess we each have to develop our own styles. Some of it, surely, I got from Murray Rothbard, the person from whom, by far, I got the most from, and not only intellectually speaking. Maybe it is a Brooklyn thing, or a Jewish thing, I'm really not sure. Perhaps being provocative is my way of trying to get through to people. I am really unaware of this, or, better, not fully aware of it. Writing and speaking are to a great degree activities that you just do automatically. The centipede was asked to explain how he coordinated all of his feet; according to the joke, he just couldn't do it. Well, I think, in like manner, all I can do is speculate about my intellectual style, as I have been doing. I really don't have a strong fix on this issue. I think what we're supposed to do, mostly, on this Earth is have fun. And my lecturing and writing style, I think, is the most fun for me. Hopefully, even, I get something accomplished, although I'm not always sure precisely what.

LMR: One of your recent books deals with the topic of total road privatization, which strikes some people as incredibly radical. Can you give a quick summary of your position and the evidence on your side?

WB: Some 40,000 people die on the government roads every year. Were highways and streets run by private enterprise, there would be a hue and cry about this to end all hues and cries. I can just see politicians whining about the "greed" of the private owners of these thoroughfares, and the need for statist intervention. But these charnel houses are now owned and managed in the "public" sector. So all these needless deaths go down the memory hole. It is too much "in your face" to point this out? My 2009C book makes and defends the claim that if this socialized sector of the economy were fully privatized, then it would benefit from competition, just as do all other sectors of the economy. If highway A killed too many customers, that corporate owner would lose profits, and face bankruptcy. I would be taken over by corporation B, which was better able to address this problem. Unhappily, there is no direct "evidence" comparing public and private roads, since there are none of the latter, at least not nowadays (the turnpike roads of our early history were private, however). The reasoning I offer is that in every other industry, competition between private owners brings about a better and cheaper good or service than socialism; why not here, too? I couple this with answers to the questions of how would these services be paid for, how would competition actually work, what might private road owners do to address issues such as speeding, drunken driving, etc.

LMR: Many of our readers are very interested in the insurance sector. Mises and Hernando de Soto praise insurance as a savings vehicle for the middle-class household, while Rothbard envisions a very large role for insurance companies in his conception of a truly free society. What are your thoughts on this apparent affinity between Austro-libertarians and the insurance sector?

WB: Hans Hoppe has also done yeoman work in demonstrating the value of a private insurance industry. I am entirely in agreement with the emphasis on this industry as a way of demonstrating the benefits of laissez-faire capitalism. When insurance companies give lower rates to those who drive safely, don't smoke, get A's in class, etc., because these behaviors are associated with lower payouts by them, then are led by "an invisible hand" to encourage these beneficial behaviors on the population at large.

LMR: It's hard to know whether to be optimistic or pessimistic these days. On the one hand, governments and central banks around the world are assuming unprecedented powers. Yet at the same time, the message of Austrian economics and political liberty seems to be reaching more and more receptive fans, especially young people. What's your take?

WB: My take on this is to be studiously uninterested in promoting the case for either optimism or pessimism. Why? Because it will not affect in the slightest what I do with my life. If, thanks to Ron Paul, we are on the verge of achieving liberty, I will work really, really hard to promote liberty. If on the other hand, I were convinced that we will never reach this goal I will still work really, really hard to promote liberty. And, I will do it in precisely the same manner: by being "in your face" about praxeology and the nonaggression principle.

But since you ask for my take on this question, here 'tis. I am a short run optimist, a medium run pessimist, and a long run pessimist-optimist. Let me explain. In the short run, say for as long as Ron Paul is active, hopefully the next decade or so, I am an optimist. When I got into the freedom movement in around 1962, there were, maybe, oh, a few score libertarians, and maybe a dozen or so Austrians, *in the entire world.* Ayn Rand's *Atlas Shrugged* came out in 1957, but it hadn't had much of an impact on the general culture five years later. The mainstream media were successfully marginalizing this book, and Rand herself dismissed libertarians as "hippies of the right." When Ron Paul ran for president on the Libertarian Party ticket in 1988, he received 0.47 percent of the vote, which I take as a proxy for libertarian interests. This was a *gigantic* increase over the early 1960s, but not really enough to write home about. How is he doing in 2012? To ask this is to answer it: his results are amazing and stupendous, compared to what went before. The mainstream media first started out ignoring him, then laughing at him, then smearing him. Although none of this has really stopped as of this writing, his vote totals typically average some 20 percent or so. He draws gigantic crowds wherever he appears, is ubiquitous on radio, television and in the print media, and a good portent for the future, he is most popular with young people and their favorite media, the internet.

What about the medium run, after the time that Ron Paul is active? Well, there is of course Rand Paul, and, hopefully, a whole bunch of other Pauls who will leave medicine for politics, but Ron is way more consistently libertarian than is Rand. I think a Ron Paul comes along only once a century or so. I am pessimistic for the medium run, since I think that biology is against us. My readings of sociobiology have convinced me that human beings are hardwired for socialism-fascism. The American Revolution was an anomaly (and hardly achieved liberty, given slavery). Ayn Rand, Murray Rothbard and Ludwig von Mises were anomalies. Ron Paul is an anomaly. Looking over all of our history over the entire globe, the light of freedom was a bare flicker. Our biology is against human liberty, and all we can do is to keep this light going. Here, I buy into the remnant philosophy. Our duty is to add to the corpus of liberty, keep it aflame, but not expect too much, except when we are in the hands of an aberration, such as Ron Paul.

What about the long run? I define this as over the next 100,000 years or so, time for biological constraints to be lifted. If we don't blow ourselves up, first (the pessimistic scenario), I think that the prospects for natural liberty are positive. Intellectually, freedom makes sense. There is all the empirical evidence that anyone would want that liberty is efficacious. Only think of the "natural experiments" of East and West Germany, North and South Korean. Morally, there is no question that voluntary interaction is vastly preferable to coercion, to socialism, to fascism. Hopefully, the human race will prosper, and one day be found on all inhabitable planets, and many that are not now inhabitable (we will make them so) throughout the universe. But will the forces of evil, of unreason, of anti-libertarianism prevail? Then, we will either all die of poverty or nuclear Armageddon.

To summarize: in the near time, I am a wild-eyed optimist, thanks to Ron Paul. I am a medium run pessimist, due to considerations of sociobiology. In the long run, I am a pessimist-optimist. The former if we blow ourselves up, the latter if not.

Blogs

This section is devoted to blogs I have made about Ron Paul. Please, let no one think that I maintain every word I ever wrote about this man is precious because I wrote it. Rather, every word I ever wrote about this man is precious because of who *he* is.[43] I am fortunate that I have lived during the era he lived, and that I actually know him, and consider him a friend. What more could a libertarian want to make him happy, apart, of course, from the actual liberty for which Ron works so hard. (These blogs all appeared on LewRockwell.com; the "Lew" referred to below is Llewellyn H. Rockwell, founder of the Mises Institute.)

Blog 1. News Flash! Ron Paul Is a Pacifist

Gosh. Golly. Gee whiz. I didn't realize that Congressman Paul is a pacifist. I wouldn't mind him taking this position as an individual, but as president of the U.S.? Turning the other cheek when other nations attack us? I don't think so. I am going to have to rethink my previous support for Dr. Paul.

How do I know that this is true? Why, the newspaper of record says so. Read this article and you will see the following, and I quote: "If there is one area where Mr. Paul, a pacifist, is weakest in this heavily military state, it is national defense." As is well known, the New York Times is the gold standard of newspapers. They never lie. They give us all the news that's fit to print.

I wonder why soldiers donate to the Ron Paul campaign more than they give to the other contenders, all of them put together? When the members of the military learn that this Texas congressman is really a pacifist, I'm sure they will send their money elsewhere.

Could it be that the New York Times is lying though its teeth? Nah. Couldn't be. Imagine that. Ron Paul a pacifist. Who would have thunk?

43It may appear to some that every word I ever wrote about Ron Paul has been placed in this book. Not so, not so. There are at least a dozen words or so that have not made the cut. On a more serious note, I have viciously culled what I have written about him; and each word I deleted cut me to the quick.

I suppose he has changed his views on this matter since his own military service.

Blog 2. Wormhole economics

Here (http://libertybullhorn.com/2012/01/03/ron-pauls-1-trillion-cut-a-case-of-wormhole-economics/) is a despicable, ignorant and economically illiterate attack on Ron Paul, written by one Sven R. Larson, Ph.D., Research Fellow, Wyoming Liberty Group. This latter organization is one of the state free-enterprise think tanks, and, indeed, they often do good work. Not, however, in this particular case.

Larson's "argument" is that Ron Paul wants to reduce the size of government too quickly and that this is equivalent to "wormhole economics."

For an incisive antidote to this Keynesian gibberish, see this. Also see this material:

Blanchette, Jude. 2004. "The Trouble With the EU," June 16;

Erhard, Ludwig. 1957 [1975]. Prosperity Through Competition, Greenwood Press;

Formaini, Robert L. 2005. "Germany: Doomed by Schmollerism," November 4;

Higgs, Robert. 1996. "Reform Is Not Possible;";

Hodgson, Fergus. 2012. "Ron Paul walks the talk: Rebuttal to the Liberty Bullhorn;";

Tucker, Jeffrey. 2010. "Erhard Persuades the Business Class," June 3;

Vogelgesang, Frank. 2002. "Ludwig Erhard, We Need You," April 24.

Blog 3. Ron Paul Anonymous

In a previous blog of mine, I had occasion to say this: "I'm setting up a new Twelve-Step program, modeled after Alcoholics Anonymous. It will be called Ron Paul Anonymous. We will be dedicated to not allowing him to ruin our lives by devoting practically all of our time to reading about him, watching him, donating to his money bombs, working tirelessly on his campaign."

A reader of this blog, Doug, sent me what could well become The 12 Steps of our new group, Ron Paul Anonymous (at his invitation, I have very slightly edited his suggestions). Here they are:

• Step 1 We admitted we were powerless over our leaders — that our government had become unmanageable

* Step 2 Came to believe that Ron Paul could restore our government to sanity

* Step 3 Made a decision to support Ron Paul's candidacy with our time, money, and energy

* Step 4 Made a searching and fearless moral inventory of our candidate — and found him to be far superior in every way to every other candidate, as well as the incumbent

* Step 5 Attempted to convince other human beings the wrongheadedness of their support of the welfare/warfare statists

* Step 6 Were entirely ready to remove all these defective politicians from office

* Step 7 Humbly asked God to help us remove them

* Step 8 Made a list of all persons harmed by the state, and became willing to put a stop to the madness, for their sakes

* Step 9 Made amends to such people by electing Ron Paul and any candidate he endorses for any other office

* Step 10 Continued to take personal inventory and when we were wrong in our efforts to promote the candidacy of Congressman Paul, promptly admitted it

* Step 11 Sought through prayer and meditation to emulate Ron Paul, praying only for knowledge of Austrian Economics and libertarian theory

* Step 12 Having had a political awakening as the result of these steps, we tried to carry Ron Paul's message to other citizens, and to practice his principles in all our affairs

We are of course not serious about this proposal. And, we hope and trust that no one in any real twelve-step program will take offense at these remarks, which are only an expression of our love for this man.

Love is part of the Twelve-Step programs, and, for many supporters of Ron Paul, it is part of our support for him, as this word "rEVOLution" expresses.

Blog 4. Herman Cain

Did Herman Cain sexually harass those women? I don't know. But, I do know that Cain is a liar. And, if he lied once, blatantly and publicly, I don't trust that he wouldn't lie again.

Here is his demonstrated lie (from Doug Wead; http://www.newsmax.com/DougWead/ron-paul-rand-straw/2011/10/14/id/414543):

"Ron Paul had asked Cain why, in the past, he had opposed an audit of the Federal Reserve and why he had belittled those who were calling for it. Cain flatly denied he had ever said such a thing.

"But here is Cain's exact quote:

"Some people say that we ought to audit the Fed. Here's what I do know. The Federal Reserve already has so many internal audits it's ridiculous. I don't know why people think we're gonna learn this great amount of information by auditing the Federal Reserve. I think a lot of people are calling for this audit of the Federal Reserve because they don't know enough about it. There's no hidden secrets going on in the Federal Reserve to my knowledge."

Cain's first lie was this denial of his. Cain's second lie was his accusation that Ron Paul had misquoted him. Again, this episode hardly constitutes proof that Cain is a serial harasser of women. But, it does call into question his veracity. If he would lie to Ron Paul's face, why wouldn't he incorporate this practice in other contexts?

Blog 5. (T)reason

We all know that Reason magazine is anti-libertarian. Its editor Katherine Mangu-Ward infamously rolled her eyes at even the outside possibility that Ron Paul could become the next president of the U.S. Of course, she was not merely prognosticating; she was actively attempting to undermine his chances. (This isn't a horse race. The commentary from the sidelines can affect the outcome). Did Mangu-

Ward get fired for her anti-libertarian act? Of course not. But everyone knows about this act of treason against the free society.

Blog 6. The Fed: Independent, Accountable, and Transparent — So Take That, Ron Paul!

Lew gets upset with bloggers if they just present material without comment. The material, below, on the Fed, cries out to be presented on its own, without comment. However, Lew is bigger than me, so I had better comply with his wish.

Here we have perhaps the most self-serving commentary on the Fed by an adherent of that evil institution. The Fed is to the U.S. economy as was the old central planning authority of the U.S.S.R. What controlled substance are these people imbibing? And, to add insult to injury, this "scholarly paper" contradicts itself all over the place. How can an institution, any institution, be independent, and yet accountable to anyone else? If the Fed is so transparent, why do they resist Congressman Paul's initiative for an audit?

I give you fair warning, you had better be sitting down when you read this material. There's a good chance you'll keel right over in a hysterical fit of the giggles, and the floor is closer when you're seated. Ah, would it be possible that Murray Rothbard were alive at this moment.

Waller (2011): "Over the years, there have been changes in the Fed's structure to improve its independence, credibility, accountability, and transparency. These changes have led to a better institutional design that makes U.S. policy credible and based on sound economic reasoning, as opposed to politics. In times of financial and economic crisis, there is a tendency to re-examine the structure of the Federal Reserve System. To the uninformed observer, the Fed's structure is in many ways mind-boggling. In particular, it seems counterintuitive that, in a democracy, the central bank should have independence from Congress. Yet, this independence is the result of Congress trying to avoid making monetary policy mistakes for political gain. Of course, accountability of public policymakers is a fundamental principle in a democracy. It is the tension between independence and accountability that led to the design of the Federal Reserve, and it has been an ever-present force in U.S. monetary policy for the past century.

"In the end, the Federal Reserve System is a well-designed institution, created by Congress, that keeps the government from relying on the printing press to finance public spending. It is independent, credible, accountable, and transparent. It is a nearly 100-year-old success story that has served the nation well."

"In 1913, Congress purposefully created the Federal Reserve as an independent central bank, which created a fundamental tension: how to ensure the Fed remains accountable to the electorate without losing its independence. Over the years, there have been changes in the Fed's structure to improve its independence, credibility, accountability, and transparency."

I owe this to Bill Barnett II and his son Michael Barnett

Blog 7. Gaydar

In chaptger 26 I stated: "Gay people, it is said, have a radar system (gaydar) which enables them to discern anti-homosexual bigotry, even when it is not in your face...." I was very much in error on this, and I apologize for my mistake. (My "motto" in writing is that nothing stops me, even total ignorance, as in this case. I have been corrected on this matter by several blog readers. The correct interpretation of "gaydar" is the ability to tell whether a straight-acting person is actually gay; or the ability/gift of being able to detect homosexuality in other people. However, there SHOULD be a word, I suppose a different one, to describe gays who can discern people who hate homosexuals even when they try to hide this behind a facade. Linguists, get to work on this! Where is Noam Chomsky when we need him?

Blog 8. Ron Paul Is Right To Dis FEMA

I don't put FEMA right up there (down there?) with the Fed. I imagine that we will see the beginning of the end of the Fed within a month of Ron Paul taking office. But FEMA should also be on the list of government departments scheduled to be closed. What follows is an excerpt from this paper of mine, which appeared in a peer-reviewed journal (Rockwell and Block, 2010):

If New Orleans were turned into a free port, a city state all on its own, its chances for a rosy financial future would be much improved. Instead of relying on millions of dollars, perhaps billions, from Washington, to be misspent by FEMA (a four-letter "F" curse word in some southern parts of the country), the Big Easy would be far better on its own.

He who pays the piper calls the tune. This is no less true of public finance than of any other field of endeavor. With federal money, comes federal control. Often, all too often, this 'aid' comes not in the form of dollars given to recipients, but as in-kind goods. But the latter is necessarily less efficient than the former, save in the rare cases where the recipient would have spent the money in exactly that format. For example, which would the average person rather have, one violin, one motorcycle, a year's supply of beer, two suits of clothes, 1,000 Frisbees, 10 steaks and 100 bowling balls, or, the exact amount of money necessary to purchase these things, to use exactly as he would like? The answer is obvious. And, yet, FEMA gives residents of New Orleans mobile home campers, costing some $70,000 each, that will blow away in the next strong wind, when they might have offered lower-priced, sturdier prefabricated cottages costing around $5,000 each. Better yet would have been cash on the barrel head.

Political separation is the ultimate in decentralization. If the latter is a plus in terms of economic development, then this applies, in spades, to the former. Why should the people of New Orleans be dependent upon the largesse of officials thousands of miles away from them, when local control and self-reliance is a far better recipe for success?

The obvious objection to this element of the free market plan is that it is too extreme. However, this may well be the window of opportunity for separation. If New Orleans were to renounce all promised aid funds from the United States, there is at least the chance that they would let my people go. When South Carolina attempted to utilize its Constitutional right to this end, there was no big financial gain to be made by the federal government in acquiescing. That is no longer the case.

It cannot be denied that there is a sense in which New Orleans homeowners are owed federal money, and would be foolish to renounce it for what might be seen as pie-in-the-sky benefits of separation from the United States. After all, the levees that were breached by the hurricane were built, owned and operated by the federal government. There is, however, another side to this issue. First of all, many of the laws under which Crescent City dwellers are to be compensated were illegitimate in that they improperly subsidized irrational geographical settlement patterns. Encouraging people to live in a flood plain simply makes no sense. Second, and more pertinent, the nature of the governmental beast is that these funds will not and cannot be forthcoming without committing further rights violations. How will Washington, D.C., collect the funds it is promising to rebuild the Big Easy? Why, from other taxpayers. And this in turn amounts to no less than theft. In the very nature of things it is impossible to be compensated by the actual perpetrators who are far too few to make up for the vast damage they have perpetrated. So, in justice, New Orleans residents will not be giving up anything that properly belongs to them in any case.

However, the federal government may well be more willing to cede control of the Big Easy in lieu of paying out these vast sums of money already promised, particularly in contrast to the case if this situation did not occur. Not that it is likely in any case; but we are attempting to map out the ideal road ahead whether or not it is politically feasible.

With New Orleans the southern U.S. equivalent of a Hong Kong or a Singapore, the inhabitants of this city will be in a position to pursue a much more radical free enterprise route than would otherwise have been the case."

Blog 9. A FEMA story

This story, also about the incompetence of FEMA, was written to me in response to my other FEMA blogs, by Jack Harrison. I pass it along without comment, except to say that it shows that Ron Paul was EXACTLY on target when he recently criticized FEMA:

"Your blog reminded me of my 'volunteer' experience with FEMA after Katrina. I was sent first to Atlanta for staging, inoculating, indoctrinating, orientating, etc. Then after a few days on hold, I was told to rent a car for 30 days and drive to Jackson, Mississippi, rent a hotel there for 30 days, and wait further orders. After a week in Jackson, I was told to drive to Biloxi to FEMA's local HQ. Upon arrival in Biloxi, I was told I'd be driving back and forth, two hours each way, to Mobile Bay, Louisiana, where I'd work on one of the FEMA-leased Carnival Cruise Line ships as 'head of security' — meanwhile I was originally brought on for my computer and technical networking skills and told I'd be helping rebuild the damaged infrastructure. Yup, an IT geek somehow wound up as head of security on a floating trailer park. Two solid weeks of time and money wasted before I even arrived on duty to do a job I had no business doing.

Lew always wants us bloggers not merely to report material, but to add our own commentary to it. In this case I will ignore Lew's request, and, instead, merely inform you of a passage that appears in this refereed journal article (Block and Rockwell, 2007):

One week after the hurricane, FEMA ordered the Army Corps of Engineers to buy 211 million pounds of ice from IAP Worldwide Services of Florida. Trucking companies were notified of a grand opportunity since the government was paying the bills for delivery, and the dispatchers sent out the word. There is no space to explore the workings of IAP Worldwide, but the company, which relies heavily on tax dollars as a federal contractor, has a new CEO who most recently held the position of vice president of national security programs for the notorious Kellogg Brown and Root. His name is David Swindle.

But back to the story of the ensuing chaos. One trucker picked up ice in Greenville, Pennsylvania, and was told to drive it to Carthage, Missouri. But when he arrived in Carthage, he was told by a FEMA official to go to Montgomery, Alabama. After a day and a half sitting in Montgomery, he was told to go to Camp Shelby, Mississippi, after which he was sent to Selma, Alabama, after which he was sent to Emporia, Virginia, where he stayed for a week burning fuel, until he was sent to North Carolina, and finally to Nebraska, where he dropped the ice in a government storage unit. That's 4,000 miles over a period of two weeks. This was hardly the only case.

The news media chronicled the stories of these truckers. A truck full of ice was sent from Dubuque, Iowa, to Meridian, Mississippi, then to Barksdale Base in Louisiana, then to Columbia, South Carolina, and finally to Cumberland, Maryland, where he waited for six days before being sent to Bettendorf, Iowa, where the ice was unloaded. Another truck was sent from Wisconsin to Missouri to Selma to Memphis, Tennessee, before finally dropping off the ice in a storage unit. There were 4000 drivers enlisted in this incredible charade. No one knows for sure how much ice ever got through or how much, if any, good it did.

In one of the first incidents reported of what was to be two weeks of catastrophe, a group of volunteer firemen from Houston came to New Orleans wanting to help. They were told to wait. They waited 48 hours and were ordered to go back. A group of doctors from Maryland tried to get in but FEMA sent them on to the Red Cross, which said it could do nothing without the approval of federal health officials.

After the New Orleans mayor made a call for firefighters to come help, 1,000 volunteers were sent to Atlanta, where they were put in a conference room at the Sheraton Hotel and subjected to seminars on sexual harassment and other bureaucratic matters. They were then told that their job would be to distribute fliers with a message on it: call 1-800-621-FEMA. Many or even most of these well-trained people left town. Those who stuck it out and headed for Louisiana were aghast that their first assignment was not to fight fires, which had been raging for a week, but to escort President Bush on his TV-laden tour of the area. All the photos can be seen on WhiteHouse.gov.

In fact, FEMA refused offers of help of all sorts, mainly because of issues of control. FEMA declined help from Amtrak in evacuating people from New Orleans. The Chicago municipal government wanted to send volunteers from the fire department, police department, and hospitals all over town, but FEMA said no. The same happened to New Mexico, whose governor volunteered equipment and personnel.

FEMA prevented Wal-Mart from delivering three tank trucks full of water, and the Coast Guard from delivering diesel fuel. As for the National Guard, for days it would not allow reporters into the Superdome where tens of thousands were trapped. People were hungry and thirsty, but the National Guard would not allow the Red Cross to deliver any food. Here is the astounding statement from the spokesperson of the Red Cross: "The Homeland Security Department has requested and continues to request that the American Red Cross not come back into New Orleans.... Right now access is controlled by the National Guard and local authorities.... We cannot get into New Orleans against their orders."

The Salvation Army attempted to rescue two of its own officers trapped in a building and on dialysis. They rented three boats for a rescue. But they were not allowed through , though to be fair the Salvation Army didn't specifically name the government as at fault, but it did point out that all private efforts were running into similar kinds of obstacles, so the message was clear. Meanwhile, the USS Bataan, a floating hospital for 600 patients, that happened to be at sea and rode out the storm, was still sitting empty by the third day, not permitted to do its job.

An astounding case of ineptness comes to us from the case of three Duke University students who drove to New Orleans to help but were turned away by the National Guard. They had seen the news and knew that they could help, and wondered why they should be pushed around by bureaucrats. Being college sophomores, they took a risk. They forged press credentials, with fake IDs and shirts and the works. They went back and adopted a haughty tone. The National Guard waved them through immediately. Then the students drove to the Convention Center. There they found thousands of sick, hungry, thirsty, and dying people in desperate need. They found a man who had welts all over his body. He was in a tree covered with fire ants as the flood waters rose, and there he stayed being bitten repeatedly for up to 24 hours.

The boys picked him up along with three others and drove them to a Baton Rouge hospital. They made another trip there and back with more people before they began to become frightened of what the government might do to them. On one return trip, they observed 150 empty buses driving the other way – and they have a video to prove it.

One can only express astonishment at how the government treated the tens of thousands of people it had herded like cattle into large public spaces. For reasons still unclear, the government couldn't seem to get its act together on transporting them out even as the people themselves were forbidden to leave. Once the central planners decided to move all these people from the Superdome to the Astrodome, no means of transport arrived, even as aerial photos showed miles and miles of public buses available.

Indeed, the first bus to reach Houston was not driven or approved by the government. It was commandeered by 20-year-old Jabbar Gibson, who drove it from the floods and picked up as many people as he could and drove all the way to Houston, a 13-hour drive. He beat the government's system by a day. Meanwhile, the tens of thousands of people who had been shoved into the Superdome on Sunday, before the floods came, were still suffering in that massive calamity by Friday and Saturday.

Perhaps the most astounding case of incompetence has received the least attention. It relates to a 500-boat flotilla stretching over five miles that left for New Orleans from Lafayette. It involved 1,000 people who had hoped to rescue hospital patients and take them to safety. It consisted of private boaters, fishermen, hunters, and others who had spent their entire lives navigating Louisiana waterways. Once this caravan arrived, they were turned away by the Department of Wildlife and Fisheries, which was now being run by FEMA. All five hundred boats were turned away and ordered out.

Now, keep in mind that this was three days after the hurricane hit. There were hundreds of people inside Charity Hospital in New Orleans alone. They had no supplies and only three had been rescued. At this very time, the head of the FEMA-ized Wildlife and Fisheries Department announced to the world on television that it needed no help from anyone and that it had all matters under control."

Ron Paul's criticisms of FEMA were VERY accurate, the MSM to the contrary notwithstanding.

Blog 10. Nigeria

As you can see from this series of letters between me and Mr. Michael Onasanya of Nigeria, appreciation for Congressman Ron Paul is by no means limited to Americans. I greatly hope Mr. Onasanya sends me a YouTube talk on this matter. When and if he does, I will certainly blog it.

My thoughts on this correspondence: It had been my view, before reading his initial magnificent letter, and his follow-up responses to me, that I stood second to no one in my own appreciation of Ron Paul as a man, as a friend, and for what he has done for libertarianism. After reading what Michael Onasanya has to say, I realize I am now in a horse-race as far as the Ron Paul appreciation sweepstakes are concerned.

-----Original Message-----

From: Michael Onasanya

Sent: Fri 8/19/2011 1:00 PM

To: wblock@loyno.edu

Subject: Ron Paul

Dear Mr. Block, my name is Michael Onasanya, I am Nigerian and an ardent fan of Lewrockwell.com. Please tell Congressman Ron Paul that there are those, though not American, who however, adore him to pieces. Just so you know, I learned everything about true freedom from the articles by the wonderful people who write for Lewrockwell.com. This email, however, is about that courageous and celestial human called Ron Paul. , From him and his activities, I learned courage, fortitude, patience, humility, kindness in the face of opposition, gentleness and a host of other things too numerous to list, I sometimes envy his children and if I ever come back to this world, and he was here before me, I would request God make me his son.

Concisely, Ron Paul is the rarest of men, one who inspires, motivates, and restores belief in the goodness of man. I have benefitted a lot from you all and I would like to contribute my widow's mite to the pollination of minds so please, let me know how I can be of worth to you. I deliberately wrote this email to you in the hope that you would know how to get it across to the 'man' himself, the great Ron Paul, thank him for me and others like me who understand, thanks to you, that freedom is all about 'live and let live' and 'first, do no harm'...

cheers,

Michael Onasanya

Dear Michael:

May I please have your permission to blog the material you sent me?

Best regards,

Walter

On 8/23/11, Walter Block

Dear Michael:

May I suggest, no, urge, you to create a youtube talk of your views on Ron Paul? If you do this, please send me the url for it, so that I can broadcast it, send it to the Ron Paul campaign, etc.

Best regards,

Walter

-----Original Message-----

From: Walter Block

Sent: Tue 8/23/2011 1:21 PM

To: Michael Onasanya

Subject: RE: Ron Paul

Dear Michael:

Thanks for your lovely, lovely letter. I will indeed share it with Dr. Paul and some Ron Paul people.

What kind of work do you do?

Best regards,

Walter

Dear Mr. Block, thank you for taking the time to respond to my email, I am highly gratified. As to what I do, I am an information systems architect, specializing in the practical implementation of Artificial (synthesized) intelligence technologies.

Unfortunately, Nigeria, my country, does not seem ready for people like myself as the country is neither interested in advanced research, nor development of anything but still, those like me persevere after all. The world is truly connected now and globalization is a fact. With a big market we'll survive and even thrive.

I will endeavor to make the video as advised, extolling the proven virtues of Ron Paul, and I dearly hope Americans can open their eyes long enough to see what we foreign observers see. Ron Paul truly cares about America and humanity, in a way no other American politician does. He can make us (Americans and foreigners) believe in America again, the city on a shining hill, the light of humanity that was once America.

Cheers,

Michael Onasanya

Dear Mr. Block, you may do as you wish with the correspondence. Do edit the typos though lest some left-wing good-doer, or right-wing chicken-hawk (LOL) accuse me of illiteracy. The feelings expressed within are genuine and heartfelt, and the intention is to let Congressman Ron Paul know that beyond the shores of America, he is adored intensely… A prophet has no honor in his country after all....

Cheers,

Michael Onasanya

Blog 11. Supreme Court

Four days ago, on July 22, 2011, I wrote a column for LewRockwell.com in which I speculated about President Ron Paul's likely appointments to fill vacancies on the U.S. Supreme Court. That article was very much a first draft. I knew that I was committing errors both of omission and commission. I called for help from the readership of LRC. I now input information I was given as a result of that request.

If you go back to that url, you will see the results. Here are some teasers. (1) I added 19 new names. (2) I had almost two dozen objections to my omission of one of these libertarian lawyers. Guess which person received all of these "votes" (3) I added two people to my list of "libertarians" that Ron would never in a million years appoint. Who were they? (4) The article I cited as a reason for not appointing one of them to the Supreme Court was written by Matt Mortellaro. I asked the subject of that article (one of the two I added as nonlibertarian "libertarians") if he would publish a reply to it. He said he wouldn't, because the Mortellaro critique of him was so poorly done. In my view, however, this one article is worth the entire price of admission. It is really an excellent defense of Ron Paul, one worthy of the widest dissemination possible.

Lew Rockwell asked me to follow up my Supreme Court nomination article with another, this time on Ron Paul's cabinet. I must decline, due to the press of other commitments. However, I now turn around and suggest that other people take up Lew on this suggestion of his. While I am on the subject, however, of follow-ups to this column of mine, let me add a few more to the mix. Who will candidate Ron Paul, choose as his running mate? Andrew Napolitano? Rand Paul? Gary Johnson? Lew Rockwell? This would make a good column, in my humble opinion, for LRC.

Here is another possibility. Will Ron rescind the Council of Economic Advisors? If not, then who will he pick to join this group? Who are the economists that President Paul will likely rely upon? (Hint: all those he has so far chosen to testify on the hearings he has so far conducted on the Fed should appear front and center on any such list.)

Here is yet another possible entrant for these "What Will President Paul Do" sweepstakes: What will Ron do first? Get up a list of the order in which his first dozen or two initiatives will appear. Will he first bring the troops home? Which countries first, given that he cannot do this for all of them in the very first day? Or, will his first act be to abolish the Fed? The much beloved Department of Agriculture? The Department of Education?

The fun here is not so much in making up these lists, although that can indeed be a blast, but in the reasons given for these choices.

My expectation is that if enough good LRC columns are written on these subjects, Lew will highlight them in a special session on his web page. Then, the Paul Administration will find in one handy place information of possible use to it.

Blog 12. George Will's Republican Candidates for President in 2012

George Will, in his article, "The GOP's weirdness faction," states as follows: "Let us not mince words. There are at most five plausible Republican presidents on the horizon — Indiana Governor Mitch Daniels, Mississippi Governor Haley Barbour, former Utah governor and departing ambassador to China Jon Huntsman, former Massachusetts governor Mitt Romney and former Minnesota governor Tim Pawlenty." This, after bashing Mike Huckabee and Newt Gingrich as potential candidates. Notice any missing name from this list? I'll give you a hint. His initials are R.P., he is a congressman from Texas, and the father of a newly elected senator from Kentucky, also with the same initials. If you haven't guessed yet, you probably had a public school education. Go to the back of the class!

Blog 13. Dime's worth of difference

Here is a great quote from USA Today from an article entitled "Governors head to D.C., minds on the economy":

"Most of the … nation's governors are leaving their state capitals for the annual winter meeting here of the National Governors Association. … The 103-year-old group has a reputation for bipartisanship. 'If you were to sit in on one of those governors-only sessions, if you didn't already know, you wouldn't be able to tell who the Democrats and who the Republicans are,' Scheppach said." (Ray Scheppach is the executive director of the association).

I am tempted to leave things just at that. But, Lew insists that we bloggers not merely report things, but comment on them as well. (Lew can get pretty vicious about this, resorting to violence against those who disobey him on this matter, the petty tyrant that he is. See David Kramer's exposé of him in this regard).

Scheppach, obviously, doesn't realize he is giving away the store. A certain ex-governor of Alabama (George Wallace) famously said, "There's not a dime's worth of difference" between the two political parties. With the exception of Ron Paul, Rand Paul, and maybe one or two others, there really *is* no difference between the leadership of the two parties, and even their respective followers. Surely, on foreign policy, Obama is a Bush clone. Ok, ok, there might be a subtle difference in what they want to spend taxpayers' money on, but they are as united as they can be with regard to their views that they know better than the long-suffering taxpayer how to spend his money. And, yes, there is the present brouhaha in Wisconsin. But the altercation does not involve principle. Rather, it concerns which gang members shall get which shares of the stolen money.

Blog 14. Cuts in *defense* spending?

In an otherwise very good effort, the author of this article commits a major howler. No, let me correct that: he is guilty of a gargantuan, despicable error. The author, one Alexander Mooney, says that Ron Paul "has long argued for drastic cuts in defense spending."

Ron has long argued for "drastic cuts in DEFENSE spending?" No, Ron has NEVER done that. Never in a million years has he come even CLOSE to saying anything of the sort. Rather, Congressman Paul has argued for drastic cuts in (rather, elimination of) OFFENSE spending. As far as I know, Ron might even agree to INCREASES in DEFENSE spending: buffing up the Coast Guard, as part and parcel of the process of pulling back to our own borders ALL our troops, and closing down our some 800 foreign military bases. No, this is precisely what our ENEMIES accuse Dr. Paul of, and it is CRUCIAL that Ron NOT be linked with cuts in DEFENSE spending in any manner, shape or form.

The reason I am so exercised about all this (apart from my usual hysterical personality) is that Mooney does not appear to be an enemy of the Ron Paul movement but, rather, a friend, as can be seen by perusing the remainder of his article. But if even FRIENDS can make such appalling errors, there is little hope for Ron in 2012.

Blog 15. Libertarians are neither right nor left

There is a very interesting letter from a conservative now making the rounds, asking for a divorce from liberals; it is addressed as follows: "Dear American liberals, leftists, social progressives, socialists, Marxists and Obama supporters, et al:"

It is well worth reading, in that it does indeed make some good points against the self-styled "progressives."

Here is my open-letter response to this author:

"Who is this ignorant young man? He doesn't seem to realize that there are not only two political economic philosophies in play in the world today, but three: left-liberal-pinko-socialist-progressive-Marxists, right-conservative-patriotic-warmongering-imperialist-fascists, but, ALSO, libertarians, who are members of NEITHER of these first two groups. It is my considered opinion that we libertarians are equi-distant from both socialist Democrats on the left, and fascist Republicans on the right."

Blog 16. It is all the government's fault

It is the government that is responsible for hurricanes, earthquakes, tornadoes, volcanoes, flooding, storms, rain at inconvenient times, and other supposed acts of God; and also for AIDS, cancer, heart disease, and other diseases. As well, the state is responsible for the fact that we have not yet colonized the moon and Mars. Why do I make these hysterical sounding claims?

Because the state has taken in compulsory taxes, some half of our GDP for lo these many years, and used it to further reduce our prosperity by regulating us and bombing innocent people in other countries. Does anyone doubt that if the world's wealth were, oh, 4-5 times higher than it now is (my guesstimate of what it would be but for this pernicious institution), that we would have at least been way further ahead in dealing with the issues mentioned above?

Blog 17. Libertarian like dad?

Here is the part of a NY Times interview with Rand Paul that I found most interesting:

NYT: As someone who has opposed all tax increases, the Department of Education and the invasion of Iraq, do you consider yourself a libertarian like your famous dad, Representative Ron Paul of Texas?

RP: I call myself a constitutional conservative.

Well, as far as I am concerned, Rand is WAY better than his opponent on libertarian issues, and, if elected, would very likely be the SECOND most libertarian member of the Congress.

Blog 18. Ron Paul, slippery mainstream politician

Tom Woods recently asked Ron Paul a very important and incisive question. Tom couched it in a way cleverly designed to elicit an answer from Ron. But Congressman Paul, slippery mainstream politician that he is, managed to (well, at least partially) evade this ingenious query.

Much as I appreciate Tom's attempt to pin Ron down, I say that the time has come to cast off Woods type of namby-pamby pure libertarianism. No, if you want to accomplish anything in this world, I have now been convinced by the neo-cons: pure naked aggression is the only way to go. So, I am now calling for the setting up of a new group: Draft Ron Paul for Presidential Candidate in 2012. But, this will not be the usual sissy type of "draft," where we whine, plead, and beg Ron to run in 2012, never threatening him with bodily harm since we respect the libertarian nonaggression principle. That is for wussy libertarians. No, now that I have been converted to neo-conservatism, I am calling for the government to pass a law compelling Ron to run in 2012. I think that life in prison for Ron if he refuses is too harsh (I'm no extremist!); I have a lesser penalty in mind: a day in the stocks (I'm an old-fashioned kind of guy).

So, Ron, be warned: we're coming to getcha. We'll be armed with pitchforks and torches. Rotten vegetables will be your punishment should you disobey this new law. Ron, on a more serious note, please read this wonderful essay.

(To the readership of this blog: please do not write me telling me I'm a disgrace for abandoning libertarianism; I'm just kidding here. Of course, I'm very serious about the importance of Ron running in 2012. That would be sooooo wonderful. As Tom says, if Ron did, we could possibly triple the present size of the libertarian movement.)

Blog 19. The Libertarian Party

(This is a letter I wrote to a 2012 candidate for the Libertarian Party ticket for president; this is not Governor Gary Johnson; I thank my friend Dr. Michael R. Edelstein for bringing this issue to my attention; I also urged the LP to hold their convention after the one organized by the Republicans, so that they could see if Ron won or not, but their leaders declined to do so):

Raise the issue: suppose Ron wins the Republican nomination. The LP standard bearer can then do one of several things.

a. run against Ron

b. quit and support Ron

c. stay in, and support Ron

d. call Ron, ask him what to do, and do whatever he says

You should announce as part of your platform that you'll choose option d. I'll bet you Johnson will not go along with that. And, I'll betcha, this option d will be very popular in the LP.

The challenge facing the Libertarian Party is how best to promote libertarianism. How do you do that? Why, by converting people to libertarianism. And who is doing that, par excellence? Why, our man, Ron, of course. If Ron wins the Republican nomination, he'll surely be a better converter of people to libertarianism if the LP candidate, possibly you, supports Ron, rather than runs against him. This being the case, would you not be a better promoter of libertarianism if you helped Ron, rather than ran against him? I think that is very clear.

The LP is NOT a goal, it is only, merely, a MEANS. A means toward what? Toward liberty. Toward limited government. If liberty can best be promoted via the LP, I support the LP; that is USUALLY the case. But, if liberty can best be supported via Ron Paul, as it most assuredly is, in this present case, then I support Ron. I urge you to do so.

Blog 20. Convert a Friend bomb

Dear Raymond:

I think that your idea is SUCH a good one that I am sharing this with my Ron Paul contacts. An Excellent idea. Costs nothing. Gets publicity. Maybe, the Paul campaign can give a prize every month to the person who converts the most people; a prize such as a dozen copies of Ron's books, so that this person can convert even more people with these books next month.

Best regards,

Walter

-----Original Message-----

From: Raymond A. Gazzara

Sent: Friday, February 10, 2012 10:18 AM

To: wblock@loyno.edu

Subject: Ron Paul conversion Bomb idea

Good Morning,

Mr. Block, I am a fan of yours through your articles on LRC. I have yet to purchase your books, but Defending the Undefendable is on my wish list. I'm just waiting for my brain to feel up to the task.

I had an idea that I was hoping to run by you, and if you like it maybe you can get it to the right someone. I know money is important to Ron Paul's campaign hopes, but ultimately what is more important is getting more and more people to our cause. In addition to his Money Bombs (which I always support), how about a Convert a Friend bomb, held maybe every month??

I know you and the many dedicated friends of LRC & MISES have spent a lifetime educating the "rest of us" and converting many, but if the "rest of us" make some more converts, we can increase our numbers, hopefully dramatically.

Say there are 10,000 of us (hopefully there are many more) and month 1 we have a 25% success rate, well there would then be 12,500. Next month with a 25% success rate there will be 15,625 … like the magic of compounding interest and with even greater benefits.

Again I want to thank you for your great work for the libertarian cause.

Regards,

Raymond

Blog 21. Ron Paul and Gandhi

According to Gandhi "*First they* ignore you, then they *laugh at you*, then they fight you, then you win." How does this apply to Ron Paul? Well, it is a bit more complicated than that in this case. Here, the "ignoring" certainly fits. The mainstream media talks about everyone else under the sun except for You Know Who. And who can forget the "laughing": he is a crazy old uncle, his suits don't fit, his eyebrows aren't "presidential" enough, etc. The "fighting" is clear: he has been smeared with everything in the book they could throw at him, and with lots of stuff that isn't in the book, too. But in the Gandhi case, each of these things occurred pretty much one at a time. *First,* they did this, *then* they did that. The implication is that after they finished the first thing, they stopped it, and then went on to the second; ditto for the third and fourth. Not so in the case of the congressman from Texas. Even now, amidst all the laughing and the sneering, they are *still* ignoring Dr. Paul. How many stories about the presidential campaigns of Romney, Gingrich and Santorum (notice who is missing?) must we read from the *New York Times* and the *Washington Post*? How many times must we be reminded that Dr. Paul has not yet won any state election outright? (Maine doesn't count. Vote fraud is yet another issue that did not beset Gandhi.) Why is it that the major media almost entirely ignored that magnificent and unprecedented march of his supporters in the military on Washington, D.C., on February 20, 2012? Don't ask me how these people can at one and the same time ignore Ron, smear him and laugh at him. To the uninitiated, this sounds like a logical contradiction. But, it would appear, our powers that be are even capable of ignoring the laws of logic.

But there are at present two more altogether different deviations from the Gandhi scenario now in play.

The first is that Ron Paul has "elevated" to the status of "power broker." No. This is just another attempt on the part of the ruling class in our society to deflect Mr. Paul from his goal. First, to *win* the Republican nomination for president, then to gain a landslide victory over Mr. Obama in the fall, and finally to turn the U.S. and the world, too, into a free, peaceful, prosperous place where there is liberty for all. And, he will do it, too. Yes, the Texas congressman will have a difficult time attaining the first of these goals. But when and if he does, it will be all downhill after that, as he cashes in on his additional support of first Independents, and second, disaffected Democrats. The status of "power broker" implies that the next president of the U.S. will take Paul's calls; that he will have some input into the party platform (which is almost totally ignored in any case); that, perhaps, there will indeed be some sort of luke-warm oversight placed on the Fed; that there will be yet another blue-ribbon commission instituted to study whether marijuana shall be legalized (which will also be ignored). No. "Power broker" is a mere booby prize. Ron is in this for the long haul. For him it is "President or bust." "Power broker," along with ignoring, laughing at, smearing, are just attempts to deflect him from his this magnificent goal of his.

The second non-Gandhian scenario being experienced by Ron Paul is that he is now in cahoots with Mitt Romney. Mitt Romney? Bosh and tosh. Yes, there is a lack of personal antipathy between the two men; indeed, there is some sort of grudging respect between them. Their wives are friendly. Yes, Ron sees in Mitt a person who is less of a loose cannon in many ways than either Scam or Noot. So what? When it comes to matters of substance, in terms of foreign policy, economic principles, personal liberties as Ron never tires of telling anyone who will listen, there is as much of a unbridgeable a gap between Ron and Mitt as there is between Ron and either of the two others (notice, I'm not mentioning their names? Hah! Take that). This collusion scenario, too, is an attempt to deflect the congressman from his goal of bringing liberty to the world. For surely Dr. Paul would be the *junior* partner in any such amalgamation, at least in the eyes of the mainstream media and the real power brokers in the Republican Party. Maybe, possibly, he or his son, Senator Rand Paul from Kentucky, will be offered the *vice presidential* spot on the ticket.

Well, maybe, who knows, the future is uncertain. But at this point in time, there is no doubt about it. Ron Paul is in this game for all the marbles. And power broker, along with junior partner, are only obstacles in his path, along with ignoring, laughing at, smearing, and other such impediments.

Blog 22. Porter of the *New York Times*

According to Porter, 2011:

"Gold can't be smoked away. Yet, as money, it shares tobacco's basic drawback: It would shackle the economy to how much gold we could get our hands on. Today, the Fed can print dollars at will to meet the growing demand for money as the economy grows, or even to encourage growth. Under a gold standard, the economy couldn't grow faster than the supply of gold.

"To a large extent, the Great Depression happened because the Fed was required to keep enough gold to cover 60 percent of money in circulation, at a fixed price. This forced it to raise interest rates to attract gold reserves and forced the money supply to shrink when banks started hoarding gold. F.D.R.'s decision to jettison the gold peg in 1933 was essential to end the Depression, allowing a major devaluation of the dollar and boosting the amount of money in circulation. This lowered interest rates and primed a surge in investment.

"It seems perplexing that Mr. Paul would want to try something that so clearly failed before. We wonder if the fact that much of his wealth is tied up in gold mining stocks — and that he would certainly benefit if even more Americans caught the gold bug — might have influenced his judgment."

There is more fallacy here in these few words than you can shake a stick at. If new gold discoveries (including conversion of this metal from jewelry and teeth fillings, etc.) kept pace with the growth of the rest of the economy, prices would tend to be stable. If new gold discoveries were greater than the growth of the rest of the economy, the tendency would be for prices of other goods and services to rise in terms of gold. What if Porter's scenario were correct? Then, the rate of new gold discoveries would be less than the growth of the rest of the economy. Would this mean that the growth of the rest of the economy would have to be reduced to the level of new gold discoveries (and conversions)? Of course not. The clear implication, instead, is that prices of other goods and services would tend to fall in terms of gold. That is, we would be able to buy horses, houses and hosiery at cheaper prices. Each ounce of gold would trade for more of these items. What is wrong with this sort of "deflation?" Nothing at all. When cars, air conditioners, television sets and computers were first introduced to the market, they were very expensive. They were playthings of the very rich. But with specialization and the division of labor and mass production, their prices all fell until the middle classes and now the poor can afford them. This is hardly to put handcuffs on the expansion of the economy.

Roosevelt took the U.S. off (the remnants of) the gold standard (that still existed then) on June 5, 1933. If it were true that gold was like an anchor that kept us economically depressed, it could only have been until that time. That is, *at most* Porter's "analysis" could account for the Great Depression from its start in 1929 until that date four years later. But this contraction lasted far longer than that. (Some economic historians date the end of the Great Depression at the beginning of World War II. Better historians, such as Robert Higgs, place this date at the *end* of that war). So, even on the assumption that this author's economic theory is correct, he can account for only a small proportion of this economic debacle.

But Porter's analysis is fallacious. According to Austrian economists such as Hayek, Rothbard, Garrison, Barnett and Mises, the cause of the Great Depression occurred in the 1920s, when the runaway Federal Reserve System artificially lowered interest rates below the levels that would otherwise have obtained, thus inter-temporally misallocating resources on a vast scale (toward unjustifiably greater, roundabout methods of production, involving heavy industry). The Depression was the economy's attempt to cleanse these misallocations, but was tragically lengthened by Hoover's and FDR's New Deal attempts to prop up prices and wages, and companies that should have been allowed to go bankrupt. (In the modern era we see shades of these policies in Obama's bailouts of Wall Street and Detroit.) The Smoot-Hawley tariff of the 1930s did not help one bit, very much the reverse, and we see vestiges of this in Obama's attempt to subsidize "insourcing." His support of green industries (think Solyndra), unions (his attack on secret ballots), female wages and crony capitalist bailouts, etc. only exacerbates the situation.

Yeah, yeah, the reason Ron Paul supports the gold standard is because he has "much of his wealth … tied up in gold-mining stocks." If Dr. Paul is known for anything, it is hardly for amassing gobs and gobs of wealth; not for making Mitt Romney look like a pauper, and Bill Gates, too. Nor is it reasonable to think that the Texan accomplished this by pursuing policies as Dr. No in Congress, aimed at maximizing the value of his portfolio. If you want to lay a glove on his candidacy, you will have to do lots better than this, Mr. Porter.

Blog 23. More Advice for Ron

Based on the magnificent insights of Justin Raimondo (2012), I am convinced not, as he says, that Ron should drop out of the Republican race for the presidential nomination and go third party, but, rather, he should *stay in* this race, but, *also*, seek the nomination of the Libertarian Party. I don't much care if this is legal or not. If it is, fine; if not, even the *attempt* to do so will garner benefits for Dr. Paul in particular, and for the spread of liberty in general.

There is certainly precedent for this sort of thing. In New York State for example, there are *four* major parties: Republicans, Conservatives, Democrats and Liberals. It is far from unusual for a person to run for statewide office on *both* the first two of these tickets, or with the latter pair. In any case, by the time the courts pass judgment on this, it will be long past the election of 2012.

So, Congressman Paul should seek to run for President of the U.S. in November 2012 on both the Republican and the Libertarian Party tickets. If he gets the nod from each of them, well and good, he runs on both tickets. If he is nominated by either one but not the other, then he runs in November on the one ticket that supports him.

What are the benefits of seeking the LP nomination while continuing to seek Republican delegates? It will put the GOP on notice that they can no longer trifle with Ron Paul, changing the rules of delegate elections in mid stream, (allegedly) stealing votes from him (as in the case of Massachusetts, among others), and in every other way they can to undermine his candidacy. It will guarantee that the rEVOLution will continue long past Tampa in August, 2012.

What are the benefits of seeking the LP nomination in May 2012? This party is already on the ballot of most of the fifty states; that is a great advantage over running as an Independent and struggling for ballot status everywhere. And the philosophy of the Libertarian Party, despite putting Gingrich supporter Bob Barr at the head of their 2008 ticket, is certainly more in conformity with Dr. Paul's than is that of the Constitution Party.

What are the disadvantages of such a course of action? For one thing, it might well reduce votes for Congressman Paul in upcoming Republican state elections. But this is a minor loss, in that his motivated minions will still try to squeeze out as many delegates as possible, and Ron's main supporters are not within the GOP; rather, they are to be found among Independents, and disaffected Democrats unhappy with Obama's foreign policy. Another disadvantage will be the disappointment and opposition of New Mexico Governor Gary Johnson, who would otherwise likely obtain the LP nomination. But, Dr. Paul could choose Johnson as his Vice Presidential running mate, whether for the GOP or the LP, or both. Do NOT expect Johnson to step aside for Paul if the former wins the LP nomination due to the procrastination of the latter. So, the time is now: my advice for Ron Paul is to stay in the Republican race, and also seek the LP nomination, a.s.a.p.

Conclusion

I Hate Ron Paul

Before the Paul campaign of 2012, I was a reasonably productive researcher and writer. Nowadays, that has all changed: I have become a Ron Paul junkie. I must, I simply must read everything written about him in the mainstream media. I am forever watching him on television. I just "wasted" almost half an hour watching him on the Jay Leno show. Of course, Ron was magnificent on that occasion. But that is the trouble with him. For addicts like me, this just makes it even the more difficult to carry out my ambitions with regard to reading, writing, teaching and promoting libertarian theory and Austrian economics. Why, were it not for Ron Paul, I'd probably have written 5 more books and 100 more articles in scholarly refereed journals this past year. These are my main goals as an academic, and I have slackened off, perilously, in fulfilling them. So, I hate Ron Paul. I wish he'd stop tweaking all those pompous noses. I wish he would stop proving wrong all those who kept, and keep, saying, "Congressman Paul can't win." I wish Ron Paul would leave me in the peaceful and quiet atmosphere I used to enjoy before his magnificent campaign to turn the entire world in the direction of freedom, personal liberty, peace, private property rights, and sound economics. Just who does he think he is, disturbing not only me, but also the powers that be? We were all doing just fine until Dr. Paul came on the scene, disquieting all of us. Can't the man leave us all alone? Is that too much to ask? We were all happy, each of us in his own way, before he brought us all this intellectual, moral and spiritual turmoil. I'm setting up a new Twelve-Step program, modeled after Alcoholics Anonymous. It will be called Ron Paul Anonymous. We will be dedicated to not allowing him to ruin our lives by devoting practically all of our time to reading about him, watching him, donating to his money bombs, working tirelessly on his campaign. Our motto will be, of course, "We hate Ron Paul." (Yes, yes, of course I'm speaking in jest here; I simply don't know how else better to express my appreciation for the man from Texas.)

Postscript:

I feel it appropriate to end this book with one of the most magnificent defenses of Ron Paul ever written. It was penned by Joe Salerno, an old friend of mine. Although he is a bit younger than I am, I have always looked upon him as a mentor and guru, particularly in the area of Austrian macroeconomics. Here he is, in my opinion, at his wittiest and brilliant best.

Ed Crane's Remarkable Hit Piece on Ron Paul

By Joseph T. Salerno

The Wall Street Journal published a remarkable hit piece on Ron Paul (on 12/31/11) cntitled "Why Ron Paul Matters." It is remarkable because while purporting to be a defense of Ron Paul's ideas, it subtly portrays Ron Paul the real candidate as unelectable while distorting or dismissing outright some of his most important positions.

The author of the article, Ed Crane, begins with a solemn expression of regret over the hoary and irrelevant newsletters of yore to "which Paul lent his name" and which contained allegedly "bigoted" and "intolerant" material. Crane concedes that the objectionable ideas expressed in the newsletters are not consistent with what he knows of Ron Paul's current views and, moreover, that Paul "disavows supporting them." And yet Crane makes sure that the reader knows that Paul "refuses to repudiate" his association with the "likely source" of this secular sin of intolerant speech. Crane has somehow divined that this cardinal sinner against the official state creed of political correctness is none other than Lew Rockwell—who just happens to be the leading critic of neoconservatism and of its offshoot big government libertarianism that Crane's Cato Institute promotes so zealously. So, by the end of the first paragraph we know exactly where all this is heading—and exactly why the neocon Wall Street Journal published it.

In case the reader does not get it, however, Crane continues to prattle on for another paragraph about these "unsavory writings." He dredges up a recent editorial by the New York Times that absurdly claims that the newsletters will leave an indelible stain on the libertarian movement. The editorial, Crane opines, "adds to the background noise surrounding Mr. Paul's candidacy, obscuring the real libertarian policy initiatives . . ." But Crane's handwringing is disingenuous. For when has the Times editorial staff ever cared a whit about the fate of libertarianism? Furthermore, one has to be politically naive—which Crane surely is not—to truly believe that the opinions expressed in New York Times editorials matter any longer to most American citizens not comfortably ensconced within the Beltway or Manhattan's Upper East Side.

What is Crane's purpose, then, in obsessing about the newsletters? His purpose is two-fold: first, to portray Ron Paul as a tainted and dubious, and ultimately unelectable, candidate; and, second, to "co-opt" Paul's consistent and radical libertarian ideology. Crane seeks to court and bask in the increasing popular appeal of Paul's ideology by presenting it as a disjointed series of "libertarian policy initiatives" that are palatable to the neo-con right, which still maintains a tenuous hold on the Republican Party.

Thus Crane achieves his first goal by insinuating that Ron Paul's moral judgment is at best suspect for remaining loyal to a friend and associate whom, Crane asseverates—without a shred of hard evidence—decades ago violated the sacred canons of the American welfare-warfare state's official speech code. Crane next busies himself contorting Paul's ideology to suit his own big government libertarian (BGL) agenda. He describes, via school-boy bullet points so beloved by policy wonks, the four "messages" of the Paul campaign that "Americans respond to" and of which he, Crane, approves.

Three of the four points that Crane lists accurately reflect Ron Paul's positions. And Crane does manage to take a mild swipe at "so many neoconservatives" who want the U.S. "to be the world's policeman." Crane here hopes to establish his credibility as an anti-interventionist. Evidently, he has finally realized that Ron Paul's hard-core, old-right anti-interventionist stance has struck a responsive chord with an American public seething with frustration over the seemingly endless wars in the Middle East. These U.S. military adventures have succeeded only in wasting enormous amounts of blood and treasure while transforming practically the entire Muslim world into an implacable enemy. This is somewhat inconsistent with Crane and Cato's earlier ambivalence toward the U.S. invasion of Iraq. Although Cato formally opposed it, a staff member traveled to Iraq twice in 2004-2005 to advise the Iraqi puppet government and other U.S.-

approved Iraqi organizations on the virtues of constitutions, limited government, and religious tolerance. In a surreal spectacle the Cato staff member handed out pocket-size copies of the U.S. Constitution to a civilian populace whose city had been bombed and invaded by U.S. troops less than a year earlier. In 2005, the quarterly Cato's Letter (http://www.cato.org/pubs/catosletter/catosletterv3n3.pdf) called for the suppression of the spreading Iraqi insurgency against the U.S. occupation, while most libertarians were clamoring for an immediate withdrawal of all U.S. Troops.

The fourth bullet point labeled "Austrian economics," however, wildly misrepresents Paul's views while conflating Austrian economics and monetarism. Crane asserts, "Mr. Paul, like Austrian school economists, understands that we would be better off with a gold standard, competing currencies or a monetary rule than with the arbitrary and discretionary powers of our out-of-control Federal Reserve." Now Crane carefully avoids mentioning the position and slogan that is most popularly associated with Ron Paul's campaign: "End the Fed." In fact all three monetary reforms that Crane attributes to Ron Paul are consistent with the continued existence of the Fed. After all, the gold standard, to its great detriment, operated under Fed control, from 1913 to 1931 and from 1946 to 1971. "Competing currencies" could mean simply permitting U.S. citizens to choose to make their monetary transactions in checking deposits denominated in foreign currencies and commodities like gold and silver, while the Fed continues to operate and crank out fiat dollars. Yet Ron Paul has repeatedly and explicitly stated that he favors the abolition of the Fed and its legal monopoly of the issue of fiat dollars and the restoration of a gold standard in which the dollar is once again legally defined as a specific weight of gold. It is true that he also favors the repeal of legal tender laws and all other laws and regulations impeding American citizens from using any type of commodity or foreign currency in their monetary transactions. In this latter sense, he does support "competing currencies" as a necessary preliminary step toward, but not a permanent alternative to, abolishing the Fed and restoring a completely unregulated and private gold standard.

Furthermore, Crane's suggestion that Ron Paul, let alone Austrian economists, ever did or would view a monetary rule as even a tiny step in the direction of monetary reform is simply ludicrous. A formal rule that would limit the Fed to issuing fiat money according to some pseudo-scientific and arbitrary criterion, e.g., the Friedmanite quantity rule, the Taylor rule, a nominal income target, etc., only serves to more deeply entrench the Fed in the American economy and disguise its inherently inflationary proclivities.

Now Ed Crane is a smart, if not a notably erudite, man who surely knows that Ron Paul does not espouse a monetary policy rule as a viable alternative to the abolition of the Fed and the return to a gold dollar.

He also knows that it is primarily monetarists and the more conservative of some of their New Keynesian offspring who advocate such policy rules and that Austrian economists favor the abolition of monetary policy altogether rather than its formalization in a rule. So why would he say otherwise? This takes us back to the fact that Crane and the Institute he presides over promote big government libertarianism in all areas. In the monetary area this is manifested in the roster of participants at the Cato Institute's prestigious annual conference on monetary policy. This roster routinely includes many high-profile monetarists and Fed insiders. For example, at the last two conferences alone, participants included four current or former Federal Reserve Bank presidents, three high officials of foreign central banks, and the president of the World Bank. Indeed, both Alan Greenspan and Ben Bernanke spoke at earlier Cato monetary conferences while each was a sitting Fed chairman. Additionally, a former president of the Federal Reserve Bank of St. Louis is currently listed as a senior fellow of the Cato Institute. None of this implies that central bankers or monetarists should be unwelcome at conferences run by libertarian institutes. But it surely suggests a strong motive for Crane's gross misrepresentation of Ron Paul's views on the Fed and monetary reform.

Crane magnanimously credits Ron Paul "for his efforts to promote these ideas and other libertarian policies," that is, those that do not conflict with Cato's BGL policy agenda. But Crane then gratuitously comments: "He'd [Paul would] be the first to admit he's not the most erudite candidate to make the case, but surely part of his appeal is his very genuine persona." Really? Which candidate (or former candidate) has displayed greater erudition than Ron Paul in making the libertarian case for sound money, economic freedom and a noninterventionist foreign policy? BGL favorite Gary Johnson? Or maybe imploded Tea Party stars like Michele Bachmann or Herman Cain? Using Merriam Webster's definition of "erudite," we may also ask which of any of the

Republican candidates currently in the race has shown more knowledge gained from studying economics and political philosophy than Ron Paul? As an Austrian economist and longtime libertarian who has heard him speak on many occasions and who has conversed with him on a few, I am deeply impressed with the breadth and depth of Ron Paul's knowledge of the works of Mises, Hayek, Hazlitt, Rand and Rothbard. Crane would be better served by immersing himself in these works rather than obsessively perusing old newsletters. Then, maybe, he would be able to formulate "policy initiatives" founded on sound economics and a coherent libertarian ideology—and not confuse Austrian economics with monetarism.

Crane's crypto-Paul bashing also rears its head in his denial that "Mr. Paul is always in sync with mainstream libertarians." Here "mainstream" refers to libertarians of the BGL variety who are mainly denizens of Beltway think tanks and a few academic outposts in the hinterland. Crane excommunicates Ron Paul from "mainstream" libertarianism for his heretical positions on three issues.

First is Paul's "seeming indifference to attempts to prevent Iran from obtaining nuclear weapons." But Paul has stated again and again in public forums that he is against Iran obtaining nuclear weapons and, as president, would use all diplomatic means at his disposal to prevent such an outcome. For Crane then, Ron Paul's "seeming indifference" boils down to the fact that Paul has stated without reservation that he would not abuse his executive power to launch an unconstitutional war on Iran to achieve this result. We might turn this issue around and ask Crane if his BGL "libertarian policy initiatives" include an unconstitutional invasion of Iran to pre-empt its development of nuclear weapons. We might also query Crane about his seeming indifference to his own affirmation of Paul's anti-interventionist foreign policy earlier in the same article. I suspect Crane's anti-interventionism only extends to the point just short of which it would bring the wrath of the neocons down upon his head.

The second issue that offends Crane's BGL sensibilities is Paul's "support for a constitutional amendment to deny birthright citizenship to children of illegal aliens." Here again Crane's ignorance, willful or otherwise, of libertarian political philosophy and ideology is his undoing. For libertarian philosophy maintains that purely political "rights" involving citizenship, voting, eligibility requirements for appointed or elective office, etc. are not absolute and inviolable rights on a par with rights to one's person and property and to speak and worship freely and exchange with anyone of one's choosing. Thus libertarians can certainly have legitimate disagreements over whether, under prevailing concrete circumstances, it is prudent to support the expansion, restriction, or outright denial of certain political "rights."

Now Ron Paul has stated publicly that he is against both federal financing of building a wall on the southwestern border of the U.S. and a concerted federal campaign to round up and deport illegal aliens already in the U.S. This seems to be at odds with his support for the constitutional amendment denying birthright citizenship to the children of illegal aliens. But this inconsistency is only superficial. For Paul's positions on all these issues cut against an increase in the size and scope of the federal government financed by the siphoning off of resources from the private sector. This is obvious in Paul's opposition to the absurd plans to wall off the U.S. from Mexico and to conduct a mass deportation of illegal aliens. But it also should be evident in his support for making citizenship more restrictive. U.S. "citizenship" is the open sesame to all the goodies dispensed by the federal government including welfare payments, Social Security benefits, unemployment insurance, Medicare and Medicaid, affirmative action programs, higher education grants, military pensions, and so on. Until the American welfare state is dismantled, leaving peaceful and self-supporting illegal immigrants unmolested while restricting citizenship is both a prudent and a reasonable libertarian policy. The knee-jerk BGL policy of defending expansive citizenship under all circumstances is neither.

Crane's third reason for banishing Ron Paul from mainstream libertarianism is Paul's "opposition to the NAFTA and CAFTA free trade agreements." Crane is here employing a sophomoric semantic trick to imply that Paul is against free trade because he opposed NAFTA, which stands for North American Free Trade Agreement. This is like saying that someone is against a republican form of government because he opposes the government of the Democratic People's Republic of Korea. In fact, just as the North Korean government is not in reality a republican government but a brutal and repressive dictatorship, so NAFTA is not a "free trade agreement," as Crane claims, but in reality a managed trade agreement. As such the NAFTA treaty comprises hundreds of pages of restrictive and regulatory provisions that benefit the governments and the corporate and organized labor interests of the U.S. and other signatory countries.

Ron Paul opposes NAFTA and CAFTA because he favors genuine free trade, Crane's silly argument to the contrary notwithstanding.

Now, Crane might respond that opposition to these treaties on "purist" ideological grounds ignores the fact that they are practical, incremental steps in the direction of extending free trade. But I would demur. NAFTA and CAFTA are a step backwards in practice. Unifying and incorporating restrictions and regulations on foreign trade in complex, multilateral trade agreements make them that much harder to get rid of. More important, these agreements further conceal the domestic beneficiaries of these trade barriers under an added layer of impenetrable legalistic jargon. It is better to allow tariffs and quotas to stand alone and be seen as the naked rip-off of consumers by special interests that they really are.

At the conclusion of his article, Crane returns to the issue of the newsletters, like a dog compulsively worrying a favorite bone. Crane quotes a paragraph from a three year-old blog written by a Cato subordinate in which libertarians are earnestly exhorted to "make it clear that the people who wrote those things are not our comrades, not part of our movement." So there we have it. Crane himself does not trust his substantive arguments and his big government libertarian agenda to inspire the growing number of real libertarians leading real lives outside the beltway to forsake Ron Paul's "purist" libertarian ideology. Hence, Crane's desperate attempt to smear and excommunicate his opponents within the libertarian movement. But his shameful tactics only prove that Crane understands one thing for sure: Ron Paul matters—and Ed Crane does not.

Dr. Joseph T. Salerno is Professor of Economics, Lubin School of Business, Pace University, New York, New York and Academic Vice President, Ludwig von Mises Institute.

About the author

Walter Block is Harold E. Wirth Endowed Chair and Professor of Economics, College of Business, Loyola University New Orleans, and senior fellow at the Mises Institute. He earned his PhD in economics at Columbia University in 1972. He has taught at Rutgers, SUNY Stony Brook, Baruch CUNY, Holy Cross and the University of Central Arkansas. He is the author of over 400 articles in professional journals, two dozen books, and hundreds of op eds. He lectures widely on college campuses, delivers seminars around the world and appears regularly on television and radio shows. He has been a friend of Ron Paul's since the 1970s.

Block is a leading Austrian School economist and an international leader of the freedom movement. His earliest work *Defending the Undefendable* (first edition Fleet 1976, latest edition Mises 2008, translated in 12 languages) is now, more than 30 years later, regarded as an overlooked classic on libertarianism. This collection of essays, which argues for societal villains as economic scapegoats based on the principles of nonaggression, forces its reader to think and to rethink his or her initial knee-jerk emotional responses, and to gain a new and far sounder appreciation of economic theory and of the virtues and operations of the free market economy. Block's writing was inspired by Henry Hazlitt, the author of the most widely read economics text *Economics in One Lesson.*

Block has been a fixture in the libertarian movement for some four decades. He actually met Ludwig von Mises and F.A. Hayek, and was friends with Murray Rothbard. His contributions to academic libertarianism and to Austrian economics have been prodigious.

Block's writings continue to challenge the conventional wisdom (or ignorance) of how economics works and will retain its freshness for decades to come.

XIV. References:

Bagus, Philipp. 2003. 'The Commons and the Tragedy of Banking,' November 12; http://mises.org/story/1373

Bagus, Philipp, David Howden and Walter E. Block. Forthcoming. "Deposits, Loans and Banking: Clarifying the Debate," *American Journal of Economics and Sociology.*

Barnett, William II and Walter Block, 2005. "In defense of fiduciary media— a comment; or, what's wrong with "clown" or play money?" *Quarterly Journal of Austrian Economics*; Vol. 8, No. 2, Summer:, pp. 55-69.; http://mises.org/journals/qjae/pdf/qjae8_2_4.pdf

Barnett, William II and Walter Block. 2008. "Time deposits, dimensions and fraud," *Journal of Business Ethics;*

www.WalterBlock.com/publications; http://www.springerlink.com/content/100281/?k=walter+block&sortorder=asc&v=condensed&o=20; www.WalterBlock.com/publications

Barnett, William II and Walter Block. 2009. "Financial Intermediaries, the Intertemporal-Carry Trade, and Austrian Business Cycles; or; Crash and Carry: Can Fraudulent Time deposits lead to an Austrian Business Cycle? Yes." *Journal Etica e Politica / Ethics & Politics*, Vol. XI, No. 1 . 455-469.

http://www2.units.it/~etica/2009_1/BARNETT_BLOCK.pdf

Bauer, Peter T. 1981. *Equality, the Third World, and Economic Delusion.*, Cambridge, Mass.: Harvard University Press.

Bauer, Peter T. 1982. "Ecclesiastical Economics is Envy Exalted," *This World,* No. 1, (Winter/Spring): pp. 56-69.

Bauer, Peter T. 1984. *Reality and Rhetoric: Studies in the Economics of Development*, Cambridge, MA: Harvard University Press

Bauer, Peter T. 1991.*The Development Frontier: Essays in Applied Economics*. Cambridge, MA: Harvard University Press.

Bauer, Peter T. and Basil S. Yamey. 1957. *The Economics of Underdeveloped Countries.*, Chicago: University of Chicago Press.

Baxendale, Tony. 2010. *Free Banking, the Balance Sheet and Contract Law Approach.* March 15, http://www.cobdencentre.org/2010/03/free-banking-the-balance-sheet-and-contract-law-approach/.

Block, Walter E. 1972. "The Polish Ham Question." *The Libertarian Forum,* June-July, Vol. 4 No. 6-7, p. 5;

http://www.mises.org/journals/lf/1972/1972_06-07.pdf;
http://mises.org/daily/4054;
http://www.lewrockwell.com/block/block143.html

Block, Walter E. 1998. "Environmentalism and Economic Freedom: The Case for Private Property Rights," *Journal of Business Ethics*, Vol. 17, No. 6, December, pp. 1887-1899

Block, Walter E. 2002. "Accepting Government Subsidies.," *Fraser Forum*, February, p. 27;

http://oldfraser.lexi.net/publications/forum/2002/02/section_13.html

Block, Walter E. 2004. "Radical Libertarianism: Applying Libertarian Principles to Dealing with the Unjust Government, Part I." *Reason Papers*, Vol. 27. Fall, pp. 117-133; http://www.walterblock.com/wp-content/uploads/publications/block_radical-libertarianism-rp.pdf

Block, Walter E. 2006A. "Radical Libertarianism: Applying Libertarian Principles to Dealing with the Unjust Government, Part II." *Reason Papers,* Vol. 28, Spring, pp. 85-109;

http://www.reasonpapers.com/pdf/28/rp_28_7.pdf

Block, Walter E. 2006B. "Fanatical, Not Reasonable: A Short Correspondence Between Walter Block and Milton Friedman (on Friedrich Hayek)." *Journal of Libertarian Studies*, Vol. 20, No. 3, Summer, pp. 61-80;

http://www.mises.org/journals/jls/20_3/20_3_4.pdf

Block, Walter E. 2007. "Ron Paul and Matching Funds.," October 1;

http://www.lewrockwell.com/block/block86.html

Block, Walter E. 2008A. *Labor Economics from a Free Market Perspective: Employing the Unemployable.* London, UK: World Scientific Publishing

Toh Tuck Link, Singapore: World Scientific Publishing; http://www.mises.org/store/Labor-Economics-From-A-Free-Market-Perspective-P516.aspx

Block, Walter E. 2008B. "Replies to readers." September 23;

http://www.lewrockwell.com/block/block108.html

Block, Walter E. 2009A. "Libertarian punishment theory: working for, and donating to, the state." *Libertarian Papers,* Vol. 1 (2009).; http://libertarianpapers.org/2009/17-libertarian-punishment-theory-working-for-and-donating-to-the-state/

Block, Walter E. 2009B. "Toward a Libertarian Theory of Guilt and Punishment for the Crime of Statism." Hulsmann, Jorg Guido and

Stephan Kinsella, eds., *Property, Freedom and Society: Essays in Honor of Hans-Hermann Hoppe*, Auburn, AL: Ludwig von Mises Institute, pp. 137-148; http://mises.org/books/hulsmann-kinsella_property-freedom-society-2009.pdf

Block, Walter E. 2009C. *The Privatization of Roads and Highways: Human and Economic Factors*; Auburn, AL: The Mises Institute; http://mises.org/books/roads_web.pdf

Block, Walter E. 2010A. "You are a rotten kid (rent control and libertarianism)," February 27;

http://www.lewrockwell.com/block/block150.html

Block, Walter E. 2010B. "Are unions criminal gangs?" *Global Virtue Ethics Review*, Vol. 6. No. 1, pp. 28-49;
http://www.spaef.com/article.php?id=1176;
http://www.spaef.com/file.php?id=1176;

http://www.accessmylibrary.com/archive/6487-global-virtue-ethics-review.html

Block, Walter E. 2010C. "Is Milton Friedman a libertarian? No." *Laissez-Faire*, No. 32, pp. 9-22, March;

http://fce.ufm.edu/Publicaciones/LaissezFaire/

Block, Walter E. 2011A. "It's Ayn Rand Bashing Time, Once Again." February 18; http://www.lewrockwell.com/block/block172.html

Block, Walter E. 2011B. "May a Libertarian Take Money From the Government?" March 11;

http://www.lewrockwell.com/block/block175.html

Block, Walter E. 2011C. “Ron Paul and the Self-Hating ‘Libertarians.’” August 19;

http://lewrockwell.com/block/block180.html

Block, Walter E. 2011D. "The Human Body Shield," *Journal of Libertarian Studies*; Vol. 22 , pp. 625-630;

http://mises.org/journals/jls/22_1/22_1_30.pdf

Block, Walter E. 2011E. “Hoppe, Kinsella and Rothbard II on Immigration: A Critique.” *Journal of Libertarian Studies*; Vol. 22, pp. 593–623;

http://mises.org/journals/jls/22_1/22_1_29.pdf

Block, Walter and Chris Arakaky. 2008. “Taking Government Money for Grad School?,” May 23;

http://www.lewrockwell.com/block/block100.html

Block, Walter and William Barnett II. 2008. “Continuums” *Journal Etica e Politica / Ethics & Politics*, Vol. 1, pp. 151-166 June; http://www2.units.it/~etica/; http://www2.units.it/~etica/2008_1/BLOCKBARNETT.pdf

Block, Walter and Bryan Caplan. 2008. “Walter Block versus Bryan Caplan on Fractional Reserve Banking.” Nov 1;

http://www.lewrockwell.com/block/block110.html

Block, Walter and Kenneth M. Garschina. 1996. “Hayek, Business Cycles and Fractional Reserve Banking: Continuing the De-Homogenization Process,” *Review of Austrian Economics*, Vol. 9, No. 1, 1995, pp. 77-94;

http://www.mises.org/journals/rae/pdf/rae9_1_3.pdf.

Block, Walter and John Humphries. 2008. "Humphries vs Block on fractional reserve banking." November 17;

http://alsblog.wordpress.com/2008/11/17/fractional-reserve-banking/

Block, Walter versus Eric Posner. 2008. "Posner vs. Block on fractional reserve banking." November, 29;

http://www.lewrockwell.com/block/block114.html

Block, Walter and Llewellyn H. Rockwell, Jr. 2007. "Katrina and the Future of New Orleans," Telos, Vol. 139, Summer, pp. 170–185

Block, Walter and Roy Whitehead. 2005. "Compromising the Uncompromisable: A Private Property Rights Approach to Resolving the Abortion Controversy," *Appalachian Law Review,* 4 (2) 1-45; http://www.walterblock.com/publications/block-whitehead_abortion-2005.pdf;

http://www.walterblock.com/wp-content/uploads/publications/block-whitehead_abortion-2005.pdf

Caplan, Bryan. 2007. *The Myth of the Rational Voter: Why Democracies Choose Bad Policies.* Princeton, N.J.: Princeton University Press

Conquest, Robert. 1986. *The Harvest of Sorrow,* N.Y.: Oxford University Press;

Conquest, Robert. 1990. *The Great Terror,* Edmonton, Alberta: Edmonton University Press

Courtois, Stephane, Nicolas Werth, Jean-Louis Panne, Andrzej Paczkowski, Karel Bartosek and Jean Louis Margolin. 1999. *The*

Black Book of Communism: Crimes, Terror, Repression, trans. from French by Jonathan Murphy and Mark Kramer, Cambridge, MA: Harvard University Press

D'Amico, Dan and Walter E. Block. 2007. "A Legal and Economic Analysis of Graffiti" *Humanomics* Vol. 23, No. 1, pp. 29-38; http://www.mises.org/journals/scholar/damico.pdf; http://www.emeraldinsight.com/Insight/viewContainer.do?containerType=Issue&containerId=24713; http://ssrn.com/abstract=1008525

Davidson, Laura. 2008. "Fractional Reserve Banking Is Indeed Fraudulent," November 17;

http://www.lewrockwell.com/orig9/davidson-l1.html

Davidson, Laura and Walter E. Block. 2011. "The Case Against Fiduciary Media: Ethics Is The Key," *The Journal of Business Ethics*. Vol. 98, Issue 3, pp. 505-511;

http://www.springerlink.com/content/j76323752648720g/; http://dx.doi.org/10.1007/s10551-010-0590-2; 10.1007/s10551-010-0590-2

Doherty, Brian. 2007. *Radicals for Capitalism*. New York, N.Y.: Public Affairs

Domhoff, G. William. 1967. *Who Rules America*? Englewood Cliffs NJ: Prentice-Hall.

Domhoff, G. William. 1971. *The Higher Circles: The Governing Class in America*. New York: Vintage Books

Domhoff, G. William. 1998. *Who Rules America? Power and Politics in the Year 2000*, Third Edition, Santa Cruz: University of California

Friedman, Milton. 1962. *Capitalism and Freedom*, Chicago: University of Chicago Press

Gwartney, James, Robert Lawson and Joshua Hall. 2011. *Economic Freedom of the World,* Vancouver: the Fraser Institute; http://www.freetheworld.com/2011/reports/world/EFW2011_complete.pdf

Gwartney, James, Robert Lawson and Walter Block. 1996. *Economic Freedom of the World, 1975-1995,* Vancouver, B.C. Canada: the Fraser Institute.

Hanke, Steve. 2008. "Banking Crises: Plus Ça Change…" *GlobeAsia*, November, pp. 168-169; http://www.freemarketfoundation.com/Hanke%5CBanking%20Crises--Plus%20%C3%87a%20Change,%20November%202008.pdf

Hazlitt, Henry. 2008 [1979]. *Economics in One Lesson*, Auburn, AL: The Mises Institute

Hill, David. 2011. "Debates are welfare for Paul, Perry." November 29; http://thehill.com/opinion/op-ed/196057-debates-are-welfare-for-paul-perry

Hoppe, Hans-Hermann. 1990. "Marxist and Austrian Class Analysis," *The Journal of Libertarian Studies*, Vol. 9, No. 2, Fall, pp. 79-94; http://mises.org/journals/jls/9_2/9_2_5.pdf
http://209.85.165.104/search?q=cache:K12nTci91bQJ:www.mises.org/journals/jls/9_2/9_2_5.pdf+

%22Marxist+and+Austrian+Class+Analysis,
%22&hl=en&ct=clnk&cd=1&gl=us

Hoppe, Hans-Hermann. 1994. "How is Fiat Money Possible? or, The Devolution of Money and Credit," *Review of Austrian Economics*, 7(2), pp. 49-74.

Hoppe, Hans-Hermann, with Guido Hulsmann and Walter Block. 1998. "Against Fiduciary Media," *Quarterly Journal of Austrian Economics*, Vol. 1, No. 1, pp. 19-50,

http://www.mises.org/journals/qjae/pdf/qjae1_1_2.pdf

Horwitz, Morton J. 1977. *The Transformation of American Law: 1780-1860*, Cambridge: Harvard University Press

Hughes, Jonathan R.T. 1977. *The Governmental Habit: Economic Controls from Colonial Times to the Present*. New York: Basic Books

Huerta de Soto, Jesús. 1995. "A Critical Analysis of Central Banks and Fractional-Reserve Free Banking from the Austrian Perspective," *Review of Austrian Economics*, 8(2), pp. 25-38.

uerta de Soto, Jesús. 1998, "A Critical Note on Fractional-Reserve Free Banking," T*he Quarterly Journal of Austrian Economics* 1(4), 25-49.

Huerta de Soto, Jesús. 2001. "A Critical Note on Fractional Reserve Free Banking," *The Quarterly Journal of Austrian Economics*, Vol. 1, No. 4, Fall, pp. 34-35

Huerta de Soto, Jesús. 2006. *Money, Bank Credit and Economic Cycles* (Ludwig von Mises Institute, Auburn AL.)

Huerta de Soto, Jesús. 2010. "Economic Recessions, Banking Reform, and the Future of capitalism." http://mises.org/daily/4817

Hülsmann, Jorg Guido. 1996, "Free Banking and the Free Bankers," *Review of Austrian Economics* 9(1), 3-53.

Hulsmann, Jorg Guido. 2000. "Banks Cannot Create Money," *The Independent Review: A*

Journal of Political Economy, vol. 5, no. 1, summer, 101-110; http://www.independent.org/pdf/tir/tir_05_1_hulsman.pdf

Hulsmann, Jorg Guido. 2002a. "Free Banking and the Free Bankers." *Review of Austrian Economics.* Vol. 9, No. 1. pp. 3-53; http://www.mises.org/journals/rae/pdf/rae9_1_1.pdf

Hulsmann, Jorg Guido. 2002b. "Free Banking Fractional Reserves: Reply to Pascal Salin." *Review of Austrian Economics*, Vol. 1, No. 3.

http://www.mises.org/journals/qjae/pdf/qjae1_3_8.pdf

Hulsmann, Jorg Guido. 2003A. "Facts and Counterfactuals in Economic Law." *The Journal of Libertarian Studies.* Vol. 17, Num. 1, pp. 57-102;

http://www.mises.org/journals/jls/17_1/17_1_3.pdf

Hulsmann, Jorg Guido. 2003B. "Has Fractional-Reserve Banking Really Passed the Market Test?," Independent Review 7/3, Winter, 399-422.

http://www.independent.org/publications/tir/article.asp?a=90

Hülsmann, Jorg Guido. 2008, *The Ethics of Money Production* Auburn AL: Ludwig von Mises Institute

Kolko, Gabriel. 1963. *Triumph of Conservatism*, Chicago: Quadrangle Books

Kwiatkowski, Karen. 2011. "Reason-able?" August 17;

http://www.lewrockwell.com/blog/lewrw/archives/93269.html

Lemann, Nicholas. 2012. "Enemy of the State." *The New Yorker.* January 9;

http://www.newyorker.com/talk/comment/2012/01/09/120109taco_talk_lemann

McAdams, Daniel. 2001. "The Single Stupidest Attack on Ron Paul Ever."

http://www.lewrockwell.com/politicaltheatre/2011/11/the-single-stupidest-attack-on-ron-paul-ever/

McElroy, Wendy. (undated). "Ron Paul or antiwar.com?"

http://www.thebellforum.com/archive/index.php?t-14410.html&s=d04011a6dd48755f6fbd1338870a8646

McElroy, Wendy. 2008. "Murray N. Rothbard (1926-1995) -- the greatest libertarian theorist of the 20th century -- expressed the central political issue confronting mankind." May 28;

http://www.wendymcelroy.com/e107_plugins/content/content.php?content.92; http://www.wendymcelroy.com/rockwell/mcelroy000706.html

Molyneux, Stefan. 2007. "The shape of things to come." November 23;

http://www.youtube.com/watch?v=McNo62gpw6M&playnext=1&list=PLADDEC1E9BDF4ECE0

Molyneux, Stefan. 2008. "The Stateless Society: An Examination of Alternatives"

http://www.mail-archive.com/libertarianenterprise@yahoogroups.com/msg02056.html

Molyneux, Stefan. 2011. "Walter Block vs Stefan Molyneux vs Ron Paul." August 19;

http://www.youtube.com/watch?v=O90je0Vfr20&feature=relmfu

Mises, Ludwig von. 1978. *The Clash of Group Interests and Other Essays.* New York: Center for Libertarian Studies.

http://www.mises.org/etexts/mises/clash/clash.asp

Murphy, Robert P. 2011. "The Fractional-Reserve Banking Question." June 14;

http://mises.org/daily/4499

North, Gary. 2009. "What Is Money? Part 5: Fractional Reserve Banking." October 10;

http://www.lewrockwell.com/north/north769.html

Oppenheimer, Franz. [1914] 1975. *The State*, New York: Free Life Editions

Paul, Ron. 2009A. "Earmarks Don't Add Up." March 16;

http://www.ronpaul.com/on-the-issues/earmark-reform/

Paul, Ron. 2009B. "Ron Paul on Earmarks." March 11;

http://www.ronpaul.com/2009-03-11/ron-paul-on-earmarks/

Paul, Ron. 2010. *End the Fed.* New York, N.Y.: Grand Central Publishing

Polleit, Thorsten. 2010. "The Faults of Fractional-Reserve Banking." December 23;

http://mises.org/daily/4880

Porter, Eduardo. 2011. "All that glimmers." *New York Times*, November 8; http://www.nytimes.com/2011/11/08/opinion/all-that-glimmers.html

Raico, Ralph. 1977. "Classical Liberal exploitation theory: a comment on Professor Liggio's paper," *The Journal of Libertarian Studies*, Vol. 1, No. 3, Summer, pp. 179-184

Raimondo, Justin. 2012. "Ron Paul's Hour of Decision: Is Ron Paul running for president in the wrong party?"

http://lewrockwell.com/raimondo/raimondo163.html

Rand, Ayn. 1957. *Atlas Shrugged*, New York: Random House

Reisman, George. 1996. *Capitalism*. Ottawa, Il.: Jameson Books; pp. 954-963

Reisman, George. 2009. "A Pro-Free-Market Program for Economic Recovery," November 20;

http://mises.org/daily/3870

Rockwell, Jr. Llewellyn H. 2001. "Liberty and the Common Good" December 31; http://www.mises.org/article.aspx?Id=860

Rockwell, Jr., Llewellyn H. and Walter Block. 2010. "The Economics and Ethics of Hurricane Katrina" American Journal of Economics and Sociology. Vol. 69, No. 4, October, pp. 1294–1320

Rothbard, Murray N. 1961. "A Fable for Our Times By One of the Unreconstructed"

http://www.lewrockwell.com/rothbard/rothbard22.html

Rothbard, Murray N. [1962] 1991. "The Case for a 100 Percent Gold Dollar," *In Search of a Monetary Constitution*, Leland B. Yeager, ed., Cambridge, MA: Harvard University Press, pp. 94-136, and Auburn, AL: Ludwig von Mises Institute. See also "The Logic of Action One" pp. 364-384;

http://mises.org/story/1829

Rothbard, Murray N. [1963] 1975. *America's Great Depression* (Sheed and Ward, Kansas City).

Rothbard, Murray N. 1977. "Do you hate the state?" *The Libertarian Forum*, Vol. 10, No. 7, July.

http://www.lewrockwell.com/rothbard/rothbard75.html

Rothbard, Murray N. 1982. "Law, Property Rights, and Air Pollution," *Cato Journal*, Vol. 2, No. 1, Spring; reprinted in *Economics and the Environment: A Reconciliation*, Walter Block, ed., Vancouver: The Fraser Institute, 1990, pp. 233-279.

http://www.mises.org/rothbard/lawproperty.pdf;
http://mises.org/story/2120

Rothbard, Murray N. 1983. *The Mystery of Banking*. New York: Richardson and Snyder.

Rothbard, Murray N. 1990. *What Has Government Done to Our Money?*, Auburn, AL: Ludwig von Mises Institute;

http://www.mises.org/rothbard/rothmoney.pdf

Rothbard, Murray N. [1962] 1991. "The Case for a 100 Percent Gold Dollar," *In Search of a Monetary Constitution*, Leland B. Yeager, ed., Cambridge, MA: Harvard University Press, pp. 94-136, and Auburn, AL: Ludwig von Mises Institute. See also "The Logic of Action One" pp. 364-384;

http://mises.org/story/1829

Rothbard, Murray N. [1962] 1993, *Man, Economy, and State* (Ludwig von Mises Institute, Auburn, AL.).

Rothbard, Murray N. 2005. *What Has Government Done to Our Money and The Case for a 100 Percent Gold Dollar.* Auburn, AL: The Mises Institute;

http://www.mises.org/rothbard/rothmoney.pdf

Rothbard, Murray N. 1998 *The Ethics of Liberty,* New York: New York University Press.

http://www.mises.org/rothbard/ethics/ethics.asp

Rummel, R. J. 1992. *Democide: Nazi Genocide and Mass Murder.* Rutgers, New Jersey: Transaction Publisher.

Rummel, R. J. 1996. *Death By Government*. New Brunswick, NJ: Transaction

Rummel, R. J. 1997. *Statistics on Democide*. Center on National Security and Law, University of Virginia

Salerno, Joseph T. 2010. "White contra Mises on Fiduciary Media," May 14;

http://mises.org/daily/4389

Salerno, Joseph. 2012. "Ed Crane's Remarkable Hit Piece on Ron Paul."

http://www.economicpolicyjournal.com/2012/01/ed-cranes-remarkable-hit-piece-on-ron.html

Smith, Adam. [1776] 1979. *An Inquiry into the Nature and Causes of the Wealth of Nations*, Indianapolis, IN: Liberty Fund

Spooner, Lysander. 1966[1870]. *No Treason: The Constitution of No Authority and A Letter to Thomas F. Bayard*, Larkspur, Colorado: Rampart College; http://www.lysanderspooner.org/notreason.htm

Waller, Christopher J. 2011."Independence + Accountability: Why the Fed Is a Well-Designed Central Bank"; *Federal Reserve Bank of St. Louis Review*, September/October, Vol. 93, No. 5, pp. 293–302

White, Lawrence H. 2005. "The Federal Reserve System's Influence on Research in Monetary Economics." Econ Journal Watch, Volume 2, Number 2, August 2005, pp 325-354

Williams, Walter, E. 1982. *The State Against Blacks*, New York, McGraw-Hill.

Thanks:

The author wishes to thank Anonymous, Shmuel Ben-Gad, David Bergland, Jordan Bullock, Pete Chamberlain, Max Chiz, Dick Clark, Skyler Collins, Ran Dagoni, Michael R. Edelstein, Ross Kaminsky, Stephan Kinsella, Thomas Nash, Lisa Ostroski, Max Raskin, Lew Rockwell, Shawn Ritenour, Daniel Sayani, Kay Wosewick and Mei Yao for help in the preparation of this volume, and the following co-authors of several of the chapters in it, for their permission to reprint material they have written: William Barnett II, Steve Berger; and Rafi Farber and Joseph Salerno for permission to reprint their writings as the Forward and Postscript, respectively. I am also grateful to Lew Rockwell, Ron Paul and Tom Woods for the blurbs that adorn the back cover of this book.

Printed in Dunstable, United Kingdom

89412043R00221